LESBIAN FEMINISM

LESBIAN FEMINISM

Essays Opposing Global Heteropatriarchies

EDITED BY

NIHARIKA BANERJEA, KATH BROWNE,
EDUARDA FERREIRA, MARTA OLASIK
AND JULIE PODMORE

ZED

Lesbian Feminism: Essays Opposing Global Heteropatriarchies was first published in 2019 by Zed Books Ltd, The Foundry, 17 Oval Way, London SE11 5RR, UK.

www.zedbooks.net

Typeset in Bulmer by Swales and Willis Ltd, Exeter, Devon
Index by John Barker
Cover design by Burgess & Beech

ISBN 978-1-78699-531-5 hb
ISBN 978-1-78699-530-8 pb
ISBN 978-1-78699-532-2 pdf
ISBN 978-1-78699-533-9 epub
ISBN 978-1-78699-534-6 mobi

Contents

Acknowledgements

Our thanks go to those upon whose shoulders we have stood while organising this collection, whose work we build upon and who paved the way to make this possible. We are deeply appreciative of the work, time and effort of all of the contributors whose ideas and enthusiasm made this collection a pleasure to edit. We want to thank all the activists who made it possible to produce a book on lesbian feminisms with contributions from so many different countries, contexts and realities. This is a time when it is more urgent than ever to stand up and resist the backlash against human rights, a time when activism can make a difference in the world.

Thank you to Kim Walker for enthusiastically supporting this project. We are grateful to Shirley Howe and Georgina Perryman for their excellent assistance in getting the text to publication.

Sara Ahmed's chapter is reprinted from her Killjoy blog, located here: https://feministkilljoys.com/ and was presented as a keynote at the 2015 Lesbian Lives Conference in Brighton. Thanks to her for the permission to reprint it here.

Line Chamberland's chapter was originally published in 2002 as "Place des lesbiennes dans le mouvement des femmes", in Francine Descarries and Elsa Galerand (eds) *Le féminisme comme lieu pour penser et vivre diversité et solidarité: actes de colloque* published by Alliance de recherche IREF/Relais-Femmes. It has been translated from the French by Julie Podmore with Line Chamberland.

Jules Falquet's chapter was originally published in French in 2009 in *Genre, sexualité et société* as "Rompre le tabou de l'hétérosexualité, en finir avec la différence des sexes: les apports du lesbianisme comme mouvement social et théorie politique" (http://journals.openedition.org/gss/705). It was translated from the French by Julie Podmore with Jules Falquet.

Natacha Chetcuti-Osorovitz's chapter was translated from the French by Julie Podmore.

Eduarda wishes to thank feminist activists for their resilience and for making our world a better place.

Kath wishes to thank all of her co-editors for making the process stimulating, as well as easy. Donna for her perseverance and love, and to my children, may you know the world that lesbian feminists dream about.

Niharika wishes to thank her co-editors for renewing her belief in the possibility of connections across differences. Niharika also thanks her queer human and non-human kins for making the world around her enduring and beautiful.

Marta wishes to thank all the other editors for the close and effective cooperation as well as for the lessons learnt and friendships maintained in the process. Marta dedicates her work on this book to the possibility of a distinct lesbian feminism emerging in the Polish social and academic reality in a not-too-distant future.

Julie wishes to thank her co-editors and the authors for making this collection possible. A special thanks to the Montreal lesbian activists who continue to preserve and reanimate Quebec lesbian feminisms: Johanne Coulombe and Dominique Bourque of Les éditions sans fin, Sylvie Bompis, Laure Neuville and Louise Turcotte of Archives lesbiennes, and of course, Line Chamberland.

Introduction: transnational ruminations on lesbian feminisms

Niharika Banerjea, Kath Browne, Eduarda Ferreira,
Marta Olasik and Julie Podmore

Opening remarks

Lesbian Feminisms reflects our collective conviction that gender and sexualities matter to each other, and that their intersection cannot be overlooked in contemporary nor historical contexts (see Ellis and Peel, 2011). The collection is based on the premise that lesbian feminism enables an investigation of the heteropatriarchies that continue to define everyday lives. We want to emphasise the plurality of and differences around lesbian feminisms, pointing to the importance of locality in shaping discourse, experiences and struggles with regard to the liveabilities[1] of women[2] with 'non-heterosexual'[3] expressions, practices and identities. In this context, the general objective of this book is to create a platform where discussions and the scope of perspectives could be widened to include the intricacies and varieties around lesbian feminisms. This approach can also challenge any discourses that position lesbian feminisms as static, bounded and over (see Enszer, 2016).

In their collection on *Twenty-First Century Lesbian Studies*, O'Donnell and Giffney (2007) note the self-reflexive questioning of lesbian studies, and the ways it can be energised and engaged to enable conversations rather than closing them down. As they argue, it is the indeterminacy of 'the lesbian' that has always been crucial (see for example Doan, 1994; Faderman, 1981) and that, for many, lesbian feminisms are and always have been queer, as they contest gender *and* sexual orthodoxies and normativities. Lesbian feminist theorising can take a variety of forms; thus, we did not determine its meaning in advance, and instead invited authors to consider lesbian feminisms in contemporary gender and sexual politics.

It is important from the outset to note that significant disagreements continue to be manifest in places such as the UK and the USA between some of those who might call themselves lesbian feminists *and* trans people, activists and allies. The editors and authors of this book take the position that lesbian feminism can be trans inclusive. We, and others, refuse to cede lesbian feminisms to those who are trans-exclusionary (Ahmed, 2017; this volume; O'Donnell and Giffney, 2007), and instead seek to critically explore heteropatriarchies in ways that understand gender/sex and sexualities as continually reconstituted within regulatory frames (Butler, 1990). For us, the foci of lesbian feminisms are the regulatory frames of (hetero)sexuality and patriarchies as they are manifest in a multitude of ways, and through multiple and intersecting differences and hierarchies around race, caste, class, religion, language and location.

Although the five of us differ with regard to nationality, age, academic status, activist capital, social and cultural background, and experiences around lesbian feminist thought and practices, we worked together in a transnational[4] and transgenerational attempt to draw a diverse set of authors into a discussion of the possibility of (re)claiming the multiplicity of potentials presented by the theories and praxis revolving around lesbian feminisms. We use the preposition 'around' because it creates the opportunity to incorporate discussions that may not be explicitly labelled as 'lesbian feminist', but can nevertheless contribute, as the chapters included here suggest, by expanding the theoretical and political potential of lesbian feminism.

Lesbian feminism, in its conceptual form, has a long herstory, one that is complex and geographically specific. Yet, and perhaps because of this, the story of lesbian feminism has often been told in a reductive way. We, therefore, wanted to understand a variety of practices, discourses, intersections, contexts, movements, temporalities and networks revolving around the concept. In inviting multiple activist and scholarly reflections on past and present ideas and practices around lesbian feminisms from various localities across geopolitical borders, we have created a multi-faceted conversation that seeks to counter any devaluation of lesbian feminist politics and reject the erasure of gender in sexuality discourses and queer politics. All the contributors, albeit in different ways, draw attention to the diversity of languages, national policies, and sexuality and feminist politics in which lesbian feminisms have been articulated (or not). In this way, we, as the editors, hope to ignite a wide-ranging, in-depth discussion regarding the relevance of lesbian feminisms to contemporary politics.

In seeking this multiplicity, we introduce the reader to the different contexts and partial herstories across localities. This is not a comprehensive global overview, but instead we offer partial insights from our unique perspectives. We begin by providing the general prism through which lesbian feminism tends to be remembered and interpreted. This interpretation is undergirded by a critique of power of Western and Anglophone hegemonies to produce and reproduce gender and sexualities knowledges. We then offer a glimpse into knowledges, experiences and articulations around lesbian feminisms from different cultural and social contexts. Finally, we provide the outline of how this book is constructed and what to expect from the contributions that will follow. In so doing, we challenge orthodoxies that can become solidified around discussions of lesbian feminisms, before opening the book out to further this endeavour.

Narrating lesbian feminism: transnational stories

Throughout this book, we emphasise the significance of applying local lenses to the understanding of concerns and issues that inform and can potentially revise articulations around lesbian feminisms. In this section, we offer, in no particular order, examinations of our own particular regions at various scales, including French linguistic regions; the Republic of Ireland; Southern Europe and South America (Portuguese and Spanish); Eastern Europe; and India. These geographies are where the editors' situated knowledges and contexts are placed, and they offer, often for the first time in English, an insight into lesbian feminisms' other narratives, other herstories and other realities. They are not representative or comprehensive; instead they contest Anglo-American exclusivity and offer entry points into the diverse contexts from which the authors write.

Anglo-American lesbian feminist hegemonies

The predominant story of lesbian feminism often follows a very specific narrative in the Anglo-American context (see Browne and Olasik, 2016). Simply put, the first self-identified lesbian feminist movements developed in the USA/UK in response to the lack of recognition of lesbian concerns within both second-wave feminism and the gay liberation movement in the late 1960s and early 1970s. Lesbian activists founded their own groups and, throughout the decade, the movement expanded across North America and Western Europe (Myers, 2003). It spread through submerged informal networks of activists (Taylor and Whittier, 1992) who moved between rural lesbian lands (Valentine, 1997), small towns and big cities from the United States (Taylor and Rupp, 1993; Taylor and Whittier, 1992), Canada (Chamberland, 2000; Millward, 2015; Ross 1995), the United Kingdom (Jeffreys, 2018), to New Zealand (Laurie, 2001) and Australia (Jennings, 2008; 2009; 2015), as well as the French-language contexts of France, Quebec and Belgium (Chetcuti and Michard, 2003).

In the 1970s, lesbian feminists adopted many different political positions ranging from cultural, radical and lesbian feminist (Taylor and Rupp, 1993; Myers, 2003), but the basis of Anglo-American lesbian feminisms was to challenge heteropatriarchy's sexual oppression of women. Initially, feminists and lesbian feminists used consciousness-raising, writing and study groups to begin to investigate and disrupt the very idea of femininity and female sexuality for the first time (Koedt, [1968] 2000; Millett, 1970). Based on the Radicalesbians' 1970 'woman-identified woman' principle (Radicalesbians [1970] 1992), at the core of this movement was a political identity devoted to turning one's energies towards other 'women', the collective building of women's communities and cultures, and the conceptualisation of lesbian feminist politics and theories (Jay, 1999; Phelan, 1989; Shumsky, 2009). Part of the building of this solidarity often involved the practice of separatism and political lesbianism. Soon after their break with mainstream feminism and gay liberation movements in the early 1970s, early lesbian feminist groups such as Washington DC's The Furies (Bunch, [1976] 1987; Valk, 2002; 2008) began to practise 'separatism', experimenting with communal living and working together to write an alternative world into being. Political lesbianism involved the choice to devote one's energies towards women (to be woman-identified) and to remain apart from men, not as a component of individual sexual preference, but rather as a means of challenging patriarchy through solidarity with women and "not sleeping with the enemy" (Leeds Revolutionary Feminist Group, 1981).

Both separatism and political lesbianism brought a quest for the creation of autonomous spaces, a "lesbian nation" (Johnston 1973), leading to experiments with women-only commercial, social and festival spaces and separate living arrangements including urban communal living and the building of self-sustaining rural communities (Valentine, 1997; Morris, 1999). As Enke (2007) argues, by the 1980s, the movement was powerful because it also found ways to take up public space and render lesbians and their politics more visible. Symptomatic of that era of lesbian visibility was the idea of 'lesbian continuum' as developed by Adrienne Rich (1980). In theory, it clearly showed how 'womanhood' was a product of a patriarchal social order that tied all women sexually to men through its economy, thus rendering lesbian existence an impossibility. In practice, these insights could be used to create an alternate social order that focused on building complete lesbian autonomy from the heteropatriarchal system. In this sense, the movement offered a unique critique of the systemic reinforcement of unequal gender relations by capitalist heteronormativity because it recognised the interlocking power relations among regimes of sex, gender and sexuality and the symbolic violence their intersections have created not just for lesbians but for all women (see for example Covina and Galana, 1975; Lorde, 1984; Loulan, 1987; Hoagland, 1988; Hoagland and Penelope, 1988). As Phelan (1989) argues, these early lesbian feminist theoretical projects were particularly challenging for the women's and the gay rights movements because they rejected the individual liberalism that, by the 1980s, was informing both of the latter groups.

By the late-1980s, feminist conflict generated by the 'Sex-Wars', attention to the normativity of the construction of lesbian subject brought by Third Wave Feminism, and the alliance of a new generation of lesbians with gay men around the AIDS crisis and through queer politics and theory, led many lesbian feminist groups to decline and disband. These shifts brought a rejection and devaluation of lesbian feminism by new generations who were critical of its separatisms, essentialisms and exclusions (Phelan, 1989; Stein, 1992; 1993) and, ultimately, its whiteness, cis-normativity, ableism and other exclusions (Bell and Valentine, 1995). While the sexual politics of queer activism and theory and its erasure of lesbian subjectivities was in question (Cohen, 1997; Walters, 1996), some, such as the Lesbian Avengers, did initiate new forms of lesbian activism through queer politics such as dyke marches (Currans, 2012). It was the indeterminacy of both the signs woman and lesbian that was later seen as key to the decline in lesbian feminisms (Myers, 2003). As the 1990s progressed, the coalitional politics forming around LGBT rights, the essentialism of lesbian feminism's 'subject' and its 'separatism' increasingly appeared outdated. Ultimately, however, it has been the transphobic association of gender with biology expressed through lesbian feminist texts and ideals such as those proposed by Raymond (1979) and Jeffreys (2003), in particular, that has delegitimised lesbian feminisms in Anglo-American contexts.

The delegitimisation of Anglo-American lesbian feminism has also played out in the separatist spaces it created as part of a search for autonomy from heteropatriarchy. These spaces were often problematic in terms of their inclusions of women of colour, disabled people and others (Bell and Valentine, 1995) and due to their association of womanhood with nature. Today, activist institutions such as dyke marches, scenes, dances and women's music festivals – sometimes only loosely informed by lesbian feminism – continue to struggle to find their constituency as they confront mainstream LGBT calls for coalition-building, the decoupling of gender from sexuality, queer-of-colour critiques of the movement's whiteness, and trans critiques of cis-normativity (Boulila, 2015; Brown-Saracino and Ghaziani, 2009; Lane, 2015; Podmore, 2015). The Michigan Womyn's Music Festival, which, it has been argued, closed in part because of trans/queer activisms, is a famous example (Browne, 2011; Trigilio, 2016). Such debates revolve around what can constitute lesbianism in the first place. Relying on naturalised sex categories, some lesbian feminists have seen trans women as men who are seeking access to 'specifically' women's spaces and bodies. Trans women are read as dangerous 'invaders' and a threat to women and girls (Raymond, 1994; Jeffreys, 2003). Although we take a different stance, the narrative of trans-exclusions in Anglo-American feminisms is powerful and, in the summer of 2018, resulted in direct actions at London and other pride events as well as an extensive campaign to prevent self-identification for trans people in the UK.

With all this in mind, reliance on this story does not acknowledge North American/British lesbian feminism's herstorical complexity or the temporally and geographically diverse expressions around lesbian feminisms, the interplay between lesbian and feminist politics outside of the Anglo-American context and political work in between. Even in the United States, lesbian feminism flowed through diverse networks and was reworked by African-American (Lorde, 1984; Smith, 1983) and Chicana (Moraga, 1981; 2000; Moraga and Anzaldúa, 1983; Trujillo, 1991; 1997) lesbians to address intersections between heteropatriarchy with colonialism and racism (see also Combahee River Collective, [1977] 1997 and Taylor, 2017). The diverse networks of lesbian feminists also crossed national and linguistic borders. Francophone lesbian feminisms are exemplary here as the movement emerged out of dense cross-border transnational networks of lesbian feminists on either side of the Atlantic Ocean. In cases such as Quebec, the powerful legacy of lesbian feminism among Francophone communities meant that it endured well into the 1990s and is still a means of activism for older lesbians today (Tremblay and Podmore, 2015). A similar process took place between Chicana lesbian feminists in the US and those in Mexico. We now move on to discuss lesbian feminist movements and articulations in contexts other than Anglo-America.

'French' lesbian feminisms[5]

French-language lesbian feminisms developed in tandem with their American counterparts but went in different directions due to a persistence of radical feminism, the importance of materialist feminisms (see Chetcuti-Osorovitz and Falquet, this volume) and a sustained refusal by lesbian activists to be subsumed by the gay and lesbian coalition (Podmore and Tremblay, 2015).

To linguistically disrupt Anglo-American hegemonies, we profile these histories here and include a selection of pertinent French-language translations in the collection.

In Paris, the second-wave feminist and gay liberation movements were launched shortly after the social upheaval of the 1968 Sorbonne Occupation due to a sense that issues of gender and sexuality had been marginalised during this event. Feminists launched the Mouvement de libération des femmes (MLF) in 1970, and it was out of this movement that both gay and lesbian sexuality politics would rapidly emerge. Following the famous feminist demonstration at the Tomb of the Unknown Soldier in 1970 led by Monique Wittig, study groups within the MLF formed. Les Petites Marguerites, a lesbian subgroup, began to hold regular meetings in 1970, and, in 1971, Les Polymorphes perverses was formed to study questions of sexuality in social theory (Bonnet, 1998). Exceptionally, some members of the MLF began to organise with 'homosexual' activists, eventually forming the short-lived Front homosexuel d'action révolutionnaire (FHAR) (Chetcuti and Michard, 2003; Chauvin, 2005). The first explicitly lesbian feminist group in France, Les Gouines rouges [Red Dykes], was formed in reaction to the sexism lesbians experienced within this group.

Les Gouines rouges was also a short-lived group, but over the course of its existence it made an important move that would shape the future of French feminism and radical feminism in French-language contexts. Rejecting the FHAR, Les Gouines rouges returned to the MLF, reaffiliating themselves with feminism and rejecting gay liberation. As Bonnet (1998) has argued, this had an important impact on lesbian activism in France in the 1970s where it remained firmly within the feminist coalition. Affiliated with feminism throughout the 1970s, lesbian feminists formed many activist groups, organised by city, ideology or for specific events such as the First International Feminist Conference in Frankfurt in 1974 (Boucheron, 2007). Although lesbian feminist activists remained strongly associated with feminism in the 1970s, once Monique Wittig's "The Straight Mind" and "One Is Not Born a Woman" were translated and published in *Questions féministes* (1980a; 1980b), the pivotal break between heterosexual radical and lesbian feminists would change the direction of lesbian feminisms in France leading to the development of a radical lesbian movement with the foundation of the Front des lesbiennes radicales in 1981 (Chauvin, 2005).

Francophone radical lesbians developed a materialist analysis of heterosexuality, arguing that heterosexuality is a political regime and heterosexual feminists are collaborators, thus lesbians must work autonomously from feminism (Chamberland, 1989; Turcotte, 1998). This strain of lesbian feminism developed through transnational networks among Francophone lesbian feminists in Western Europe, but especially through the interactions between France and Quebec (Podmore and Tremblay, 2015). A distinctive French-language lesbian feminism had been developing in Quebec since 1976, when Francophones attending the Pan-Canadian lesbian conference in Ottawa grew impatient with the linguistic dominance of English at the meeting (Hildebran, 1998; Tremblay and Podmore, 2015). Shortly after, the lesbian feminist space Coop femmes was created, a place where Francophone lesbian culture would flourish in Montreal until the early 1980s, when radical lesbians broke their solidarity with heterosexual feminism and the lesbian feminists who remained allied with the movement (Chamberland, 2000). They formed *Amazones d'hier, lesbiennes d'aujourd'hui* [Amazons of Yesterday, Lesbians of Today], the title of their documentary film (1981) and the periodical they published regularly from 1982 until the late 1990s.

While there were a variety of lesbian feminist practices in both France and Quebec from the 1970s onward (Chamberland, 2000), an enduring sense that lesbians needed their own autonomous spaces and political movements distinguishes French lesbian feminisms (see Chamberland, this volume). In Quebec, the creation of autonomous[6] lesbian organisations continued well into the 1990s, when in many English-language contexts, the lesbian and gay, queer and later the LGBT movement, decentred this activity (Tremblay and Podmore, 2015). In response to difficulties in organising with gay activists for the Quebec Human Rights Commission into violence and discrimination against gays and lesbians (Bonneau and Demczuk, 1998), lesbian activists returned to autonomous representation and, in 1996, formed their own provincial organisation, the Reseau lesbien du Québec [Quebec Lesbian Network]. It, along with the Centre de solidarité lesbienne, are only the most visible sites of lesbian organising in Quebec today. Lesbian publishing continues with Les Éditions sans fin (a Wittig-inspired title) and the archiving of this lesbian feminist herstory remains separate in the autonomous Archives lesbiennes du Québec. In France, the story is similar. The national Coordination lesbienne en France still serves as an umbrella for a range of lesbian feminist organisations throughout the country. In Paris, the lesbian archive remains housed in the Maison des femmes, autonomous from the LGBTQI archives movement, and the city continues to host Cineffable, an international lesbian feminist film festival. And, in Toulouse, where the only women-only café in the country flourished throughout the 1990s, Bagdam Espace Lesbien continues to organise lesbian activist events including the annual, week-long lesbian festival, Le printemps lesbien de Toulouse. While French-language lesbian feminisms emerged simultaneously and in dialogue with those in Anglo-American contexts, place, politics and language have resulted in some very different outcomes.

Ireland

Ireland's exclusionary and discriminatory past in relation to homosexuality and lesbianism were negotiated, resisted and reworked creating Irish lesbian lives, activisms and solidarities (O'Carroll and Collins, 1995). There is a rich history of women-loving women (see for example, Donoghue, 1995; O'Donnell, 2003). Despite extensive legislative changes there are continuing gendered oppositions (McAuliffe and Kennedy, 2017). Women and lesbian (feminist) organising created, and continues to create the island of Ireland, as well as more specifically the Republic of Ireland (see for example the documentary *Outitude*, www.kickstarter.com/projects/582948562/outitude-a-documentary-about-the-irish-lesbian-com). This section briefly outlines key lesbian (feminist) organising that contests Anglo-American narratives of lesbian feminisms. These organisations have various relationships with the term lesbian feminist; here, this term is used to emphasise their engagement with gender and sexual politics from a lesbian perspective.

In the Republic of Ireland, post-colonial British legislation played a part in lesbian lives until homosexuality was decriminalised in the 1990s. Lesbian activists and communities played a significant part in national politics throughout the twentieth century, working alongside gay men around issues of HIV, but also organising separately (see for example Kamikaze, 1995; Crone, 1995; Moane, 1995). What is interesting, and different to the Anglo-American narrative, is the longevity of these organisations and their continued existence as women- and lesbian-focused events and services, that can cater for the entire LGBTQ community. Some of the lesbian organising and service provision that began in the 1970s/1980s includes: the first all-Ireland lesbian conference, which was held in 1979 and continues to this day in the form Lesbian Lives; Dublin Lesbian Line, which, established in 1979, continues to run, supporting LGBTQ people and is staffed by those who are female identified (www.dublinlesbianline.ie/); LinC in Cork, which seeks to "improve the quality of life, health and well-being of all women who identify as lesbian or bisexual in Ireland" (linc.ie); and finally, the Women's summer camp, which started in 1988 and is held in different places across Ireland each year for women (including trans women) and their children. Notable, and in a marked difference to the Anglo-American narrative, is the inclusion of all those who identify as 'women', and this is reflected in national legislation in the Republic of Ireland that allows trans people to self-declare their gender identity. Beyond lesbian-specific organising, lesbians played a significant role in recent Irish sexual politics, both the 2015 same-sex marriage referendum (see Mulhall, 2015) and the 2018 referendum regarding abortion.

Irish (Republic) lesbian communities and manifestations differed from English manifestations (as did Scottish, Welsh and Northern Irish), relating their lesbian and feminism to their specific national contexts, as well as transnational events such as the St. Patrick's Day parade in New York (Conrad, 2001). However, it is often English lesbian politics that are remembered and narrated not only as the Anglo in Anglo-American dominance, but also as 'British Feminism' (to which Irishness is often subsumed and presumed to mirror). While, undoubtedly in the Republic of Ireland there were influences from England and the USA, as lesbians travelled to the USA and UK (O'Toole, 2013), the Irish nation continues to be very different to England, as O'Donnell's chapter (this volume) attests. Northern Irish lesbian feminisms contest Englishness and cannot be presumed to equate unproblematically to Irishness (see for example Duggan, 2012; Kitchin and Lysaght, 2003; Mulholland, 1995).

Southern Europe and Latin America

In the Portuguese context, the intersection of lesbian and feminist movements has provided a space for assertion for lesbian activism. The strong feminist component of Portuguese lesbian activism was particularly visible in the involvement in diverse initiatives to decriminalise abortion, including demonstrations during trials and promotion of thematic debates (Ferreira, 2014; Santos, 2012). However, the intersections of lesbian activism and the feminist movement in Portugal have not always been easy. During the 1970s and 1980s, the feminist movement in Portugal, as well as more broadly, was not open to discussing lesbian issues or even acknowledging that some feminists were lesbians. After the 1990s, along with the emergence of the LGBT movement in Portugal, there have been progressive and consistent interconnections between the feminist movement and lesbian activism (Ferreira and Silva, 2011). It is significant that most of the initiatives focusing on lesbian issues in Portugal are mainly promoted either by lesbian associations on their own, or in collaboration with feminist organisations. The joint actions of lesbian and feminist associations contribute both to strengthen lesbian political action and to push forward the critical reflection within feminist movements on the relationship between gender and sexuality.

Portugal provides an interesting contrast to other countries that are culturally close to it, such as Spain, where the joint actions of lesbian and feminist associations have not, herstorically speaking, led to a higher autonomy of the lesbian movement. The lesbian movement in Spain has come a long way from the total absence and lack of recognition of lesbian women's existence in the Franco regime's 1970 law on dangerousness and social rehabilitation,[7] to later resisting the hegemony of an LGBT movement that silences the diversity comprised within the very LGBT acronym. Lesbians have had to articulate both a political discourse and social presence for themselves in order to create visibility within both the feminist and the LGBT movements (Trujillo, 2008).

In Latin America, there are many different realities at the intersections of feminist and lesbian movements, crisscrossed by local politics and social movements. Political instability has been a frequent reality in many Latin American countries. In this context, the path to equality is not an easy one (Arcos, 2016). Social movements can be strong, but changes towards equality face increased difficulties. For example, in Brazil most of LGBTI rights are a legal reality, but the social context can be quite different. Political instability can compromise legal achievements and in a heteropatriarchal society, women and non-heterosexuals are more vulnerable to discrimination. And lesbians are located at a particularly vulnerable intersection (Silva, Ornat and Junior, 2017).

Beyond the herstorical differences in the paths of feminist and lesbian movements in the countries of the Iberian Peninsula and Latin America, there are strong cultural ties that support joint feminist actions in the present that integrate lesbian issues. One example of these actions is the Iberian and Latin American Network of Geography, Gender and Sexuality (REGGSILA). This network of researchers and activists aims to make visible the production of knowledge on geographies of gender and sexuality in these geographical and cultural contexts, to foster the development of research in this area of knowledge, to enhance synergies between Iberian and Latin American research centres, and to consolidate the presence of topics related to gender and sexuality in higher education in geography. The geographies of gender and sexuality, including lesbian geographies, have been predominantly Anglophone not only in the use of English as the working language, but also extending to cultural hegemony regarding forms of knowledge production. REGGSILA questions this Anglo-Saxon cultural hegemony, by disseminating and making visible research on geographies of gender and sexuality in Iberian and Latin American contexts.

The presence of lesbian issues in the REGGSILA network is strong and visible. One significant example is the *Latin American Journal of Geography and Gender* (RLAGG) (www. revistas2.uepg.br/index.php/rlagg) whose editorial board are founding members of REGGSILA. It has a section, "LES

Online", specifically centred on lesbian issues. This section is the result of the merging of the digital journal *LES Online* (https://lesonlinesite.wordpress.com/) with RLAGG, illustrating the importance of the continuing study of lesbian issues as well as intervention projects and opinion pieces related to lesbian issues from the Iberian and Latin American context.

Poland

Poland has not seen a distinct feminist movement in a coherent sense (Środa, 2009; Olasik, 2018). There are instances of dispersed, independent feminist authors, politicians, activists and public personas in Polish herstory that continue to be unearthed today, but the long socialist period made it almost impossible for the very idea of feminism to emerge on a larger scale. As a consequence, no distinct lesbian component emerged in a collective political form either, be it in activism or academia. It is important to understand the difference between more common developments in some of the Western societies and the historical status of Poland. When Poland was behind the Iron Curtain, human rights, minorities and personal freedoms could not be addressed. Moreover, after 1980, the Polish government was closely allied with the Catholic Church, promoting pro-nationalist values. This cut any potential feminist activists off from building political alliances. Becoming a non-communist state in 1989, the country was left with a devastated economy and deprived of a legacy of activism with regard to human rights. As a result, Poland continues to struggle to accept a multiplicity of gender and sexual expressions, and its populace remains conservative and defensive in the face of such prospects (Olasik, 2018: 50; Kossowska and Van Hiel, 2003; O'Dwyer and Schwartz, 2010).

After the fall of the Iron Curtain, the 1990s brought first local feminist initiatives as well as two major LGBT organisations, but the lesbian has not been a primary concern within their activism and campaigns. Poland has recognised a few feminists, who have been present in the public arena for the last two or three decades (Fuszara, 2006; Graff, 2001). Interestingly, they are seen and described as 'radical' for their women-centred views even though their focus never moved beyond the presence of women in politics and the public sphere (Olasik, 2018: 51–52). After the victory of Law and Justice in 2016, a radical right-wing party that has instigated aggressive homophobic and anti-woman regimes, a series of famous Black Protests began.[8] In relation to these, one feminist philosopher and activist declared, "On 21 September 2016, feminism in Poland started" (Majewska 2017: 25, the editor's translation). However, these events took the question of abortion out of the context of female sexuality, refusing the articulation of lesbian positionalities; indeed, pro-choice activists were not even named as feminists. Meanwhile, at the academic level, several gender-studies programmes are available at larger universities, but they do not cover the question of sexuality in general, nor do they specifically include non-heterosexual identities (Olasik, 2018: 207–217).

Under these local circumstances, the question of Anglo-American hegemony is a crucial one. Kulpa and Mizielińska (2011) have offered an important contestation of Western hegemonies in dealing with sexualities and genders; their English-language volume gathered voices from all around Central and Eastern Europe. However, lesbian concerns were hardly discussed and the concept of 'lesbian feminism' did not appear anywhere in the collection. That being said, while what the Global North is apparently offering can be perceived as better and more progressive, and so it is too easy for contemporary Polish activists and academics to fall into the trap of linearity, which does not take into account the specificities of the locality. With all this taken into account, lesbian feminism has no specific past here, but hopefully it will have a future.[9]

India

In India, the connections between lesbian activisms and the larger feminist movements are inextricably linked, wherein the former acquired a voice and form in conversation with the latter. Having said that, the term lesbian feminism has little traction, be it in popular parlance, in LGBTQ movements or in queer politics. Nevertheless, the intersections and alliances between women's movements and lesbian concerns have been key to the shaping of feminist politics in general and queer feminist politics in particular (see Sen, this volume; Biswas, Beethi and Ghosh, this volume).

Post 1947[10] and up until the late 1980s, autonomous women's movements[11] across India were primarily working around questions of violence (including gender, class and caste-based violence), livelihood, health, education, etc. Along the way, the question – who is the woman in the women's movements – was being put forth by individuals and collectives that were attempting to complicate the concerns of Dalit women,[12] lesbian women and disabled women within larger women's mobilisations, thereby also fracturing the dominant subject of feminist politics.[13] From within the context of women who were either desiring or loving women in urban spaces, bringing a 'lesbian perspective and standpoint' to feminist politics was key. Women-loving women who were also allied with feminist politics broadened the understanding of gender oppression by highlighting narratives of violence faced by persons who strayed from normative scripts of gender assignment.[14] This standpoint has consequently not only pointed to homophobia within women's movements but has also worked against a hierarchy of violence that preoccupied women's groups during the 1990s.

As lesbian activists who are also part of women's movements recall, these movements have long been justifying the trivialisation of lesbian issues by saying that they have greater problems to contend with, such as dowry deaths, domestic violence and poverty. Lesbian activists have had to challenge this hierarchy of violence, to be able to address violence and discrimination for persons assigned gender female at birth and straying from normative scripts. The conditions under which the women's movements constructed such a hierarchy was not solely driven by homophobia. Dave (2012:98–99) locates the need for the women's movements to prioritise poverty over questions of sexuality, in the widening gap between "elite Indian activists and their grass-roots subjects" following the economic liberalisation of the Indian economy in the early 1990s. Thus, the sharpening of lesbian politics within the women's movements has not been easy.

The defining moment, however, for the solidification of a 'lesbian community and critique', was triggered by the backlash surrounding the release of *Fire* in 1998.[15] A film by Deepa Mehta, *Fire* portrayed a love affair between two sisters-in-law in a caste Hindu middle-class household.[16] This film thus broke ground in the portrayal of sexually explicit scenes between two women in the Indian film industry. This was immediately followed by violent backlashes from Shiv Sena,[17] that, in turn, prompted women desiring women to come out on the streets with posters challenging heteronormative desires and claiming a varied 'politics of pleasure'.[18] The lesbian as a political subject and lesbian collectives in India did exist before 1998,[19] but as Chatterjee (2018:14) reminds us, the protests around the *Fire* backlash "shifted the figure of the gay and lesbian subject from a relatively hidden and obscure position in the Indian imaginary to a more public one". Since then, lesbian voices have been key in diffracting the question of gendered violence with sexuality.

Over time, concerns of transmen have come to the surface with the concerns of lesbian women, in addition to bisexual women. Perhaps because of this, a conceptual focus on lesbian feminism has taken a backseat to a much needed articulation around 'queer feminism' to incorporate a deeply layered understanding of the gendered body and sexual violence.[20] If one were to take this argument further, then it may be said that lesbian voices, in their need to include a critique of the marginalised gendered body, had to speak alongside and with the cis subject in both heterosexual and non-heterosexual relationships, as well as trans subjects that were assigned gender female at birth, as they were all impacted – though differently – by gender violence in both domestic as well as public spaces.

As chapters in this collection show, centring the lived experiences and material realities of lesbian-identified women, bisexual women, transmen[21] and genderqueer persons within women's movements can offer an entry point to the conceptualisation of a lesbian feminist perspective with its queer feminist articulation in India (see Biswas, Beethi and Ghosh, this volume; Banerjee, this volume; Karollil, this volume; Mahajan this volume). Queer movements in India, with their regional variations (alongside Dalit feminist articulations, the disability rights networks and sex workers collectives), have already fractured the essential coherence around the category 'woman'; given this, what can lesbian feminism add to the already existing queer feminist articulations within the Indian context? We choose to leave this question unanswered (but not unaddressed), with an aim to use this as an entry point to a transnational conversation about the continuing need to consider gender and sexual politics together across the differences of contexts.

Book outline

This collection brings together academics', activists' and academic-activists' herstorical and contemporary discussions around lesbian feminist theories, movements, experiences and practices. The seventeen chapters include authors from a diversity of linguistic contexts and geographical regions (including Australia, Canada, France, India, Ireland, Portugal, South Africa, the United Kingdom and Germany) who consider the role and relevance of gender and sexual politics to lesbian feminisms for their particular herstorical, social, political and academic contexts. Here we offer a summary of each chapter in turn, in order to entice the reader to delve further into transnational discussions around lesbian feminisms. We have chosen to weave the chapters together through solidarities and communities, personal accounts and rants, within/without studies/institutions/childhoods and future potentials, but of course there are multiple connections, links and divergences between these.

The first chapter, by Sophie Robinson, explores the development of lesbian feminist communities and practices in Australia between the early 1970s and mid to late 1980s. Through the Hobart Women's Action Group, the Australian chapter of 'Radicalesbians', 'Sexually Outrageous Women' (SOW), and the election of the first lesbian president of the Sydney Gay and Lesbian Mardi Gras in 1989, Sophie examines how lesbian feminism was practised in relation to other movements, such as that of the women's movement and gay liberation, as well as further examining what lesbian feminist activism looked and felt like for its practitioners. This chapter provides an example of how lesbian feminism in an Australian setting expands the connections between sexuality and feminism, thus bringing forth lesbian visibility.

In a different context, Rukmini Sen discusses the dialogues and debates between the women's movement and lesbian activisms in India. Assumptions that lesbian groups would 'naturally' find an alliance within the women's movement were dispelled where these were difficult and resisted. Rukmini offers an understanding of this 'uneasy companionship' between women belonging to different kinds of organisations, those that are marked as women's organisations and those that are lesbian women's collectives, in Kolkata, Delhi and Mumbai. To this end, this chapter addresses the following questions: (a) How is *difference* constructed and created as a political strategy in both the spaces? (b) How has the language of power shifted from patriarchy to heteropatriarchy?

Jules Falquet's chapter, a translation from the French for this collection, was originally published in the inaugural issue of *Genre, société et sexualité* in 2009. Jules proposes a reconsideration of lesbian feminist theory and activisms and American Black feminisms as a means by which to contest contemporary neoliberal heteronormativities. The discussion asks for an intersectional analysis that is critical of identity politics. Jules argues that lesbian feminisms have shown us that markers of 'naturalness' are arbitrary and created and, to disrupt them, we need to disrupt the organisation of labour, refusing single-issue politics.

The assumptions of natural alliances are traced through Katherine O'Donnell's chapter in very different ways. Exploring the politics of 'trans-exclusionary feminists' in the UK and Ireland, Katherine examines the theological basis of writers such as Mary Daly, who created specific versions of womanhood, excluding trans women. Arguing for geographic and contextual differences in the alliances with trans people between Ireland and the UK, she notes Ireland's refusal to host a debate "We Need to Talk" which sought to debate trans existence and rights to self-identification under the guise of 'women's rights'. This pertained to gender legislation coming into the UK that was already in place in the Republic, illustrating the lack of understanding of some British feminists of the independence of the Republic of Ireland. However, the 'swift' response of Irish lesbian feminists should not allow for complacency: Katherine contends that the idea of Ireland as post-colonial and post-theocratic is contingent and may not be stable.

Ranjita Biswas, Sumita Beethi and Subhagata Ghosh trace the journey of Sappho for Equality – an organisation that has engaged in the struggle for the rights of lesbian, bisexual women and trans-masculine individuals for more than eighteen years. They map out the political and theoretical framework that has informed, reformed and restrained engagements on the ground, within the LGBTQ community, with the state and with other social movements, particularly feminist movements and queer politics.

Karuna Chandrashekar and Shraddha Chatterjee further this exploration by exploring lesbian feminism through 'erotic friendship'. Their chapter presents a dialogue between friends, an attempt to navigate the discomforts, pleasures, doubts and joys of building and maintaining queer friendships in contemporary queer times as a strategy that helps reach lesbian feminist positions and counter its costs. In the process, they open up the question – how radical is queer friendship?

Shals Mahajan presents a series of episodic rants and anecdotes spread over three decades, and more specifically connected to their work as a member of LABIA – a queer feminist LBT collective, based in Mumbai since 1995. These herstories of being, both personal and political, simultaneously tangle and unravel threads of self and collective, identity and desire, gender and sexuality, naming and being.

In contrast with companionship and community, Rosie Swayne offers an activist retort to English-based lesbian activists who are seeking to refuse and refute trans rights. Seeking to pull together evidence that challenges contemporary arguments, Rosie both offers an insight into how trans-exclusionary lesbian movements are currently operating in the UK and contests their claims. She urges intersectional analysis and critique, a means by which to fight back.

In "The Butch, the Bitch, the Superwoman" Paramita Banerjee adopts a personal approach, examining her experiences with radical left politics during national Emergency in India and the first few years of the first-ever non-Congress government between the mid to late 1970s, as well as with the post-independence women's movement, as it gained momentum during the late 1970s and early 1980s. By reflecting on her experiences, Paramita elaborates on how her involvement with the LGBTQ movements in India in general, and West Bengal in particular, have shaped and sharpened her understanding of gender and sexual normativities and myriad ways of defying them.

Line Chamberland's chapter is an English translation of a French article first published in 2002 in proceedings of the conference "Le féminisme comme lieu pour penser et vivre diversité et solidarité". Using her personal trajectory as primary path, Line tells the story of the relationship between lesbian feminism and feminism in Quebec. The chapter takes us from the first generation of lesbian feminists in the 1970s through the conflicts and ruptures of the 1980s and, finally, into the 1990s when lesbian feminism in Quebec became increasingly fragmented in the face of the coalition around gay and lesbian rights, queer politics and the formation of lesbian subgroups around other interests. The chapter knits together, unravels and reknits the connections between the terms lesbian and feminist in multiple ways: feminist-lesbian, lesbian feminist, lesbian within feminism, lesbian-first-and-then-feminist etc.

In conversation with Nadika Nadja and Poorva Rajaram, Nitya V also explores the question of what or who is a lesbian feminist, questioning what it means to call oneself a lesbian and a feminist. The text explores the meeting point of these two terms, as personal-political affinities, in the context of the contemporary Indian milieu. Through reflections on diverse questions, raised by the act of articulating the being of a lesbian and feminist, the chapter thinks through the term 'lesbian feminism' in relation to the anxieties, dissonances and forms of belonging in 'our time'.

Natacha Chetcuti-Osorovitz's chapter is a translation from a French text drawn from her broader work on lesbian feminism in France (Chetcuti, 2010). The chapter presents the major currents of thought in French sociology and their rapport with social movements and theorisations of lesbian feminisms. Natacha examines the influence of key theorists, such as Monique

Wittig and Nicole-Claude Mathieu, demonstrating how this body of work made it impossible to continue to envision categories of gender and sex as they had been, because it denaturalised knowledge on heterosexualised gender.

In contrast, Asha Achutan offers an examination of the 'girl child' in Indian state policy, directing our attention to how the management of gender can restrict an articulation of lesbian feminist issues, where, politically and socially, lesbians are 'liminal at best'. In so doing, Asha opens up space to enable a lesbian feminist critique of the governance of gendered bodies. The potential of lesbian feminisms in this chapter is explored through a lacuna that is so stark that the chapter works around lesbian feminism but does not proscribe it.

Valérie Simon also explores the potential of the lacunae within lesbian feminisms to create critiques from without. Based on her personal reflection on the twelve-week lecture series she organised titled "LEARNING HOW TO SCREAM: A Lecture Series on Lesbian Lives, Theory and Activism", she explores how those excluded from the transmisogynistic, whitewashed, biphobic and classist official history of lesbian theory and activism are the ones engaging and critiquing it. Valérie argues that for contemporary manifestations of lesbian feminism to flourish and grow, we must conceive of lesbian feminism as a theoretical, political and personal standpoint from which to think through contemporary issues.

Mamatha Karollil's chapter also asks us to consider the potentials and futures of lesbian feminisms. It is a reflective account of her experiences and observations of queer women's organising within LGBT/queer activisms in India, and specifically, Delhi, over the last decade. She looks at the tensions and contradictions between organising around identities and the necessity of introducing an intersectional lens drawn from queer theory. Mamatha questions what woman-identified political organising or lesbian feminism can offer to the practice of politics in a context of increasing right-wing fundamentalism that provokes the need for collaborations across a range of activisms such as feminist, queer, anti-caste and anti-communal politics.

Sara Ahmed's rich speech at the Lesbian Lives conference in 2015 is reprinted here because it offers powerful and important insights into the potential of reclaiming lesbian feminism, Sara calls for a revival, for a 'bringing back to life' of lesbian feminism for queer times. Her lesbian feminism forms a necessary alliance with transfeminism wherein anti-trans becomes anti-feminist. Ahmed sees the potential and possibility in lesbian feminisms, in its small actions, its ordinariness where the raising of an arm from the ground becomes a call to arms, a call for a lesbian feminist army to chip away at the 'Master's house'.

Nadine Lake analyses how the increased visibility of lesbian, gay, bisexual and transgender (LGBT) sexual minorities in post-apartheid South Africa has been met with vitriolic public speech and violence aimed at Black lesbian women. Nadine focuses on deconstructing the term corrective rape and explores how the emergence of a counter archive of lesbian activism and solidarity in South Africa may contribute to the reconceptualisation of national and transnational lesbian sexualities.

Conclusion

Overall the chapters in this collection offer rich and varied explorations of and around lesbian feminisms, refusing their static definition and demonstrating how they are redefined through their locations. We have sought to build an interdisciplinary approach, where a diversity of scholarly and activist perspectives within and across the humanities, social sciences and cultural studies could be adopted so as to disrupt Western and Anglophone hegemonies and explore the multiple ways that lesbian feminisms are employed and may contribute to contemporary sexuality politics in diverse contexts. Beyond multiplying and expanding the geographical portrait of lesbian feminisms, the collection addresses key debates in contemporary gender and sexuality praxis as well as around collectivities and solidarities. Although the collection is far from exhaustive, we hope that it can contribute to contemporary debates about the role of gender in sexuality politics by enriching the portrait of lesbian feminisms, opening up new dialogues, and encouraging further reflection and even reconsideration. The collection's transnational context further permits the exploration of multiple but interwoven pasts as they intersect with varied presents in search of alternate futures.

Notes

1 We use 'liveability' to refer to the optimal conditions required to live a life that is worth living.

2 'Women' is used as a gendered category in this book.

3 We use the term 'non-heterosexual' in single quotations to specifically refer to sexual and gender practices, identities and expressions that are outside the dominant heteronormative model. In doing so, we do not deny the usage of the term 'heterosexual' to signify an identity, practice or expression by those outside the dominant model.

4 We deploy 'transnational' as a political concept that includes connections and solidarities across borders around geopolitics, ethnicities and institutional locations.

5 'French' feminisms here refer primarily to the French-language feminisms that developed in France and were extended by Francophone lesbian feminist activists in Quebec.

6 In this context, 'autonomy' refers to lesbian organisational independence from the growing gay and lesbian and LGBT movements as well as from the feminist movement.

7 This was an act of the Spanish penal code adopted by the Franco regime in 1970 used to define particular groups, including queers, as "dangerous subjects".

8 The Black Protests were a mass social reaction to sudden proposals on total abortion bans; they were organised events that took place several times in almost all the major cities in Poland simultaneously. Dressed in black and holding black umbrellas, people marched for hours, protesting with shouts and banners. It is believed that one of those marches actually stopped the Law and Justice party from adopting the law, which is unprecedented.

9 One hopeful example is the recent emergence of a lesbian-centred organisation, named 'SISTRUM Association: The Space of Lesbian*

Culture'. Not only is it the first such initiative, but it also seems to break with the above-mentioned Western linearity, since it calls for a diversity of lesbian expressions rather than a fixed interpretation. For more details see Olasik (2018: 190–197).

10 India gained political independence from England in 1947.

11 Autonomous women's movements refer to mobilisations that emerged independently of political party affiliations after 1947.

12 Dalit women, also known as 'untouchables' or 'outcastes' because of the Hindu caste hierarchy, are among the most economically, socially and politically oppressed groups.

13 The subject of feminist politics within women's organisations was primarily middle to upper caste, Hindu, heterosexual. For some notable publications in this regard, see Ghai (2002; 2005), Guru (1995), Menon (2007), Rege (1998; 2006).

14 To further understand the lesbian perspective and standpoint, including their connections with women's movements see Biswas (2007), Chatterjee (2018), Dave (2012), Menon (2009a; 2009b), Narrain and Bhan (2005), Shah (2005).

15 For some notable references in this regard, see Bose and Bhattacharya (2007), Dave (2012), Menon (2007), Narrain and Bhan (2005).

16 'Caste Hindu' refers to the folds of the caste system, in relation to its outside, to which the Dalits are relegated, and hence, abject.

17 A Hindu right-wing political organisation.

18 For detailed accounts of lesbian organising, see CALERI (1999 [2011]), Dave (2012).

19 Notable among them are Sakhi formed in 1991 in Delhi, Stree Sangam (later LABIA) and the Forum Against Oppression of Women in 1995.

20 It is important to note here that in addition to lesbian voices, sex workers' voices have been equally crucial in bringing the question of sexuality to the centre of the women's movements. Further, on the conceptual forefront of queer politics, transfeminism is gaining some traction as well.

21 Including transmen in this narrative in no way means that political articulations of trans men in separation from lesbian activisms do not exist or are insignificant in the Indian context. The dynamics between queer feminist collectives and trans men are complex, indicating the constant need for queer feminist politics to not become complacent when thinking about the gendered body and violence associated with that.

ONE | Sisterhood, separatism and sex wars

Sophie Robinson

Lesbian feminism emerged in Australia during the early 1970s via enhanced lesbian politicisation (and following this, separatism) in Women's Liberation, the homosexual political organisation Campaign Against Moral Persecution (CAMP) and Gay Liberation. Homophobia and sexism within these movements, which reflected broader social and cultural prejudices, caused some lesbian activists to explore their dual oppression and different political futures compared to gay men and heterosexual feminists. By the end of the 1970s, lesbian feminist collectives, protests, conferences and communities, underpinned by explorations of sisterhood and separatism were emerging across Australian states and territories. Drawing on several oral histories I conducted over a four-year period with women in Australia who identify, or did, as lesbians and feminists, this chapter traces some foundational moments in the history of Australian lesbian feminism during the 1970s and 1980s. Some of my informants were politicised and radicalised during the 1970s as participants in Women's Liberation, CAMP and Gay Liberation, and some were politicised via the 'sex radical' lesbian scenes that emerged in Australia during the 1980s and 1990s.[1] These scenes spanned leather, kink, sadomasochist (S/M) and fetish subcultures, and were primarily linked with gay male sexuality at the time. However, Australian lesbian sex radicals claimed them as their own.[2] Lesbian sex radicals are not typically considered part of lesbian feminism, or rather sex radicals and lesbian feminists are seen as combatants. This is because of a dominant narrative, and for some an experience, of lesbian feminism as a political position without any necessary connection to sex or desire. As has been widely covered in the context of the United States of America (US), the 1980s saw some watershed moments for feminism. Sexual practices such as sadomasochism as well as pornography were increasingly politicised, which seemingly divided lesbians and other feminists across lines of pro-sex and anti-sex. However, these debates were much more complex, varied and, as I will show, localised. Tracing these nuances in an Australian setting can challenge our understanding of the links between lesbian feminism and lesbian sex radicalism.

I explore the dynamic history of Australian lesbian feminism via four foundational events that took place between the early 1970s and in the mid to late 1980s. Two of these events centre around conferences during 1973. Here I introduce the Hobart Women's Action Group (hereafter referred to as HWAG), as well as an Australian chapter of the 'Radicalesbians'. My other two examples are the lesbian sexual sadomasochism (S/M) group which formed in Sydney in 1984, 'Sexually Outrageous Women' (SOW), and the election of the first lesbian president of the Sydney Gay and Lesbian Mardi Gras in 1989, Cath Phillips. I argue here for reconsideration of a distinct lesbian sexual and cultural revolution in Australia, and more specifically, in Sydney. Sydney has some considerable claim as the Australian 'lesbian capital' since the 1970s – although there was inevitable movement out of Sydney as lesbians and their activism moved interstate and internationally. Together these four examples trace how Australian lesbians generated unique debate about the connections between sexuality and feminism, challenged sexism and homophobia within their communities, and promoted lesbian visibility. The developments in lesbian feminist politics and activism in this period were a remarkable advance, given the historic and enduring silence around lesbianism and female sexuality in Australia and elsewhere. While there is a tendency to only focus on experiences from the Global North in histories of feminism broadly, this chapter offers a vital and localised reinterpretation of lesbian feminism's expansive origins, reach and trajectories in an Australian setting.

A lesbian presence emerges

From the early 1970s, lesbian activists in Women's Liberation, CAMP and Gay Liberation attempted to redefine lesbianism in more positive terms, and not, as the medical establishment and wider society had treated homosexuals thus far, as deviants.[3] While Women's Liberation was a particularly empowering space for some lesbian activists, namely through its specific cultivation and celebration of women-only spaces, there was also some significant hostility towards lesbians in the movement in its early stages and concern over how to integrate lesbian 'issues'. For Thelma, interviewed for the 1996 exhibition portraying lesbian existence in Australia *Forbidden Love, Bold Passion* (Ford et al., 1996) she had not been 'out' prior to involvement in Women's Liberation. However, within Women's Liberation consciousness-raising groups:

> I developed a whole new understanding of women's place in the world. Being a lesbian became the most natural thing in the world. The women's liberation movement gave me the confidence to be an open lesbian. From then on, I have never been anything else. (Thelma, quoted in Ford et al., 1996:14)

Not all identifiably feminist lesbians were enamoured of this development. Lesbian activist, and founding member of the CAMP Women's Association (CWA),[4] Sue Wills, recalled:

> For some women, the early 1970s was a time of sexual liberation
> in the narrow sense of a fairly new-found freedom to experiment.
> Women you'd met once or twice would suddenly bowl up to
> you and say something like, "I've decided I'm a lesbian and
> you're it. Teach me". – which is equally offensive ... these
> reactions stem from the same view of lesbians as being defined
> purely in terms of sexuality, as women sort of permanently on
> heat. (Wills, 1990:5)

Indeed, lesbian was a contentious term in the early 1970s,
so much so that the CWA used 'female homosexual' instead
for their early literature. As Wills explained, "this was only
partly in order to make the link with male homosexuals in
the organisation – gay had been taken by the Gay Liberation
movement" (Wills, 1994:21). The word lesbian had "negative
connotations" (Wills, 1994:21). An emerging lesbian feminist discourse within Women's Liberation, CAMP and Gay
Liberation centred on dispelling the various myths and prejudices about lesbianism that informed such discomfort. It also
enabled lesbian activists such as Wills to differentiate their
separate struggle from heterosexual feminists and gay men.

Emerging historians Beverly Kingston and Jill Roe, the latter
a member of CAMP, pioneered an analysis of lesbianism from a
feminist perspective as early as 1971 (Roe, 1971; Kingston, 1974:5).
Along with international feminist writers and theorists, Kingston
and Roe furthered Women's Liberation's critique of femininity
and the nuclear family, articulating "the relationship between
dichotomous sex roles and compulsory [hetero]sexuality" (Lake,
1999:243). As Australian historian Marilyn Lake noted, albeit
briefly, in her comprehensive history of Australian feminism, *Getting Equal* (1999:243), the theorising around femininity and sex
roles that took place in Women's Liberation owes much to such
early theoretical interventions by lesbians. By the mid-1970s,
circulating radical feminist ideas and texts from overseas, such

as *Sisterhood Is Powerful*, a collection edited by Robin Morgan (1970), and "The Woman-Identified Woman" by the New York-based group the Radicalesbians (1970) further inspired several participants in Women's Liberation, Gay Liberation and CAMP to take lesbian politics and activism more seriously.

In January 1973, the Hobart Women's Action Group (HWAG), established in Tasmania (an island state off the mainland of southern Australia), made a further bold intervention into Australian feminist discourse at a Feminist Theory Conference held in Mount Beauty, Victoria. The conference was organised by a group of feminists from Canberra who self-mockingly described themselves as 'The Hevvies' (Magarey, 2014:37). Akin to the more well-known and historicised zap action staged by the 'Lavender Menace' group at the Second Congress to Unite Women in the United States in 1970 (Jay, 2013), HWAG's presence at the Mount Beauty conference challenged patterns of homophobia within Australian feminism. Their paper, formally titled "Sexism in the Women's Liberation Movement", with an additional title of "Why Do Straight Sisters Sometimes Cry When They Are Called Lesbians?" (HWAG, 1973:8–12) listed a range of issues and structures defining Women's Liberation at that time in which they felt lesbians were silenced. This included consciousness-raising groups, interpersonal conflict and discrimination, uses of the feminist term 'sisterhood' and,

> Being called a bull dyke for speaking out at a Gay Lib/women's
> Lib session on sexism ... Being told lesbianism is a 'passing
> phase' in women's lib. Finding out that the lady you're in bed
> with is a 'real woman' (liberated variety) and you're only a
> hardened lesbian (sick variety). (HWAG, 1973:8)

In their paper, HWAG rearticulated a fundamental tenet of Women's Liberation – the inclusion of all women in definitions of sisterhood (Magarey, 2013). While HWAG opened a space to consider the lesbian presence in Australian feminism, many around them and after them were also exploring lesbian feminism for themselves.

Radicalesbians

In 1972, the year before the Mount Beauty conference, a group of women in Melbourne, known at the time as the 'Gay Women's Group', started to meet separately from the men of Gay Liberation, namely because they found some to be sexist and ignorant of lesbian oppression (Melbourne Gay Women's Group in Mercer, 1975:441–446). After some significant clashes at their shared meeting space in the Gay Liberation Centre on Davis Street, Carlton, some of the Gay Women's Group moved over to the Women's Centre. This was a symbolic shift, and one uniquely influenced by the recent arrival of three women, Robina Courtin, Jenny Pausacker and Kerryn Higgs, who had each been away in London and influenced there by radical feminism. Courtin and Pausacker were particularly emphatic about the benefits of a radical feminist lens, Higgs recalled (2017), and they encouraged the Gay Women's Group to engage with international radical feminist literature circulating at the time. Australian historian Jill Matthews has historicised this as "productive misreading" whereby texts were not "simply copied or borrowed wholesale from abroad" but redefined locally (Matthews, 2017:4).

One such text included "The Woman-Identified Woman" by the New York-based Radicalesbians that provided a "nascent definition of lesbian separatism" (Enszer, 2016:182) which resonated transnationally.[5] Kerryn Higgs, author of Australia's first lesbian novel *All That False Instruction* (Riley, 1975), published under pseudonym 'Elizabeth Riley', recalled that in addition to the Woman-Identified Woman, Robin Morgan's book of poems *Monster* (1972) was another source of inspiration (Higgs, 2017). The group had managed to publish *Monster* with Morgan's direct consent as it was unavailable locally. Already under threat for being sued by Ted Hughes due to the defamatory content of "Arraignment", Random House publishing had decided to "remove all copies from every market in the Commonwealth" (Morgan, 2014: Preface). In Canada, a group of women decided to nonetheless publish a pirated edition with Morgan's consent. Soon after, Morgan recalled,

> Australian women and New Zealand women had contacted me wanting to publish their own pirated editions, which they did, also with my permission. This happened all across the Commonwealth – spontaneously, furiously, wonderfully. (2014: Preface)

During this time some in the Gay Women's Group also began debating whether they too should reclaim the word 'lesbian'. Lesbian seemed radically different to "camp, gay or woman-identified", Chris Sitka recalled, and was a positive and more explicit term used to define their identities and politics (Sitka, 2011:123–125). In early 1973 a few chose to start calling themselves 'Radicalesbians' specifically. Sitka noted that this was "the most out and outrageous name we could confront our various oppressors with" (2011:125). In July 1973, a national Radicalesbian conference was held at a guesthouse in the beachside town of Sorrento in Victoria. Just over sixty women from Sydney, Adelaide, Canberra and Melbourne attended (Sitka, 1989:3). "We had big plenary sessions and discussions", former participant in the Sydney Radicalesbians Diane Minnis recalled (Minnis, 2017), and topics ranged from bisexuality, to non-monogamy, to women's refuges, to how to develop a feminist culture across music, writing and other mediums. "It was kind of like a flowering of lesbian feminism really", Minnis explained (2017).

A Radicalesbian manifesto was developed at the conference, unique from the New York Radicalesbians' "Woman-Identified Woman". The core message of the Australian version was to link

'gay consciousness' with a 'feminist consciousness' and to redefine relationships between women.

> We want to overcome the division between women – to touch,
> relate, to give strength and validity to each other. We want
> women to be able to relate on all levels. We want to relate as
> individuals, not as elements in a correct ideology ... We do not
> want equality, but liberation.
>   We want a distinct feminist community where we can learn
> to be/act ourselves ... no point conquering male culture when
> we can create our own. (Radicalesbians, 1973, cited in Willett,
> Murdoch and Marshall, 2011:126–127).

One session at the conference explored prospects for establishing women's refuges across major Australian cities. Refuges and
women's services broadly are areas of feminist activism that lesbians have been very active participants in founding and running
in Australia since the early 1970s, the first being Elsie's refuge
for women and children in Sydney in 1974. In another session,
participants explored the topic of 'relationships' and whether
'warm and real sisterhood' was in fact 'non-genital', though not
necessarily non-sexual (Karen, in *Vashti's Voice*, 1973:12). Such
questions pointed to broader discussions about the parameters
of feminist sexuality and an emerging concern with the politics of
lesbian sex radicalism. These are known as the 'Sex Wars'.

Australian lesbian sex wars

In 1982 US scholar Gayle Rubin presented a paper titled
"Thinking Sex" at the international feminist academic forum,
"The Scholar and the Feminist Conference IX", held at Barnard
College, New York. Rubin's paper, later published in a collection of the conference proceedings, *Pleasure and Danger*, edited
by Carol S. Vance (1984a), theorised a pervasive sexual hierarchy that differentiated sexual behaviours and relationships into a

binary of good vs bad, normal vs deviant (Rubin, cited in Vance, 1984a:267–321). It also identified how lesbian sexuality, and namely lesbian S/M,[6] had become a specific fault-line.[7]

While the charged US debates in the lead up to and the aftermath of the Barnard conference cannot be mapped neatly onto the Australian context, there are nevertheless some general shared features in terms of the regulation of lesbian sexuality at this time. In the interviews I conducted with Australia lesbian feminists and sex radicals, for example, all recalled debates emerging in the early 1980s, and some before, about whether lesbian sex and relationships should specifically *not* incorporate power-dynamics, role playing or indeed penetration. These potentially continued the power differentials inherent to heterosexuality and patriarchy, some argued. One of my informants, Katrina Harrison, a lesbian sex radical from Sydney, indeed acutely recalled such debates "as a sad and confusing time" (Harrison, 2017). Women who had been "happy to participate in covens and group sex in the 1970s", perhaps suggesting an earlier history of sex radicalism, "suddenly became quite puritanical in their outlook", she noted (Harrison, 2017). During the 1970s, Harrison was active in feminist groups at Sydney University after the birth of her three children. She helped to establish a 'women's room' on campus, a parent-operated child-care centre, and staffed women's refuges and women's health and rape crisis centres. Katrina also co-founded *Mabel*, the Australian feminist newsletter, produced in Sydney which ran from 1975 to 1977, and she had her first sexual experience with a woman at a feminist conference. By the 1980s and 1990s, Katrina's activist trajectory had shifted. She got involved in running women's sex and play parties in Canberra, such as the "Ms. Wicked" contests associated with Sydney-based lesbian pornography magazine, *Wicked Women* (Henderson, 2013) and became a member of Sydney Leather Pride. Harrison recalled feeling ostracised by parts of the lesbian and feminist community during this time.

> Women who had been sexually adventurous (participating in
> multiple relationships, engaging in bondage etc, etc) suddenly
> became evangelically monogamous and 'vanilla'. Those of us
> who had been open about what we liked were shunned and
> ostracised by some of our friends. (Of course, we suddenly
> had other friends because they were curious or wanted to
> experiment). (Harrison, 2017)

From the early 1980s, spaces for lesbians to experiment with their sexuality, an environment lacking in sexually explicit resources by and for lesbians, were emerging and expanding. This included discussion and consciousness-raising groups for exploring S/M, workshops on sex toys for lesbians and how lesbians could use them, parties where women were encouraged to indulge in their 'wickedness' through enacting and/or watching sexually explicit performances, and also via the promotion of leather clothes and goods by and for women (Blackman and Perry, 1990:67–78).

The entry of group 'Sexually Outrageous Women' (SOW) into this terrain "was a somewhat awkward attempt to create a degree of sexual sophistication amongst lesbians", according to activist and former participant in both Sydney's lesbian feminist and lesbian sex radical scenes, Kimberly O'Sullivan (1991:22). SOW also represented a "coming out", O'Sullivan explained, of lesbians who wanted to explore their sexuality beyond sisterhood and separatism (1991:22).

Challenging the notion that lesbians have safer, non-penetrative and less recreational sex than gay men was core to the expansion of lesbian sex radicalism in the 1980s. At a time when gay male sexuality was linked to illness and disease in Australia and elsewhere due to the emergence of the HIV/AIDS crisis, some lesbians were meanwhile embracing gay-male-dominated sexual subcultures (as well as caring for their dying gay male friends) such as the leather and S/M scene and redefining these for themselves. In doing so they also challenged some degree of invisibility of lesbian sex and desire in feminist discourse and refocused it as a feminist issue. In 1984 a notice in Sydney feminist newspaper *Girls Own* in 1984 introduced SOW as a group "for women interested in exploring/experimenting in diverse sexual practices (including SM)" (*Girls Own*, 1984; SOW, cited in O'Sullivan, 1997:120). Kate Rowe was in her early thirties when she came across one of these notices and soon made contact. At the time, she was new to lesbian feminist activism, having been radicalised by her participation in the first Mardi Gras parade in Sydney in 1978. Prior to this she had not engaged in any political activism and had been a very heavy drinker. After deciding to become sober Rowe soon found she "was up for exploration" (Rowe, 2016). She described her experience of expanded sexual possibilities in this period.

> I was very interested in exploring stuff sexually and I wasn't really thinking about it in political terms ... It seemed like a lot of women were going down that path ... it was a lot of women, like me, who were being tentatively explorative. (Rowe, 2016)

Sexual health resources by and for lesbians, including pornography, were largely non-existent in this period, and SOW attempted to fill this gap. One of the group's founders, Robyn, brought back a copy of the lesbian magazine *On Our Backs* after a trip to the US (Rowe, 1991). This gave Rowe her first bit of exposure to lesbian pornography. She also recalled Robyn bringing back an "amazing dildo, the first lavender silicone dildo ... It came with a leather harness" (Rowe, 1991). SOW eventually held their own sex toy workshops, with dildos and other instruments donated by 'Numbers', a gay male sex shop in Sydney. They hosted sexually explicit performances, by and for women, demonstrating various sexual acts incorporating bondage and sadomasochism.

S/M was provocative territory for the lesbian community in Sydney. As Rowe highlighted, it was especially so "in the context of everything that was going on at the time ... You know the whole violence against women thing and all that sort of stuff ... so this [group] was antithetical to all of that, and I wanted to understand [it]" (Rowe, 2016). S/M, which encompasses a range of practices, became the target of widespread feminist criticism in Australia, the UK and the US in this time. S/M seemed antithetical to a feminist politics that had, thus far, been working to make visible a vast array of evidence of violence, sexual abuse, incest and emotional abuse against women since the early 1970s (Ward, 1984; Murray, 2002). Reflecting on SOW with me, some thirty years later, Rowe indeed recalled how subversive it felt to be involved. And yet, she also credited the group for giving her certain training and an "attitude ... of not being a prude ... it was 'a great piece of history'. I am glad it happened" (Rowe, quoted in *Wicked Women*, 1991:24). However politically 'unsound' it may have seemed to her and other lesbians initially, SOW offered Rowe a pioneering space for women to 'watch and learn' lesbian sex radicalism in the short time that it operated (Rowe, 2016).

The lesbian presence in Sydney's Mardi Gras

From the mid-1980s another terrain in which Australian lesbian activists challenged their invisibility was the annual Sydney Gay and Lesbian Mardi Gras. Sydney's Mardi Gras has become the definitive social and cultural event representing Australia's LGBTIQ+ communities since it first began on the evening of 24 June 1978. While organised to be a street party celebrating gay and lesbian visibility and solidarity it swiftly developed into a violent battle between paraders and police (Harris, Witte and Davis, 2008). Lesbians played a significant role on that night, namely through resisting and fighting back against the police; however, it was not until the late-1980s that the lesbian presence in Mardi Gras reaffirmed itself. Gay activist Ron Smith, who, with artist

Peter Tully, worked on various parades during the 1980s, recalled that with election of an "all dyke committee" in 1988, and the election of Cath Phillips as president in 1989, Mardi Gras was repoliticised and "brought Dykes seriously back to it" (Smith, 2007).

In 1988 – the year of Australia's Bicentenary – Kimberly O'Sullivan, Cath Phillips and Celia Hutton were elected to the Mardi Gras committee. The Dykes on Bikes (DOB) also emerged that year as a definitive lesbian presence in the parade. DOB first formed in San Francisco in 1976, when it was only a group of around twenty to twenty-five women, remaining small and informal in its organisation or structure at least until the early 1980s (San Francisco Dykes on Bikes, 2016). Kimberly O'Sullivan recalled seeing the San Francisco DOB and feeling inspired to start a Sydney contingent. Today, the original San Francisco group is considered the 'mother chapter' for the broader Dykes on Bikes community, which extends across the US, Australia and England. O'Sullivan had also been present for the first Mardi Gras in 1978, crawling under a car with her girlfriend to hide from police (Harris and Witte, 2018:11). She recalled the moment that Cath Phillips called her in the late 1980s to ask if she would stand for a position on the Mardi Gras committee, and if she could get another woman to join them on the ticket. "I had another friend called Celia Hutton", she noted,

> And, so, I rang up Celia … We fronted up to this [Mardi Gras Committee] meeting with all these boys … There was one guy, I think it might have been Anthony Babicci … He was very old, gay liberation, liked women, that kind of stuff. (O'Sullivan, 2015)

Babicci was supportive of having the three women on his ticket for the upcoming election; however, O'Sullivan recalled that other men in the committee were less enthralled. As O'Sullivan noted, this had something to do with their political training and context, and more specifically their proximity to women as activists and allies. "The others were more clone-era guys who'd come out in the Eighties and never had anything to do with women ... so, they came out into a solely gay male world" (O'Sullivan, 2015), she explained.[8]

In the same year that Phillips, Hutton and O'Sullivan were elected to the committee, Cath Phillips spent two days in gaol. At an art show in Mildura, a town in the north east of Victoria, she had been "charged with two counts of obscenity because of a sculpture she entered in the show that included a caption with the word 'cunt'" (Macken, 1988:245). Phillips refused to pay a $400 fine in relation to her charges, which led to her gaol sentence. According to Phillips, there was a rush to get her released on bail in time, as she was to be the last speaker in a Special General Meeting of the Sydney Gay Mardi Gras Association to decide whether they would finally include the word lesbian in the title. She was released in time and attended the meeting on the 6 December 1988. After a tense vote, it was determined that the name be changed to Sydney's Gay and Lesbian Mardi Gras. However, "the schism split Sydney", O'Sullivan recalled, and there was big "fallout" (O'Sullivan, 2015):

> I looked across at all the guys I'd been sitting at a board table with for two years [and who had moved against the change]. Anyway, it got through, by some miracle ... It was really, really unhappy. The fallout from that was really big. (O'Sullivan, 2015)

For Cath Phillips, Mardi Gras was an organisation and culture that needed significant structural change. "The profile of women needed to be raised and people were feeling disenfranchised, which troubled me" (Phillips, quoted in Wright, 1990). When asked in 1988 why lesbians "took so long to get back into Mardi Gras?" Phillips explained that "we had our own problems with sorting out our own dogma and the sort of sex we would be associated with" (Phillips, quoted in Macken, 1988:245). For example, "if you went to your friends and told them you'd just been to the Mardi Gras, they'd say, 'That's not right, they're all boys, they're horrible, they all have penises and stuff'" (Phillips, quoted in Macken, 1988:245). When Mardi Gras "started ten years ago, almost half the people arrested were women because dykes had a high profile in the event. That was the only year we had input into it" (Phillips, quoted in Macken, 1988:245).

For Sydney's lesbian community, the late 1980s was a definitive period for reaffirming the lesbian presence in the gay commercial and cultural scene. Phillips becoming the president of Mardi Gras, and Mardi Gras' name change to include 'lesbian', were crucial aspects of this. Indeed, they are moments in Sydney's gay and lesbian history still recounted by activists from this time. The backlash and interpersonal struggles that O'Sullivan, Phillips and others had to negotiate within the gay and lesbian community as they asserted a lesbian presence indicated ongoing areas in which these political communities were divergent, namely due to unresolved issues of sexism that lesbian activists had been illuminating since the early 1970s.

Conclusion

The four examples examined in this chapter trace Australian lesbian feminism in its earliest formations in the 1970s, and its later development during the 1980s, a decade typically narrated for its significance in the lives of gay men. I have charted some of the ways that lesbians sought to alert gay men and other feminists to their unique experiences of sexism and homophobia, and how they started to form a movement focused on lesbian politics, culture and liberation. Furthermore, these earlier examples of a developing lesbian feminist consciousness in the 1970s can be linked with various efforts in the 1980s and 1990s to address lesbian invisibility in the Sydney gay commercial and cultural scenes, including sex radical subcultures. Over a period of twenty years, lesbian activists of different political training and backgrounds contributed to more expansive understandings of lesbian identity in Australia, both in relation to and beyond explicitly feminist activism. Tracing this history indicates an expansive lesbian presence in Australian feminism and offers new examples of lesbian feminism's diverse trajectories and genealogies.

Notes

1 Sex radicalism as examined in this chapter refers to those who were experimenting with sadomasochism and/or leather as part of their sexual practice, and to signify that they were part of a sex radical community.
2 In *Kink*, Kerry Bashford (1993) and other writers associated with Australia's first lesbian sex radical publication explore this historical moment in which women were challenging the boundaries of sexual subcultures to include women, and to reclaim such spaces for lesbians especially. For studies that explore sex radicalism and the rise of lesbian sex radical subcultures during the 1980s and 1990s see, Califia-Rice (1980), Vance (1984a), Rubin (1984), Thompson (1991), Faderman (1992) and Taylor (2008).
3 See for example Clarke (1975), Ross (2009), and Jennings in eds Willett and Smaal (2013).
4 CWA is the same acronym used for another Australian women's group, the Country Women's Association. Founded in the 1920s, The Country Women's Association of Australia incorporates various CWA chapters around Australia that each work to support and advocate for regional, rural and remote women and their families.
5 While "Woman-Identified Woman" emphasised "the primacy of women relating to women … [as] the basis for cultural revolution" (Radicalesbians, 1970, in Enszer, 2016:194). Julie Enszer has highlighted that the lesser known "How to Stop Choking to Death", written by Lois Anne Addison and her lover ('Revolutionary Lesbians' as they called each other) advanced the notion of lesbian separatism as "working directly only with women" (Enszer, 2016:182).
6 See Ardill and Neumark (1982), Ardill and O'Sullivan (1986).
7 See also Duggan and Hunter (2006), Ferguson (1984).
8 For further insight into the 'clone' subculture, an import from San Francisco during the 1970s, and its relationship with a new masculinity amongst Australian gay men see Willett (2000).

TWO | Is there a new language in hesitation?

Rukmini Sen

Dialogues and debates between the women's movement and lesbian movement in certain locations in India have been both hesitant and complicated. As much as there may have been an assumption that the lesbian groups will 'naturally' find an alliance within the women's movement, it did not happen easy or without resistances. This chapter will try to understand this 'uneasy companionship'[1] between *women* belonging to different kinds of organisations (those that are marked as women's organisations and those that are lesbian women's collectives) in different parts of India. When saying organisations and collectives, the intention is not to hierarchise, rather to think whether internal structures got created within women's groups over years of functioning and funding. On the other hand, lesbian groups did begin as support systems, as safe spaces to converse, as *loose* collectives engaging with questions of care and support. In the Indian context of political mobilisation, these were much less structured, somewhat in the lines of autonomous women's groups of the early 1980s. However, the latter became very rare by the late 1990s or early 2000s, when we see the lesbian collectives starting a discussion on (impossibilities of) love. By looking at some publications and interviews emanating from these 'lesbian' spaces this chapter will want to interrogate the following:

a) How is *difference* constructed and created as a political strategy in both the spaces?

b) How has the language of power shifted from patriarchy to heteropatriarchy?

This chapter reflects upon some (im)probable conversations in the course of alliance building especially in the context of groups and mobilisations in the metropolitan urban cities of Kolkata and Delhi, one in the eastern part of the country and the other in the north and also the capital.

Uneasy beginnings

My own involvement with a women's organisation in the city of Kolkata through the decade of the 2000s provides me with certain insights and experiences about how I am approaching this chapter. This is, primarily, a reflexive essay, which draws from being associated with some protests and observations on activities of sexuality rights organisations in Indian cities. Clearly, women's organisations and gender – and sexuality-profiled organisations like PRISM, Sappho or LABIA (in Delhi, Kolkata and Mumbai respectively) – emerged at different time periods, have existed parallel to each other and came together on certain common issues around violence (like the repealing of Section 377 of the Indian Penal Code) and marginalisation. The uneasy beginnings and the hesitant continuities between the otherwise 'natural' allies seem to be the direction that has been taken in many parts of the world.[2] Why are some groups and movements considered to be 'naturally' in alliance? Autonomous women's organisations came into existence due to their disillusionment with (progressive) leftist organisations in the early 1980s. Dalit women questioned the universal category of women that mass women's organisations or autonomous organisations seemed to represent till the early 2000s. This was

happening in different ways, through the formation of National
Federation for Dalit Women and also epistemologically inaugurating the *difference* question through Sharmila Rege's essay
(1998) "Dalit Women Talk Differently". So, even when alliances happen, they result from unease and differences, and not
necessarily from similarities. Difference, therefore, is an important political basis for aligning – processes, programmes and
possibilities. These methods of coming together, due to difference, are never smooth, in fact always messy and complicated.
Thus, it is important to understand that any politics of coming
together of organisations and ideologies with multiple positionalities is invariably fraught with discomfort and unease, and the
possibilities for future lie in how to converse within these.

Attempts to converse: creating spaces

There are clear differences between the issues that women's
organisations in the city of Kolkata highlighted and those that
lesbian women's collectives focused on in the initial years of the
latter's coming into visibility. The autonomous women's groups
in the city started by responding to the question of dowry-related
violence and rape in public spaces.[3] The monogamous, heterosexual 'family' although interrogated, the structure never really
got challenged – practices within it like dowry and bride burning were considered evil problems. The patriarchal hierarchy that
dominated heterosexual families was questioned. However, the
movements did not really imagine an alternate to the heterosexual
monogamous biological kin-based families. In fact, heterosexual marriage seemed a given, raising biological children was
common among left and women's groups, and negotiating one's
selfhood and personal identity in order to raise the child was common among women in left organisations and women's groups in
Kolkata definitely, throughout the 1980s, until the 2000s. Within
this larger political context of the city, love, sexuality and intimacy

were not really political issues, but, rather, individual matters, just like domestic violence was at the start of the women's movement and it took so many years to break the silence around it and make it a part of the public, political agenda. Thus, although the lesbian collective Sappho created a community space to begin with, in the city of Kolkata in the late 1990s (starting with a helpline number advertised in a local Bengali newspaper, to hawking their newsletter in the book fair, to gaining an office space to establish a resource centre (www.sapphokolkata.in/sexuality-resource-centre/), to finding a space on the lesbian women's question in the leaflet of a women's platform in West Bengal), it did not come easy. All of these happened through the 2000s in Kolkata after the release of the film *Fire*.[4]

Whether the foregrounding of sexuality happened in women's organisations directly or in a more unconscious assimilative mode is subject to discussion. In a 2014 interview, Malobika, who is a founder member of 'Sappho in Kolkata', suggested that, "It was, therefore, an absolute necessity to be a part of the women's movement. That is why, immediately after the formation of Sappho, we became part of Maitree[5] ... the idea is to create spaces like Max Mueller Bhavan[6] and the Academy of Fine Arts.[7] Also, we want to engage with colleges here, which could be through films or discussions" (In Her Voice, 2014). The connection between the concerns of lesbian women and heterosexual women was understood by members of 'Sappho' early and that established their camaraderie with existing women's groups as well as the need to align with women's groups in the city on the question of violence against women, while pushing the contours of who could be at the receiving end of this violence. Trying to equate food, clothing and shelter with sexuality in the same breath was tough in the city which had a history of left trade union politics, radical student movements during the 1970s through Naxalite movements,[8] autonomous women's groups and then NGOs working on women's rights, as well as the state government that had belonged to the communist tradition for thirty-four years. One of the reasons for the growth of autonomous women's groups in Kolkata (like in other parts of India such as Delhi, Bombay and Hyderabad) was the disappointment with the mainstream political parties as well as radical left groups and their indifference to specific questions related to women – sexual violence, torture and humiliation experienced by them due to dowry.[9] If this 'shift' and creation of autonomous women's groups happened in the early 1980s, the other shift/split happened around early 2000s – this was the split-scepticism related to what the *real* women's issues are – sex, desire, love, violence, suicide, rape, dowry, foeticide? It may not be correct to identify a split, but surely a rupture in the women's movement emerged with sexuality, love or desire being part of the conversation. The question of difference and sexual identity being the basis for the difference was squarely put in the landscape of social movements through lesbian collectives. Did the women's movement ever really imagine the existence of the (desiring) lesbian women and the violence faced by them from members of the parental family? Did they consider suicides as a result of parental pressure or perceived social pressure about the stigma around same-sex love as (domestic) violence? Was it through films like *Fire*, reporting of incidents of suicide in Kerala and later in other parts of the country and the continuous foregrounding of the lesbian women by Sappho in the women's movement agenda that spaces got created? So, all of this happened through time as well as with hesitation rather than in haste. Chayanika Shah, one of the founding members of LABIA (Mumbai) in an interview articulates:

> For me, the articulation of the queer voice within women's movements dates back to '87 as a campaign issue. But conversations around being lesbian, and the knowledge of

lesbian women within the groups were there even when I had joined. For example, the Forum would meet in a household of two women, who we all knew were a couple. And for me the fact that they met in a lesbian couples' home made me think that this group is welcoming to lesbian women and that all was fine. My understanding at that time was also that we didn't need to be very open and out, and that I don't need to label myself; I can be in a relationship with whoever, it really does not matter. But there was a lot of conversation, and there was a feminist understanding of sexuality and of relationships. Though there was an acceptance of being lesbian, there was no foregrounding of issues. (Mathew, 2017)

The objective has been to need an accommodative space to meet, to push the boundaries of the existing collective spaces as well as to create new public spaces, *counterpublics*. It is nearly like forging solidarities through alternate kinships, much in the sense of making/choosing families. Through lesbian lives and living therefore, counter and alternate discourses on personal living and collective living emerge. The Sappho collective becomes a shared, safe, supporting, nurturant space together with trying to build and choose families which are not biologically constructed. Constructing and strategising on conversations has constantly been the way in which gender and sexuality rights issues found room within and outside women's movements.

Building friendships and communities

From hesitant beginnings and conversations, there have been multiple methods and moments of emerging – through political and legal efforts made by lesbian groups in alliances with women's groups, other sexuality rights groups, mental health groups, child rights groups, disability rights groups or transgender groups. What is important to understand is that forging alliances has always been the way through which lesbian collectives have organised themselves. One such moment was post the 2009

Delhi High Court judgment decriminalising Section 377 of the Indian Penal Code. In the first issue of 2010, Sappho's newsletter *Swakanthey* (i.e. "In My Own Voice") contained an entry:

> 2nd of July 2009, all LGBT groups gathered in front of Academy of Fine Arts, a set of people labelled as 'criminals' without performing the crime, who were now freed. As humane citizens of India we gathered to wish each other … Who are we? And how are we with ourselves? In the politics of NGOization of HIV/AIDS organization, where is our movement for sexuality rights? The gathering at the Academy was an appeal to community, or rather the promise of a community that refuses to remain non-existent within the folds of the city, loving, laughing and seeking to change the norms of social interaction right at its heart. This collective was not a fiction, but a reality that with all its territoriality and face-to-face interaction became a site for political re-imagining. (Sappho, 2010:1)

The questions of community and identity were both significant in the 2009 moment. This was because the law was both constructing a community while also 'freeing' people in same-sex relationships or LGBT as the law understood them. It is through the Naz Foundation judgment that legally a group was being constructed, of people who were in 'same sex' sexual relationships, although of course that meant only men in the eyes of law. Lesbians did not become visible through law, the lesbian question was more discursive, created through deaths or being present in various kinds of mobilisations. The law, however, was present, as a (cultural) framework, which could harass many kinds of living. Through the *Swakanthey* statement it is necessary to understand that there was a rearranging of the community identity that the court had constructed; the felt need to step away from the HIV/AIDS construction while claiming a movement and moment for sexuality rights. This was momentous, since there was a clear rupture marked as well as a connection established.

Rupture from the health framework to sexuality and connection with more women wanting to claim their gender orientation. On its website, LABIA[10] talks about the interconnections that a sexuality rights organisation needs to make:

> We believe that our freedoms are not singular, and neither are our identities. We are queer, we are people of different sexualities and genders; we are also people being thrown out of our jobs because of corporate takeovers; we are people from different castes, regions and communities; we are people with disabilities; we are people losing our lands to development schemes or SEZ plans; we are people spending endless time filling water for our families; we are still being forced to marry against our wills; we are citizens of this country, struggling to survive and fighting for our rights. (LABIA, 2010)

There is a need therefore to connect with and critically engage with 'others' or locate oneself with/in other people who also rearrange domesticities.

> For a progressive sexual movement ... even if the question is not one of marriage, but of legal contracts, of augmenting domestic partnership arrangements as legal contracts, certain questions still follow: why should it be that marriage or legal contracts become the basis on which health care benefits, for instance, are allocated? If one argues for marriage as a way of securing those entitlements, then does one not also affirm that entitlements as important as health care ought to remain allocated on the basis of marital status? What does this do to the community of the nonmarried, the single, the divorced, the uninterested, the nonmonogamous, and how does the sexual field become reduced, in its very legibility, once we extend marriage as a norm? (Butler, 2002:21)

Consolidating within and pushing the contours of alliances remains the critical objective with which conversations could happen.

One of the members of Sappho talked about the support system that the organisation had provided over the years:

> Emotionally [I think of] Sappho as a group coz it comes almost like a family. You have drama, everything happens here, is just amazing. But people will support you, if you do something wrong, people will still talk to you it doesn't matter. And there's a lot of friendship and everything. Might sound odd but we also have these somebody somebody's brother and somebody somebody's mother [to connect with] and I don't know, I think maybe because in everyday life something is missing somewhere that we try to find or make relationships over here, not necessarily just friendships and finding a partner and stuff. But you will always find someone calling each other by your, some sort of a term which you would be like some sort of a family member thing. (Banerjea, 2011)

Establishing friendship or kinship relationships through a collective or trying to establish a sense of belonging in a city which is also the home to most of the members, is one of the fundamental roles that many of the queer feminist organisations perform. Thus, it is necessary to understand how the home, family, kinship, relation, possession, connection and compromise are all experienced by the transgressor – the member of the queer feminist organisation. I have "Friendship As a Way of Life" (Foucault, 1997) here as a reference point to the argument being made – the need to look at lesbian queer lives as rearranging kinship structures and family arrangements, not merely a transformation in the legal sphere. The role of the transgressor here is not merely to be a member of a queer feminist organisation, rather to imagine that through the collective what are the possibilities of co-existence and new forms of living.

New marches, new colours, towards more conversations
The rearrangement of loving and living needs to happen in multiple forms, even in the ways in which queer groups protest and/

or celebrate – protest about homophobia and celebrate diverse living. The first time I participated in a pride march was in the city of New Delhi. The march was from Mandi House Metro Station to Jantar Mantar Road (all in central Delhi), a common distance travelled during marches in this city. Having previous experiences being part of marches, and protests that have been organised by women's groups in Kolkata and Delhi, my first reflection was to compare a queer pride march with a women's movement protest rally or remembering 8 March (International Women's Day). The use of colours in the dresses, the rainbow flag being waved, the colourful masks or hairdos – it was all striking. The fact that there were many people in masks represents how difficult it still is to come out of the closet; the masks could keep the secret but could be the gateway towards unravelling it as well. The covering of the face and the articulation in the voice co-exist. Multiple gender identities perform in public spaces, where the co-relation between the face and the voice remain clandestine, the use of *dholaks* (drums) and *dafli* (tambourine) and the practice of participants stopping regularly in the middle of the march to dance to the rhythm of the *dholak* also gave the pride a 'carnivalesque', celebratory essence. This is usually uncommon in women's movement rallies – there's a lot of song and sloganeering, but dance while marching is an unusual sight, at least at the ones I have attended in Delhi and Kolkata. I have, however, personally performed dance in women's movement meetings in Kolkata, dancing either to the poem titled "Pashani Ahalya" of Salil Chowdhury (written in the context of the Kakhdwip massacres in West Bengal during the Tebhaga movement). I have also performed to the song "O Alor Pathajatri", again composed by Salil Chowdhury, in various centrally located Kolkata protest sites; this is a song calling the masses towards transformation beyond the darkness that engulfs the society. Both these performances 'fit' the radical nature in which women's movement protests happened in Kolkata in the 2000s. This poetry or song composed through the left-oriented Indian People's Theatre Association, and the autonomous women's movement's political alliances with left politics, made these protest songs and dance acceptable within women's movement spaces. Many years have passed, and it was in 2014 that I spontaneously danced to "Premero Joare Bhashabe Dohare" ("The Love between the Two Would Create New Waves"), together with a Sappho member, during a protest march organised on International Human Rights Day, which took place after the Koushal judgment of the Supreme Court that recriminalised same-sex sexual acts. To perform a (heterosexual) love song of the Rabindranath Tagore style (performed by two women) in a protest march was not the most usual form of protesting. Yet it could happen since there was a substantial presence of members from sexuality rights groups and transgender groups in that march. The creation of a space for a subversive love song marked an important dialogic moment and reminded me of what I observed as well as how I participated in the Delhi queer pride mentioned previously. There was such a significant performance of/through the body which seemed to be an integral component of the pride. The erotica in shaking the belly or the bosom, the sensuousness in the red lipstick, the appeal in the black *surma* (kohl) or the caressing of the rainbow pride flag – they were all spectres of performance and acts of claiming and reclaiming a public space which humiliates, victimises, coerces and punishes the 'queer'. The Delhi pride in its plurality and unfathomable energy expressed love through posters like "Pyar Kiya to Darna Kya?" ("What Is There to Fear While in Love?"), "Pyar Huya Iqrar Huya" ("There Is Love and There Is Acceptance of That Love"), "Queer Huya to Kya Huya" ("So What If Love Is Queer?"), "Love over Bigotry" or "Love Is a Human Right". It all emphasises the freedom to love, across bodies and genders. On the other hand, claiming that "Genders Are Diverse Not

Disordered", "Stop Assuming My Gender" or "Be Straight Not Narrow" encompasses a strong message sent to the heteropatriarchal structure that by default assumes two genders, a heterosexual union and a marriage among these two genders, and procreation as a result of that marriage. One common slogan that I have given voice to in the course of my being part of women's movement's rallies has been "Awaaz do, hum ek hain" ("Raise your voice to say, we are one"). Here, while I was about to echo "*hum ek hain*", someone pointed out to me that *ek* could be changed to *anek*, making the slogan "Awaaz do, hum anek hain" ("Raise your voice to say, we are many"). It was a meaningful changing of the original slogan and reminded me of the title of the 7th National Conference on Women's Movement in 2006, Kolkata, which was "Affirming Diversities, Resisting Divisiveness".

There has been an interesting change or proliferation of colours in protest marches. Being part of women's groups in the city of Kolkata throughout the 2000s, one realised that the colour red was marking protest; it was also the colour of the Communist Party flag. Red also signified blood, and because of this it has historically been associated with sacrifice, danger and courage. Red is also the colour most commonly associated with passion, sexuality, anger, love and joy. In China and many other Asian cultures, it is the colour of happiness. Since the French Revolution, the red flag has been the symbolic colour of revolution, and, in the later nineteenth and twentieth centuries, the symbolic colour of socialism and communism. In the twentieth century, red was the colour of revolutions: it was the colour of the Bolshevik Revolution in 1917 and of the Chinese Revolution of 1949, and later of the Cultural Revolution in China. Red was the colour of Communist parties from Eastern Europe to Cuba to Vietnam to India. The song "Bhoy ki laal ronge, amader priyo rong laal" ("There is nothing to fear in the colour red, our favourite colour is red") also exemplified the closeness of the colour red with protesting forms. With the inclusion of pink, both separately and together within the rainbow flag, a new set of colours gets associated with protest, where pink clearly refers to sexuality. Pink, when combined with white or pale blue, is the colour most commonly associated with femininity, sensitivity, tenderness, childhood and the romantic, while pink combined with black or violet is commonly associated with eroticism and seduction. These changes in marches and colours are also represented through some of the posters that have come up most recently in the wake of the post-2012 Delhi gang rape.[11] There seems to be a language of protest emerging across various cities and towns in India which is bold, sexual and thereby political. Some of the posters that young women in the streets of Delhi carried while protesting against the Delhi gang rape in 2012 read, "My outfit, being drunk, great boobs, flirting does not cause rape" or "Meri skirt se unchi meri awaz hai" ("My voice is higher [louder] than my hemline"), "My body my right, my city my right", "Ignore my lipstick and listen to what I have to tell", or "Even at 12 am this city is mine". There is a strong reference to the body, the dress code or claiming of public spaces in these posters and slogans. It seems to inaugurate a new moment, a moment where the boundaries between queer feminism and feminism get blurred, where conversations between women's groups, lesbian women's groups or transgender groups create new languages of protest.

These articulations resonate with the contemporary times where young, sexually conscious women are trying to construct dialogues between differences, or converse despite differences. Movements have progressed a lot from the initial periods of hesitations. There are clearly new distances and discourses, and bridges have been built – alliances across groups are always complicated and yet when today a voice says "*mahila mange azaadi*" ("women desire/demand freedom") the imagination of this contemporary woman is not the early 1980s, or even the 1990s. It is a new fractured identity where she inhabits plural self(s) and community, where hesitation and not certainty is the way towards multi-logues.

Notes

1 I am influenced by and will draw upon the 1979 Heidi Hartmann essay, "The Unhappy Marriage of Marxism and Feminism: Towards a More Progressive Union".

2 A certain type of women's movement in India looked at the left ideology as the 'natural' home for talking about women's emancipation. However, the autonomous women's groups in the early 1980s emerged from a disillusionment with the left parties, although may not be with left ideology. In the late 1990s when lesbian support groups or resource centres were emerging, women's groups were considered to be the 'natural' home/allies and not always gay groups. Similar experiences of being with as well as being apart from women's groups have happened in the US – the Lavender Menace turned Radicalesbians is a good example of a 1970s New York-based lesbian collective. The Combahee River Collective was a Black lesbian group of 1974 which also later took up Black lesbian women's questions.

3 A series of bride-burning incidents were being reported in Bengali dailies in the early 1980s and women's groups in the city of Kolkata formed platforms to talk about bride burning, dowry-related murder or dowry death. Rape of women political prisoners became an important rallying point in Kolkata as a consequence of the atrocities committed on Naxalite women. It may be worthwhile to note that dowry death as an issue was troubling many north Indian states as well in the early 1980s and the rape of a tribal girl in a police van in Nagpur became the basis of making custodial rape a political issue for the women's movement. As a result of some of these mobilisations, there were changes in rape laws of the Indian Penal Code as well as introduction of a specific provision of dowry death also in the criminal law in the 1980s.

4 Arguably the first film to represent lesbian love in Hindi films in India released in 1996. There was tremendous controversy and protests after the release of the film by many Hindu right-wing groups claiming the film and its philosophy went against Indian culture and tradition. For more detailed discussion on the film, please see Kapur (2000).

5 A network of women's groups in West Bengal.

6 The venue of Dialogues, India's oldest LGBT film festival.

7 An open space outside an art gallery and theatre where a lot of protest meetings have taken place.

8 Primarily landless labourers and student-based agitation against landlords originating from the mountain town by the name Naxalbari in North Bengal. The movement spread across West Bengal, Bihar and Andhra Pradesh primarily and led to a second split in the Communist Party as a result of the ideologies practised by the Naxals.

9 For further discussion on the reasons for the creation of autonomous women's groups in Hyderabad and Bombay, see Kannabiran and Kannabiran (2002) and Ray (1999), respectively.

10 LABIA (Lesbians and Bisexuals in Action) is an organisation for queer and trans-identified women in Mumbai, India. It was founded in 1995 as Stree Sangam and in 2002 changed its name to LABIA.

11 An important moment in contemporary times for the women's movement and all other forms of social movements in the form of gruesome rape and murder of a young woman in public transport in Delhi. Protests occurred all across the country and led to various changes in rape laws in 2013. Young students from various college and university campuses used an interesting (sexual) language of protest, where freedom, body, reclaiming of public spaces became part of the protestors discourse.

THREE | Demythologising heterosexuality and sexual difference

Jules Falquet

> Mixed gay movements *displace the question* of heterosexuality
> by concentrating on sexuality; part of the non-mixed lesbian
> and feminist movements place the system of compulsory
> heterosexuality and the organization of reproduction at the
> heart of the oppression of women, and that is more threatening.
> (Mathieu, 1999)[1]

The present multiplication of movements and research on sexu-
ality/sexualities is undoubtedly a positive outcome since one of
its most important benefits is to render more visible the many
practices and people who, around the world and every day, cou-
rageously contest the existing sexual order. However, by concen-
trating almost exclusively on sexuality as a collection of *sexual
practices* and/or *individual* desires and attributing considerable
importance to interventions on the *body* and its appearance –
again, principally an individual act – it seems to me that the dominant trends of these movements are missing part of their objective.
Indeed, if the idea is to contest the binarity of gender or sexes and
especially their supposed 'naturalness' – a project that large parts
of the feminist and lesbian movements have been working on for
more than four decades – by focusing on individual identity and
everyday practices we risk taking a side road leading to a dead-
end. Fascinating as the body and the human psyche can be, travelling along this side road does not, however, allow us to reach the
deep roots of the problem. Therefore, the argument that I would

like to defend here is that the problem lies not in the body nor in persons … So, where does it lie and how can we solve it?

To answer this question, I propose a rediscovery of other paths of analysis and struggles, which began in the second half of the 1970s, but despite this early development, are almost unknown today and rarely used. The possible reasons for this involuntary or intentional ignorance are multiple. First, the unequal circulation of the different perspectives depends upon their subversive potential and the positions of power (notably of sex,[2] class and 'race'[3]) of the people and groups that defend them, as well as their position within the academy or the activist world, and in the North–South divide.[4] Next, there is the weakening of the social movements that they stem from and that could support them, which is related to the decline of 'progressive' and 'revolutionary' movements and the growing conservatism since the 1980s in the context of the rise of neoliberal globalisation.

However, the main point is not to try to know why this or that orientation is today the dominant one in social sciences or in the social movements, but rather to respond to the intellectual and moral urgency to understand and transform reality. Actually, the enforcement of neoliberalism leads to a staggering rise of inequalities alongside sexual, racial and class divides. In the face of this brutal deepening of exploitation and misery, ignoring the legacy of the radical struggles is a luxury that we cannot afford.

First, in order to put the current dominant occidental understanding of sexuality and its ties with sex, gender[5] and the mechanisms of matrimonial and/or political alliances into perspective, I will provide some socio-anthropological reminders and present a brief review of the main results of the fundamental work that Nicole-Claude Mathieu developed throughout the 1970s and 1980s and that she brought together in 1991 in a book that she eloquently titled, *L'Anatomie politique* [Anatomy is Political]. Next, I will present what seems to me to constitute the most important theoretical and political insights of the lesbian, radical and feminist[6] movements of this period, both in the United States and in France.[7] To conclude, I will demonstrate to what extent these findings are particularly valuable in the context of contemporary neoliberalism, and how they can be enriched to help us face the analytical and political challenges posed by globalisation.

The diversity of matrimonial and sexual practices between 'women' and the meanings that are attributed to them

The historicity and multiplicity of sexual and matrimonial practices between women

The economically privileged, contemporary, 'white', urban, occidental world is far from being the first or the only one in which 'women' established among themselves sexual, loving and/ or marital relationships. Different poets have described in the first person their carnal love for other 'women', from Sappho of ancient Lesbos to African-American author Audre Lorde (Lorde, 1982; 1984). Despite their later destruction, the pre-Vedic period in India's history left behind very sexually explicit sculptures depicting sexual relations between 'women' (Thadani, 1996). In Zimbabwe, lesbian activist Tsitsi Tiripano (who died in 2001) and the gay and lesbian group GALZ, with which she fought, provide resounding proof that lesbianism exists in the African continent (Aarmo, 1999). In Sumatra, Indonesia, 'tomboys' are 'masculine women' who establish couple relationships with other 'women' (Blackwood, 1999).

Lesbianism, as it is defined in the dominant Western thought today, is a recent category. It is based on numerous, highly social premises that have been progressively established in different societies. Some are largely shared beyond the Western world – the belief in the existence of 'women' and 'men', and that these women and men are such because of the 'sex' that was conferred upon them by Nature. Others are more specific: *sexual practices* being supposedly what confer a sexual *identity*[8] upon an individual; sexual identity as stable and permanent (or even innate); and, finally, sexual 'identity' made to correspond with a type of character or personality.

In contrast, practices that could seem lesbian according to contemporary Western logic, such as sexual or matrimonial practices, may not necessarily be so for some societies that implement them. Thus, in at least thirty African societies, as among the Nandi of western Kenya, there are forms of marriage between 'women', that do not necessarily involve sexual practices between the women (Amadiume, 1987; Smith Oboler, 1980). Generally, the reason is a rich, older woman wanting to have progeny with a younger woman who provides children by having sexual relations with a man. Also, among the indigenous population of the northern plain of the American continent, shamans, referred to as 'berdaches', establish couples with people of the same 'sex' precisely because they are considered socially as belonging to a gender that is the opposite of their own 'sex' (Lang, 1999). It is exactly this great diversity and complexity of past and present cultural arrangements, whether dominant or marginal, regarding sex, gender and sexuality, that Nicole-Claude Mathieu's work allows us to discover (1991).

Mathieu's analytical framework

The analytical framework proposed by Nicole-Claude Mathieu is especially interesting because it includes both Western and non-Western, current and past societies, to which she applies the double sociological and anthropological lens that is so typical of her perspective. The core of her analysis on the articulation between sex, gender and sexuality, appeared in her "Sexual/Sexed/Sex-Class Identity: Three Ways of Conceptualising the Relationship between Sex and Gender".[9] Here she responded to a hypothesis of

Saladin d'Anglure (1985) according to whom a 'third sex' existed, as in Inuit society, invalidating the idea of a binary between the genders and the sexes and reducing notably and strikingly, according to Mathieu, the theory of 'women's' oppression. In her article, Mathieu worked on a whole range of practices concerning sexuality, gender or sex that contemporary Western thought would more readily describe as queer. In fact, she analyses:

- 'institutionalized deviances', whether permanent or occasional, trying to establish whether they are an inflection of the norm or, on the contrary, its essence;
- the self-definition of groups or individuals considered deviant or marginal, trying to establish if they constitute 'normalized' solutions to perceived inaccuracies, or forms of subversion. (Mathieu, 1991:230)

In studying these forms of "deviance" in quite varied societies, Mathieu shows (1) that most are actually institutionalised mechanisms of adjustment and/or are functional or functionalised within the social systems considered, and moreover, (2) there is no single way to believe (or not) in the naturalness of sex and of gender. Mathieu's article is especially interesting because it effectively demonstrates the limits of the "vulgate of the 'sex-gender-system'" that, starting in the 1980s, tended to replace other analyses that were properly speaking feminist: the "sex-gender-system" analysis becomes inoffensive and dull when we remove the dimension of sexuality. But, moreover, as Mathieu demonstrates, it is not queer sexualities or genders that are really key in understanding the structural social relations of sex, but rather the norm that they reveal, namely the central principle of *heterosexuality* that haunts 'gender theories' like a ghost. It is in unmasking this spectre and all its diverse manifestations that Mathieu succeeds in revealing not one but three major modes of the articulation of sex, gender and sexuality:

Mode I: *'Sexual' identity*, based on an individualistic consciousness of sex; where sex and gender are homologically
connected: here gender translates sex.

Mode II: *'Sexed' identity*, based on a group consciousness;
where sex and gender are analogically connected: here gender symbolizes sex (and, vice versa).

Mode III: *'Sex-class' identity*, based on a class consciousness;
where sex and gender are socio-logically connected: here
gender constructs sex. (Mathieu, 1991:231)

This typology permits an important distancing from the ethno-
centrism and flawed universalism that characterise the dominant
contemporary Western view of sexuality and especially its beliefs
regarding sexual identities. This decentring shift reveals the emi-
nently relative, historical, cultural and, in the end, non-absolute
character of sex, gender and sexuality. Simultaneously, Mathieu
allows us to understand that a large portion of heterosexual people,
but also many people who contest heterosexuality in the Western
world, for instance, large swaths of the global gay, queer and trans
movements that are developing today, adhere in fact to Mode I
and sometimes to Mode II of the articulation sex-gender-sexuality.

In contrast, here I propose to re-examine the logic developed
in other strands of the movement that for a long time have developed, like Mathieu's thinking itself, within what she describes
as Mode III, the anti-naturalist and materialist one.[10] However,
before taking any further steps, it is necessary to make a few
important points regarding the material and conceptual context
in which these analyses are situated.

The three modes of conceptualising the relations between sex,
gender and sexuality described by Mathieu are inscribed within a
framework in which there is a clear predominance (numerical and
political) of societies organised in favour of people who are considered

as men and as males. This hegemony, which we observe almost everywhere in the world for the historical period that is documented, functions due to a closely intertwined combination between (1) social relations of sex that are varied but all patriarchal[11] and (2) for women, the general imposition of procreative heterosexuality as well as a strict prohibition and invisibilisation of exclusive female homosexuality.

Certainly, exceptions exist. As the collection of texts brought together by Mathieu (2007) demonstrates, some matrilineal and especially uxorilocal[12] societies do experience social relations of sex that are clearly less unequal than those that exist in patrilinear and virilocal systems. Regarding sexuality, male homosexuality (certain sexual practices, in certain stages of life) and moreover, homosociability, are not uncommon, being socially integrated within mechanisms of patriarchal power, as among the ancient Greeks, the Azande, the Baruya or in some exclusive male clubs found in many contemporary cities, as Mathieu reminds us (1991). In contrast, sexual practices between 'women' are scarcely tolerated, and only as long as they are private, invisible and clearly separated from homosocial practices and/or moral and material solidarity, let alone visible matrimonial and political alliances[13] between 'women'. Because, it is precisely by deliberately and collectively conflating amorous-sexual and material-political alliances between 'women', *to the detriment of the compulsory relationships with men,* that is, stepping from lesbianism as a political movement, that the real practical and theoretical revolutions that I will further present, could occur.

Lesbianism as social movement and political theory

The emergence of an autonomous social movement and the critique of other movements

The semi-public existence of lesbian collectivities in different Western countries (and others) pre-existed, notably, the development of the feminist movement, as we can clearly see for example in Davis and Kennedy's (1989) study of the small city of Buffalo in the McCarthy-era United States of the 1950s, which demonstrates the existence of working-class and racialised lesbian communities organised around 'butch–femme' codes. However, it was at the end of the 1960s and the beginning of the 1970s that the lesbian *movement* appeared, in the North as well as in the South, in a climate of economic prosperity and profound social and political change: the development of a consumer society, triumphant 'modernity', and the emergence of diverse progressive and/or revolutionary movements. In the United States, movements for civil rights, Black liberation, the independence of Puerto Rico or Indigenous rights, revolutionary struggles and decolonisation, the opposition to the Vietnam War, feminist and homosexual movements finally, served as political 'schools' for a generation of activists. Nevertheless, for a variety of reasons, these movements left many women and lesbians unsatisfied. It is precisely the critiques of the inadequacies, contradictions and silences of these movements that led them to seek organisational and especially theoretical autonomy.

Regarding lesbians, the first very visible expression of the necessity for autonomy was made by the white North American journalist Jill Johnston, who simultaneously critiqued the gay movement that was dominated by men and the feminist movement dominated by women who were usually heterosexist and heterosexual. Her columns, published in the *Village Voice* between 1969 and 1972, were brought together in a book entitled (by her editor) *Lesbian Nation: The Feminist Solution*. Appearing in 1973 in mainstream publishing circles, it quickly became a best-seller (Johnston, 1973). In fact, in the 1970s, and not without conflict, the lesbian movement spread like wildfire in many parts of the world, establishing its autonomy from feminism and the mixed gay movement, and more broadly, from the set of 'progressive' movements from which many of its activists emerged.[14]

Thus, the first contribution of the lesbian movement to other social movements was nothing other than permitting them to reflect on the limits and gaps in their thinking, as much in their everyday practices as in their political objectives, especially in the domains of sexuality, the family, the gender division of labour or the definitions of masculine and feminine roles. The countless critiques formulated on these topics by lesbians, with most of them also being articulated by the feminist movement, are like a mirror held up to the face of many movements and activists which should permit them to really bring coherence into their political projects.

Theorisation of interlocking power relations and the necessity of alliances

In the same spirit of building autonomy and deepening reflection on the long-term objectives and everyday practices of social movements, the Combahee River Collective, one of the pioneer Black feminist groups, appeared in 1974 in Boston. It was born out of a quadruple critique of the sexism and the middle-class character of the Black movement, the racism and middle-class perspective of the feminist and lesbian movements, the reformist orientation of National Black Feminist Organization and the blindness of socialist feminists to questions of 'race'. In response to all these insufficiencies, the Combahee River Collective affirmed for the first time in a manifesto that became a classic, the inseparability of racism, patriarchy, capitalism and heterosexuality – and thus the inseparability of the struggle against each and every one of these systems.

> The most general statement of our politics at the present time would be that we are actively committed to struggling against racial, sexual, heterosexual, and class oppression, and see as our particular task the development of integrated analysis and practice based upon the fact that the major systems of oppression

are interlocking. The synthesis of these oppressions creates the
conditions of our lives. As Black women we see Black feminism
as the logical political movement to combat the manifold
and simultaneous oppressions that all women of color face.
(Combahee River Collective, 1979)

Many lesbians and feminists 'of colour' rapidly echoed them.
Among the initiatives that had the greatest impact was the collection *This Bridge Called My Back*, edited by two Chicana lesbians,
Gloria Anzaldúa and Cherríe Moraga, that brought together the
voices of a group of Black, Indigenous, Asian, Latina, migrant and
refugee feminists and lesbians, that affirmed that they also found
it impossible to choose between their identity as woman and their
identity as a person of colour (Moraga and Anzaldúa, 1981).

From a theoretical point of view, the perspectives developed
by these activists marked an actual change of paradigm, with
the Combahee River Collective's pioneering formulation of the
concept of the four interlocking forms of oppression (Combahee
River Collective, 1979). It should be noted that this fundamental
contribution to the social sciences is inseparable from their point
of view as 'outsiders within', as women, Blacks, lesbians and pro-
letarians. Their capacity to see and articulate the interlocking of
these oppressions was also the product of their *collective activism*. There is actually an additional contribution: the Combahee
River Collective reminds us that if we take standpoint theory[15]
seriously, it is necessary to bring at least three elements into play
in order to understand the reception of a theory: the social position of who formulate(s) the theory, the individual or collective
character of their thinking, and its connection with social transformation projects.

Politically speaking, the contribution of a group such as Combahee is also considerable. First, these activists asserted that it
was necessary to struggle simultaneously on several fronts. Next,
they insisted on the necessity that everyone take on the different

struggles. Fighting racism, for example, is as much the responsibility of white people as anyone else and it is incumbent upon men as well as women to oppose patriarchal social relations of sex. However, and this is another central point, they highlighted that the organisation of these struggles should respect certain rules. The goal is not that each group closes itself off and isolates itself in specific struggles, as Barbara Smith, one of the key activists from Combahee, explains:

> I have often addressed the pitfalls of Lesbian separatism as practiced by mostly white women ... Instead of working to challenge the system and to transform it, many separatists wash their hands of it and the system continues on in its merry way ... Autonomy and separatism are fundamentally different. (Smith, 1983)

The distinction that Smith makes between separatism and autonomy is especially useful. Indeed, like separatism, autonomy implies that groups have the right to choose their own inclusion criteria and their way of working. On the other hand, unlike separatism, it permits, and should lead to, the creation of meeting spaces and alliances:

> Black women can legitimately choose not to work with white women. What is not legitimate is ostracizing other Black women who have not made the same choice. The worst effect of separatism is not upon whomever we define as 'enemy', but upon ourselves as it isolates us from each other. (Smith, 1983)

Finally, and it is one of the logical and particularly important consequences of all that was said, in the face of the simultaneity of oppressions and to guarantee political autonomy, the strategy that these Black lesbian feminists suggest, is actively seeking and building coalitions that are not based on an addition of identities and of infinitely fragmented organisation, but rather on concrete actions in order to collectively formulate a political project (Smith, 1983).

The denaturalisation of heterosexuality and sex

The third important contribution of the lesbians is the complete reversal of the naturalist and conventional understanding of sexuality, gender and especially sexes. This reversal is accomplished by calling into question the idea, ostensibly simple and innocent, that heterosexuality is a *natural* mechanism of attraction *between the two sexes.*

The first attack on the idea of the supposed naturalness of heterosexuality, the genders and the sexes, was launched in 1975 by the white anthropologist Gayle Rubin in her essay "The Traffic in Women: Notes on the 'Political Economy' of Sex" (Rubin, 1975). In this audacious work, Rubin demonstrates the profoundly social character of heterosexuality. She emphasises that Claude Lévi Strauss himself was dangerously close to saying that heterosexuality was a socially instituted process, in affirming that it was *the sexual division of labour, socially constructed*, that forced the formation of 'family' units that included at least one woman and one man. More precisely, what the anthropologist argues, is that in terms of biological and social reproduction, *it is necessary to compel* individuals to form social units that include at least one 'female' and one 'male' – social units that individuals do not form spontaneously. Following Lévi Strauss, Rubin demonstrates that the role of the sexual division of labour, understood from this perspective as the prohibition for each sex to master the complete set of tasks necessary to survive, is precisely to render them materially and symbolically dependent upon one another. It is also and especially, explains Rubin, the reason that similarities between men and women are taboo, which is intimately linked to the taboo of homosexuality – this taboo being more ancient and fundamental than the taboo of incest (Rubin, 1975).[16]

A few years later, it was in finally placing *lesbianism* at the heart of the argument that two writers and white feminist activists, Monique Wittig and Adrienne Rich, were able to push the analysis further. While it is common to view these two theorists as representing opposing positions,[17] they both engage in a particularly heuristic repositioning of lesbianism following a three-step process. First, they extract lesbianism from the narrow field of strictly sexual practices. Next, they displace attention from this 'minority'[18] practice toward 'the majority', that is, focusing on heterosexuality. Finally, and especially, they show that what is really at stake, both in lesbianism and in heterosexuality, has much more to do with power than with sexuality. For Rich as much as for Wittig, heterosexuality, far from being a natural inclination existing in human beings, is imposed *on women*[19] by force, meaning both by physical and material violence, including that of economics, and through a strong ideological, symbolic and political control which uses an array of devices that range from pornography to psychoanalysis.

Thus, in her article "Compulsory Heterosexuality and Lesbian Existence", Rich (1980) denounces *compulsory* heterosexuality as a social norm made possible by the *invisibilisation* of lesbianism – including within the feminist movement. She positions lesbianism from the perspective of a "lesbian continuum", bringing together all women who, in different ways, distance themselves from compulsory heterosexuality and attempt to develop links between themselves to struggle against the oppression of women independent of their sexuality. Rich has critiqued certain essentialist aspects of the concept of 'woman-identified woman' (Koedt, 1968). In her article, on the contrary, she highlights the existence of solidarity practices between women, described among and by Black women such as Toni Morrison or Zora Neale Hurston. And it is this, in a way, that she would like to see develop: a real solidarity between women, not 'natural', romantic or naïve, but actually deliberately and clearly political, which opens space for all in the struggle for common liberation. In a later work she affirmed:

> It is ... crucial that we understand lesbian/feminism in the deepest, most radical sense: as that love for ourselves and other women, that commitment to the freedom of all of us, which transcends the category of 'sexual preference' and the issue of civil rights, to become a politics of asking women's questions demanding a world in which the integrity of all women – not a chosen few – shall be honoured and validated by every aspect of culture. (Rich, 1979)

Meanwhile, Monique Wittig starts from one of the main proposals of materialist feminism – developing around the publication *Questions féministes* where her two foundational articles were published:[20] women and men are not defined by their 'sex'. For materialist feminists, far from any naturalist reference to the body, women and men are defined through a class relation that produces the positions they occupy in the social relations of power. This class relation is defined by Colette Guillaumin as a direct physical appropriation, which she called *sexage*, that also has an ideological component: the naturalisation of the dominated group and people (Guillaumin, 1978). In Wittig's terms, "what creates a woman is a specific social relation to a man, a relation that we have previously called servitude, a relation which implies personal and physical obligations as well as economic obligations ('forced residence', domestic work, conjugal duties, unlimited production of children, etc.)" (Wittig, 1980b). Women and men are political categories that cannot exist without one another. Lesbians, "by escaping or by refusing to become or to keep on being heterosexual", by challenging this social relation, heterosexuality, question the very existence of women and men. But individual escape is not the solution, because there is no place outside of society: to exist, lesbians must wage a political struggle of life and death to put an end to the existence of women as a class, to destroy the "myth of woman", and to abolish heterosexuality:

> [O]ur survival demands that we contribute with all our strength to the destruction of the class of women within which men appropriate women. This can be accomplished only by the destruction of heterosexuality as a social system which is based on the oppression of women by men and which produces the whole set of doctrines around the so-called *difference between the sexes*[21] to justify this oppression. (Wittig, 1980a)

What Wittig shows is (1) that heterosexuality is not natural but social, (2) that it is not a sexual practice but an ideology which she calls "the straight mind", and, above all, (3) that this ideology, based on the patriarchal oppression of women by the class of men, is based on the fervent belief in the existence of a *difference des sexes*, and ceaseless renewal of this faith. Wittig stresses that this "sexual difference" constitutes an underlying assumption not only in common knowledge but also throughout all Western "sciences", from psychoanalysis to anthropology. Moreover, she affirms that this belief, the actual cornerstone of heterosexuality, is never subject to analysis, and furthermore, that it is contradicted, day after day, by the *political* existence of lesbians and their movement.

Contemporary challenges

Today, what is the legacy of the theories that I presented above, that could constitute a basis for feminist and/or lesbian, materialist, anti-naturalist and radical, theorisation? How does it enable us to attack the roots of the "main problem" that I mentioned in the introduction? Moreover, this problem, what is it in the end?

The first legacy, as Black lesbians and Black feminists, among others, repeatedly insist, is the interlocking dimension of the social relations of power. This fundamental element profoundly calls into question the orientations of an entire portion of the LGBTQI movement, that focus on a single type of social relations (sex) and is always based on and reinforces, at the same time, white, 'patriarchal-gay-male' and middle-class perspectives. Needless to say, here it is not in the absolute, about contesting the legitimacy of the struggles of any sex or gender minority, but rather to urge vigilance, in order to avoid losing in terms of race and class, what we can win in terms of sex relations. Simultaneously, awareness of the interweaving of power relations demands that we extend the perspectives of Wittig, Rich and Mathieu. Specifically, we must continue to analyse how heterosexuality, as an ideology and as a social institution, constructs and naturalises not only sexual difference, but also differences of 'race' and class. It is a field that is especially wide and stimulating, and where most of the analysis remains to be done.

Today, it is all the more vital, to explore this field because nationalism, xenophobia and essentialism (of 'race' and 'sex') are rising up again along with globalisation and the development of reactionary political thought, that is naturalist and ahistorical and linked to the rise of religious fundamentalisms, in the United States and the world, a rise that is morally and financially encouraged by successive North American governments and/or exacerbated by their politics. The work of Colette Guillaumin on the naturalisation of 'race' and sex, which is one of the primary sources for materialist feminism and lesbianism, constitutes a very solid basis upon which to rely. Meanwhile, let us not make a mistake about the 'principal enemy': what underlies this ideological process (the naturalisation of the social positions of individuals, with the rise of religious power as its maximum political expression), is actually a material process of exploitation, extraction and concentration of wealth that is intensifying with neoliberal globalisation.

Precisely, a third series of challenges (the heart of the 'problem' perhaps) concerns the hardening of social relations of power and the deterioration of the living conditions of a large part of the world's population. The brutal impoverishment of most 'women' (and men) in the world is forcing many people into mobility just when international migratory politics are becoming more restrictive and the internal control of the population's movements is being strengthened in many countries (through legal minoritisation, forcing people into refugee camps, prison confinement, the erection of walls everywhere, the ghettoisation of many working-class districts, as well as the threat of murder-femicide based on Ciudad Juárez's 'model', the enforcement of 'ethnic' separation, the lack of financial means to move, etc.). Work is modified and informalised while a larger and larger portion of the workforce is pushed toward what I called elsewhere "the continuum of work that is considered feminine", that is neither completely unpaid nor actually salaried, and that brings together a set of 'services' that are required and extracted at low cost from the people who are socially constructed as women (Falquet, 2008).

In this regard, the work of Paola Tabet (2004), extending directly from the analyses presented here, could prove to be very useful, especially her concept of the "continuum of economic-sexual exchange". In fact, it could permit a better understanding of the new logics of matrimonial, sexual and labour alliances of impoverished and racialised women (and therefore, a better understanding of an important part of sexual and gender practices), especially the few possible 'choices' of these women. Lacking legal autonomy, they have scarce choices and oscillate between marriage with richer and whiter men, eventually of other nationalities, and sex work in all its traditional and newer forms. Simultaneously, it is necessary to directly use the perspective of the co-formation of social relations, to analyse the way that this economic-sexual exchange works and how it operates in conjunction with more 'traditional' salaried work. For example, to understand interventions on the body, does creating or improving breasts or lightening the skin allow them to find a husband, a client or a job as a receptionist, or to become or remain a 'white/beautiful' 'woman'?

As we have seen, the problems are numerous and complex. To guide us, we do have tools – which still need to be improved: the theories of the interweaving of social relations of sex, 'race', class *and* the analysis of 'the straight mind'. These theories encourage a distancing from 'identitarian' politics that gets obsessed with reclaiming (or contesting) the symbolic, physical or psychic attributes of a sex, a 'race' or a class. As lesbian feminists have well demonstrated, Nature does not exist, and its attributes are nothing more than markers and consequences of the assignment of particular positions in the social organisation of work. These markers can change without disrupting the organisation of work. Moreover, as long as we fight only against a single dimension at a time, the interweaving of social relations permits their re-accommodation without the basis of its logic (appropriation and exploitation) being thoroughly modified. And, it is therefore, appropriation and exploitation that we must attack, if we want to effectively fight their effects. In other words, we must fight to change *the organisation of the division of labour as well as access to resources and knowledge.* And, to start, we can reclaim for ourselves the analysis of the social movements that propose to directly attack the core of power relations.

Notes

1 Although this text exclusively reflects my personal positions, I could not write it without having taken part in the lesbian-feminist movement. I would like to highlight the theoretical and political importance that the following groups have had for me: Comal-Citlalmina, Archives lesbiennes, La Barbare, Media Luna, Próximas, 6 novembre et Cora.G [play on words in Spanish about rage and the G spot]. I would also like to thank Nasima Moujoud, Florence Degavre, Ochy Curiel, Natacha

Chetcuti, Cécile Chartrain and Nicole-Claude Mathieu for their valuable comments.

2 To counterbalance the strong tendency to naturalise the many categories of analysis, which are often confused with everyday categories, I often employ them using quotations in this text. I will refer to 'woman' in quotations as a person who is socially considered to be a woman, in a given society, independent of any naturalist considerations.

3 Here, I use the concept of 'race' to refer to the product of a *social relation* that includes diverse dimensions such as 'colour', but also migratory status or nationality, among others.

4 The categories South, North and West are political categories. They can never be considered monolithic and ahistorical blocks. The West is multiple and full of contrasts as well as the South and the North; they are criss-crossed with contradictions of sex, class, 'race', region, etc. and are in permanent transformation.

5 In this article, I will sometimes use 'genders' in the plural (which is nonsensical if gender is (correctly) understood as a concept meaning a social relation of power), to retain the 'common sense' usage. Some people use 'female gender' and 'male gender' to refer to a set of social characteristics that are supposedly feminine or masculine, and in this sense, one could say that two genders exist. According to the same logic, sex relations (in the singular) refers to a structural social relation, when sexes (in the plural) refer to what is commonly conceived of as females and males.

6 Here, I cannot address the complexity of each lesbian and feminist political and theoretical position. For greater detail on the various currents within the lesbian movement, see Falquet (2004) or Turcotte (1998).

7 Of course, the world is infinitely larger than just these two countries, but the United States and France are the countries in which the majority of the activists and theorists whose work I have decided to present here were living. I am fully aware of having set aside other important reflections on these questions.

8 In French, it is possible to distinguish between *identité sexuelle* and *identité sexuée*. The first would correspond to female-woman (or male-man) and the second to sexuality (heterosexual, lesbian, homosexual, bi-sexual and so on). It is more difficult to make this distinction in English, where sexual identity is likely to refer to both levels and create confusion. In this case, I refer to *identité sexuelle* (sexual 'preferences').

9 It was in 1982, during the 10th World Conference of Sociology in Mexico City, that Nicole-Claude Mathieu presented the foundations of this work for the first time. It was then published in a collective book (1989) and taken up again in 1991 in Mathieu's aforementioned book that provides an overview of her research: *L'Anatomie politique*.

10 "In Mode III of the conceptualisation of the relationship between sex and gender, the dual division of gender is understood as alien to the biological 'reality' of sex (which becomes, moreover, more and more complex to define), but not, as we will see, to the efficiency of its ideological *definition*. And it is the very idea of this heterogeneity between sex and gender (of their different natures) that lead to the idea not that the sexual difference is 'translated' (Mode I) or 'expressed' or 'symbolised' (Mode II) through gender, but that gender constructs sex. Between sex and gender, a *sociological* and political *correspondence* is established. Mode III constitutes an anti-naturalist logic and a materialist analysis of socio-sexual relations" (Mathieu, 1991:255–256).

11 I use the adjective patriarchal not to refer to a *system* that is supposedly universal and ahistorical (an idea that has largely been critiqued and discredited, and is moreover, incongruent with the idea of the co-creation of the social relations of power), but to describe patterns in the social relations of sex that are unfavourable to women (social relations in a given group at a given time can be more or less patriarchal, in the sense that they can be more or less oppressive for women just as social relation can be more or less racist).

12 Matrilineal: a system in which group affiliation is defined by following the matrilineal line. Uxorilocal: a system in which, after marriage, the husband goes to live in the spouse's place of residence.

13 This is why the transgression by some 'women' of the prescribed social appearance for women and moreover, the transgression of their place in the division of labour, is specifically sanctioned in most societies ('women' who refuse maternity and/or the raising of children, domestic labour, the economic-sexual exchange with 'men', or who dare to earn a better salary than the 'men' and occupy positions of power). To avoid these sanctions requires a great deal of talent, collective support and/or benefits from the privileges of age, 'race' and/or class.

14 For Latin America, see the pioneering work of Norma Mogrovejo (2000).

15 The diverse standpoint theories developed especially by Patricia Hill Collins, Sandra Harding and bell hooks, refer to (1) the reflexivity of the researcher in relation to her/his own position in terms of sex, class and 'race', among others, during 'field work', and (2) taking into account the standpoint from which theory has been developed, in order to decide how to use it for formulating the analysis.

16 From the 1980s on, Rubin developed an analysis that departed from the theoretical position that I present here, reducing lesbianism to a sexuality, one (oppressed) sexuality among many others.

17 Indeed, after having published Wittig's two articles and as a result of a broader conflict within the feminist movement in France in relation to the issue of so-called 'lesbian separatism', which was actually radical lesbianism, *Questions féministes* exploded. When it reappeared under

the name *Nouvelles Questions féministes*, it published as its first article, the translation of Rich's work, presenting it in the editorial as its "new political perspective" (*Nouvelles Questions féministes*, 1981). Rather than exploring the (supposed) opposition between Wittig and Rich, it would be important to analyse more deeply the causes and consequences of this split, which profoundly impacted the theoretical development of French materialist feminism. It would also be interesting to conduct a parallel analysis of (1) the invention, in the United States, of "French feminism" (Delphy, 1996; Moses, 1996), (2) the theoretical evolution of authors such as Gayle Rubin and the North American feminist and lesbian movement regarding sexuality following the conference on 'sexual politics' at Barnard College in 1982, and (3) more recently and in another disciplinary field, the growing legitimacy of Butlerian theories, that are in part based on an interpretation of French authors, including Wittig.

18 This concept of 'minoritisation' and minority/majority is based on the French materialist feminist theorist Colette Guillaumin. It refers not to 'numbers' but rather to a position of less or more power, and the social relations that dialectically create these respective positions.

19 Wittig writes that women embody both heterosexuality and sex. They *are the sex*. Saying "woman" is equivalent to saying "heterosexual". Very differently, men can *practise* sexuality the way they like without being labelled since they are not playing the role of a 'female'.

20 "One Is Not Born a Woman" and "Straight Mind" were the products of a paper presented in English during a 1978 conference in the United States which were published in French in 1980 (Wittig, 1980a; 1980b).

21 Italicised by the author.

FOUR | The theological basis for trans-exclusionary radical feminist positions

Katherine O'Donnell

Introduction

This chapter argues that Irish lesbian feminism has been largely anti-theocratic and post/colonial in its perspective and has therefore remained opposed to current UK trans-exclusionary radical feminist (terf) activism, which has received much media attention. We examine how the Radical Lesbian Feminist, Mary Daly, engaged with the theology of St Thomas Aquinas to provide crucial conceptual underpinning of terf perspectives. We see how Daly's rigid adherence to her metaphysical concepts, designed to refute Aquinas, meant that she was unwilling to engage with evolving feminist theory on gender, and unable to respond to feminist critical race theory. As Irish lesbian feminism has remained conscious of its post/colonial legacy, it is characterised by a political practice of building alliances, coalitions and by an intersectional thinking that is critical of claims to supremacy and hierarchy. Irish lesbian feminism has also been generally engaged in an oppositional politics to theocratic rule. This essay argues that an intersectional post/colonial lesbian feminist politics and an anti-theocratic perspective that is critical of categories such as the pure and impure (the real and the fake; the true and the dissembling) means that Irish lesbian feminist culture has not proved amenable to terf activism which rests on the version of Radical Feminism espoused in the work of Mary Daly.

When I refer to Irish lesbian feminism, I am referring to the participation of lesbians in feminist activism on the island of

Ireland on *either* side of the border where to the north are the six counties of Northern Ireland, under the jurisdiction of the UK, and to the south are the twenty-six counties of the Republic of Ireland. Irish feminist activism has often been led and fuelled by Irish lesbians since the revolutionary decades at the start of the twentieth century (O'Donnell, 2003). In using the slashed term 'post/colonial', I refer to the political context where the Republic of Ireland won independence from the UK less than a hundred years ago while the six counties of Northern Ireland currently enjoy the benefits of a twenty-year-old peace settlement which ended a bloody and bitter sectarian British and Irish nationalist conflict. So post/colonial refers to the differing experiences of colonial settlements on either side of the Irish border. In using the term 'anti-theocratic', I refer to Irish feminist activism that opposes the power of the Catholic Church so strongly evident in the Republic as well as fundamentalist Protestantism in Northern Ireland.

I use the term 'trans-exclusionary radical feminist' (and the lower case acronym, terf) as a descriptor of active positions and not as an identity category to denominate people. I have a number of reasons for using 'terf' to describe *perspectives and activities* rather than as an *identity* label. Firstly, if we understand that Radical Feminism means a commitment to focus first and foremost on the oppression of females and femininity from patriarchal oppression, then we must accept that there are Radical Feminists who are trans women, cis women, or queer-identified Radical Feminists who do not wish to exclude trans women from women-only spaces and the category of 'woman'. Secondly, I am mindful that in some quarters (generally restricted to social media platforms) the neutral (and precise) acronym TERF has, according to socio-linguist Deborah Cameron, been used in a manner "which has clear similarities with hate-speech directed at other groups (it makes threats of violence, it includes other slur-terms, it uses metaphors of pollution)" (Cameron, 2016). My prime motivation for using terf as a description of activities and perspectives is to avoid reifying it into a fixed identity in order to cool heated polarisations and provide more opportunity for those who currently hold terf views to change their mind. I use the acronym in the lower case to better deploy terf *as an adjective rather than a noun* and for the same reasons that some authors speak of aids rather than AIDS: I think the acronym when capitalised conveys a tenor of gravity and alarm.

UK trans-exclusionary radical feminism

There has been a recent upsurge in terf activity in the UK (Ntim, 2018; Hinsliff, 2018). A strong argument might be made that terf activism in the UK is being generated through media provocation as there is a small (though highly visible) number of participants involved and UK feminist and queer activism is generally and significantly trans inclusive (Anderson, 2018; Lees, 2017). An op. ed. in *The Sunday Times* written by Jenni Murray, presenter of BBC4's "Woman's Hour" provides a typical case study of terf rhetoric current in the UK: the central argument being that trans women "are not real women" (Murray, 2017). Murray's piece is routine in its terf tropes, such as her dismissal of trans women as being vacuous, superficial and hyper-feminine, who think that being a woman is all about frocks and make-up. Murray uses a generic terf argument in stating that trans women do not have enough experience of gender oppression to call themselves women and again she is also typical in naming particular trans women as examples to prove her assertions. Murray also fulfils the generic conventions in declaring that she is not anti-trans and that she is being brave in speaking out even though she is an eminent broadcaster and confidently assumes the position of speaking for all 'real' women. Murray maintains a terf perspective in homogenising all trans women, without taking into account a wide variety of trans female embodiments, and without reading cis or trans women feminist scholars who might provide her with some nuanced thinking on the issue of trans women's relationship to biology and the experience of gender oppression and male violence (Connell, 2012; Cooper and Trebra, 2006). Murray's piece is also typical of terf discourse, by invoking the spectre of trans women as a potential violent threat to 'real' women, thereby displaying a confused understanding of gender. For example, Murray calls for protection from bullying and violence "equally for transsexuals, transvestites, gays, lesbians and those of us who hold to the sex and sexual preference assumed at birth". It remains unclear how at the moment of birth one might assume a "sex and sexual preference". With this confusing clause Murray might be making the case that cis heterosexuals also need protection from bullying and violence, though it is not stated why cis straight people might need such protection.

I was surprised by the surge of UK terf activism, perhaps in part, because most of my feminist activism takes place in Ireland where trans and non-binary people have played active roles as leaders and participants in queer and progressive social movements and communities. Terf views have never had a public expression in Ireland (Mulcahy, 2013). This is evident in the *Lesbian Lives* conference which was run annually at University College Dublin since 1993 and since 2011 is now co-organised with the University of Brighton. Also, the annual Irish Women's Camp, which is over thirty years old, last year decided to make explicit its queer and trans femme inclusivity. However, my surprise was largely grounded in my experience of regular participation in research events and projects with feminist academic colleagues in the UK where inclusive participation of diverse, minority and marginalised identities is a central organising principle. I read widely in feminist academic publications and was not aware that any UK-based feminist academic held a terf position and indeed it was very difficult to find any UK-based feminist academic who was putting forward a terf position.

Terf positions within the academy: Jeffreys, Daly and beyond

Terf positions within academia (and indeed within Radical Feminism) have always been a minority and are now a rarity. A recent guest post on the *Daily Nous* blog site by a number of academics who have terf arguments signal that they intend to write an essay elaborating their broader philosophical concerns but the main focus of their post on *Daily Nous* (which broadcasts "news, for and about the philosophy profession") is to claim that the term TERF is "at worst a slur and at best derogatory" (Weinberg et al., 2018). Hence, a blog by feminist analytic philosopher Dr Kathleen Stock where she muses on the Radical Feminists' 'Gender Critical' stance has proved to be the most comprehensive introduction by a UK academic who finds herself drawn to a terf position (Stock, 2018). What Stock's notes reveal is a confusion on the part of those who take a terf position in how the term 'gender' is defined in feminist theory as well as a yearning for a taxonomy that can provide for *stability, hierarchy and purity*. People taking terf positions claim they are 'gender critical' but they misunderstand feminist gender theory which has followed the work of Judith Butler and think that such theorists talk about gender as if it is a term which describes (or indeed recommends) that we can (or must) choose and change the expression of our gendered embodiment *easily and at will*. In fact, Butler and post-structuralist and queer gender theorists more generally are interested in how embodiment entails human engagement in forming ourselves within the pre-existing constructs of vocabularies and practices that we find ourselves inhabiting (Butler, 1993; 1999). Those gendered discourses are inflected by a range of values at work in the societies and cultures in which we live. Those discourses institute certain norms and limits for gender expression that we might find oppressive and so gender theorists are concerned with how we might reject those discourses or, in solidarity with others, create new ones: *this is not a facile endeavour, and for some this is a matter of life and death.* There is a momentum among feminist and queer gender theorists to elaborate how social movements, communities and cultures might develop languages, establish social institutions, and create political imaginaries in order to bring into practice categorisations of embodiment and kinship that make a greater diversity of lives possible (if not flourish), and to resist those conceptual categories that discriminate, harass, injure, patholo-gise, criminalise, marginalise and oppress us and others (Martin, 1994; Butler, 2004). Some of us may feel and experience more strongly than others that our gendered and sexed embodiment is more fixed or more fluid. While these experiences are interesting to examine it is more important for feminist and queer gender theorists to co-create contexts and grammars of gender, sexuality and kinship so that we can all live the reality of our experience of such embodiment.

The 'gender critical' terf stance insists that there is an innate, unchangeable, binary gender (male or female) which is based on biological sex characteristics. The 'gender critical' nomenclature is meant to signal a disbelief that a conscious identification with a gender identity is felt by all. 'Gender critical' feminists who main-tain a terf stance claim that they do not strongly identify with the gender they perform or were assigned. Yet, they are essentialists who believe that there is only an immutable 'hard-wired' consti-tutive sense of a gendered self based on chromosomes, genita-lia, reproductive capacities and hormone levels. The essentialist terf position brushes aside varieties in chromosomal makeup and intersex embodiment more generally, as well as the fact that reproductive capacities and hormone levels may vary greatly according to age, pathologies, contraceptive medication, surgeries, treatment therapies and menstrual cycles. The emphasis on the importance of genitalia as a fixed marker for identity is also less than obvious, considering that most of us rarely reveal our genitalia to other people. When we argue for the necessity of natural characteristics to establish and secure social identities we operate a *cordon sanitaire* exclusion policy and we run the risk that the policing of this boundary becomes the focus for our politics. For example, the terf definition of who is 'really' a woman excludes many who live their lives as women, not merely trans women (including this author who does not have the uterus or ovaries that Stone says are essential. I don't have a cervix either.) Moreover, discourses that presuppose that there are personality, behavioural and intellectual differences between naturalised and fixed ethnicities and genders are routinely used to support racism and sexism. So it should be no surprise that the terf essentialist position is welcomed and promulgated by the alt. right and ultra conservatives (Parke, 2016; Duffy, 2017). Yet, Sheila Jeffreys, a British-born academic who spent her career in Australia and who maintains a terf position, expresses such surprise:

> Now one of the things I find puzzling about it is that, when I look at the House of Lords debate on this legislation, those I agree with most are the radical right. Particularly the person I find that I agree with most, in here, and I'm not sure he will be pleased to find this, is Norman Tebbitt … Tebbitt also says that the savage mutilation of transgenderism, we would say if it was taking place in other cultures apart from the culture of Britain, was a harmful cultural practice, and how come we're not recognising that in the British Isles? (Jeffreys, 2006)

Terf activists insist that the rich complexity of gendered expression is a black and white certainty; it is a moral perspective that often refers to the inherent violence of men. I first encountered this potent cocktail of ideas in the late 1980s when I was a student of the theologian and feminist philosopher, Professor Mary Daly, at the Jesuit-university Boston College (BC). While Robin Morgan is referred to as the first second wave feminist to publically agitate for removing trans women from lesbian and feminist spaces (Stryker, 2008:102–104), her friend, Mary Daly, was the first high-profile feminist theorist to publically voice a terf position, a position she articulated occasionally in the lectures I attended at BC in the late 1980s and early '90s. In the 1960s and early '70s, trans people were visibly active in the women's and lesbian and gay liberation movements in the USA and elsewhere. The famous 1960s rebellions of the Compton's Cafeteria and Stonewall provide us with evidence of trans people taking leading roles, such as Stonewall veteran Silvia Rivera who was a founding member of the Gay Liberation Front and the Gay Activist Alliance, and women like Beth Elliot of the Daughters of Bilitis, and Sandy Stone of Olivia Records. However, during the '60s, Daly was living in Europe and was a lone female graduate student studying Catholic theology at the University of Fribourg. The university can trace its roots back to a sixteenth-century Counter-Reformation Jesuit foundation, and it remains famous for its faculty of Catholic theology (now under the auspices of the Dominican Order). Daly was ultimately awarded a total of three PhDs for her seven years of work in theology and philosophy.

It seemed in the liberal glow of Vatican II that women would be called to ordination in the Catholic Church, and for some on-lookers Dr Mary Daly, who had been in Catholic education from primary school, would appear to have been first in line. Yet to be a priest was not Daly's ambition; she was purely enamoured with mastering theology and the philosophical underpinnings, the ethics and metaphysics, of Catholicism. Even in her women-only feminist ethics classrooms at Boston College, Daly would continue to teach, with relish, the virtue ethics of Aristotle and the

Summa Theologica of St Thomas Aquinas (Madsen, 2000; Plaskow, 2012). Her first book, *The Church and the Second Sex* was published in 1968 and Daly became internationally recognised as a foundational feminist theologian. In this book she critiques the sexism of the Catholic Church and argues for equality between the sexes. Her second book, *Beyond God the Father*, published in 1973, had an even greater impact, where Daly calls for the full-scale exodus of women from Christian churches. Drawing on the methods of the existentialist theologians Paul Tillich and Martin Buber, Daly not merely analyses the misogyny and androcentrism of Judeo-Christian religions, she elaborates her own systematic theology, based on a metaphysics that offers a praxis for women's liberation from patriarchal control.

For the rest of her career Daly would continue to extend and develop the template of reality, transcendence and revolutionary redemption that she systematised in *Beyond God the Father*. Throughout her writings Daly postulated that the 'Foreground' of false, oppressive images and simulacra is the 'necrophilic' male-centred realm of patriarchy. The Foreground creates toxins that are destroying all the natural life of the planet. However, in the 'Background' (behind the scenes of the Foreground, in the revolutionary underground) all living things are co-creating deep connections, this is the world of 'bio-philia', an on-going communion, a 'Voyaging' in true 'Be-ing' and this is the realm of 'Woman'. However, according to Daly, most women remain trapped in the Foreground, they are distorted in their being and they have no real 'life energy'. In later works Daly would describe the women entrapped in the Foreground as 'Painted Birds', promoted by men to be 'Token Torturers' (of Radical Lesbian Feminists such as Daly, 1984; 1987). These women were 'fembots'. In her *Wickedary*, Daly glosses 'fembot' as: "a female robot: the archetypical role model forced upon women throughout fatherland: the unstated goal/end socialization into patriarchal womanhood: the totaled woman" (Daly, 1987:198). Throughout her writings Daly exhibits an eye-popping level of misogyny towards the women of the Foreground; she displays no tenderness towards the women who operate under the false consciousness of patriarchy. Daly celebrates the Crone, the Hag, the Revolting Woman, the female Lunatics and Angels (who are the messengers we must listen to).

The *éminence grise* of Daly's gender politics is St Thomas Aquinas. Daly conceptualises gender in order to engage with and refute the constructions of male and female in Aquinas' *Summa Theologica*. Aquinas (in)famously argued that men rule over women because men have far more intellectual capacities than women and they were created first and in God's image while women derive from men (being created from Adam's rib) (*Summa Theologica I*, qu. 92, art. 1; qu. 92, art. 1, ad. 2; qu. 92, art. 2; qu. 93, art 4 ad. 1). Aquinas argues (by paying close attention to the etymology of Biblical terms) that women are created to be helpmates for men, but in a servile capacity rather than as true equals. However, Aquinas continues to worry that women are "deficient and unintentionally caused. For the active power of the semen always seeks to produce a thing completely like itself, something male". However, Aquinas goes on to reason that the female is not (entirely) accidentally caused but "is intended by Nature for the work of generation" (*Summa Theologica I*, qu. 92, art. 1, ad. 1). The passage goes on to declare: "So if a female is produced, this must be because the semen is weak or because the material [provided by the female parent] is unsuitable, or because of the actions of some external factor such as the winds from the south which makes the atmosphere humid" (*Summa Theologica I*, qu. 92, art. 1, ad. 1) (Daly favoured this translation by the Dominican Order who educated her at Fribourg). Daly's preoccupation with answering Aquinas limits her conceptualisation of gender in that her thinking remains polarised in a Thomist binary of male and female. In her first two books she explores androgyny as an ideal but she disavows this work in her third book, published in 1978, *Gyn/Ecology: The Metaethics of Radical Feminism*, which was one of the most eagerly anticipated books of second wave feminism: "The second semantic abomination, androgyny, is a confusing term which I sometimes used in attempting to describe integrity of be-ing. The word is misbegotten – conveying something like John Travolta and Farrah Fawcett-Majors scotch-taped together – as I have reiterated in public recantations" (1978:1). However, many of Daly's Radical Feminist contemporaries continued to creatively theorise (through science fiction and essays) on androgyny and 'transsexuality'. For example, Andrea Dworkin's essay "Androgyny: Androgyny, Fucking and Community" in her book *Woman Hating* (1974) remains a brilliantly perceptive (and indeed prophetic) reading of how trans women might be seen to provide emancipation from repressive gender norms. Yet, from 1978 Daly continues to maintain a strict demarcation between the pure categories of male and female.

Furthermore, while Daly appeared in her first book to be an astute reader of Beauvoir, in her second book (and thereafter) she seems not to worry about Beauvoir's insight that the body is not a thing but "perspective" and "situation" (1973:8), in short, that biology is not destiny (1973:40–41). Instead Daly worries about technological control of biology, which she regards as a defining feature of patriarchy. Daly always took seriously Aquinas' insistence that God/males would seek to beget others in their own image and likeness. She inverted this Thomist paradigm in her idealisation of the Background with its untamed, unfarmed, ecological natural forces which gave to her liberated women a separate sphere in which they could enjoy their powers of generation and creativity. Like Aquinas, Daly was prone to magical, miraculous thinking, and parthenogenesis (virgin birth) was a keen point of interest for her. She promotes the idea that as more women make the creative 'Leap' from the Foreground and go 'Wild' to the Background we will see parthenogenesis become the norm as Spinning, Spiraling Hags, in communion with their true Spirit Energies are liberated from men and release their own powers of reproduction. In the classroom, Daly frequently quoted Aquinas on the necessity of hope in the movement towards the Good, and in Daly's vision, she envisages that the increasing (patriarchal) contamination of the Earth will be halted by a feminist revolution in consciousness where women will share Daly's conceptualisation of reality and make a collective Leap into the separate sphere of Woman in the Background. With this collective Leap a new evolutionary process would emerge that would result in a massive reduction in the population of males.

Daly's work depends on belief in the fundamentally different 'energies' of male and female and in the power of the 'force fields' of energy created when women live absolutely apart from men and the man-made. In her penultimate work, *Quintessence*, Daly celebrates this imagined future: "Those who have any awareness of the heinous crime of reversal which is patriarchy must be in a state of deep conflict and fear of ... Her" (Daly, 1998:91). In interviews about the book, she freely spoke about her glee at the elimination of the Y chromosome (something she believed was already happening, which was why fearful men were so invested in reproductive technologies and cloning). With regards to those who bear a Y chromosome Daly declares: "But I do think there's something wrong with that life form, to be honest. You know, in the '70s we commonly called them mutes [short for mutants]" (Madsen, 2000).

Daly's metaphysics draws on a neo-Romantic idealisation of the natural world to describe generation as the domain of Women and a loathing of technological intervention as the domain of the patriarchy and is bound in a refutation of Aquinas that is ultimately an unhelpful inversion of his pernicious binary of male supremacy and female inferiority. The thought-praxis that Daly's writings outline calls for an ethics of separatism from men and a deep aversion to popular expressions of femininity. When Daly references mundane examples of femininity (such as make-up and high heels) her visceral loathing of such femininity is religious in its fervour, and therefore it is hard to defend her characterisations of everyday femininity from charges of misogyny. From these bases we can see how it became logical for Daly to promote a hatred of trans women, whom she stereotypes as the quintessential hyper-feminine creations of patriarchal technology who seek to deliberately contaminate the pure energetic field of Woman. The first clear statement of Daly's transmisogyny is to be found in *Gyn/Ecology*:

> Today the Frankenstein phenomenon is omnipresent not only in religious myth, but in its offspring, phallocratic technology. The insane desire for power, the madness of boundary violation, is the mark of necrophiliacs who sense the lack of soul/spirit/ life-loving principle with themselves and therefore try to invade and kill off all spirit, substituting conglomerates of corpses. This necrophilic invasion/elimination takes a variety of forms. Transsexualism is an example … Transsexualism is an example of male surgical siring which invades the female world with substitutes. (1978:70–71)

The quote is typical of Daly's work; she rejoiced in coining neologisms such as 'phallocracy' ('cockocracy' and 'flopocracy' being favoured synonyms). Daly said that her feminism was radical in being concerned with fundamentals and the way that she returned to the roots of words and pulled them apart from their contaminated constructions formed within the toxic contexts of patriarchy. Daly was happy to be called a fundamentalist: she believed in purity (Daly, 1984). Her argument, very much in favour among Francophone feminists at the time, was that language was structured to uphold all the explicit laws and implicit rules and assumptions of patriarchy. Every symbolic system, including our languages, operated to underpin the dominance of the interests and perspectives of males and masculinity and the concomitant subjugation of females and femininity. The call went out to invent new forms of language to articulate the feminist revolution and Daly responded with verve. The quote above is also exemplary of Daly's lesbian feminist war talk. Daly excelled in presenting her feminist vision as the war of the "Spinsters, Lesbians, Hags, Harpies, Crones, Furies who are the Voyagers of Gyn/Ecology, Hags, Crones" (1978:1) who will 'Spin' away, apart but also against the 'ruling/snooling class', the 'Big Brothers of Boredom'. Daly's metaphysical apocalyptic rapturous mystical separatist vision was, for a time, wildly popular in feminist circles: she provided a mythic vision of embodied womanhood that promised a return to the time before the Fall into Patriarchy, that is a matriarchal world where men were few and of little consequence.

Daly's biggest influence on formulating the creed of transmisogyny can be found in the work of her PhD student, Janice Raymond, who published the dissertation that Daly supervised, as *The Transsexual Empire: The Making of the She-Male* in 1979 with an ecstatic dedication to Daly. With this book Raymond, a former nun in the Mercy Order (founded in Ireland), became the chief theorist of trans-exclusionary radical feminism (Raymond, 1986:79). The book presents feminism as a war of the good against the evil of patriarchy, the purity of creative women (particularly lesbians) against the impurity of destructive men, and in the belief that the battle of feminism involves fundamental transcendental universal constants fixed in a stable and uncomplicated conceptualisation of male and female. Like Daly, Raymond has a visceral loathing of popular expressions of femininity which she regards as being constructed by and for males who have a rapacious desire for the appropriation of women's bodies and energies. A second edition "with a New Introduction on Trans-gender" was issued in 1994 where Raymond seeks (and fails) to defend her work against charges of essentialism and remains, frankly hateful of trans women. Her work is lacking in empiri-cal or anthropological evidence and remains staunchly oblivious to feminist gender theory. For example, Raymond quotes John Money and Anke Ehrhardt to define gender identity and gender roles and moves on to give an illogical and scant discussion on why the term 'gender' is problematic for the feminist critic – without citing any feminist work on the concept (1994:9). Raymond's work is also replete with opinions that offer no justification. To give just one example, she states:

> The reason that women wear pants is mainly comfort and convenience. Pants are practical in all types of weather and don't make women physically vulnerable or encourage sexual harassment, as certain styles of feminine clothes do. More significantly, a woman putting on a man's clothes [sic] is, in a sense, putting on male power status, whereas a man putting on women's clothes is putting on parody. (1994: xxviii)

Raymond's mentor, Mary Daly, was gloriously contemptuous of 'academentia', of being schooled and disciplined. So Raymond's stern pronouncements on trans women and Daly's rhapsodic writings both remain impervious to critical engagement by aca-demics: you rejoice in or reject their work, there is no carefully critical middle ground.

Given the recent rise in transmisogyny in the UK, we might wonder if Raymond's work might ultimately have more durable impact than her inspirational mentor, as Daly's relevance to the feminist movement saw a steady decline through the 1970s until few feminists (bar feminist theologians) were reading her by the late 1980s. The reasons for the decline in Daly's position within feminism may be three-fold: first, her vision demands a degree of faith and practice of a belief in transcendence and separatism that is perhaps too demanding for many to fully live. Second, Daly was disinterested in engaging as a peer with other feminist theorists; she was a creative, imaginative thinker, a prophetic, poetic, playful preacher who sought audiences and acolytes who would further amplify and elaborate on her vision. Daly quoted feminist and lesbian separatist creative writers to illustrate her ideas but as she had an inspiring metaphysical and ethical system already worked out she had no need to further engage with feminist conceptual thought. Third, Daly was never able to adequately answer Audre Lorde's devastating open criticism of *Gyn/Ecology* which Lorde first published in 1979. Lorde pointed out that Daly ignored all of the powerful mythic archetypes of female goddesses in African traditions: "What you excluded from *Gyn/Ecology* dismissed my heritage and the heritage of all other non-European women, and denied the real connections that exist between all of us" (1983:95). Lorde also noted that Daly did not quote Black women except one quote from Lorde which prefaced a discussion of African female genital mutilation. Lorde said:

> I felt that you had in fact misused my words, utilized them only to testify against myself as a woman of Color … So the question arises in my mind, Mary, do you ever really read the work of Black women? Did you ever read my words, or did you merely finger through them for quotations which you thought might valuably support an already conceived idea concerning some old and distorted connection between us? This is not a rhetorical question. (1983:95)

Lorde (unfairly) claimed that Daly never responded to her initially private correspondence even though Daly did leave a phone message and wrote a letter of reply and arranged a meeting with Lorde. Daly maintained a strict silence on her efforts to find a rapprochement with Lorde, even to the extent that she never defended herself from Lorde's charge that she had never made a response. However, Lorde's charge still has some validity in that the extant letter from Daly to Lorde shows Daly repeatedly saying that she is unsure how to respond (De Veaux, 2004:46, n.21). Even though subsequent work by Daly drew on indigenous, African, and other 'non-European' sources, Daly never engaged with *intersectional* feminisms, anti-racist or Marxist feminisms, or gender or queer theory. Moreover, in thrall to her own systematised categories she was never able to move away from thinking of 'Black' and 'Women' as two separate categories of experience. In her lectures Daly would dismiss anti-racist feminism as a distraction from the main goal of Leaping and Be-ing and Wilding. She offered the example of Susan B. Anthony (the nineteenth-century American white feminist) as someone who had disastrously deserted feminism (that is her work on female suffrage) for the distraction of working for the abolition of slavery. Lorde's words in her "Open Letter to Mary Daly" were to prove prophetic: "When patriarchy dismisses us, it encourages our murderers. When Radical Lesbian Feminist theory dismisses us, it encourages its own demise" (1983:96). Daly insists that our terms and concepts should be dynamic: women must use verbs rather than nouns and keep Spinning and Weaving and Voyaging into creating new languages but her rigid metaphysical transcendental taxonomies of gender brooked no intersections with the construction of social realities.

Reflecting through Irish lesbian feminism

For me, attending Prof. Daly's lectures was regularly a disconcerting experience. I often enjoyed the first twenty minutes when Daly would give wonderful incantations and exhort Voyaging into the transcendental Background where women would Spin and Weave and Be together. Her metaphysical poetics incited further my lesbian chauvinism. I found her exhilarating, but she also made me very uneasy: she reminded me too much of the nationalist religious rhapsodies that saturated my lifetime of twenty-two years in the theocracy of the Republic of Ireland. I had been actively involved in Irish feminism since 1983 and that meant that I was part of a movement profoundly critical of the oppressive force (brutal and total) wielded by Catholic churchmen. Daly seemed to me to be like a Catholic cardinal, replicating all tropes of the religion she thought she had surpassed: a bulwark of immense ego that admitted no doubt, and loftily ignored what did not pertain to its perfect metaphysical system; an obsessive preoccupation in the hermeneutics of transcendental symbols, myths, prophecies, goddesses, apocalypse and miracles; a focus on ritual and the creation of sacred spaces and a specialised language for those who would partake in realising the vision; an almost autistic disregard of emotion and affect; and a sublimation of women's actual various, varying and complex embodiment into a transcendental reification of 'Woman' as a pure symbol of energetic life force, nature and generation. I could see in Daly's imagined vision all the glories and grotesquery of Catholicism and her theological imagination held no promise of liberation for me. Without irony, Daly had her students read Margaret Atwood's *The Handmaid's Tale* even though it seemed to me that Atwood must surely have been (at least partially) satirising the work of Mary Daly. For me, Daly's vision of the real Women of the Wild Background vs the fembots was uncomfortably close to the venerated good women (that is nuns, respectable wives and mothers) and the ghosted legions of bad, fallen, shameful women of Ireland, who were driven into silence, held in institutions or fled into exile. Such binary theological thinking had put the failed and deficient women of Ireland into Mother and Baby Homes (from where their babies would be taken from them and given to 'real' and deserving mothers); and had relegated socially vulnerable girls and women to a lifetime of penance through hard unpaid labour in Ireland's Magdalene Laundries (especially those who were considered as having 'fallen' or being in danger of falling into sexual immorality). Twentieth-century theocratic 'Republican' Ireland ensured that married women would be legally prohibited from paid work and systematically denied control of their bodies so that they would fulfil their natural destiny of being dependent wives and mothers to many children. Burdened with the legacy of these moral demarcations between women who count and those who are discounted, Daly's feminist ethics (my lesbian chauvinism notwithstanding) created divisions between women that ran along those tracks of the pure and the impure women, a pernicious demarcation which had caused so much suffering to Irishwomen. The hierarchy enacted in current UK terf pronouncements about 'real' cis women as opposed to the 'artifice' of trans women has a deeply uncomfortable resonance for Irish feminists who are still dismantling theocratic categorisations and addressing our legacy of terror and shame. I believe that my reaction to Prof. Daly's lectures would have been shared by many other Irish feminists if they had also been in those classrooms: as far as I was concerned Prof. Daly was modelling the repressive thought structures that had severely subjugated women in the Irish theocratic state and a dazzling dance with St Thomas Aquinas was not going to lead us along a path of liberation.

I also shared Prof. Daly's confusion in reaction to Lorde's challenge. My professor was not a racist *in the way that I understood the term*: she clearly did not hate or despise African Americans. But like Prof. Daly I had a deep sense that Lorde was right, *but I didn't know how Lorde was right*. I realised that if I could not entirely understand and hence respond to Lorde's challenge this meant that I had to do some serious *reading, listening and thinking*. I still accept the fundamental tenets of Radical Feminism that the oppression of females and femininity is the oldest and most widespread oppression. Yet African American feminists illustrated for me how Beauvoir is right in her statement that "one is not born but rather becomes a woman" (1973:301). There is no pure category of 'woman' and our politics must pay attention to the complex, changing and messy places that Prof. Daly considered irrelevant: that is in the mundane world where class and race and embodiment differently positions us.

Conclusion: states and stakes

UK feminists taking terf positions have become active in organising against progressive gender identity legislation being introduced to the UK to enable people transitioning gender categories to swear an affidavit on their gender change (Hinsliff, 2018). One of the key benefits to this legal process is that it erodes the medical pathologisation of trans subjectivities and it allows trans people more options on what kind of medical supports and interventions they themselves deem necessary. One particular terf organisation in this movement organised a speaking tour of the UK and added Dublin to their itinerary. It is unclear if they forgot that Dublin is in the Republic of Ireland and not under the jurisdiction of the UK. The response by Irish feminists was swift: within a few days over 1,000 cis feminists had signed a statement in solidarity with trans women, anybody who was arguing to exclude trans women from events, spaces or the category of woman was going to be robustly challenged. This groundswell of Irish feminists also pointed to the fact that the progressive gender identity legislation being introduced in the UK was already in place and not merely uncontroversial but welcomed law in Ireland (Redmond, 2018; Donohue, 2018). Chief among the arguments made by the multitude of cis Irish feminists was that the Republic of Ireland is post/colonial and therefore sensitive to those, such as trans people, who suffer stigma, oppression and marginalisation. This large cross-section of Irish feminists was going to resist the colonising tool of false universals and demarcations that divided us from our friends, colleagues, lovers and allies. The Irish feminists expressed annoyance at the timing of the interference of British terf activists as all were involved to repeal the eighth amendment to the Irish Constitution which prohibited abortions: an amendment that had been inserted due to campaigning by Catholics. The cis Irish feminists further remarked that the activists who sought support for their terf campaign in the UK had not been allies in the Irish feminist struggles to get justice for the Magdalenes or in supporting Irish women travelling to the UK for abortion services.

When Mary Daly visited Ireland in the 1980s and '90s she had been warmly welcomed by Irish lesbian feminist activists (Daly, 1992; 2006). Daly was witty and charismatic, persistent in her work, with a zeal for women's liberation and infectiously exuberant about the superpower of lesbianism and its transcendental potential. What was not to love? Yet, Irish lesbian feminists did not entirely follow the Spinning Spiral paths charted by Daly: there was no anti-trans activism in the Republic of Ireland. Further, Irish lesbian feminist activists throughout the 1970s, '80s and '90s did not have any divisive breaks on the issues of S/M, pornography and sex work that marked the lesbian and feminist sex wars among our large Anglophone neighbours in the UK to the east and the US to the west. Many Irish feminists during these decades were living in poverty and activism was focused on peace initiatives to address the colonial conflict in Northern Ireland; on fighting the immense social and political control of the Catholic Church in the Republic; and maintaining lesbian communities and lesbian visibility while emigration was rife (GLEN and NEXUS, 1995). Yet while Irish feminists have successfully repealed the 8th Amendment to the 1937 Irish Constitution, and the proposed legislation looks set to include trans, non-binary and intersex bodies, trans inclusivity must remain of vital concern for Irish feminism as coalitions between Christian religious and feminists are so strongly in evidence in the two countries that continue to exert so much economic, political and cultural control and influence over the island of Ireland (Parke, 2016; Duffy, 2017). Moreover, a recent alliance between feminists (many of them lesbian) and Catholic religious orders which ran the notorious Magdalene Laundries saw Ireland enact legislation which aims at abolishing sex work (TORL, 2018). We may not be as post/colonial and post-theocratic as we imagine.

Acknowledgments

The author would like to acknowledge the UCD Newman Centre for the Study of Religion and Faith for the support received in bringing this work to completion.

FIVE

Manoeuvring feminisms through
LGBTQ movements in India[1]

Ranjita Biswas, Sumita Beethi and Subhagata Ghosh

Our journey: introduction

The year was 1999. A film called *Fire* released the previous year
sparked off a chain of events in different directions and with
different consequences: the Hindu right wing objected to the
film's depiction of same-sex love between two Indian women
and showed their displeasure through vandalism; individuals
and groups came out in support of the film and in protest of
the Hindu right-wing forces;[2] the common folk woke up to the
reality of women desiring women in a country whose sculptures
and texts had for a very long time borne witness to the same;
nationally and locally many groups collectivised themselves to
speak publicly about the sexual rights of lesbian women (Dave,
2012; Chatterjee, 2018); a group of six women came together
in the following months to form a lesbian support group and
named themselves Sappho (Akanksha and Malobika, 2007),
inspired by the Greek poet who lived on the island of Lesbos
and wrote in celebration of women loving women (Boehringer,
2014; Mendelsohn, 2015). Retracing the journey of Sappho and
Sappho for Equality (henceforth SFE) over the last eighteen years
is therefore an act of reflecting back on a time that holds many
stories in its folds, that speaks multiple queer tongues and that
etches diverse shades of memories. It is also a doing, undoing
and redoing of histories and herstories. Taking a sidestep from
personal journeys, though not in any way suggesting ruptures

between the personal and the political, this piece recounts the stories made and unmade by Sappho and SFE (the latter being an activists' forum created out of Sappho, the more informal collective) over the last nineteen years. While a chronicle inheres in itself the promise of a smooth and linear narrative, the fact is that these nineteen years have been marked by rough edges, detours, somersaults and impasses. The crossroads have been many, appearing at regularly irregular frequencies.

Our tryst with feminism

In a way, Sappho's political journey took off in 2000, allying with Maitree, a West Bengal based network of women's rights activists and organisations. At that time, locating politics in identity seemed the way forward, and we decided to build our space as a lesbian women's group. Though also known as an LBT group within the broader, what was back then called, the 'LGBT movement', we invested heavily in putting forth the 'same-sex loving woman' as our political protagonist. The point of reference for garnering support was violence – violence on same-sex loving women. Our proximity with the women's movement was conflictual and a productive one at that. Though some sections in the women's movement expressed incomprehension about women desiring women, the leadership in Maitree demonstrated their openness in welcoming Sappho as another women's rights organisation. The acceptance of lesbian women within the women's movement came from a liberal framework of sexuality being one's private choice and, therefore, nobody's business. Inclusion was however, conditional; solidarity and support were extended to lesbian women in situations of discrimination and violence. The issue of sexuality remained an uncomfortable idea, where sexual acts between men and women were only to be discussed within the framework of violence and desire had next to no locus standi. On the whole, the women's movement in Kolkata,

West Bengal distanced itself from any critical engagement with the issue of sexuality in general, and heterosexism in particular. The naturalisation of heterosexuality within the women's rights movement functioned to silence lesbian practices, experiences and identities and focused merely on their identity as 'woman'[3] and their experiences as battered women. Notwithstanding such reservations about lesbian desire, there was also the warmth of alliance that became evident when Sappho carried its banner in the 8 March 2001 International Women's Day march. This hesitant hand holding, on the one hand, and silencing on the other, continued until 2006 and, in a way, defined the relationship between lesbian rights activism and mainstream women's rights activism. It was the 2006 Autonomous Women's Movement Conference[4] where SFE finally got the chance to prove their seriousness and credibility when they became part of the organising committee and co-organised a session on 'marginalised genders and sexualities' with LABIA, a Queer Feminist LBT Collective. Since then, SFE has raised many an issue in meetings, collaborated on events and programmes, and matched steps in protests with the women's movement in Kolkata.

Our political activism stemmed from our experiences which actually positioned us squarely in opposition to the heterosexual women's movement who welcomed us, but, with some incomprehension. We also found ourselves in conflict with the gay movement where we understood each other but did not find convergences beyond our location outside peno-vaginal sexual practice. We, on our part, were staunch in our convictions. Our political journey, charted through our demands for an acknowledgement of our sexual difference and also our lived experiences that were gendered, brought us closer to the women's movement in Kolkata and took us away from the larger gay movement.[5]

In our political articulation of a lesbian identity within both gay spaces and women's rights spaces, the transgender experience/presence within the group (few and not well articulated till then) inadvertently got subsumed within the category of woman. Words like cis and trans held no or little meaning respectively then. Butch was the operative term then for female-to-male trans-identifying persons, though it was used more in terms of giving meaning to what we understood as 'biological' women unhappy with their gender expression/role and preferring women as sexual partners. But their 'unhappiness' did not stop us from branding them as women, or as lesbians. Our political commitment, at that point in time, lay in the argument that one need not be a man to love or have sex with a woman. We[6] remained unaware of the innumerable possibilities in the sphere of gender and sexual expressions/identities and, also, failed to differentiate between sexual preference and gender identity. For most of us, those who did not fit into the gender binary of 'woman' were the butch lesbians, 'performing' as men.

Bisexual women had the most confusing status in our political and organisational imagination. Their 'ambiguous' desire made them non-monogamous by default and caused moral and ethical conflict among the rest. The possibility of a sexual relationship with men was seen as throwing a spanner in the lesbian works. A few married women who wanted to belong were instinctively identified as 'lesbians forced into marriage'. The term bisexual became a holding place to acknowledge and accommodate the differences in the lived experiences of married women's same-sex desire and single women's same-sex desire. We either remained oblivious to the political valence of this identity or deliberately refrained from staking a claim to its politicisation. We caught on to the understanding that because lesbian women were forced to marry they were by compulsion 'bisexual in practice but lesbian in identity'. We did not address the complexity of bisexual lives; as and when bisexuality emerged as a choice we became guarded, suspicious and jittery.

So, we, if not so much by design, but by sheer pragmatic compulsion, suspended some of our own desires, practices and expressions to carve out a sexual-political reality that fitted albeit awkwardly into the larger politico-legal picture. And so, our concerns, our activism revolved around people who are 'biological women in erotic/sexual relationships with biological women', in other words, the L world, which subsumed the T and ignored the B. Lesbian for us then was the all-pervasive category that could accommodate all gender-sexual expressions, identities and practices within its fold as well as its political aspirations. The rights language became our tool to fight oppression and discrimination in a way leading to the further consolidating and freezing of identities. We found no way to bring the transmasculine or the bisexual woman into this precariously positioned lesbian subject for fear of losing authenticity. Though we still described and named ourselves as an LBT rights organisation, we were not able to bring into the fold of the organisation or political space the experiences of the B and the T. However, on a more pragmatic level we tried to remain open and keep the space as inclusive as possible to a variety of experiences and expressions of gender and sexual identities.[7]

The sky is not the limit

Despite such limitations, we as an organisation (the core of which was ever expanding, and yet, remained interpellated by the lesbian subject) managed to make friends with people who were like us and unlike us – binary/non-binary trans, bisexual, cis, heterosexual, gender-fluid, queer and so on. So, almost organically we opened few windows, we responded to the calls of affinity and bonding till the boundaries between Sappho and Sappho's friends blurred, calling for a shift in our political journey. We put our heads together to frame our vision and mission, and we formed SFE (2003), a platform welcoming all people irrespective of gender and sexual orientation who believed in questioning oppressive normative structures and institutions of discrimination. This was perhaps one of our earliest tentative steps taken to think beyond identities and question hegemonic structures. This step ironically provided scope for many identities and practices to come together in introspection and resistance.

Positing sexuality as a critical category of analysis, we began using the conjoined lens of gender-sexuality in our interfaces with community members, activists, researchers, students and the state. Our interactions and activities no longer talked about lesbian positionality only; we did not even talk about homosexuality or sexual orientation per se. Gender-sexuality became our entry point to understand, on the one hand, the fluidity of practices, expressions and identities, and, at the same time, provided us with conceptual and political resources to question the organised workings of homophobia, heterosexism and their alliances/intersections with other systems of oppression. Gender came to be understood more in its possible porosities and trans experiences started getting a foothold in discussions and interactions.

Issues like livelihood, class, caste, disability, regionality and political/racial/religious marginalisations did come into discussions and in solidarity-building efforts with other movements, but not so much directly in our political consciousness. Intersectionality, not then a buzzword as today, came in the form of matching footsteps with other movements, raising voices in each other's support and reacting in solidarity to crises. In these hand holdings, violence was the binding force, but what was lacking on both sides was critical engagement with issues other than what was considered core, those fundamental to one's own movement.

Our journey from lesbian identity to lesbian standpoint happened almost imperceptibly, spontaneously, through learning more about ourselves and others, about the plurality of identities and responding to a call for solidarity and bonding with differences and diversities.

With the joining of new members, novel experiences of intimacies, sexual practices and living arrangements brought with them a questioning of the hitherto known and the always-understood. The pressure to etch out distinct separateness in theory as also in lived lives between heterosexuality and lesbianism gave way to the need to bring to crisis essentialist ideas of identity[8] and discover overlaps, contradictions and newer instabilities. Ashwini Sukthankar in her short piece in Swakanthey (June 2004) writes, "This necessity to define a politically active community tends to reify difference by not only essentialising and naturalizing but also by homogenizing, and in the process, erasing all possibilities of polymorphous contradictoriness". Arriving at the instability of a 'true' lesbian identity proved exhilarating as our relationship with the rights framework shifted. Our discomfort with lesbian as just a sexual-political identity brought us to the lesbian standpoint. We moved from identity to a standpoint because we "wished to propose another worldview, another 'picture' different from the *One* presently holding us captive" (Achuthan, Biswas and Dhar, 2007:39; emphasis in original). We believed it was important to revert the gaze as it existed, from the centre to the margins, and re-view the centre from the perspective of the margin. Through a critical interpretation from the perspective of lesbian lives and loves we hoped to inaugurate a radical rethinking of the hegemonic sexual; we wished to posit the lesbian standpoint as the counter-point to the heterosexist-phallocentric imagination of the social.

This difficult work of rethinking the hegemonic from the standpoint of lesbian lives, however, was not to beget a "faithful description of their marginality, their experiences and their micropolitics" (Biswas, 2011:429). Nor was it to ensure more tolerance and empathy by the mainstream towards the margins. For us then, imagining politics from a lesbian standpoint implied a collaborative re-construction of the world of intimacies, kinship ties and living practices (Biswas, 2011:432).

Spreading tentacles was necessary and, with the help of some funding, SFE began treading into spaces that unfolded in front of us. Co-versing and traversing we arrived at 'Queer', sometimes loosely using it as identity and sometimes as political possibility. Our co-versing and traversing with queerness found wings with a few very individual personal experiences of friends, some of whom self-identified as gender non-conforming men with lesbian desire, or our heterosexual friends with queer sexual practices and lives. Queer, for us, worked as a place holder. It allowed us to soak in different experiences of gender and sexuality within individual and collective spheres. Just as it was difficult but not impossible, to embrace experiences of a 'born-woman' wanting to become a 'man' and be in a straight relationship with another woman, so too it was the case with trying to understand friends who practised pain, bondage and domination in sexual pleasure. Transmasculinity and transfemininity entered our individual and organisational life-worlds. Following the NALSA verdict of 2014 and the bill drafts that followed on protection of rights of transgender persons, the transgender community consolidated themselves further, especially the transfeminine community who were already present in public visibility and enjoyed some form of collectivisation since the times of the HIV/AIDS campaign in the 1990s. Though the transmasculine community showed less motivation in claiming public visibility, in general there has been an overall prominence granted, and what was previously just personal and anecdotal came to be organised, mobilised into narratives of discrimination, violation and invisibilisation. Our participation in the trans rights movement (mostly spearheaded by the transfeminine community) pushed the understanding from gender binary to gender fluidity where gender is also understood as a choreography of shaping bodies, beings and relationalities.

On the one hand, we found ourselves being pushed from different directions to give up the search for an authentic name, a label that could define and contain myriad sexual practices and behaviours.[9] On the other hand, in the larger political scenario labels and identity tags multiplied and the movement came to be defined as LGBTIHKQA+.[10] The political interface became complicated as a result, and tentative alliances and sharp divides came to be drawn on terms of authenticity, authorship and authority to represent. Who is a more authentic subject of politics; who has the right to speak for whom; who is acting as the gatekeeper? Such questions only multiplied.

To queer or not to queer, that is not the question

Presently we find ourselves at queer crossroads. We began our journey as primarily a lesbian political group; today, we are divided on how to best describe us in terms of affiliations, ideologies and political commitments. Some of us who identified previously as lesbian have started re-describing ourselves as queer and some who announced themselves as queer all along, have chosen to rename themselves lesbian! This rethinking and renaming, though done in a playful mode sometimes, has not been a mere play of words. It conveys how our personal and political lives have shifted, crisscrossed and interfaced. It also indicates how our political selves try to negotiate different subjectivities while imagining and materialising social justice. We have added the prefix 'Q' to the organisational tag (LBTQ) to indicate tentatively our movement both in thoughts and politics.

Feminism has remained our primary touchstone for political mobilising and queer theory became a collaborator-in-arms. Feminism honed our critique of patriarchy in its multiple avatars; it reiterated the need to reclaim gender as a category of analysis in a time when gender runs the risk of becoming a descriptive category only; it suffused our politics and ethics with a certain criticality. Queer theory helped us understand how social theories are rooted in heteronormativity with its binary oppositional categories of self and world. The concept of queer as an identity and/or a political practice prodded us to delve deeper into our existence; questioning and challenging existing identities and practices proved to be philosophically and politically enriching.

As an organisation we are trying to understand the promises of queer in praxis and politics, which has opened our own standpoints towards newer possibilities – more inclusive, dynamic and intersectional. Our politics today is informed by the fact that there can be no single-issue struggle, i.e. different dimensions of social life cannot be separated out into discrete and pure strands. Hierarchies of caste, race, class, gender, (dis)ability, sexuality, religion or location generate diverse structural inequalities for particular groups. Different kinds of alliances need to be built across different groups to effectively address 'non-normative' people's intersectional inequalities. Linking gender-sexuality with other axes of power such as caste, religion, location is therefore necessary where each needs to be prepared to be destabilised by the other.

Again, while queer theory provides us the tools to think out of the box, it also sometimes proves to be paralysing. Its promise of privileging structurelessness can often become pathways of remarginalisation. As Darnell L. Moore (2013:259) puts it:

> Yet, and again, even in its quests to resist structures, the 'queer' exists as another space wherein structure is once again reconfigured and operationalized, particularly as it relates to the ways that some bodies and political interests are made visible in queer movements while others are not.

While we pick our steps tentatively, we cannot give up the insights from lesbian feminism. Lesbian feminism is not about identity categories, of women loving women only, but also about keeping the lesbian lens/perspective alive within feminism. The lesbian feminist standpoint helps keep alive the questioning of marriage and family; it disturbs the oft seen tendency to anchor our politics in aspirations for queer families, queer kinships, queer marriages etc. without so much as questioning families, marriages and kinships. The slippage between queering and quer(y)ing can occur too often and too easily unless we remain aware of our impulse to create 'alternative' normativities and structures that seek conformation as a pre-condition for belonging. The lesbian standpoint moored in an incestuous intertwining of gender-sexuality adds to the criticality of our political–personal life-worlds.

As we try to queer our understanding of the trans (binary and not), the barely-there bi, the quietly watching asexual, the totally misunderstood pan or poly (amorous/sexual), the choice in our case is not between queer feminism or lesbian feminism; it is perhaps about queering our understandings of feminisms, lesbian feminism and queer theory. The lesbian lens is as much needed as the queer lens, and we have no qualms in wearing either and more.

Notes

1 We submit that this account is only partial. It does not express the travels/travails of all members of the organisation. In a way, it is the journey of the authors and that too only somewhat. It is a fact that however homogeneous it might read, the three have not had completely synchronous or similar impressions of the movement(s) nor did we agree on all interpretations and accounts of the movements. Also, when we say India in the title we do not claim to be in any way representative of the myriad strands and loci of what is known as the queer movement in India. This account is just one such multifarious strand and a product of our efforts to braid together tentative threads of histories, experiences and anecdotes.

2 There are many newspaper reports and texts that discuss the aftermath of the release of *Fire*. For example, see Sohini Ghosh (2010) and Brinda Bose (2006).

3 The body marked female at birth seemed to be the point of connection between the various women's groups that came together under the banner of Maitree. Trans women did not find any place, because they did not qualify to the category of woman, defined by the presence of

female genitalia. But then again, sex workers were not included in this network either. Perhaps, the subject of feminist politics remained marked by the trope of the deserving female-bodied victim of violence.

4 The Autonomous Women's Movement in India emerged in the 1970s and marked a radical shift in the women's movement compared to its character in the pre-independence times. This was the time when Indian politics came to a crisis with the declaration of emergency and fracturing of the Indian left; a number of social issues like price rise, dowry deaths, rape in police custody etc. grabbed headlines; and the post-independence dream of gender equality and women's development lay sadly unrealised. A number of locally organised movements were born, some of them led by women's groups, and the erstwhile women's wings severed their links with the political parties and declared themselves autonomous. The first conference was held in Bombay in 1980 and the seventh National Conference of the Autonomous Women's Movement was held in Kolkata in September 2006 (Sen, 2000).

5 The gay rights movement in India focused on delinking homosexuality from the disease–danger–death conundrum and worked to build a strong campaign in the sector of health and hygiene against HIV/AIDS. The lesbian rights movement, on the other hand, found solidarity with the women's movement through the shared experiences of gender oppression (Achuthan, Biswas and Dhar, 2007:3-4).

6 When we use 'we' as a pronoun for the collective the fact is that we are a mixed bag of gender-sexual identities, expressions and practices. On the one hand, many among us, but especially some with non-conforming gender expressions and identities, could not access the multitude of names or identity tags, available so easily today, to make sense or describe our experiences. On the other hand, the ones that could be accessed fell short of approximating our lived experiences.

7 The organisational Trust Deed, which was an official document used to register with the state in 2003, has mention of various categories like, "women who are gender variant"; "alternate sexualities"; "same sex preference" etc. in the description of the organisation.

8 Identity politics rests in the ability to carve a political legitimacy based on an authentic self – be it the gay gene, the gay pride, the lesbian culture etc.

9 On our part, every time we tried to take refuge in an identity-name that could be abstracted out of practices and politicised, we found them getting more and more parochial and exclusive.

10 Lesbian, Gay, Bisexual, Transgender, Intersexed, Hijra, Kothi, Queer or Questioning, Asexual. The plus sign denotes the expansiveness of the acronym and the identity terms.

SIX | Speculations on lesbian feminism as erotic friendship

Karuna Chandrashekar and Shraddha Chatterjee

> When a life is what we have to struggle for, we struggle against structures. (Sara Ahmed, *Living a Feminist Life*, 2017)

These words are a direct defence of why lesbian feminism remains relevant for feminists today. The everydayness of lesbian lives is an exercise against heteropatriarchy, perhaps because heteropatriarchy works insidiously through inter-personal and intra-psychic sites, marking the personal and political as battlegrounds of challenge and transformation. In this chapter, it is this struggle for everyday life with which we wish to engage, contending that to adopt a lesbian standpoint or orient a life towards lesbian feminism is to struggle with, and for, (a way of) life. To think of lesbian feminism in today's times also requires us to consider the radical post-essentialist possibilities that *queer*[1] offers to us. This is to already put lesbian feminism or a lesbian standpoint in some crisis, and to ask, what does lesbian feminism look like today? We contend that the particularity of lesbian feminism is its fidelity to community building. Therefore, to reach a standpoint, however contingent, requires a network of care and desire that makes visible the dangers of compulsory heterosexuality even as it rejects it. Written as a dialogue between friends, in this chapter we attempt to navigate the discomforts, pleasures, doubts and joys of building and maintaining queer friendships against the backdrop of contemporary times as a strategy that helps reach lesbian feminist positions and counter its costs, in the process also opening up to question, how radical is queer friendship? Phrased differently, what does queer friendship offer to lesbian feminism, and how is the praxis of such friendships radical, insofar as it works against heteropatriarchies?

I

S: Growing up, I always found myself most wounded by the female friendships I lost to men, or because of them. These were the friendships I grieved the most, despite how normalised their loss had become; in this grief was also the sadness of how it was understood and acceptable that, throughout my life, I would lose women as they developed relationships with men.

K: I always regarded the loss as partial; my friends drifted away but remained tethered to me by a slowly thinning wire. A wire thinned by a desire that was redirected, almost, as if, naturally. Desire redirected to a boyfriend, husband and/ or children. Our attachment remained as melancholic. As much as I have begrudged this displacement, my replacement, I know the lives of friends loving men or married to men aren't perfect. In some manner, I have ended up being witness to the failure of The Heterosexual Dream. I have mourned this loss for my friends; it is devastating to watch a dream die even when that dream was never one for me. I also know the courage of picking oneself up from a broken illusion; every divorced woman, every single woman in India is painfully aware of this reality.

We start our journey towards an imagination of lesbian feminism with a conversation about women[2] in heterosexual relations, and our relations with them, because we wish to think about lesbian feminism as an ongoing and dynamic practice in friendship, rather than as a standpoint based in identity. For us, this involves holding on to, and building, friendships with women in heterosexual relations, because we recognise that something about those friendships can be queer, and therefore, incorporate and expand a praxis of lesbian feminism. In part, our turn away from politics or standpoints solely determined by identity as a marker for lesbian feminism is in line with critiques of identity, where identity can be considered a 'necessary fiction' at best (Butler, 1993). Following that, we acknowledge that sometimes political mobilisations based on identity are necessary, perhaps especially so in intersections with the law, but we also want to mark our difference from such politics. How we imagine lesbian feminism does not fall within this domain of identity as necessity.

In part, this is because for us, lesbian feminism does not converse with, or respond to, the state or its mechanisms, even while existing in relation to those mechanisms, being shaped and hurdled by them.[3] We move away from identity because it is useful to think about how a framework of identity is invested in fragmenting our experiences, while giving the illusion of centredness, authenticity and wholeness (Scott, 1992; Chow, 2001; Chiesa, 2007). As such, identity politics can be seen as fragmenting our relationships to each other rather than intensifying them, albeit under the guise of arbitrary solidarities (however necessary they may be). This is partly because as we begin to wonder if our experiences fit within a certain framework of identity we narrativise our lives against certain formulations of goodness and badness of our fit within that identity. We become assailed by questions such as "Am I queer enough?" or "Am I radical enough?" These are not productive questions as they can never be answered satisfyingly, and they go against solidarity by virtue of centring the subject rather than focusing on how particular subjectivities emerge in relation with the collective.

As we shift away from identity, we are also able to shift away from a centred, autonomous, agential and rational understanding of the subject. This allows us to focus on how the subject comes into being relationally, in how it is oriented differently towards or away from different people, non-humans, things and phenomena. To turn away from identity allows us to think of these queer relations beyond the act of having sex, and mark friendship at the heart of lesbian feminism as we attempt to understand it. In doing so, we do not make a distinction between sex and friendship, but rather try to expand the logic of queerness to include friendship, and to expand the logic of friendship to include erotics. For us, this lends new significations to queerness and sexuality, and therefore, tries to widen the scope of lesbian feminism beyond identity and sexuality, even as we attempt to occupy the same space from which it arose before – the intersection of feminist and queer politics.

Each of these relations may have its own pace, sense of time and space, and culture, geography and history; the subject, conceived through relationality (rather than rationality) is therefore, at once determined by many temporalities, linearities and orientations. Ahmed discusses such an orientation as being "turned towards certain objects, those that help us to find our way" (2006b:4). Sexual orientation – or to be oriented as lesbian – is then to be oriented towards space in a certain way, but is also a series of choices determining, and determined by, the people with whom we inhabit that space. The proximity or distance from certain spaces and people are negotiated within this logic of orientation. Ahmed (2006a; 2006b; 2017) asks us to consider orientation in thinking through who we direct our energies towards, what acts and relations we invest in, who we keep close to and turn away from, and whom we open ourselves to. In other words, lesbian feminism is about who we relate to, and who we find unrelatable.

To imagine being oriented in lesbian feminism (as opposed to being oriented 'as lesbian feminists') is to begin from a place of disorientation: "[t]o inhabit any place is a dynamic negotiation between the familiar and the unfamiliar" (Ahmed, 2006b:8). For example, writing on friendship within the discourse of queerness can feel like a moment of disorientation, because the predominant focus of queerness has hitherto been sex and sexuality. However, if we think of identity as a fragmentary experience, always in the process of becoming through relationality, then queer phenomenologies help us understand what Ahmed calls "the politics of discomfort" (Ahmed, 2006b).

However, before we expand on queerness as friendship, we need to explain the reasons for this journey. They lie in the persistent questions that remain with us as we try to orient ourselves in queer spaces (which is often a demand to orient ourselves to inhabit and perform a particular kind of queerness): why are some of us always uncomfortable with conflating 'being queer' with having sex with others who also identify as 'queer'? Why is it that the logic of sexuality as sexual act feels like it is not enough? Why is Pride not enough, or sometimes, too much? Why is queer sex not 'queer' enough, and so often, hetero- or homo-normative? Why do queer spaces, where we would hope to find the most comfort, make us uncomfortable?

For us, then, these discomforts lead to speculations that to experience queerness is to be non-aligned, to be turned away from the logic of heterosexuality, wherever it operates. This includes being disoriented by queerness in its homonationalist manifestations (Puar, 2007; 2017), in its exclusions of class, caste, disability and race, in its insistence on performing and demonstrating a 'good queerness', in its reliance on law and its demand to be included in frameworks of the nation state (Chatterjee, 2018), in its assumption that queerness is always about sex and not about an overarching way in which we relate to others and orient ourselves to the world. Therefore, for us, lesbian feminism inaugurates another way of "friendship as a way of life" (Foucault, 1997): a robust orientation to, and enactment of, erotic/friendship as politics, care and ethics.

Lesbian feminism, to us, means a turning towards and nurturing of what is queer in our friendships with women and womxn, and turning away from what is heterosexual in our relations with them. Since kinship has historically and cross-culturally mostly positioned us in relation to men, we see the potential in lesbian feminism as a praxis of friendship among women and womxn to be queer because it turns away from relations among women and womxn being oriented through men. These turns in such erotic/ friendships are also momentary, and lesbian feminism relies on its repeated utterances. Rather than fitting ourselves as lesbian feminists into a predetermined and static field of what constitutes lesbian feminism, and its goals, utopias and futures, we recognise that *lesbian feminism is a praxis we are always working on.* In our imagination, lesbian feminism is not a politics aligned towards futurity, an impossible future always yet-to-come. Rather, it is in the everyday decisions through which we live our lives; who we live with, who we meet, who we speak to on the phone, who we stay in touch with, and therefore about who we allow to touch us. Therefore, it is also about how we plan our lives, and with whom, how we orient ourselves to decisions on marriage, children, couple-hood, family.

Yet, heteronormativity and its terms are always-emerging knowledges, and it is in our disorientation that we know where we align with a frame, whether we fit in the frame at all (Ahmed, 2006b). To be turned away from heteronormative goals – marriage, compulsory heterosexuality, property ownership and childbirth is to turn away from the present script that builds these decisions as a network of care and support. Queer people are often abdicating certain discourses of care and love in the search for other ones. For example, single and queer womxn will often be asked by close friends and family about their plans for marriage and family. Even among close friends it becomes common to hear different iterations of the same complaint, "It's time to get serious now", or "What are you doing with your life if you're not getting married and starting a family?" The assumption here is that there are only a few metrics by which we can assign meaning to our lives, a code of acts and alliances that make us recognisable to others as worthy of belonging. For single womxn (where queer womxn get read as single womxn often), the question of care and love becomes a pressing reality because our inability to fit the heteronormative frame is seen as our unworthiness to receive support and care, rather than being seen as a problem born out of the smallness of the frame itself. For example, in India, there are many of us who give up on being single because of a fear of being alone and uncared for.[4] One can only imagine, thousands of married women were single once, and in some manner single still, insofar as they are married but remain uncared for. Perhaps the choice between being single womxn and married women is to negotiate with which forms of loneliness one can live. To make this bargain and get married is to trade being marked in a certain way for a mark of marriage. In this context, unmarried womxn, single womxn, queer womxn and divorced womxn are marked by a similar disobedience.

This is why it is useful to imagine lesbian feminism in India as a turn away from identity and towards relationality, because as queer womxn, sometimes we are more oriented towards our heterosexual women friends than those who come to be seen as 'authentic' or 'good' queer subjects. Having been asked the same questions as our heterosexual women friends, with the same gendered orientations towards the 'tragedy' of our single-hood, the same expectations of gender roles and subservience, sometimes we have more in common as queer womxn with heterosexual women than with 'good' queers who may be misogynistic, homonationalist and uncritically willing to fit within the narrative of having a happy marriage, children and comfortable middle-class lives.

II

S: It feels difficult to meet the demands of the heterosexual women who have managed to remain in my life over the years. In their friendship, they demand that I be okay with being displaced once they become a couple or marry, and my decisions to not follow that path are sometimes seen as a personal attack on their decisions to do so. These friendships feel extremely precarious, and swing between companionship and loneliness. On the other hand, with my queer friends, where things should feel easy, or at least, more comfortable, they do not. Building an imagination of the future is so often impossible, and mired with psychic and material hurdles. Also, sometimes our queerness feels so precarious that we are utterly unforgiving of, and cruel to, those who can be our friends. How do I imagine a life with a friend who may want to become a couple some day? How do I think of owning a house with friends; how would we live there, who would it go to when we die? These friendships are draining in a different way, in that the labour required to sustain them cannot be anticipated. Where does one go when one is tired, and needs to rest? Where does queerness find a home?

K: Whenever I feel burdened by the demands of being a good queer subject I turn to the past. My friends have been there for me when I have felt, as Barthes (1978) says, "annulled by love". I am rescued by friends but moreover rescued by the possibility that feminist friendships keep open possibilities that (hetero) romantic love closes for me. Perhaps it is easier for me to believe in the friend than in the lover. In friendship the violence of love loses some of its colour. I don't mean to say I have not hurt, nor that I have not been hurt by my friends, sometimes profoundly so. But I have not yet been annulled by a friend. If there is a lovers' discourse, is there a discourse of the friend?

What does it mean to love a friend? Is it very different from what happens between two lovers? Why do we ask this when thinking through lesbian feminism? Why do we consider friendship to be a practice that, for us, defines lesbian feminism? In her work on female friendship, Faderman (1981) details the accounts of love between women in nineteenth-century England and America. Not burdened by concerns of abnormality or identity, literature from that time details passionate attachments between women reflected in the lives of writers like Emily Dickinson and Virginia Woolf. We know of this because of the letters they wrote to the women in their lives expressing yearning and desire. Faderman's work (1981; 1993/1983) shows us that our categories for discerning between different kinds of love have caused us some trouble. Perhaps, in our time, it is important to ask, what does it mean to choose our friends over lovers or partners? Further, what determines who we choose as friends?

In the 1897 novel, *Diana Victrix*, Florence Converse writes of a woman, Enid, rejecting a proposal for marriage because she is attached to her work, but also because of her profound attachment to a female friend. The man is bewildered by the second reason and asks, "Only a woman?" (Faderman, 1981:168). To this Enid responds, "The reason the woman separates us, ... is because the woman and I understand each other, sympathise with each other, are necessary to each other. And you and I are not. It is not simply her womanliness, it is her friendship" (Faderman, 1981:168). Friendship is not a substitute for love as this character would have it. It is already its own world, rich with desire, meaning and care. It has its own meanings, and perhaps, we would like to contend, its own logic of signification. This logic of signification is antithetical to the logic of lack which is bound by its affiliation to the phallus. It also has no need for a substitute attachment (heterosexual love and marriage). For Enid, it is not possible to imagine a man replacing her friend and the care and companionship that she provides. Moreover, why should she? To imagine such a possibility would require her to imagine a lack that marriage to a man can help fulfil. We do not believe that friendship can exist in the framework of lack.[5]

Yet, all womxn cannot make, nor do they desire to make, Enid's choice. In another book from that time, *Anne of Green Gables* (Montgomery, 1976), the titular character of Anne falls in love with her female friends frequently. Anne, unlike Enid in *Diana Victrix*, gets married to her childhood sweetheart. Yet, the entire series dedicates the bulk of her story to the girls and women she meets before and after her marriage. Anne's desire (which, we argue, reads as queer almost immediately) is not to get married but to find 'kindred spirits', people like her (they often turn out to be women), those she recognises and is recognised by. Between womxn who choose their friend and womxn who get married, is it possible to see a spectrum of the place of friendship in the lives of both queer and heterosexual womxn?

In our turn to relationality from identity, we situate an ethics and practice of lesbian feminism in who we turn to in times of despair; who we show up for, who we make plans with, who wounds us, and finally, who we spend our lives with. These examples are to say that there is simply no script for how these friendships should operate, nor what it takes for them to survive, but that womxn are trying out, and failing at, what works for them as they go against the grain. This writing and rewriting of newer scripts includes passionate attachments, love, sex and everything in between. Between friends, sex can become another elaboration of attachment, but it need not be the only one, nor the most significant.[6] Unlike in love, at least as it is normally understood, where the absence of sex gains meaning as a problem or difficulty, between friends the presence of sex, or the possibility of sex, may be just one way to navigate desire. Here, we demarcate between friendships that begin with, and circulate around, a sexual encounter, where sex is an integral part of the relation between people, and between a relations that may include the sexual act as one of its facets.

III

K: All the friends / that I ever lost / laid their hearts / bare / like the relief of trees / against bodies of backlit skies / there is an insurmountable darkness between us / and we forget forgiveness / this skin still feels too thin for the wind

S: dearest saudade, how could you fail me, how could you turn away from the lies? I lay there for so many lifetimes, preserved perfectly, cauterised in my pain ... How could you leave me, my beloved, to be plucked apart by vultures and men who feasted on my skin? Where did you go, even now these words are thrown into the void with deep faith that you will hear them someday ... Saudadethenamealreadyrollsunfamiliarlyonmytongue.

Whenever there is possibility, there is also melancholy.[7] Lesbian feminism could lie between friendship as possibility and melancholy, and this oscillation colours such relations with responsibility.[8] For all of those friends that stay in our lives, there are those who do not choose us back; to discuss the affective attachments of queer friendship would be incomplete without the veil, and weight, of loss that we carry into our new relationships. Sometimes this loss comes from us being passionately attached to friends who are not attached to us in return. At other times, this loss comes from moments when those we considered our friends fail to understand our orientations, creating a failure where two erstwhile friends now look away from each other, become strange. At yet other times, this loss comes from losing queer friends to suicide or death after illness, leaving us with no hope for recovery. As such, much of coming to terms with queerness so often involves mourning unrequited feelings or 'feeling backward' (Love, 2007) (feelings that are later mirrored in the near universal experience of watching our heterosexual friends getting married). Our queer friendships carry our navigations through this loss, sometimes by being shadowed by it, and sometimes by helping us surpass it. Moreover, we often do not – or are unable to – speak of this loss to the friend, and it becomes melancholy precisely because it contains a forgetting, and a revealing that who we are attached to (as friends/lovers) have forgotten us. Unlike the character of Enid, we so often find that we are replaced.

Further, we find that this melancholy is not just individual, but also historical, and remnants of it determine who we choose as our friends.[9] History and geography often have a bearing on who we are able to call a friend; lesbian feminism as erotic/friendship, therefore, bears witness to the fissures and fractures we are born into, and that continue to determine who we touch or do not, and who touches us or does not. This paleonymically burdens our (in)ability to be friends across caste, class, racial and religious lines; *sometimes the work of lesbian feminism is to work against the grain of history.* Choosing our friends and lovers based on similarities in the positions we hold with respect to various power structures, for us, goes against a praxis of lesbian feminism as we seek to embody it. This makes erotic/friendship and lesbian feminism less utopian than we would like it to be. Yet, these are the stakes we continue to contend with – even as we are discontented; this is the world we live in, and we believe our feminism(s) are better off for knowing these stakes as they stand.

These constant displacements of, and failures in, love and friendship that are part of our lives build the grounds for lesbian feminism as a responsibility we become oriented towards, to care for our friends, even in the possibility that they may leave us some-day. It is to give an account of oneself as someone who forgives a friend, who continues to turn to friendship as hopeful, despite the constant threat of disorientation and disavowal. Lesbian feminism, then, is also about being weighed down, or anchored, by friendship in a way that it is friendships that circumscribe us (however provisionally), giving us the opportunity to escape the signifiers of patriarchal kinship that have hitherto determined womxn's existence. This is where feminism comes in yet again, by the way it charts our course (of love and loss) differently. Therefore, we write this not just in the hope of expanding meanings of what is 'queer' and 'lesbian', but also as subjects of feminism attempting to imagine more ethical forms of relating as gateways to friendship, care and finding homes when our struggles for survival have made us too weary. For us, lesbian feminism as an ethics of friendship not only includes what we continue to struggle for, but also includes those dreary afternoons when we are comforted by a cup of tea and some conversation. It includes those evenings of laughter among friends that make us feel the world is more alive and hopeful. Many of us will know that sometimes even the existence of such moments has been made possible by a struggle.

In the end, we would like to say that it is not enough that the queerness of friendship exists, or even that passionate attachments between people exist, but that they can be mobilised to explore different forms of relating and caring that move beyond turning against the structures that have hitherto shackled us; lesbian feminism is to turn away from those structures, refuse them as interlocutors that we must work against, or work around. This also means turning away from anger and antagonism. Too long we have imagined queerness as death, loss, abjectness and failure (Edelman, 2004; Halberstam, 2011; Berlant and Edelman, 2014; Penney, 2014); too long we have thought of ourselves as forever destined to traverse the Möbius of love and loss. It is time to turn towards the power of erotic/ friendship as pleasurable, as a way to be happy, despite, or rather because of, our disorientations.

Notes

1 We see queer as a shifting signifier, sometimes taking it to mean embodiment and praxis, sometimes responding to its deployment as an identity. We recognise that queerness is dynamic, changing "forms and articulations upon each utterance; and yet, queerness is also stable, marked in difference to heterosexuality and, sometimes, heteronormativity" (Chatterjee, 2018:1). In this chapter, we also find ourselves closer to an understanding of queerness as a dynamic yet stable material embodiment that directs how we relate to, and make sense of, the world around us. We find ourselves away from an understanding of queerness as identity. This understanding is in part a response to the contexts that we occupy as Indian womxn living in cities where we are often read as single women (or unmarried women) rather than as queer. Rather than insist that we be read as such, we have sought to understand the challenge of being marked in this way and how it shapes our relationships to others. For us both are true, the silence of our queerness and the ways in which they reveal themselves in relation to heteronormativity and patriarchy in India. This particular location has pushed us to re-examine our place in different discourses of queerness which travel to us easily through both academic and NGO discourses. For both of us, the challenge of friendship has been in the ways it fails us but also in the way heteropatriarchy does not consider friendship a viable relationship to invest in. The loss we feel is doubled, both by the loss of friends and the uncertain place it has in heteronormativity.

2 Throughout this chapter, we use the terms 'woman/women' to mean cis-gendered, heterosexual women, and 'womxn' as a broader term that addresses cis-gendered queer women, persons assigned female at birth, trans women, and those who position themselves somewhere on the transfeminine spectrum.

3 Here, we share an understanding of the relationship between the state and the subject in a Foucauldian way, insofar as the subject is shaped by, and in response to, power/knowledge. We depart from Foucault where he does not make room for desire and the psyche in understanding this subject; in this departure, we come close to a psychoanalytic understanding of the subject, albeit with other departures.

4 In countries where queer marriage is legal, many also choose to marry because the script of marriage is strong, and repeatedly insists that we will be unloved and alone without it.

5 Those familiar with Lacan will realise that here, we are responding to his framework of psychoanalysis to say it cannot theorise friendship, or rather, it cannot theorise friendship the way we are imagining and living it.

6 Audre Lorde (1984) has already awoken us to the danger of the separation of the erotic from all aspects of life except for that of sex.

7 As Winterson (1992:9) asks: "Why is the measure of love loss?"

8 Here, we turn away from Derrida's understanding of friendship as responsibility (2005/1994), and instead of focusing on the limits and impossibilities of friendship in the larger backdrop of state and democratic discourses, we focus on the possibilities of friendship as a promise of ethics and care.

9 Lorde (1984) writes about the historical inability of white women to listen to Black women in her open letter to Mary Daly. In such contexts, listening becomes a praxis of keeping oneself open to the other, which grounds the basis for friendship.

SEVEN | Once upon a time I was a lesbian, now I am genderqueer and feline

Shals Mahajan

Imagine a game, a version of spin the bottle. When the bottle stops and points, you have to say who you are – the identities you admit to (or care to articulate) in the here and now. In a room full of queer bodies and deeds, you might find a lesbian or two. Or maybe not. It may be that we never get to that point, 'cause I suspect it might be easier to get stuck at human and caste and nation and end up in a discussion on borders and boundaries and the inevitable limits of identity or …

But even if desire does enter the room, and knowing our unruly selves, I am fairly certain that it would, given the complexity of our desires and the instabilities (diversities) of gender, lesbian is going to be in short supply.

Imagine in this crowd, tagging along in a less than graceful manner, my touching-47, greying-rather-handsomely (to make up for the rest of the bumblingness I suspect), feline genderqueer self. A self who has repeatedly spoken of how both masculinity and femininity are alienating to them at a personal level; and who has, since the beginning of queer memory, been tongue tied at discussions of "who are you attracted to?", trying a breeziness born of experience rather than clarity.

I came out in the early 1990s in Bombay, and lesbian was at that time exciting, but also a little too womanly (or womynly, what with the 'womyn loving womyn' definition that was being bandied about). In the high articulation of youthfulness, I called myself a desi[1]-dyke and then just dyke (the *desi* sounded silly in the *des*). I was also part of that fiercely feminist lesbian gang, who was discovering the joys of women-only spaces and feminist movements, and for whom lesbian meant everything – sort of.

Desiring women made one lesbian and, more importantly, connected us to the silent, longing, aching, lonesome parts of ourselves and to each other. Lesbian was hot, happening, sexual, desiring. It was the only word we had in common in our myriad languages obsessed with keeping women pure, asexual and repro-ductive within marriage. From the Kerala schoolgirls who called themselves "The Martina Club", to those of us finding names for groups that might reflect some connect between women (Sakhi, Stree Sangam, Sahayatrika, Sappho),[2] lesbian was the identity that defined our difference. Or, this particular difference.

In the space and time between then and the room of the imag-ined game of spin the bottle, lie the lives being lived, and those who found voice in some of these names, or who changed the names with the power of their voices and of their lives. This is the space that the stories I go back to, personal and political, come from. These stories/histories are also deeply connected to my work as member of LABIA – *a Queer Feminist LBT Collective* that I was part of from the very first meeting in 1995, when it was formed in Bombay, to its twenty-year celebrations a couple of years ago, and now again after a break of two years.

The hair, the hair (since 1995)

I keep on telling C that she can never be more butch (though of course she is) than me because I have the hair. In fact, I have coined this term – the haircut butch. It describes me more exactly than butch does, a term I hate to have applied to myself. As I keep telling a friend I have known for ages – my looking butch is always taken to mean I am butch, but I know I am not, and the other butches definitely know it. I neither fit the brotherhood, nor do I want to. But it puts me in a curious place which is almost asexual. And yet, it is the visible marker that sometimes gives me and others the courage to reach out to someone who looks like 'that' or gives a stranger the courage to approach one of 'us'.

Over the years I also settle into an 'aesthetic', for want of a better word, that I feel comfortable in: short hair cut at a local men's hair cutting salon, cargo shorts, collar or V-neck tees or bush shirts. The odd jeans when it is not too warm. The classic butch aesthetic, incidentally. And yet, it is during these very years that I begin to say clearly, "I am not butch. Do not call me so". And begin to find that friends do understand.

On the one hand, I am out of the butch–femme dynamic (which we spend endless hours discussing and fighting over). On the other, despite all my passionate feminism, I am so uncomfortable being a 'woman' that I cannot have the ease of camaraderie in spaces that are only for women.

Strangely, I am not articulating any of this at the time. We are at the heady point of finding and creating spaces for lesbian and bisexual women. We are meeting people like us and learning autonomous feminist politics.[3] We are reaching out to more and more women, and we are also talking about 'women who look different'. We have yet to learn that actually, what we are talking about, is that 'we feel different'.

The difference in feeling that we are able to articulate then, is that of sexuality. And it has taken me so long to find women who understand and even celebrate my difference, including that of my looks, that I do not find the space within me to say that I do not feel 'woman', let alone celebrate my woman self. I seldom call myself lesbian or do so only when I am articulating a politics or taking a specific position in a discussion. For me, I am a dyke.

It is this euphoria that those of us who've met some les-bi-an folks (yes, we did that too then to talk of lesbians and bisexuals together), carry with us when we start phonelines, try to follow every case reported in the news, and write back to every letter that follows the smallest news item that journalist friends write in different regional language newspapers. It is this euphoria we carry with us when we start a homemade zine and invite these women to write not just letters to us, but to write for each other.

These are our lifelines to each other as we are confronted with more and more news reports of two women, or sometimes more, attempting suicide. We learn fact-finding and documentation from the women's movements and reach out to groups that will listen to us. We hope these already established women's groups will be able to give support wherever they are, since LB groups are less than a handful, and the rest of the organising only focuses on HIV/AIDS.

Meanwhile, as Stree Sangam, we also meet many people whose relationship with the term 'lesbian' is even queerer – we need that word badly, without knowing it, almost as badly as we need trans at this point – than mine is. They run away as 'lesbian' couples, not quite butch–femme, not man–woman, but not two women either. We are learning about the complexity of gender from hijras *and* kothis,[4] *but not this closely. These people are close to us, and somewhere in our fumbling dialogues we begin to understand gender more, theirs and ours. LesBiT[5] in Bangalore (2005) begins with the term transgender firmly in their name, and we all go through stages of finding terms that fit the widening 'us'. Our language and our understanding of gender begin to shift radically.*

Being feminist and queer

We are fortunate to be part of an entire culture of activism because of the groups around us (Forum Against Oppression of Women, Saheli, Aawaaz-E-Niswaan).[6] That and our feminist moorings lead us to seek answers and change beyond our most intimate and immediate environments. As LABIA, we find shared ground with various women's groups. We participate in discussions on family laws, connect our experiences of sexuality to critiques of marriage, production and reproduction, and take part in discussions on sexual assault laws and child rights campaigns. When 2002 Gujarat[7] happens, we put all our energies as LABIA into doing the work needed there. We also work with these groups and with human rights groups to create support for LBT individuals in different places.

The first big conference we are part of as Stree Sangam is the 6th National Women's Movements Conference in Ranchi in 1997. While such conferences earlier had sessions on 'women who love women', this time a session with this name is put on the schedule. What surprises me most is the number of women, from so many places, who stop those of 'us' who seem visibly queer/lesbian/something, to ask us when 'that night' session is. This session has been publicised with all the other sessions and deliberately kept as a night session so that it does not run parallel to other sessions running through the day. We communicate, often using someone's help to translate the question, or through gestures and languages we do not share. I am thankful for looking outsider enough to be identified as such.

A few years later, in April 2004, when we have changed from Stree Sangam to LABIA, we do a skit on "I don't look lesbian enough", in an open-mic/performance space. Many of us are still battling the stares for not looking 'women'. Others are also fighting the battle of being invisible as queer, as lesbian, of being seen as 'straight', even within the larger LGBT-KQH spaces. Two decades later, I am not surprised when a non-binary gender-identifying person speaks of not being seen as non-binary or trans* because of their appearance. So much has happened and still most people, even queer and trans* or QUILTBAG[8] identifying, prefer to assume rather than ask a person about themselves.

When we finally meet, those of us organising the evening are gobsmacked to see over a hundred women in attendance. While some of us are sure that people are here by mistake, the people themselves are not. No one knows how, but conversations take place, multiple, but also with a lot of silences. In a world where desire is tough to talk about, it is even more difficult to be identified as a lesbian, a woman-loving woman, in a space where people from your community, group or city might be around. It takes us ages to understand the impact of this moment of euphoria. Of course, in the larger organising, there are attempts to keep reports of 'these' sessions out of the press conference and such like, but there are enough allies too who ensure such things do not happen. We do get written in the history of these amazing conferences.

When the 7th National Women's Movements Conference, held in Kolkata in 2006 (the last of these nationally organised, non-funded huge conferences) is organised, LABIA is not just part of the national co-ordination committee but at the forefront of pushing for all transgender persons to be able to attend the conference. After much struggle several trans men and trans women do attend, but not all who want to can. 'Marginalised genders and sexualities' is firmly on the agenda with other identities and locations and we also manage to have a well-attended discussion challenging the long-held feminist line that sex is biological and gender social, thus opening out the dichotomy of the categories of 'sex' and 'gender'. Finding space for sexuality, we begin to understand, was easier than opening out gender will be.

Understanding different identities and locations that each body occupies, and the personal and political meaning of intersectionality is perhaps what we learn most in these interactions. It is something that is clearly missing in the larger LGBTIKQH organising and campaigns, even though most funded groups work on HIV/AIDS with very marginalised people. Few such groups see the necessity of intersectional politics then, and LABIA gets the tag of 'radical lesbian'.

Stone butch blues (neither stone nor butch but still having the blues) 2009

"I do not like to go out with stone butches", she says, somewhat self-consciously, and I stop myself from bombarding her with questions that are both barbed and bewildered. The reason I am being 'good' is simply that I am interviewing her for my work and this is not the place to interrogate her with my usual abrasiveness. So, I try humour and gently ask her if she is talking about being seen socially with those she calls stone butch or dating them, and she says socially, since they out her inevitably. Or, so she thinks.

Then feeling that perhaps she has been very brash, she adds, "you know I do not really understand about gender, I am a lesbian".

I suppose that before 2000 (though our conversation is happening almost a decade later), when we still were a group of lesbian and bisexual women and had not started to think of genders other than the binary, we too might have sounded as uncertain. Remembering this, I ask her, "who do you think is a stone butch?" and, seeing her hesitate, add, "do you think I am one?"

To my utter horror she says, "yes, very much so". My first reaction, absurdly, is a stern desire to convince her that I really love, I mean *love*, to be touched, penetrated and brought to orgasm multiple times, so hello, who are you calling stone? For one frantic moment I teeter on the edge of hysteria and paroxysm.

Curbing both, I finally ask her how she understands the term and whether she is aware of how it is used. It turns out that my 'butch' persona is yet again to blame. And it is all about the looks. She does not understand stone sexually, but since I never dress in any other way, I am a hardcore butch.

The year 2009 is the euphoric year of the Delhi High Court judgment on Section 377, the point from where many LGBTIKHQ's histories and stories will begin. This is the beginning of the explosion of what will soon spread to several cities and towns – pride marches (later parades), more queer parties in the metro cities, access to internet and the legitimacy of connecting as LGBT/Queer (which seem synonymous at most times), and many Q-themed endeavours. It is also the time when we begin to see how normative the demands and the representation of this 'queer' is becoming. It is no wonder then, that in 2009, in a metro like Bombay, a trans-looking person is not an acceptable lesbian.

What a drag! (2010)

At a mad drag party at a friend's backyard, several of us are drinking and dancing. The invite had sent us into a tizzy: a beloved friend is leaving town and we all want to say goodbye in a dynamic fashion, but the drag question is … well, dragging us down.

What is drag for a person who wears everything? What is drag for one with short hair who does not identify as either woman or man? What is drag for one who is most comfortable in trousers and tucked in shirts? And so on and so forth.

I reject the long-standing drag idea for me – a Parsi aunty in a silk sari, with a string of pearls (and curly hair if we can manage to do it) – because it requires more chutzpah than I have. Have ever had! And then I waver between a sari, which I know I could never wear (what if I do not look like a *hijra*? What if I actually pass as an aunty?), and a *salwar kurta* which sounds like a cop out, but I can wear a pink and blue one!

I settle on the *salwar kurta* and lots of *kajal*[9] lining my eyes and then, on a whim, darken my upper lip with it as well.

The thing is that I actually do have a lot of hair on my upper lip. It is not seen much since most of it somehow blends with my skin. But when I darken it, it becomes a surprisingly real moustache. Trimmed, understated and most 1960-ish, or so I think. It gets me noticed.

And when I look into the mirror, I see an image of my handsome father from his wedding studio photograph. His moustache is just as thin and sharp, his smile larger, his eyes twinkling quite so.

At some point during the party, the conversation turns to gender and, based on that, who X, a trans man, would like to date or not. What a surprising turn of events, that! Not.

The intense discussion that follows also necessitates identifying the genders of the others so as to decide whether one wants to date them. The conversation meanders long and precarious down several paths and stirs something quite intense: one friend is bugged at X's inability to hug her since she has abandoned her regular open-necked shirts and jeans for a dazzling sari showing her broad shoulders to their best. Another is flirting quite deliciously in a mini-dress with lots of chains around her, a complete contrast to her usual tough *bhai*[10] (though woman-identified) self, until I unwittingly call her *janaab*[11] and she cuts me down with a sharp look. Yet another has involved herself in such an elaborate turban that one is forced to talk to the turban. And a pretty boy has finally unbuttoned his sharp shirt to reveal the lace underneath. Much is happening.

Somewhere in this "who will you date?" affair, the conversation reaches me. X (or perhaps someone else, by then) rejects me by saying that I am too butch. At this, much to my astonishment, I find several of the bunch burst out in loud laughter. "You have to be joking", is the common refrain. Someone raises a beer bottle up in the air and says, "All those who think S is butch, raise your hands". There are none. And then, the next question, as naturally: "And those who think that she is a queen?" Most of the hands are in the air, accompanied by much laughter. And I think to myself, "Damn! I should've worn that sari after all!"

Loss

The year 2009 is also a year of deep loss and pain as we lose our feline familiar we have lived with for sixteen years. As C and

I relearn to live in our own skins and spaces, a part of me that had never needed expression in the world of humans until then, begins to seek articulation: my feline self. It is as if that which was so far content to be now does not know what to do with itself. With my closest familiars, I begin to express myself slowly. As I mourn, I give myself space to be without Chintoo, the person I was with him. I become more peaceful over the years, the question of gender becomes easier, when I see my feline humanness. It even helps me sleep better. I realise that perhaps feline is the closest to describing myself. Maybe that is what my gender is, really. I begin to share this in small bits. It seems frivolous and easy to dismiss, and often I feel too fragile to say it as a politics of being. It takes several years for me to be able to say this to even my closest circle of friends. When I do, they surprise me with their understanding. I still do not know how to connect this being to the politics around me. Yet, this is me too, and in the queer spaces I inhabit, I find myself saying this more and more. And I find that there is respect, and often, understanding too.

But there is another loss in these very years. The women's group that I have been part of for more than fifteen years becomes a difficult place to belong to. And, it is on the question of gender. Several of us have, over the years, raised the issue of Forum Against Oppression of Women remaining a group of 'women' alone. We have had many discussions on gender, and while all of us understand the need to articulate politics specific to the location of 'woman' in the present, we also feel that we should as members expand to include trans-identified persons, like many of us.

But these discussions lead us back to some of the usual cis-feminist articulations that many of us had thought had been dealt with in this group – aren't trans men availing of male privilege? Don't trans women have male privilege as they grow up as men? Some women might not feel safe if a man comes into the room.

This from a roomful of mainly cis, upper-caste, educated, autonomous women feels particularly obtuse. "You are okay as you don't have a beard or look like a man." Really, is that all my being genderqueer all these years has meant? And how have all our personal and political conversations come to this!

It is not as if we do not try, again – those of us who understand gender differently and want change, and those who do not. We watch films, we share our lives, we open ourselves to each other. In the end, we are still backed against a wall of insularity that does not shift. The group will remain 'women' only. It does. Several of us leave. We still remain comrades in the long struggles and join hands in different campaigns, but the hurt and the cracks remain. Persons who took years to understand their *savarna*[12] privilege will perhaps take some more to understand their cis privilege too. In any case, intersectional politics in action means that we maintain dialogue and work together where we can, even if the particular intimacy of that 'we' is broken.

Some of those same comrades insist on calling me by my earlier name, despite multiple corrections, and using female pronouns (which we have long rejected) for me and others too. That at least is something they share with a large part of the world!

Bees saal baad (December 2015)

Twenty years of the collective now known as LABIA – *a Queer Feminist LBT Collective*; twenty years of my being queer in this city, with these peoples. A time to reflect, to celebrate, to reconnect with fellow travellers; to strengthen some ties, break others, yet again see how the confines of the familiar can be shifted, expanded, and how spaces to talk and hear be created – collectively, individually, in multiple ways.

This was also the last year when we marched as a collective in the Bombay Queer Azadi[13] March (QAM, also known as the Mumbai Pride), one which we had been an intrinsic part of organising in the first few years. We had moved out of the organising several years ago but had still been participating in the march with our 'political' slogans and banners, despite repeated digs at our 'politics'. The first time we wore T-shirts saying "the right to dissent", we were asked what dissent had to do with a queer march. But, in January 2015 things reached a strange impasse. In this march, we'd carried banners claiming "Gender, Sexuality, Dharm:[14] Where I am Respected, that is my Ghar",[15] in several languages and distributed leaflets connecting the 'ghar wapsi'[16] campaigns of the Hindu right to the increasing violence against trans women and Dalits and Muslims. For us these issues were queer issues and several people in the march joined us in wearing the stickers and carrying the banners. When a news report (Deshpande, 2015) focused on this campaign, the QAM organising committee, of which we were no longer a part, issued a statement distancing themselves clearly and saying that the QAM does not stand for it. This was absolutely fine with us, since it was done in the name of LABIA and other political groups who agreed with this politics and not under the umbrella of QAM.

It was fascinating that the presence of our politics was seen as inflammatory and diversionary, while the presence of the wedding procession of two Hindu men, in full Hindu costumery and paraphernalia, horses, dresses etc., was not just welcome, but a highlight of the march with several supportive voices from the 'community' appearing on television and other shows to talk about it.

Clearly, the same march of queers no longer had the wherewithal to include both these voices, and no conversation was possible anymore. This, more or less, had become the norm in several other cities and states, though with differing degrees of possible conversation and visibility. Thus, in December, as we readied to celebrate twenty years of the collective, we also worked towards creating a space for conversations. As our invite read:

This current scenario – more visibility, stronger voices and mainstream demands – is located within the larger political climate of increasing right-wing agendas. Any kind of dissenting voices that do not agree with the Hindu, upper-caste, hetero-patriarchal worldview are being suppressed. There is increasing censorship and clamping down on freedom and rights, and dissent is viewed as sedition, as anti-national. From the State and within the queer movement too, we have a push towards mainstreaming. In such a context, if we are queer and we are feminist, then we need to define our politics and clearly delineate where we stand vis-à-vis both these contexts.

This 20-year celebration of LABIA is for all of us – to define Feminist Queer Activism as distinct from the State and the mainstream queer voices, to feel resonance, have conversations, express solidarity and get a sense that we are a robust, consolidated voice in this country as well, even when we disagree with each other. These two days are for all of us!

Almost ninety-odd persons, from different parts of the country, different in their locations and identities, spoke and listened to each other for two days. Our differences were evident, articulated even, but our attempt was to create a space for sharing, reflection, resonance, a space where we could listen to each other with respect and care, often lacking most in our material lives.

As the report later circulated to the participants said:

> Somewhere in these threads emerged what a participant called the inseparability of empathy and political commitment. We might read this as an inspiration to articulate models of living different from the rationalised individualist models available in the heteronormative mainstream today.
>
> ...
>
> While listening to one another, we might not have had answers, but perhaps we were struggling to find newer ways of articulation. Acknowledging, without getting defensive, and seeing from these different experiential locations helped us see better. And maybe then the issue, as one participant reminded

us, was that even as we talk of rights we seem to forget rights *for what* – for us to be able to be "who we want to be" and recognise the wide diversity of these aspirations. As someone said, "Maybe commune is a better word than community, because community limits individuality".

It is not surprising that, in such a space then, the tears and laughter were both held warmly.

LBT* meet Kolkata (March 2018)

When you are in a hall filled with more than seventy LBT* activists from around the country discussing queer and trans* politics in the current situation, immense frustration and stunning insights are both very likely. I was part of such a meeting a few weeks ago and found myself in a completely unexpected discussion.

Over the last day and a half, we have been discussing the ins and outs of law, trans* rights, what it means to be a woman in the present moment, how we understand gender, and sexuality and how we see ourselves (anti-right, left-leaning, queer feminist for the most part) within the larger queer and trans* organising and other movements. All this with the growing Hindu right-wing discourse of intolerance and impunity.

At some point it becomes clear that we need more intensive discussions around the terms L, B and T*, to try to articulate what each of these locations sees as concerns and needs. Perhaps that will help us come to a larger understanding of what we are fighting for together. All these three larger groups come with a long and splintered history of feeling marginalised within the larger queer organising, demands and campaigns, especially those around Section 377 of the Indian Penal Code (IPC) which has clearly overshadowed the demands and needs of LBT* persons. But, if we are united by our difference and sense of otherness from the mainstream, we are also clearly divided, not just by our separate locations, but also due to our mistrust and mutual lack of understanding of these locations as well as the deep experiences of loss and pain we feel within what are 'community' spaces.

Within our discussions over the last day and a half, another clear locational split has been drawn between the binary trans* and non-binary trans*. This has not sprung up in this room as such, but is a reflection of the fraught and difficult spaces that are being created, virtually and in real space, on trans* issues. There is a difference of language, of understanding, of gate-keeping. The most hurtful of all is the question of "who is really trans?", which then also translates into "who can speak of and for trans?" So, the four groups are – lesbian, bisexual, binary trans* and non-binary trans*. The most important point to note, though, is that each person can choose the group they want to be in, and it needn't be based on their personal identity.

Of course, we are tempted to run to the groups we feel like we belong in, and I walk towards the non-binary trans* corner of the hall. I have never really been part of a group discussion on this with persons from so many different places. But I soon realise that most of us are doing exactly what we said we'd try not to, and also, that the bisexual corner is rather lonely, and I leave this corner to join that.

Now get this: if anyone had ever suggested to me that I might consider calling myself bisexual, I wouldn't have precisely socked them one in the jaw (not being that kind of person), but I would've, at the very least, raised an eyebrow to ask, "do you know me?" I have never been in too many such discussions either, except to agree that bisexuals are very much part of all spaces and we should fight biphobia and so on.

Our group is the smallest in numbers and we all begin by talking about that and the fact that some of us came to this group precisely because it seemed unfairly small. Some of us identify as bisexual while others have been working with the 'bisexual community'. Our first discussion then centres around the use of the term 'bisexual' and its meaning, especially when most of our shared understanding of gender has moved beyond the binary. In a world of more than two genders, how does one make sense of bisexual?

Clearly, many who identify as part of the bisexual community do not see the world as only bi-gendered, just as most of us do not. At the same time, the language of desire is complex and there is a diversity of articulation. It strikes me that my trajectory has never traversed into bisexuality because when the world was just men and women, and I was trying hard to find myself as 'a different kind of woman', bisexuality was not part of my personal identification. Cis men were quite outside the realm of my geography of desire. Today, I might say that perhaps cis men are my hard limit.

Even before I reached the word genderqueer for myself, let alone admitted to my felinity, I began seeing myself as queer – a word that fit my sexuality so much better than lesbian, or even dyke. It made sense of that part of me who was always clueless in discussions of butch–femme, or "who's my type?", who found various transgressions fascinating and who never felt comfortable as a woman-loving woman. We speak of the journeys of opening spaces from only lesbian and bisexual to queer and questioning, of continuously breaking and reformulating our languages, our spaces and ourselves. In these journeys, the bisexual has had to fight for space and understanding with the lesbian too, and the necessity of keeping bisexual (because of its historicity) as a term or reference made perfect sense in the discussion that followed.

But what really opens the space for me is the definition of bisexual that a group in Delhi has been using – bisexual is being attracted to your own gender and other genders. A part of me leaps at that – yes, that could easily be me. Of course, I belong in that space. And that is new. There is a difference in how queer becomes me and how this particular definition of bisexual does. It just goes to show how little one knows.

Live and learn

It has been a few months since, and the years of seeing bisexual as necessarily belonging in a bi-gendered, cis world have not quite gone away. So, I am not jumping about proclaiming myself a bisexual quite yet, but I can see the possibility of this location, as well as the politics of it for perhaps the first time. I think of all the possibilities that queer opened up in our discourse and bisexuality has some of those too. Who knows, I melodramatically think as I write this, a new way of being lesbian, or as a friend insists on calling it, lesbianly, might be next.

But my politics also reminds me, more and more, as we ready ourselves for the boil of the next general elections in the country early in 2019, and as the count of atrocities increases, that this is no time for queer euphoria. Even though we, the now much made of 'queer community', have never felt more optimistic that the dreaded Section 377 of the IPC will finally be removed by the Supreme Court. The hearings of the case, that took place in July 2018,[17] point to this clearly. A positive judgment will inevitably lead to much rejoicing and a push for more 'equal' rights, perhaps towards partnerships and same-sex marriage. It will also give more space for the queers who support the present right-wing government to come out openly in support of it.

The fractures that already exist will deepen, the mainstream 'gays' (also perhaps some lesbians and trans persons) will take more centre stage. The queer dissenters, the even more fractured rest of 'us' will have to try harder, with more self-reflexivity, with more empathy and compassion for each other, to find both common ground and support across differences. To learn every day, to work with differences, even, with some incomprehension.

So, this genderqueer dyke is not hanging up their suede shoes quite yet!

Notes

1 *Desi* is a term generally used by people of Indian origin in the USA (from the Hindi word *des*, meaning country).

2 These terms come from different languages: Sakhi refers to a woman friend, Stree Sangam can be translated loosely to 'a confluence of women' and Sahayatrika to women fellow-travellers. Sappho refers to the Greek poet from the island of Lesbos.

3 The autonomous women's groups emerged in the late 1970s and '80s in various cities and towns. Many of the women who began these groups had worked with left parties, trade unions and people's movements and found that women's issues were being relegated to the background and thus felt the need for groups and politics autonomous from the political parties and larger structured organisations. Most of these groups began as voluntary, nonfunded collectives. For a brief history, please read Saheli Women's Resource Centre (2000).

4 Hijras/Arawanis/Kinnars/Thirunangai, and many others are socio-cultural identities that have existed in different ways in the subcontinent. Most of them are transgender persons assigned male at birth who usually express feminine characteristics, may or may not have surgeries, but usually live with others like themselves forming community households with one guru (head of the household). Their practices are not uniform across the geographical region but almost all of them hold the promise of some sort of a community. *Kothis*, who also sometimes find space within the *hijra* communities, are persons assigned male at birth who may take on feminine characteristics with others like them but may also continue to dress and live as men otherwise.

5 LesBIT was to begin with an acronym of lesbian, bisexual and transgender and later the I also referred to intersex.

6 'Saheli' translates as 'female friend' and 'Aawaaz-E-Niswaan' as 'Voice of Women'.

7 There was a targeted violence against Muslims in Gujarat in 2002 by the Hindu right-wing forces. It was triggered by an apparent burning down of a train compartment carrying a few Hindu right-wing persons returning from Ayodhya allegedly by some Muslims. What followed was ghastly violence with state complicity for many days after in which thousands of Muslims were killed, many injured and large amounts of businesses and households devastated. Please refer to Saheli Women's Resource Centre (2003) and other extensive work done by groups and movements.

8 Acronyms/alphabet soups of identities as more and more get added with time and articulation. These include, but are not limited to: Queer,

Questioning, Lesbian, Bisexual, Transgender, Intersex, Hijra, Kothi, Genderqueer, Asexual, Non-binary and many more and are used in differing combinations.

9 *Salwar kurta* and eyes lined with *kajal* are clearly culturally feminine even though many people use them; on me they become highlighted because I never wear either these clothes or any make-up whatsoever.

10 Bro/dude.

11 While *janaab* could be used for people of all genders, my use of this word rather than a clearly feminine term of address was not appreciated. Acknowledgement of the gender performance is as much part of drag as is the performance itself, and clearly with that word, I broke the contract!

12 *Savarna* is used to refer to persons from dominant castes in the Hindu caste hierarchy. Dalit movements and activists have popularised the use of this term to refer to those who are not Dalit and to push the awareness of the constant structural and therefore personal presence of caste in all our lives, regardless of our personal beliefs.

13 *Azadi* refers to freedom.

14 *Dharm* refers to religion.

15 *Ghar* refers to home.

16 *Ghar wapsi* is the Hindu right-wing campaign, often violent, to 're-convert', or bring back to the Hindu fold, people who have been following other religions, especially Christianity and Islam. This is based on the understanding that Hinduism is from the region, whereas other religions have come from 'outside' and people (especially the marginalised) have been 'coerced' or 'misled' to convert to these religions.

17 Subsequent to the writing of this essay, the Supreme Court delivered a positive and affirming judgment on Section 377 of the IPC on 6 September 2018 in the *Navtej Singh Johar & Ors. v. Union of India thr. Secretary Ministry of Law and Justice* case.

EIGHT | Unqualified, middle-aged lesbian swerves abruptly out of her lane to talk about trans issues

Rosie Swayne

Introduction

A conflict is occurring within my own UK lesbian/feminist community that makes heated, emotional Brexit debates seem like a casual exchange over preferred brands of fairtrade marmalade. I first became aware of the growing hostility towards trans people when an old friend with ordinarily shared values shared a *hilariously* misaimed article on social media that appeared to hold Caitlyn Jenner personally responsible for systemic misogyny, specifically because she appeared on the cover of *Vanity Fair*. I reacted with the appropriate amount of sarcasm (i.e. ALL of the sarcasm) and promptly experienced for the first time what I now know to be an aggressive 'dog pile'. And let me tell you, being dogpiled by lesbians is not nearly as sexy as it sounds. I wrote this piece primarily as a resource that pulls together a formidable collection of works created by highly qualified (academically and/or through lived experience) writers that serves to challenge the dangerously misleading narratives of trans-exclusionary feminism. However, rather than simply write a list of links, it also felt important to add my own voice – that of a middle-aged cis-gender lesbian feminist who will not tolerate the vicious malignation of fellow LGBT members in the name of 'radical feminism'.

In fairness, a huge transphobic lorry is shedding its load right in front of me so I kind of have to

Yeah, about this whole transphobia within feminism thing. I'm not really enjoying it to be honest. It was kind of funny for a while, but then I read an earnest think piece on the "inherent dangers" of 20-year-old non-binary YouTuber Milo Stewart, and realised we might be in trouble. I'm seeing so much misinformation flying around every day that I'm compelled to write this piece even though I usually only write in song form – and while "Terfandot" is absolutely an opera that needs writing, I wanted to pull together some thoughts and information right now in the hope that it might be a helpful resource to friends in my community who I know are increasingly seeing others swayed and/or confused by this pervasive trans-exclusionary rhetoric.

I don't know what it's like to be trans, but I do have the relatable experience of having something integral to my life called into question, *because biology*.

My adopted son is my son. I know it, he knows it, and it is an unshakable truth to us. Yes, it is possible for a child to have two mothers. No, this is not because I 'identify' as being the actual person who gave birth to him and/or believe the sperm was conjured up with pure lesbian enthusiasm. But our children have two mothers and we have two sons – this is a reality, and we expect the same legal protection and respect as any other family.

However, if we apply *because biology* to my family (and there are plenty who are keen to), it isn't actually a family at all – we're just a couple of single mothers with bastard only-children in an unusually cosy house-share situation.

Luckily for us, we live in a time (2018) and place (UK) where the law actively protects our family from this wilfully ham-fisted interpretation of how biology relates to actual human people. It is not something we take for granted.

We owe a debt of gratitude to our elders in the LGBT community who fought through decades of activism to help achieve the security my family enjoys today. Trans people have been intrinsic to this movement from the very beginning, and so to defect from the fight for trans equality at this point would feel rather like pulling the ladder up behind us.

But it is not due to blinkered loyalty that I oppose this growing hostility coming from areas of my own community. It is because the issues being presented are distorted, divisive and alarmist.

Gender and sexuality are of course not the same thing. However, there is a relationship between the two that is especially pertinent when comparing the shift in social attitudes concerning sexuality in the last fifty years, and the kinds of claims that are being made about trans people today.

Dismissing LGBT lives as ridiculous: "Enabling transgender people is like the Emperor's New Clothes!" is the new "Equal marriage? We may as well let people marry their dogs!"

There is evidence of trans people existing in almost every culture throughout human history. It's not just a new Western trend those spoilt, blue-haired millennials have invented to annoy you.

There are various hotly contested hypotheses regarding the existence and potential cause of trans tendencies, based on elements such as brain structure / foetal hormone levels / androgen receptor genes / cerebral blood flow / psychological disorders / gender socialisation / blue-haired millennials just trying to annoy you.

There are also hotly contested hypotheses regarding the evidence and potential cause of homosexual tendencies based on elements such as the search for the 'gay gene' / prenatal environment / chromosome linkage / psychological disorders / satan … just trying to annoy you.

While neither have a clear, singular, conclusive biological trait or explanation as to their existence, it is widely believed that a combination of genetic, hormonal and social influences are at play.

The interplay between social factors and human biology is increasingly understood as a highly complex relationship, and so 'because biology' can't really serve as the definitive answer some want it to be. Current scientific understanding suggests that my being a lesbian will have been influenced by social as well as genetic/biological factors. This doesn't make my sexuality a delusion – I'm still a lesbian, regardless of how I became one.

In her acclaimed book *Whipping Girl* (Serano, 2007:29), writer and biologist Julia Serano refers to opening talks with the question: "If I offered you ten million dollars under the condition that you live as the other sex for the rest of your life, would you take me up on the offer?"

The majority of people of course say no, because changing something so fundamental is unthinkable to them. Most of us do not experience what Serano refers to as 'gender dissonance' – when someone's deep-rooted sense of gender (or 'subconscious sex', to use the book's 2007 language) contradicts their assigned gender.

Even without knowledge or experience of any trans issues whatsoever, surely anybody can recognise that someone making the decision to transition – with all the complications, danger, discrimination, social insecurity and risk of rejection that is likely to entail – is highly unlikely to have come to that decision for any lighter reason than that living as their assigned gender is impossible to them.

If "WELL maybe *I* 'identify' as a *wooden spoon* today!" is your preferred stance on the realities of the issue, you're deriding a wealth of research, evidence, lived experiences and ultimately social progress towards better inclusion of a highly misunderstood minority group – but congrats on being hilarious.

Interpreting growing LGBT numbers as contagion: "The Trans Lobby are turning our children trans!" is the new "The Gay Lobby are turning our children gay!"

Remember before the 1990s when there were 0 per cent gay youths and then Beth Jordache kissed another girl on C4's *Brookside* and suddenly 100 per cent of children were homosexual and society collapsed and we all died?

Well the same diabolical model is in place now, only this time it's being spearheaded by the 'Trans Lobby' who apparently exist for some reason.

Rather than recognising the rise in young people 'coming out' as trans as the positive outcome of a society growing to understand and support trans youth, it is being suggested that actually those crazy kids are just copying each other, mainly to annoy you.

There is talk of a condition called Rapid Onset Gender Dysphoria (ROGD) – whereby teens meet trans teens online and then catch teen trans from out of the interwebs, like something out of the spoof alarmist TV news show *Brass Eye*. Here is a quick list of important facts about ROGD:

1. It isn't actually a condition.

It's premise is obliterated with glorious precision in articles such as "'Rapid Onset Gender Dysphoria' is Biased Junk Science" from *The Advocate* (Tannehill, 2018) and "'Rapid Onset Gender Dysphoria': What a Hoax Diagnosis Looks Like' from *Gender Analysis* (Jones, 2018), but to summarise:

The entire theory is based on a single poster abstract of an online survey completed by 164 *parents* of gender questioning teens. The surveys were only posted on three websites that are specifically aimed at parents who do not support their child's transition – a bias that is not acknowledged anywhere in the abstract. None of the actual children concerned were involved in the collection of information on them.

As Jones (2018) observes, 'rapid onset gender dysphoria' actually perfectly matches the description of the already established condition of late onset gender dysphoria, where dysphoria reveals itself in puberty or much later, due to an individual perhaps remaining closeted or having not yet identified their experience as something that has a name / that others also experience.

There is a belief that so many teens assigned female are wanting to transition that it is causing 'lesbian erasure' (which is also the name of a tribute band I totally want to exist, by the way – please make it happen for me).

The idea is that in UK society, as we all know, becoming a trans man holds wayyyy less social stigma than being a lesbian – so teens are taking the easy road and simply tra- ... wait ... what!?

"Oh it turns out my child simply wants to change genders which is SUCH a relief because I was terrified they were a lesbian, which would have been devastating – but I was worried for NOTHING! More T dear?", said no parent ever.

According to some media sources, gender clinic statistics do currently reveal a higher number of youths who were assigned female at birth 'coming out' as trans as teens. While there is currently no consensus on the reason for this, it is suggested the intense social stigma is even higher for youths assigned male at birth, and so it often takes significantly longer for them to 'come out'.

A nuanced and thought-provoking angle on butch women and trans men can be found in Mark Mulligan's (2018) article "Fight and Flight: 'Butch Flight', Trans Men, and the Elusive Question of Authenticity".

It's really important to note that there is no discernible evidence that a person can be 'convinced' to change their gender identity. The highly documented case of David Reimer, summarised in his tragic obituary "David Reimer, 38: After Botched

Surgery, He Was Raised as a Girl in Gender Experiment" (Woo, 2004), and also the track record of gender-reparative therapy as outlined in Stonewall's material on "Conversion Therapy" (Stonewall, 2017) reinforce the idea that it's just not possible.

You might hear a frequently recited statistic that some 80 per cent of trans teens would desist in time if they weren't coerced into transitioning by their gaudy, infectious interweb pals and weirdly completely-homophobic-yet-incredibly-trans-inclusive parents and go on to "just be gay or lesbian" (I think we're supposed to ignore that trans people aren't necessarily straight at this point).

This 80 per cent desistance figure refers most commonly to a study entitled "Desisting and Persisting Gender Dysphoria after Childhood: A Qualitative Follow-up Study" (Steensma et al., 2011), which relies largely on information gathered in the 1980s. It is strongly contested for a number of significant reasons, such as that the majority of children involved were simply untypical in their gender expression, rather than appearing to suffer from dysphoria – meaning it was inevitable the majority did not want to transition in later life – i.e. it's not 'desistance' if they weren't trans in the first place. There are a number of detailed and qualified articles challenging the credibility of the study, a particularly easily accessible example being "Detransition, Desistance, and Disinformation: A Guide for Understanding Transgender Children Debates" (Serano, 2016). However, a great promoter of the statistic has been Kenneth Zucker, whose reputation as an advocate of reparative therapy and other questionable practices are summarised in "The End of the Desistance Myth" (Tannehill, 2016). BUT such challenges are notoriously challenged by Jesse Singal in high-profile articles such as "What's Missing from the Conversation about Transgender Kids" (Singal, 2016). BUT these challenges of such challenges are robustly challenged in "Media Misinformation about Trans Youth: The Persistent

80% Desistance Myth" (Winters, 2016) . AND THEN there is the SMALL MATTER of Singal (2018) admitting he has been presenting the data inaccurately ALL ALONG in "Everyone, Myself Included, Has Been Misreading the Single Biggest Study on Childhood Gender Dysphoria Desistance and Persistence"; AND THEN FINALLY, chuck in the … oooh trifling matter of … *The International Journal of Transgenderism* recently publishing a peer-reviewed article entitled "A Critical Commentary on Follow-up Studies and 'Desistance' Theories about Transgender and Gender-nonconforming Children" (Temple Newhook et al., 2018) that meticulously and comprehensively addresses the problems and inaccuracies associated with the 80 per cent desistance statistic, and I think we're done here. Go home, famous desistance statistic, you're drunk.

Erroneously conflating untypical gender expression with an intense gender identity issue like this enables the wilful misinterpretation of the current situation from those acting like they believe all 'tomboy' girls and 'effeminate' boys are in danger of being marched off to the gender clinic for reassignment surgery.

In reality, the majority of young people who are even referred to the NHS Gender Identity Referral Service leave again with no medical intervention whatsoever. For example, based on 2016 figures via "Britain Needs to Stop Freaking Out about Transgender Kids" (Dodds, 2016), of the 605 young people who had been discharged from the programme in the last three years, 160 had gone on puberty blockers and ninety-two of those continued onto hormone replacement therapy. The UK has 13 million kids in it by the way.

The reason that transition (medical or non-medical) is the clinically approved response to intense gender dysphoria is that from over fifty years of clinical studies, it is the only action that has proven to help alleviate dysphoria and the associated depression, self-harm and suicide risks.

And if you're now thinking "YEAH but everyone knows those suicide stats are COOKED" don't worry, I'm coming to that in a bit.

Oh and if you're thinking about THAT Swedish study (Dhejne et al., 2011), where the results are used to argue against transitioning, you can read the frustrations of Cecilia Dhejne, the author of the study, on the many ways it's been deliberately misinterpreted in the article "Fact Check: Study Shows Transition Makes Trans People Suicidal" (Williams, 2015).

The NHS will not perform any form of gender surgery on anyone under 18, and will not prescribe HRT to anyone under 16. Even then, an individual will have had measured and thorough psychiatric/clinical assessments and observations from a number of professionals who all need to agree on the course of action. They will have to have counselling and have displayed an *insistent*, *consistent* and *persistent* belief that they are not the gender they have been assigned, and expressed a *constantly strong* desire to transition. It's common that they will have already been living as their identified gender for some time.

For someone outside the situation, it's understandable to think "surely just let them make the decision when they are adults" – but the reality for many is that (a) their child's dysphoric misery is so profound that making them wait an agonisingly long time to reach an arbitrary date seems cruel and impossible and (b) going through the 'wrong puberty' not only massively intensifies dysphoria and so can be extremely traumatic, but will also have a big impact on a future transition once secondary sex characteristics have developed.

It is standard practice to let the teenager enter the first phase of puberty, to see if the dysphoria dissipates or exacerbates. If it exacerbates, they will be offered puberty blockers to put puberty 'on hold'. The idea with this being that it gives the individual more time to decide if this is what they want, and allows them to reach 16 without having already gone through puberty if they remain determined to receive HRT.

While the NHS refers puberty blockers as a safe and fully reversible treatment, it is still seen as controversial as the long-term effects are not fully established. The reason the NHS can refer to the treatment as safe is that it's been in use for over twenty years, is approved for use by the General Medical Council and there is not sufficient cause to deem them unsafe. The drug is also used to treat precocious puberty, endometriosis and prostate cancer – but there isn't a large body of evidence of it's long-term effects yet (though there is a concern that it has an impact on bone density). As unsatisfactory as this sounds, it is not a particularly unusual scenario in modern medicine – there are hundreds of treatments that have not been in practice for more than one or two decades, so naturally there is a limit to how much information there is on long-term impact. Potential side effects of any treatment are often worrying and/or uncertain, and one can only weigh up the issues and make a decision based on the information that IS available, hopefully with the guidance of an experienced professional.

If I'm honest, I can't imagine how hard it must be to see your kid go through this kind of anguish, and be confronted with these kinds of decisions – asking your teenage kid if they understand that they're signing something to say they're aware this treatment might make them sterile? or cause other health problems down the road? It sounds incredibly difficult.

And the really hard part? Doing nothing isn't a neutral option

Whenever I see the vile attacks on parents for finding themselves at this juncture and choosing to support their child in transitioning, I always wonder at the arrogance of the person doing the attacking who clearly thinks they are in a better position to judge the best course of action. It reminds me of the people shrieking

"What kind of a parent would take their child on a dangerous journey like that!" about fleeing refugees – and the question I want to ask back is "In what situation would YOU make that decision? What would the alternative have to look like for YOU to make that massive choice?"

There does seem to be a small percentage of those that transition who experience regret, as acknowledged in Brynn Tannehill's (2014) summary of media narratives "Myths about Transition Regrets".

Julia Serano (2007) points out that those who do indeed experience regret need to have their voices heard – not only so that improvements to treatment can be made in the future, but also because those individuals need support from the LGBT community and not to be simply brushed under the carpet. She also observes that within the number of those who detransition, a significant proportion do so due to how intense their experiences of rejection and transphobia are – and so then actually *retransition* further on in life.

While the potential for sensational headlines is less for happy trans people, it is important to place detransition figures alongside the *overwhelming majority of trans people who do not experience regret*, (and also of those that regret not transitioning earlier) as rigorously documented in "How Transitioning Leads to Better Mental Health – and Job Satisfaction" (Drydakis, 2017).

Belittling LGBT problems /dismissing discrimination:
"All those trans suicide/violence/discrimination stats
are exaggerated/flawed/made up" is the new "Do they
REALLY need a parade and a 'gay rights' movement?
They're not oppressed, they're just attention seeking"
There is a charity called Mermaids UK that works with the NHS in assisting young people and families of 'gender questioning' children/teens. It is suggested by anti-trans groups

such as Transgender Trend that they use a highly questionable statistic regarding the risk of suicide in trans teens. In a section entitled "Suicide Facts and Myths" (Transgender Trend, 2018), Transgender Trend claim that Mermaids are saying 48 per cent of ALL trans youth attempt suicide, and that this was supposedly extrapolated from a sample group of just twenty-seven individuals (an allegation that Mermaids themselves contest, asserting instead that their data comes from a much larger sample group via Stonewall).

But let's go with the idea their data is wrong for a second – because then we could just forget about dysphoria-related suicide altogether, right? There's a dodgy stat and that's that. Phew.

While misrepresented figures are unhelpful they do not negate the fact that even the briefest Google search reveals similar sounding results in multiple research projects in the last decade from the US, UK, Ireland, Sweden, New Zealand and Australia all citing the suicide risk in trans people to be around eight to ten times the national average.

It's been somewhat bluntly asserted that the actual body count does not match up to this repeatedly occurring statistic. The suggestion is that if 1 in 10 suicide attempts result in death and 1 per cent of the population is trans (current estimates range from 0.4 per cent to 2 per cent, but it's not actually possible to be certain) then that would mean there should be an astronomically higher number of deaths by suicide than are actually showing up in national statistics.

First, I don't know if this '1 in 10' figure has come from anywhere legitimate – the American Association of Suicidology estimates 1 in 25 suicide attempts result in death and the World Health Organization estimates 1 in 21. Second, comparing ANNUAL suicide statistics with the percentage of trans people who have attempted suicide at least once IN THEIR LIVES is automatically going to produce a major flaw in the calculation.

Taking these points into consideration, it IS possible to put forward a credible calculation that debunks this idea that it's 'impossible' that young trans people are at a massively higher suicide risk than the national average. However, when the figures have such vast uncertainties (e.g. how many trans people there actually are, over what timespan, how we are dividing age groups etc.), I would argue that this morbid number crunching is significantly less worthwhile than simply *listening* to the people who have the lived experiences of being trans, and the severity of personal and social difficulties they are confronted with when attempting to navigate simply existing.

There seems to be a determination to render every single piece of research regarding the vulnerabilities of trans people as flawed or dishonest. Stonewall UK's 2018 Trans Report (Stonewall, 2018) interviews 871 trans people and finds results such as 1 in 4 of them have been homeless at some point in their lives, 1 in 8 employees had been physically attacked in the last year, 1 in 10 had been rejected by their families. The 2017 School Report (Stonewall, 2017) involved nearly 600 trans-identified 11–19 year olds and yes, here it is again, almost half of them had attempted suicide. These reports and many more are subject to this same criticism whereby it's claimed the results of these reports are null and void due to the sample groups being too small.

It really does beg the question – how many survey groups of tens, hundreds or thousands where a consistently large proportion of participants refer to suicide attempts, violence, instability and discrimination does there need to be before they might *possibly* be considered genuinely representative? Have you ever seen a survey of trans people that presents the community as NOT suffering much higher instances of these adversities?

Rejecting repeatedly occurring evidence that a marginalised group is at risk or needs help makes them easier to vilify.

See also: most rape victims actually lying / depressed people actually lying and lazy / people on benefits actually lying, lazy and greedy / refugees with smartphones actually lying, lazy, greedy and rapists. Etc.

Equating LGBT inclusion with various forms of violation: "Those scary trans folk want access to our children / changing rooms / quivering cis bodies" is the new "Those scary homosexuals want access to our children / pets / irresistibly standard hetero bodies"
sigh

First off, if you think you've never been in a public toilet or changing room with a trans person, you're mistaken. Because – plot twist – trans people have been here this whole time. So ladies, if you object to sharing these spaces with trans women, you're actually just objecting to sharing these spaces with trans women that don't meet your criteria of how a woman should look.

Are you trying to uphold oppressive binary gender standards? Because that's how you uphold oppressive binary gender standards.

Proposed changes to the Gender Recognition Act 2004 would mean that an adult trans person will no longer need a diagnosis of gender dysphoria or to have lived as their identified gender for two years to have their gender recognised legally. This alteration would be similar to legislation already in place in Ireland, Denmark, Portugal, Norway, France, Belgium, Malta, Argentina, Chile, India and Pakistan.

The reason this change is welcomed is that it will remove the medical gatekeeping and the associated arbitrary obedience to gender stereotypes and performative hoop-jumping inevitably required to meet a gender recognition panel criteria of how an individual should present themselves.

Gender dysphoria is a symptom of being trans and not the state of being trans itself – therefore the requirement to be 'dysphoric enough' to have one's gender legally recognised is inherently problematic.

The fear is that this means 'just anyone' can change their gender. Well ... 'just anyone' who wants to legally change their gender on every form of official identification and commit in the presence of a solicitor that they intend to live as that gender for the rest of their lives with the threat of prosecution if they're found to be insincere, yes. But as there's not even the aforementioned 10 million dollar prize on offer for doing this, it seems highly likely that such an action will only appeal to trans people who need to legally change the gender on their documents to match their gender.

There's a great deal of concern for what this means for women's spaces – but the impact this change in law would have on current rules is actually commonly misunderstood, as observed in the highly concise and informative human rights article "Gender Recognition, Self-Determination and Segregated Space" (Dunne and Hewitt, 2018).

To paraphrase the piece: although the belief seems to be that this change in the law will create a new right for trans women who reject medical transitions to enter women-only spaces, the reality is that section 7 of the 2010 Equality Act already affords trans women the right to access gender appropriate spaces and services, regardless of their medical status or if they have a gender recognition certificate. The assertion that there is a risk of cis-gender men abusing this legislation in order to cause harm overlooks the fact that (a) there is little to no evidence to support this proposed scenario as being a legitimate concern and (b) denying the trans community beneficial reforms because of a perceived potential of abuse perpetrated by cis-gender males is not rational or fair – the government should rather address that risk through appropriate channels such as existing criminal law.

Professionals who work in women's spaces such as refuges have a duty of care to protect their service users and therefore make risk assessments on individuals when they are referred – if it seems there is reason to suspect someone's presence will be problematic for other service users, it is dealt with accordingly, regardless of whether or not they are trans.

"Frequently Asked Questions: Women's Equality and the Gender Recognition Act" (Mumford, 2018) is an informative piece on women's equality and associated frontline services in Scotland – to quote part of the statement:

> All violence against women organisations that receive Scottish Government funding provide trans-inclusive services. The requirement for trans inclusion plans has been in place for six years, and has not given rise to any concerns or challenges of which we are currently aware. Rather, trans women have added to our movements through their support, through volunteering, and as staff members of our organisations. In order to provide a definitive statement on this in our consultation response(s), national umbrella violence against women organisations will be systematically gathering data on how well these plans are working at the frontline.
>
> The social media discussion on the proposed changes to the Gender Recognition Act has included concerns that victim-survivors of sexual violence and domestic abuse may be placed at risk. Rape crisis and women's aid services prioritise women's safety, confidentiality, privacy, dignity, and wellbeing above all else. Over decades of practice, services have developed ways of managing any risk to individual women's wellbeing that may arise from interacting with other service users.

It seems that rather than fighting to exclude a small subset of vulnerable women from these spaces, energies might be more positively directed towards fighting for more resources for all.

There was a recent furore in the UK tabloids that "Up to Half of Trans Inmates May Be Sex Offenders" (Gilligan, 2017). Maybe.

The data that these articles were based on came from "Fair Play for Women" – an organisation who are specifically interested in excluding trans women from women's spaces. As Owl Fisher points out in the article "A Recent Study Claimed That 41 Percent of Transgender Prisoners Are Sex Offenders – This Is Why It's False" (Fisher, 2017), the report claims that at the time the study was made there were there were 113 trans women in prisons in England and Wales – whereas the Ministry of Justice records there being seventy trans-identified prisoners in total (not just trans women). Fisher also observes a significant inaccuracy regarding the prisons they claim exclusively house sex offenders – and as records available to the public do not state what actual offences have been perpetrated, we can see that a lot of guess work has led to that "may be". The fact that prisons that house sex offenders will often also house non-sex-offending inmates who need to be kept separate from more standard prisons for other reasons is also very relevant.

As with the women's refuges, risk assessment should dictate decisions regarding placement, rather than whether a woman is trans or not. Those decrying 'men' entering women's prisons seem to overlook the fact that actual men are systemically present in women's prisons in the form of prison guards – and that abusive sexual behaviour is all too common – as explained in Shon Faye's excellently articulated article "If You Really Want Women to Be Safe in Prisons, It's Not Transgender Prisoners You Need to Be Wary Of" (Faye, 2017), which gives some much needed perspective on the issue of trans women in women's prisons.

When mistakes happen it is very easy for the media to point the finger at trans inclusion rather than at the catastrophic system failures that articles such as "Loss of Senior Managers Led to UK's Prison Crisis" (Yeung, 2018) attribute to severe management/ staff shortages related to devastating austerity policy. High-profile cases such as that of Karen White, where a convicted rapist was housed inappropriately and raped two women (BBC, 2018) create understandable outrage which is then used to fuel further attempts to reject trans inclusion. In her article "Brian Paddick Is Right - Karen White Is Not an Excuse to Label Transgender People Sex Offenders" (de Gallier, 2018) Thea de Gallier highlights the problematic nature of attributing the actions of an individual to an entire marginalised group.

What I'm really struggling with is this idea that changes in legislation that look to improve the lives of a vulnerable minority group can be framed as being in direct opposition to women's rights. That trans women are being vilified to such an overwhelmingly hysterical degree that educated people who enjoy accusing the rest of us of 'rejecting science' for accepting trans women as women simultaneously cling on to outdated theories like Blanchard's "concept of autogynephilia" (Blanchard, 1989) to justify hyper-sexualising/fetishising the 'motives' of trans women (and totally ignore trans men).

Accusing a trans woman of being autogynephilic requires the belief that her need to transition has merely derived from sexual arousal based on 'imagining' she is a woman. Blanchard's case for the condition relies heavily on assuming that participants that didn't fit his model – who conspicuously appeared in EVERY ONE of his studies – were lying to him. This echoes historic studies of homosexuality when participants were assumed to suffer from a depraved mental illness which would naturally also affect their ability to tell the truth. Throughout the history of investigating transgender tendencies, there seems to be a habitual lack of actually listening to the experiences of the people involved. Julia Serano beautifully annihilates the autogynephilia theory via "The Real 'Autogynephilia Deniers'" (Serano, 2015) in which she lists six peer-reviewed scientific articles (one of which is her own) that roundly relegate the theory to junk science history.

The sexuality of trans women is being policed to such a degree that any conversation that seeks to investigate their place in lesbian communities is twisted into an unpleasant hyperbolic caricature, unrecognisable as mature discourse. I'd like to think it would not be necessary for me to utterly condemn any form of sexual coercion between individuals based on any form of ideology whatsoever, but hey, this might be on the internet – and where the 'cotton ceiling' is concerned, woe betide anyone who enters the conversation who doesn't want to be accused of being 'rapey'. But if you want to read some clarification on the issue, *The Transadvocate* offers some perspective with "Cotton Ceiling: Uncovering the Trans Conspiracy to Rape Lesbians" (Williams, 2013).

I got a small look into this dumpster fire of a conversation when I recently found myself being told in no uncertain terms that I am not a lesbian if I am attracted to trans women. And it's just, like, uhhh … really? Does this really feel like a worthwhile pursuit? A lesbian using their time and energy to aggressively tell another lesbian they are not a lesbian? Is this honestly where we are?

Fear is being used to convince us that the progression of trans rights threaten our safety. We are familiar with the old trope, of painting the 'enemy' as a threat of sexual violence against women – it is used to justify war, it is used to justify racism and it is being used here to justify transphobia. The heated discourse on social media often sees the progression of trans rights being presented as the biggest threat to women right now – and well … wouldn't life be awesome if that were true? Alas no. The biggest threat to women right now is climate change ("Why Is Climate a Gender Issue", UN Women, n.d.), war ("Fact & Figures", Women's Refugee Commission, 2018) austerity politics ("Women Bearing 86% of Austerity Burden, Commons Figures Reveal", Stewart, 2017), and the toxic combination of capitalism and patriarchy under which ALL women suffer.

Let's imagine the anti-trans movement succeeds in convincing the world that trans people do not deserve to have their lives made any easier though social inclusion and legislation – or, hell, let's go the whole hog and imagine they succeed in erasing trans people altogether. Who would win? Would women no longer need to be wary of male aggression? Would sexual assault no longer happen? Would the gender pay-gap close? Would women's bodies cease to be objectified? Would lesbians cease to be ignored in media representation aside from the occasional sexual distortion from the perspective of the male gaze? Would lesbophobia cease to exist? A feminism that is grounded in reductive, biological essentialism will never combat the problems of oppression inherent within a heterosexist, misogynist society – it will only ever serve to reinforce toxic, patriarchal norms.

The progression of trans rights is the progression of human rights. When we fight for equality we strengthen our intersectional alliances and increase our power to achieve common goals.

I urge intersectional feminists to speak out against this distorted, divisive and alarmist anti-trans rhetoric. It's subscribers do not speak for all women, and they do not speak for feminism. And anyone who says women don't have penises have obviously never looked in the trunk under my bed.

Now if you'll excuse me, I have an opera to write.

NINE | The butch, the bitch and the superwoman

Paramita Banerjee

The world as it exists is not okay: this is a feeling that had first struck deeply when I was about 8 years old and it persists to date – though I've traversed more than half a century in the meantime. The feeling has not just remained but grown stronger. It has evolved like a spiral to include more and more variables. Interwoven into that spiralling journey are my experiences with radical leftism during the only period (so far) of national emergency in India in a non-war situation, followed by the first ever non-Congress government of the country;[1] with the women's movement as it gained momentum in India in the early 1980s; confronting – though rather late – my own queer sexuality; my professional engagement in the social development sector; and my layers of involvement with the LGBTQ movement/s in India in general and West Bengal, my home state, in particular. These experiences have shaped and sharpened my understanding of normativities and myriad ways of defying them; of patriarchy and transcendence; of different forms of non-heteronormative sexualities and gender expressions, along with the varied strands of politics used/involved in these communities' struggles for rights. It is through all of these that my comprehension of lesbian feminism – as also my getting past it – has happened. The only way I can write anything about lesbian feminism is through a personal narrative of certain life events that I consider benchmarks in that entire process.

I'm not a boy and don't want to be called one

Eight is the age when I realised that I was being called a tomboy and many adults around me – though not my parents, I owe it to them to underline – were often remarking that my daredevilry in the wide range of pranks I was pretty much always up to made me equal to, or even surpass, boys. It rankled. And rankled deep. I was quite happy to be a girl; I loved my silky tresses longer and more voluminous than many of the other girls around me; I loved wearing frocks and skirts and other trendy dresses just as much as I enjoyed the freedom to wear shorts when engaged in sports and games … Boys around me had none of these advantages. They wore their hair short; their clothing was boringly limited to shorts, trousers, tees and shirts – with one set of Sunday best *kurta-pajama*[2] coming out on special occasions … I did *not* want to be a boy, or even be called one. In retrospect, I can trace the roots of my gender-fluidity – my discomfort with the gender binary – back to those days. I can, and want the freedom to, traverse the entire gender spectrum – *except* the archetypal termini called 'female' and 'male' – even as I retain my identity as a woman – a woman who does not, and doesn't want to, fit into the stereotypical box called 'feminine'/'womanly'.

Growing up in a Bengali family of two girls with both parents in academia, I hardly faced any of the "girls don't do this" staff. True, I was regularly punished for my unruly behaviour – but never was I told that such naughtiness doesn't befit a girl. Still, the feeling that there is something wrong with the world kept recurring due to various incidents. I was at pre-puberty, transitioning from an 11-year-old to 12. We were returning to Calcutta (not yet officially christened Kolkata) and I was taking admission tests in several schools. In one of the renowned coeducational schools in the southern part of the city, the copy on which I had to write my answers had instructions to examinees printed on the first page and they all used the pronoun "he". In complete sincerity, I had reported to the invigilator that I had the wrong copy – one meant for boys, only to be reprimanded for acting over-smart. The word 'gender' did not exist in my conceptual world beyond English grammar books – but I did feel affronted when told that "he" covers both girls and boys. As if being labelled a tomboy wasn't bad enough – there was also this bitter pill to swallow that girls don't need to be addressed specifically by the pronoun assigned to them in the English language; that "she" is subsumed by "he" – though, by letter composition it is the exact opposite!

Varied experiences of such heteronormative gender labelling, in combination with its inevitable bedfellow – patriarchy – constitute the foundation on which my understanding of gender politics and feminism is based. My self-confidence, my courage to question norms that make no logical sense to me, my need for personal space, the importance that I attach to being economically independent – pretty much everything I consider positive in me are supposed to be 'masculine' traits. By the time I was in my twenties, I was no longer sure what irked me more – this ascription of masculinity to so many of *my* traits in particular, or this general privileging of almost everything socially acknowledged to be positive as masculine. I wasn't angry just at being called masculine for being independent and assertive, but also because the qualities of 'independence' and 'assertiveness' were believed to be masculine *per se*. That anger was yet to find its theoretical framework, for the word 'feminism' had not entered my universe of discourse till then. I was too busy being a radical left revolutionary.

A revolution shrouded in puritanical patriarchy

Between 9 and 11 years of age, I was in northern Bengal – very near Naxalbari, the epicentre of the uprising that would sway West Bengal and several other states of India, with the dream of the 1970s becoming a decade of revolutionary liberation for the country. This is the village that would give the movement its name; those involved in it would come to be known as the Naxalites. I was mesmerised by them. Through pure serendipity, I had a chance to observe and interact with some of the stalwarts of this movement up close and personal. And, they seemed to have an answer to the riddles that bothered my young mind. I was disturbed by the fact that children my age would work at tea stalls and motor garages, as domestic help in people's houses – deprived from everything that I had access to: from food to school to playtime to movies ... These heroes told me that such differences would vanish once the revolution succeeded. I was deeply agonised by my rural cousins' refusal to relate with me as equals – forever labelling me as city bred and superior therefore, which meant they would keep me at an arm's length. These heroes told me villages would be as polished and prosperous as cities after the revolution. Photographs from the People's Republic of China were shown to reassure me that women and men, girls and boys in post-revolutionary India would wear similar dresses and do the same things – which I interpreted as the subversion of the gender binary that I found so disturbing. These fantasies so caught my imagination that I was determined to become a Naxalite by joining a particular college for my graduation. Those heroes of mine were all from that college. And I did. Both – join that college and become active in radical left student politics during the Emergency in India, which made my involvement that much more risky. Those risks I was aware of, but I faced a whole new set of challenges that I had not apprehended at all.

In the five-odd years of radical left activism, I learnt more about patriarchy and extremely regressive puritanical attitudes than I had needed to so far. Lessons that would push me towards the emergent women's movement in the early 1980s soon after my expulsion from the Naxalite outfit I was attached to. Many practices within the Party disturbed me thoroughly. Women members inevitably being asked to make tea and serve food during meetings; having to sport marriage signs when their male counterparts didn't have to; strict dress codes imposed only on women members – these are some of the most recurrent examples. These regressive practices did not match with the revolutionary zeal that we were asked to develop in self and others, but questioning was stifled rather than encouraged. The only response that could ever be elicited was that these were socio-cultural issues that were to be addressed only *after* the revolution. Even within a group of 'the vanguards of revolution'? I wasn't convinced.

Equally disturbing were the puritanical mindsets of my senior comrades – mostly male – manifested through continuous labelling of people. I would be served my first show cause notice for "Party indiscipline" when I steadfastly refused to balk down about the unacceptability of the line of criticism being taken against Madame Ching (Mao ze Dong's fourth wife and widow, now known as Jian Qing) post Chairman Mao's death. I was young – both biologically and as a member of the Party and was eager to learn about the political critique of the line she was pursuing with the (now infamous) Gang of Four. But I strongly objected to, and did not withdraw even when rebuked, points like her wearing sleeveless dresses and using lipstick being presented as markers of her being against 'revolutionary socialism'. Just one example of what I mean by a puritanical mindset.

Disenchanted with such practices and the throttling of my questioning mind, I sought answers in the writings of Marx, Engels and their followers. *The Origin of the Family, Private Property and the State* published by Engels after Marx's death first introduced me to an understanding of the systemic development of women's oppression in class society. I got my first theoretical framework to figure out that everything from the label of a tomboy to the practices I so abhorred within the Party were not stray incidents, but the inevitable markers of a social structure that treats women as inferior to men. That is also how I chanced upon the writings of Rosa Luxembourg and Clara Zetkin and found strong resonance with much of what they had to say. These writings helped me crystallise my understanding of gender as a tool of oppression much like class and led me to explore the world of feminist literature. As my comprehension of gender politics grew deeper, two things became imminent: my expulsion from the Party and my joining the emergent women's rights movement in the country. Both happened in 1981. The tomboy of yesteryears was by then a woman in her early twenties, still haunted by the spectre of being labelled 'masculine' in her demeanour. One of the many charges labelled by the Party against me read "infantile disorder: adolescent boy-type indiscipline and unruly behaviour". Ugh!

Beyond heterosexism with the butch/femme dilemma

As it happens, my introduction to same-sex attraction and the gay rights movement in the western world also happened through my readings to better understand Marxist revolutionary politics and practices. I was baffled particularly by the contrariety of these three facts: Engels' harsh comments about homosexuals being "extremely against nature"; the decriminalisation of homosexuality by the Soviet government immediately after the Revolution in 1917; and its recriminalisation in 1933 by Joseph Stalin. Since I already had many issues with the way Stalin functioned both as the USSR Premier and the General Secretary of the Communist Party of the Soviet Union (Bolshevik) – I strongly felt that Lenin's acceptance of same-sex attraction was closer to socialist ideas than Engels' and Stalin's rejections of it. It was to gather evidence for my hypothesis that I started reading about the gay rights movement in the West in general and USA in particular.

Together with my readings, a chance encounter with an elderly French woman who had been expelled from the French

Communist Party in the mid-1960s on suspicion that she was
a lesbian made me even more curious about the nature of the
relationship between leftism and the struggle for equal rights by
same-sex attracted people. The focus of my readings now con-
sisted of the tripartite discourses on Marxism, feminism and
homosexuality. Even as I began to notice the interconnected-
ness of the three in the larger struggle for equality and inclusive
social justice, the debate of the time (late 1970s and early 1980s)
around the butch/femme dichotomy disconcerted me considerably. This binary role playing immediately brought back my own
discomfort with gender labelling and stopped me from delving
deeper into the layers woven into it. I felt much more comfortable
to disparage the butch/femme binary as lesbian women playing
into the traps laid by heteronormative patriarchy (as I would later
learn to call it) – even as I gathered armour from Adrienne Rich's
(1980) "Compulsory Heterosexuality and Lesbian Existence" for
my battle with Party seniors.

More than a decade later, in the early years of the new millen-
nium, I'd be outraged by others' observation that I 'wore the pants'
in my first ever serious same-sex relationship. By then, I knew
that my desire centred on androgyny, irrespective of whether it
was embodied by a male or a female person. My rejection of the
gender binary was far more pronounced and my understanding
of both lesbianism and feminism considerably widened and deep-
ened. Within the women's rights movement in the country, I'd
increasingly begin to feel the need for including lesbian voices; of
being vocal about women's sexual rights. The argument of some
of the elders in the movement that sexuality rights were not so
pressing in a country where dowry deaths and marital rape were
everyday realities would be unpalatable to me. But my discomfort with the butch/femme dichotomy had not lessened. It still
hasn't, though my feeling of outrage has now been replaced by
that of intense sadness. In the first Pride March in Hyderabad in

February 2013, a noted leader of the LGBTQ movement in that region wore a T-shirt sporting the slogan: "Butch is the new avatar of chivalry". For me, that says it all – the homonormativity intricately interwoven in the concept of the butch, for the other side of chivalry is chauvinism and I for one do not subscribe to that.

The long arms of socialisation

In hindsight it seems almost incredible that despite my growing disenchantment with the heteronormative patriarchal world, in real life I continued playing out the most run-of-the-mill script possible. Marriage – divorce – remarriage – divorce ... I continued to think that the inevitable patriarchal contours of those conjugal relationships caused the breakdowns. That wasn't untrue – but the patterns of my own desire for androgyny, though still not consciously confronted, and gender-fluidity also contributed considerably to those factors becoming more pronounced. These connubial experiences would teach me one of the most important lessons of my life: the so-called progressive heterosexual man who chooses an 'unusual woman' as a partner wants her unusualness to showcase to the world as a marker of his liberated outlook. Within the four walls of conjugality, she is expected to be the traditionally known devoted wife – as if her 'unusualness' is a cloak she can take off at will. I do not want to commit the fallacy of a sweeping generalisation, but I'd like to underscore that I've come across many other women, and still do – even among those younger by a generation and more – who have reported this same behaviour pattern among many apparently progressive men.

This is when I'd simultaneously earn the labels of being a bitch and a superwoman – both for my inability to be submissive. I was a bitch because I refused to give up on my need for independence and assertiveness. Even the superwoman label wasn't really a compliment – it was more of a challenge thrown at me in vengeance for my gender-fluidity; to dare me to match up to impossible demands ranging from being the lone breadwinner to careful and conscious mothering to remaining a women's rights activist … Even as I burnt myself out, my understanding of the absolute claustrophobia that heteronormative patriarchal matrimony was generating in me became clearer. It is these experiences that convince me that marriage as it is institutionalised today is *not* a right, but a burden on any woman – queer, straight or trans. I wouldn't fight for it – I'd rather fight against it.

This position of rejecting marriage as an institution is as much a lesson from my real-life experiences as from my involvement in the women's rights movement in India; my involvement with women in the sex trade and their children as a social development professional; and my engagement with the LGBTQ movement in the country. As it exists and functions today, at least in India, marriage as an institution is not only heterosexist, but intrinsically patriarchal as well – based on social perceptions and belief systems that support male domination. Marriage in India is considered an essential part of the life cycle for both women and men, but the burden is far more obligatory for women. As per the Sample Registration System, 2013, the percentage of never married females in all age groups stands at 47.7 per cent, as opposed to 52.5 per cent for males (Government of India, Ministry of Statistics and Programme Implementation, 2018). Significantly, the never married category in the 15–29 age range stands at 18 per cent for females, while for males it is 21.5 per cent (Government of India, Ministry of Statistics and Programme Implementation, 2018).

The wide prevalence of women changing everything from their surnames (to adopt the husband's family name) to habitats (shifting from her natal home to that of her husband's) post marriage, even though there is no legal binding to do either, is one of the commonest examples of inequality inbuilt in the institution. This country's strict refusal to bring marital rape within the purview of a legal crime is another indicator of the intrinsic privileging of the male within marriage. Despite a law against dowry since 1961, the latest available National Crime Records Bureau Report, 2016, puts dowry deaths in the country at 11,841, with an additional 15,773 cases under the Dowry Prohibition Act. That same report depicts 162,185 reported cases of cruelty by husbands and relatives, and another 461 cases under the Domestic Violence Act (National Crime Records Bureau, 2016). Needless to say, there would be an equal number, if not more, of all these crimes that never get reported at all. Also, the report does not segregate other offences such as abetment to suicide, trafficking, forced miscarriage and death due to forced miscarriage etc., on the basis of matrimonial status. But from my interactions with women in the sex trade and with survivors of sex trafficking in the course of my work, I do know that in many cases the husband is the trafficker. Very often, someone else's husband is a non-paying live-in client of a woman in the sex trade, living like a drone and sending money from this woman's earning to support his marital family – a form of oppression of both the women involved: for the wife, directly; for the woman keeping this man – indirectly through her psychosocial need to have someone 'husband-like'. This is not an institution I want replicated for any queer person, without changing these factors of inbuilt violence first. And for that to happen, a wider and deeper engagement on the structures of the gender binary and the male privileging that inevitably goes hand in hand with that, and the degree to which marriage as an institution is a reinforcement and perpetration of both, is needed first.

Blurred boundaries beyond left, right and centre

How is this raving monologue connected with an investigation on the need to reclaim lesbian feminism? Well, first, to highlight that one may well understand and support both feminism and lesbianism on the basis of real-life experiences, even when one does not identify as a lesbian. Hopefully, that can act as an encouragement to today's lesbian activists to be inclusive in their approach beyond narrowly defined sexual-identity-based politics. Broad-based alliances on the common principles of inclusive social justice and equal rights for all marginalised population groups have possibly never been more necessary than today, for the world as a whole is experiencing an alarming rise of right-wing fundamentalism that constantly privileges one single identity over all other dimensions of a human individual. The identity varies, though: sometimes religion forms the basis; sometimes the colour of the skin; sometimes one's geographical location and language; and in a country like India – it may also be caste. As a practising supporter of non-normative gender expressions and sexual desires, I fervently hope that lesbian feminist activists manage to steer clear of such carefully designed divide-and-rule identity politics, for it never ever empowers the marginalised in the long run. History gives us many lessons in that. If there have been moments in history to rally around a sexual identity, the need today is to transcend that and find common points of deprivation and marginalisation with different population groups.

As a corollary to that, it is important for lesbian feminism to question strands of biological determinism within its discourse and practices: 'woman-identified woman' is not a simple term, for a gamut of socialised values, perceptions and belief systems are packed into that term 'woman' which need to be unpacked and carefully examined. There is a lot in the ten-paragraph manifesto published and distributed by Radicalesbians in May 1970 in New York City that I can completely relate with. (I refer specifically to this one since it is considered one of the foundational documents of lesbian feminism). The turmoil a woman has to face when she fails to comply with the role ascribed to her by society is a lived experience for me as well. I can fully understand the boiling rage generated within because of such experiences. But to claim all such experiences and outrage as 'lesbian' makes me uncomfortable, for I do not identify as one. And I feel equally ill at ease to sub-scribe to the notion of love for all women. Indira Gandhi and Margaret Thatcher are two public figures who immediately come to my mind. Both were biological women who also identified as women; but even the idea of feeling anything other than utter dis-taste for them is repugnant to me. Going strictly by the principle of 'love for all women' – I stand a chance of being labelled anti-lesbian and anti-feminist for such revulsion!

This is what I refer to as biological determinism that in my understanding overlooks how various other factors like class, religion, region, skin colour etc. shape the experiences of differ-ent biological women differently. It is this failure to understand intersectionality that would subsequently need lesbian feminists of colour to emerge as a separate subset, for instance. I'd go a step further to argue that this homogenisation of 'woman' as a category by itself allows little space for gender fluid persons to be consid-ered feminists, since the ultimate marker of a feminist woman is believed to consist in her refusal to be sexually engaged with a man. An erotic relationship between a so-called effeminate man and an apparently masculine woman would, by lesbian feminist stan-dards, not be considered non-normative – though stereotypical gender roles might be completely reversed in such a relationship. And a queer woman such as me whose eroto-sexual desires centre around androgyny beyond the male/female gender binary would certainly have no space in such a lesbian feminist world at all!

Finally, unless gender-fluidity is accepted beyond the bio-logical binary of male/female or man/woman, I cannot see much space within lesbian feminism to be trans-inclusive – trans men, trans women, transgender – whatever terminology one chooses for oneself. Lesbian feminism must take upon itself the task of deconstructing varied life experiences that go into these gender choices and the socialised values, perceptions and belief systems that remain hidden under these choices – so that patriarchal reinforcements and remnants can be challenged from a strongly feminist point of view.

This critique, however, is not to undermine that feminist discourse would remain equally incomplete and lopsided unless lesbian and trans experiences are included within the fight for women's right to social justice and equality. The experiences of persons with non-heteronormative gender expressions and sexual preferences illustrate certain façades of the layered functioning of patriarchal heteronormativity, which may not be readily available within the life situations of heterosexual women – no matter how many types and levels of marginalisation they face.

I would, therefore, pitch the idea of a kind of solidarity within both lesbianism (by sexual orientation or political choice) and feminism that Holly Lewis (2016) underlines as not a condition that results from matured humans learning to accept diversity, but a political recognition of the futures of certain population groups being tied together. A kind of solidarity that necessitates antagonism, the taking of sides in order to support one's comrades. Such solidarity recognises schisms, rather than ending them. Lesbians are comrades in the struggle for equal rights for women and the larger feminist movement must commit to supporting them. Lesbians equally need to examine their positions continuously, for homonormativity functions within the gender binary and can be as dangerous as heteronormative patriarchy, which holds the gender binary sacred for its existence, perpetration and reinforcement. Lesbian support also needs to be extended to genderqueer persons who identify as women without wanting to fit into the stereotypical box called 'feminine/womanly', who may also be sexually queer rather than lesbian – for heteronormative patriarchy marginalises them just as much as it does lesbians. To trans men, my appeal would be to remain committed to their experiences of marginalisation during socialisation as a person assigned gender female at birth and keep questioning the way heteronormative patriarchy defines masculinity/maleness. And to all of us at the edge of the strict codes of heteronormativity and gender binary, my appeal is that we first critique the institutions (like marriage) that patriarchy functions happily within, before we want them as rights.

Maybe through such support, hostilities and questioning, we could dream of a future where gender expressions and sexual relationships will be of a kind that we cannot imagine as yet. That will be answered when a new generation has grown up: a generation of humans who never in their lives have known what it is to buy another human's surrender with money or any other social instrument of power; a generation of humans who have never known what it is to give themselves to another human from any considerations other than real love or refuse to give themselves to their lover for fear of economic consequences. When these people are in the world, they will care precious little what anybody today thinks they ought to do; they will make their own practice and corresponding public opinion for each individual – and that will be the end of it (Engels, 1972).

Notes

1 Article 352 of the Indian Constitution provides for the declaration of a state of national emergency if the country's security is under threat due to external aggression or internal armed rebellion. The first declaration of a national emergency was in October 1962, when India was at war with China and it extended until January 1968 so that the Indo-Pakistani war in 1965 was covered. An emergency was declared once again on 3 December 1971 when India was at war with Pakistan. However, in common parlance, 'The Emergency' in India refers to a period of twenty-one months from 25 June 1975 to 11 March 1977 – the only national emergency declared when the country was not at war. Officially declared by Fakhruddin Ali Ahmed, the then President of India, this declaration of emergency across the nation authorised the then Prime Minister Mrs Indira Gandhi to exercise extra-constitutional authority. Elections were suspended right down to the level of students' unions in graduate and post-graduate institutions. Using her extraordinary powers, Mrs Gandhi also unleashed a massive crackdown on all kinds of

civil liberties and political opposition. Amnesty International mentions that 140,000 people were arrested without trial during this twenty-one-month period. It remains one of the most controversial periods in post-1947 India and is believed to have been one of the biggest challenges to India's democracy. The parliamentary elections held in March 1977 resulted in Mrs Gandhi losing her seat and India having its first ever non-Congress government since 1947.

2 Traditional Indian dress for boys and men.

TEN | The place of lesbians in the women's movement

Line Chamberland

During a lecture in Berlin in 1904, Anna Rüling[1] (Rueling, [1904] 1980) called on the homosexual movement and the women's movement to unite in the fight for individual self-determination. After highlighting the important contribution of homosexual women to the international movement for the rights of women, she deplored that this contribution had gone unrecognised by the main feminist organisations who, to use the language of the period, had never made any effort to defend the social status of their "uranian" members. Rüling's argument emphasised the masculinity of homosexual women and adopted a thesis proposing the existence of a "third sex", a concept advanced by Magnus Hirschfeld[2] who argued that, in addition to the male and female sexes, there was a naturally occurring third category composed of those whose physical characteristics, personality traits and sexual preferences did not conform to the attributes usually associated with masculinity and femininity.

The theory of the third sex depends on a rigid and essentialist vision of gender differences and thus appears outdated today. Nevertheless, I am still surprised by the relevance, a century later, of Rüling's nuanced observations regarding the participation of lesbians in the women's movement, clear to those who know what to look for, but a source of reticence once revealed. While such a silence may have seemed understandable when the movement had so few 'converts', now that it has acquired power and credibility, it is no longer justifiable.

In an attempt to examine the capacity of the contemporary women's movement to welcome lesbians, I start with Rüling's observation and apply it to the second-wave feminist movement that appeared in Quebec at the end of the 1960s. As my reflections on this topic are directly linked to my own path as a lesbian and feminist activist since the mid-1970s, I will describe some key moments in my personal trajectory and then identify what seems to me to be the conditions or preconditions for the actual integration of lesbians into the women's movement as well as the limits of such an integration.[3]

In contrast with other women who are said to come from minority subgroups (such as Indigenous or immigrant women), lesbians have long been an integral component of the women's movement where they have participated and continue to participate in large numbers, whether it has simply been as sympathisers, activists and workers, or as organisational directors or political leaders. It is from within this movement that they have expressed their rebellion, their anger, their dreams, with more boldness, at times, than their heterosexual sisters.

In their numerous theoretical and political texts, lesbians have named, denounced and analysed the oppression that subjugates women and thus furnished the movement with its tools, arguments and ideological weapons. I do not wish to evaluate the contribution of or the role played by one or the other, nor do I intend to open up or feed conflict between lesbian feminists and heterosexual feminists. Moreover, I do not share the opinion that lesbians have devoted or even sacrificed themselves for struggles that were not theirs. When lesbians defend abortion rights, they are fighting for their own freedom, that of control over their own bodies. When they march against women's poverty, it is because they themselves or women in their lives have confronted difficulty in ensuring their own economic independence, whether they live alone or in a couple, and even now that the couples that they form have gained recognition. The pink dollar, to adopt a recent expression used to refer to the spending power of the gay consumer, accumulates more slowly for those earning pink salaries, meaning those of women.[4]

To argue that lesbians, working with heterosexual women, have created and shaped the women's movement requires a different formulation of the question of the movement's diversity that is specific to them. The stumbling block here is not the accessibility of the movement or its capacity to reach lesbians, but rather the visibility given to their participation both within the movement and in terms of its public image. Many questions that can be globally applied to the movement and its diverse components emerge when seen from this perspective. Is the presence of lesbians stated and is their contribution recognised? Are their concerns discussed? Do service providers consider their specific needs? Is there an interest in the history and culture of lesbians? Are alliances with autonomous lesbian groups and the gay movement cultivated? What importance and what support does the women's movement give to lesbian concerns? Which concerns and which lesbians? Is there a place for debating them? Is there any feminist ideological space permitting lesbians to represent themselves as something other than 'women',[5] or even as women who are differentiated by a secondary characteristic, that of sexual orientation?

These questions have already created tensions and plenty of debates among both lesbian and heterosexual feminists. Depending on the circumstances, the lesbian question has been at times concealed or avoided and, at other times, included in the analysis and practices of groups and associations. Consequently, some lesbians distanced themselves from a feminism that they interpreted as heterosexist. The radical lesbian current would develop the most strongly articulated and vehement critique of feminism, which, according to tenets of this political position, does not call into question the political system founded on heterosexuality (Turcotte, 1998). Other lesbians continued as activists in a movement where they felt relatively well accepted albeit with discretion. Still others developed initiatives that attempted to define problems specific to lesbians, adapting or launching specific services or initiating projects that addressed their concerns.[6] In my own identity trajectory and activist projects, lesbianism and feminism were articulated differently from one decade to another.

The lesbian feminist generation

Like thousands of other women in Quebec and in the rest of North America and Europe, I identified as a lesbian feminist during the 1970s (Echols, 1984; Faderman, 1991; Hildebran, 1998; Lamoureux, 1998a; Ross, 1995; Roy, 1985). Starting with common experiences and circumstances and impacted by the feminist and gay movements, a large portion of lesbians from this generation had adopted definitions of themselves, interpretive models of their sexual desires and world views that differed radically from previous representations of lesbians. In retrospect, we can consider the emergence of lesbian feminism as a social movement that centred on identity affirmation (Stein, 1992; 1997). Through the engagement with the political and ideological struggles of feminism, a series of reconstructions of lesbian identity took place that withdrew it from medical categories and made it more universal while reversing its negative connotations. According to this new perspective, lesbianism was no longer seen as a stigmatised, pathological, sexual behaviour but as a form of resistance to patriarchal domination, a way of practising feminist ideals of independence and autonomy from men, a rejection of the accompanying imposed social roles in a search for authenticity. All women who embark upon such a path, who identify as 'women-identified',[7] according to the framework of the period, could become lesbians. Sexual categories (homosexuality, heterosexuality) that serve only to reinforce normative models were countered by an enlarged definition of lesbianism that was accompanied by the validation, albeit an idealisation, of this lifestyle.

This discourse would attract women whose desires, identities and sexual attractions varied considerably. Not all would become active militants in the women's movement. In my case, I am a product of this junction between the political and the sexual: feminism had profoundly changed my view of women and opened the possibility of desire for them while providing me with explanations for the difficulties I had until that point confronted in my relationships with men. Until the mid-1980s, the love of women and my involvement with feminism were one in my personal and political identity. As a precaution, depending on the circumstances, depending on to whom I was speaking, I omitted the 'lesbian' and retained only the 'feminist'. I did not live this half-truth as a compromise because it was feminism that gave meaning to my sexual choices. It was feminism that legitimated them, that made them acceptable in my eyes and in the image projected to others, that gave them a certain social respectability.

For myself, as for that entire generation of lesbians, primarily young and educated, the feminist discourse – which they themselves were involved in articulating – fostered a reconstruction of individual and collective identity. Until that point, the label "Lesbian" had served not only to marginalise those who felt same-sex attraction but, more broadly, to control all women by constructing the feminine gender through the establishment of a border between the normal woman, meaning feminine and therefore heterosexual – it goes without saying – and she who was abnormal or deviant. Moreover, this epithet was equally applied to frigid women whose sexual frigidity was sometimes attributed to latent homosexual desires in medical and sexology discourses and to prostitutes who would be unconsciously motivated by aggression towards men or a desire to convince themselves of their heterosexuality.[8]

Throughout the century, we can also note that the figure of *The Sexual Invert* and that of *The Lesbian* often subsumed the feminist. For example, in pamphlets denouncing the claims of the suffragettes, Henri Bourassa[9] (1925) described them as "women-men". In a critique of Simone de Beauvoir's *Deuxième sexe* appearing in *Cité libre* magazine in 1957 – one of the rare mentions given to this work before the 1960s – Dr Michel Dansereau[10] interpreted the presence of a chapter on "The Lesbian" as an indication that the author's thesis "seems to culminate, as if naturally, in inversion".[11]

We can also recall insults of this sort brandished to denigrate the actions of neo-feminists in the 1970s and after: "Nothing but a gang of damned lesbians". Even if they are just examples, they demonstrate the central role played by categories constructed around sexual practices in the definition and imposition of a feminine ideal. In the momentum gained from our radicalism, the insults hardly reached us, and it was with pride that we claimed the name lesbian. We have, I believe, underestimated the depth of these divisions that crystallised around the sexual questions lying at the heart of the women's movement.

Ruptures in the 1980s

The lesbian movement broke away from the women's movement and experienced considerable vibrancy over the course of the 1980s, a period characterised by the multiplication of meeting and performance spaces as well as the intensification of cultural production (Demczuk and Remiggi, 1998[12]). But this exciting decade, remembered today as the 'golden age' by some, also sparks in me memories of disillusionment and dissent. Indeed, the process of redefining of lesbian identity was not without conflict: after the passion of the first battles dissolved the – let's face it, utopic – hope of overcoming patriarchy within a few years, numerous political and ideological divisions appeared that created opposition between politicised lesbians: that of our visibility within the women's movement, the central or secondary character of heterosexual obligation in the process of the subordination of women, and thus the political implications of our sexual choices and alliances with the heterosexual feminists (Centre Lyonnais d'études féministes, 1989; Chamberland, 1989; Lamoureux, 1998b; Roy, 1985; Turcotte, 1998). According to Stein (1992; 1997), the movement was the victim of its own success: by expanding the definition of lesbianism, by breaking down its boundaries, it attracted women who had very diverse life experiences, for whom desire, sexual practice, personal identity and political vision were highly varied. In the face of the tensions generated by this heterogeneity, there were two different responses: one that accentuated the universality of the category 'lesbian' but risked the loss of its specificity notably by desexualising it (Calhoun, 1996); and the other that reinforced its borders by adopting political positions that bounded it more clearly even if it excluded those who did not share this point of view.[13] Finally, the intense politicisation of autonomous lesbian spaces exhausted many who had frequented them and drove away those who were less or not at all politicised.

For its part, the feminist movement had scored some points having undergone institutionalisation and professionalisation (Lamoureux, 1990; 1998b). Its audience had grown considerably, and its political power could no longer be ignored. But feminists still had to deal with the lesbian problem. From an era when contestation came from everywhere, we moved into a more conservative political climate; this was the decade of excellence when one had to prove competence and moderation. Too ripped apart, too heavy to carry in public forums, the embarrassing subject of lesbianism as well as reflection on heterosexuality as an oppressive institution for women was increasingly evacuated.

This situation made the relationship between lesbianism and feminism problematic, which unleashed an awareness in me, first in the form of a sense of unease and then in a questioning of its multiple ramifications: why did I have any shame in identifying as a lesbian without the feminist cover? How to express my solidarity with lesbians situated outside of the women's movement? What do we actually have in common? Am I not suffering the same repression as a lesbian? Am I not myself living a double life just like most lesbians and gays: feminist at work, in the women's movement, and lesbian at night, in my private life, in the bars? Are we not supposedly neighbours on the continuum of lesbian resistance, to use a term coined by Adrienne Rich (1981)? And, if we are, how is it that I know so little of their history, their culture, their difficulties of everyday life? A testimonial of Joan Nestle (1981), cofounder of the Lesbian Herstory Archives in New York, strongly affected me, where she tells her personal story while paying tribute to the courage of butch–femme lesbians who had dared to live their love in public spaces well before the rise of the feminist movement. Nestle attempts to explain the world of these women, in which she herself participated in the 1950s and 1960s, to lesbian feminist readers who perceive it as reproducing heterosexual models. This moving account gave me a means of measuring the depth of our contempt for these lesbians and the "our" included many lesbian feminists. It included me.

This move drove me to abandon the dash between lesbian and feminist. Merged as they were, henceforth, these two commitments became distinct and it was up to me to articulate them to one another. I decided to start by rebalancing the identity scale by focusing my energies on reconstructing the history of lesbians in Quebec. While pursuing my research, I devoured the writings, most of which were in English, coming from the nascent field of lesbian and gay studies in the United States and England.

Heterosexual and lesbian feminists, and the latter with each other, tore themselves apart over certain questions, especially those regarding sexuality, whose resonance was faint in the Quebec feminist movement and in its Francophone universities.[14] I cannot do more than mention these briefly here. Feminist analysis regarding pornography, rape, prostitution and the sexual slavery of women vigorously denounced their victimisation by sexual exploitation and underlined their vulnerability in this respect. By focusing on the representation of women as sexual victims, they advanced a vision of their sexuality that would be judged as reductionist by some feminists, principally by those whose sexual practices deviated from the norm, including lesbians, prostitutes and other sex workers (Bell, 1987; Healey, 1996; Snitow, Stansell and Thompson, 1983; Vance, 1984b). If the condemnation of pornography created consensus, the demand for censorship privileged by a certain feminist orthodoxy as a possible solution to its proliferation aroused reservations. What could lesbians think when, in larger and larger numbers, they hoped for explicit representations of their sexuality which were vulnerable to being judged as pornographic according to the existing canons and thus subject to censorship?[15]

Finally, the analysis of heterosexism as the ideological and institutional foundation of the hierarchical organisation of the sexes was refined and subject again to debates, notably with the rise of the queer movement, but the feminist point of view often found itself ignored if not side-lined (Chamberland, 1997; Malinowitz, 1996; Zimmerman, 1996). The more the decade progressed, the more I felt distant from the Quebec feminist movement, even if I was thrilled with its advances in many economic, social and political realms. I managed to build alliances in academia, enough to implement my research project. But here I lingered in what I call my glass closet where I put aside many of these questions.

The 1990s: visibility and recognition

The 1990s were marked by a much greater visibility of gays and lesbians in public space, notably in urban space with the development of the gay village and the annual demonstrations of Divers/Cité[16] (Demczuk and Remiggi, 1998; Higgins, 1998). The community movement branched out and consolidated. A whole series of groups and organisations were launched based on affinities or shared activities in diverse domains: sports and cultural activities, attending the same school, lived experiences or the anticipation of parenting, labour-union organising, common ethnic origins, sharing the same age group, etc.

These groups usually presented themselves as being mixed[17] even if lesbians were often under-represented. They also formed non-mixed networks around more narrowly defined concerns such as groups for businesswomen or for outdoor activities. Following the American trend, Quebec media representations gave space to lesbians and their testimonials had appeared in most of the women's magazines by the middle of the decade. Films that brought them to the screen, such as *Gazon Maudit*, reached a large audience (Nadeau, 1997).

The gay movement also took up political space and advanced demands that were primarily concerned with denouncing discrimination against homosexual persons and recognising their rights. In its orientation towards mainstreaming and through its most influential leaders, this movement prioritised reformism, striving for the recognition of gays and lesbians socially, legally, economically and politically. The radicalism of the previous decades was replaced by a desire to integrate into existing family and social structures.

Following the unravelling of the lesbian movement, lesbians found themselves divided. Some of them reorganised into ad hoc coalitions, such as around the public hearings of the provincial human rights commission (Commission des droits de la personne sur la violence et la discrimination envers les gais et les lesbiennes) in 1993. Others joined the mixed gay movement where they were occasionally allied with one another. The younger ones identified with the queer movement. Others continued to invest in the feminist movement where they increasingly assert the lesbian perspective in greater numbers. Since 1995, the Comité pour la reconnaissance des lesbiennes in the Fédération des femmes du Québec was created and recently the local Marche mondiale des femmes endorsed demands concerning the rights of lesbians (Demczuk, 2000).

In 1996, lesbians attempted to launch an autonomous movement by forming a provincial association that was open to diversity, the Réseau des lesbiennes du Québec/Quebec Lesbian Network. Finally, a large coalition stemming from the gay, lesbian, labour-union and feminist movements gave direct support to the fight for the recognition of same-sex civil unions.[18] On the whole, we can observe that many lesbians reoriented their activism over the course of this decade, focusing on pragmatic objectives and engaging in strategic alliances.

This is the case for me. For example, at the beginning of the 1990s, I was involved in the trade-union movement with the CSN (Confédération des syndicats nationaux) setting up a committee that would investigate discrimination based on sexual orientation in the workplace and clearing the ground for the demand for state recognition of same-sex couples. Through diverse projects and collaborations in the university milieu, I was promoting the development of homosexuality as a field of study. Beyond the shock that accompanied the passage from a lesbian feminist activist culture to the predominantly masculine world where the internal democratic life and the external relations of power played out in a very different manner, alliances with the gay movement offered one primary advantage: the targeting of concrete objectives that made the lesbian and gay cause a priority, even if the lesbians were in a minority there and had to fight to bring forward their specific demands such as those concerning maternity.

Conclusion

At the end of this journey, I have lost many certainties, but those that I have acquired seem to me inescapable. That is why I would like to share them with you. First, lesbians are not a homogeneous group. They distinguish themselves from each another through their life experiences, the social context in which they affirmed their difference, the ways that they construct their identities as lesbians, meaning the naming, understanding and explanation of their sexual desires, to themselves and others, its externalisation in their appearance and manner of being, and its articulation in relation to other facets of their personal identity.

Lesbians also differ in terms of their economic circumstances, where they are situated in terms of social class and ethnicity, their relationships with their family of origin, their parental status which determines whether they have children or not, whether those children come from heterosexual marriage or a relationship with another woman, or many other possible situations. They are also divided by their political visions and allegiances. Recall, for example, that lesbians did not nor do they now unanimously support the demand for the recognition of same-sex spouses. The problem does not reside as much in the absence of consensus as in the lack of a place for debate, due to the weakening of the autonomous lesbian movement and their minority position in both the feminist and gay movements. Who takes on the leadership to define their demands? The priorities of their movement? Over the last few years, the agenda has been defined by the gay movement, more precisely by the reformists that dominate this movement. Obviously, the women's movement cannot overcome this difficulty in bringing lesbians together and mobilising them around objectives that they define for themselves. The movement must at least be conscious of this difficulty and emphasise the democratic process in internal discussions and in the coalitions where it is present.

In her time, Anna Rüling's call eventually bore fruit. Indeed, in 1910, a few years after her presentation, when the adoption of a new penal code was being debated in Germany that would have the effect of criminalising sexual relations between two women, feminist organisations mobilised themselves and, working with the homosexual movement, forced the legislators to retreat (Faderman and Eriksson, 1980). Just as it was then, it is today without a doubt easier for lesbians who are participating in the women's movement to solicit and obtain its support for lesbian (and gay) demands at a time when the homosexual movement is strongly affirming itself in the public sphere and benefitting from a certain degree of popularity. This is why it is necessary for lesbians to be involved in both of these two movements.

Second, the lesbian presence within the women's movement is a source of ambiguity since lesbians participate in it most often as women and on the basis of feminist ideology. Claiming to be open to all women, including lesbians, without discrimination, without translating that concretely into practice, seems like an illusion. It seems to me that it is necessary that a movement that strives to be inclusive explicitly considers lesbian realities and perspectives in its discourse, demands and services offered. That is the project that is certainly underway, but that must again be widened to all the components of the movement, to the various terrains of intervention and struggle (Bélanger, 2000). The pursuit of such a challenge will not happen without generating its share of tensions since the question of lesbianism remains, in my opinion, a potentially implosive one inside the movement despite the progress in the last few years. It will be necessary to take time to voice fears, to create a secure climate for each other, to respect the rhythms, to understand the differences and, especially, to live with them rather than imposing an artificial consensus. I also share Calhoun's (1996) concerns regarding the possibility of representing lesbians within feminist thought when it tends to define them as being essentially women and to desexualise lesbianism.

Third, the identity and the lesbian feminist culture that I come from are the product of a particular, historic moment. Throughout the twentieth century, different conceptions of masculine and feminine homosexuality have emerged; they have competed, coexisted, they have overlapped and contradicted one another (Sedgwick, 1990). These understandings even touch at the heart of the construction of sexuality, gender (what is defined as masculine and feminine) and sexual classes: what are the borders that define acceptable, tolerated and forbidden sexual behaviours? How are sexual desires categorised? What links are there between categories of desire and the construction of masculinity and femininity? Do homosexuals and lesbians form a distinct, innocuous minority, bringing few consequences? Or, is there a continuum of sexual behaviour among human beings, a complete spectrum of sexualities and identities that can take many different configurations?

The responses to these questions are not readily apparent. They are part of our struggles during which categories, definitions and identities are produced, contested, recovered and modified. Thus, some lesbians appropriated the model of the sexual invert at the beginning of the twentieth century. This model associated feeling attraction for a woman with a form of masculinisation that permitted them to explicitly name their sexual desire in the context when desire could not be anything but masculine because women were deemed not to have any. Others distanced themselves from this model because it associated their desire with a form of abnormality, a pathology.

Today, the dominant paradigm for conceptualising homosexuality is that of sexual orientation, which dissociates sexual attraction from other elements of personal identity. This model, that came to dominate in the 1960s, reduces homosexuality to an irreversible personal trait rather than issue of character (Hurteau, 1991). This vision was warmly welcomed by the gay movement because it allows for the presentation of homosexuality as one characteristic among others, an accidental difference, and denounces any differential treatment or discrimination based on sexual orientation. The activists that adopted it stood up and demanded more tolerance for homosexuals, and more recently, access to particular types of social and institutional recognition.

This paradigm lends itself to several readings and interpretations, which doubtless explains its pervasiveness. In my opinion, this vision leads at times to very reductionist interpretations by isolating sexual orientation from its psychological, social and political components. For example, by considering it innate, we come back to the idea that a natural and accidental difference constitutes homosexuality, leaving intact the idea of a natural attraction and complementarity between men and women. Furthermore, due to a desire to show that lesbians and homosexuals are like everyone else, we end up erasing their history, their own culture, their multiple identities. These reductionist discourses avoid any interrogation of sex and gender categories, of heterosexist oppression as an ideological and institutional system which brings us to a narrow and conservative right to difference that consists only of a series of societal adaptations to us and of us to society as its objective.

Among lesbians themselves, their desire to see their lifestyles recognised, to not constantly be marginalised, stands alongside and competes with their rejection of the imposed sexual and gender order, as well as the rejection of a normalcy that is so strictly defined that it stifles their rebellion and creativity, trivialises their difference, meaning, in this context, their break from heterosexual womenhood, their refusal to be women in the social sense of the term, which, in itself, constitutes the basis of an individual and social transformation.

This tension, as far as can be predicted, will continue to carry the lesbian movement for a long time.

Notes

1 Anna Rüling (Rueling) (Theo Anna Sprüngli) was a German journalist. Due to her 1904 speech during the annual meeting of Hirschfeld's Scientific Humanitarian Committee addressing the problems faced by lesbians, she is known as the first lesbian political activist (Leidinger, 2004).

2 German doctor and homosexual Magnus Hirschfeld (1868–1935) was a pioneer of sexology. In 1897 he cofounded the Scientific Humanitarian Committee that fought for the decriminalisation of male homosexuality. He also conducted many research projects that attempted to document the existence of a third sex with many variations (sexual inversion, transvestitism, hermaphrodism, etc.).

3 In this short text, I cannot hope to comprehensively address the complex and shifting relationship between feminism and lesbianism, thus I have chosen to use the format of the personal testimonial.

4 This is an excellent example of the ambiguity created by the universal application of men's experiences. The idea of 'gay' economic power appears to include both sexes when, in reality, it refers to the development, primarily among gay men, of a stratum of consumers who enjoy higher incomes, a significant portion of which is spent on particular types of consumer goods (clothing, travel, etc.).

5 This is a reference to Wittig's (1980b) famous statement that lesbians are not women in the essay "One Is Not Born a Woman".

6 For example, in the mid-1980s, a lesbian caucus was formed within CALACS (Centre d'aide et de lute contre les agressions à caractère sexuel) as part of the fight against sexual assault. The goal was to increase the visibility of lesbians and to sensitise heterosexual feminists to their specific forms of oppression.

7 The definition of lesbian as a form of identification with women appeared, in its first iteration, in a manifesto entitled "The Woman-Identified Woman", published in 1970 by the group Radicalesbians in reaction to the homophobia expressed within NOW (National Organization of Women) in the United States (Stein, 1997:31–40).

8 There are countless examples of popular texts on sexuality and sex education manuals, particularly those inspired by psychoanalysis, that multiplied in the post-war period and were widely circulated in the 1960s. I will only mention two here. In a book entitled *Problèmes sexuels de la femme*, Dr Noël Lamare (1965) defined frigidity as a "defect of heterosexual drive" and saw the excessive attachment to one parent as a common factor determining both frigidity and female homosexuality. In his book *Female Homosexuality*, one of the works

most widely distributed on lesbianism during this period, Frank Caprio (1954) described prostitution as a form of repressed female homosexuality.

9 Henri Bourassa was a Quebec and Canadian politician as well as the founding publisher of *Le Devoir*, Quebec's intellectual and early nationalist newspaper.

10 Dr Michel Dansereau is a psychiatrist and author of works on psychoanalysis and religion.

11 The quotation is worth citing in full: "We cannot overstate, however, the subtle corruption to which the author's thesis leads. A careful scan of the titles of the chapters that deal with a woman's formative years are exemplary in this regard: Childhood, The Girl, Sexual Initiation, The Lesbian. How appropriate that all development seems to culminate, as if naturally, in inversion. Moreover, in the latter chapter, as in that of The Girl, which are the most engaging in the two volumes, the author forgets her objectivity somewhat and we sense a welling up of sympathy for her subject. Madame de Beauvoir is overtaken by a rebellion that risks engulfing her own nature while showing itself to be so unnatural" (Dansereau, 1957:66–67).

12 See especially Chapter 11, "Voix et images de lesbiennes: la formation d'un réseau de médias", by Dominique Bourque (pp. 291–311) and Chapter 12, "Le projet Gilford: mémoires vives d'une pratique artistique et politique", by Suzanne Boisvert and Danielle Boutet (pp. 313–336).

13 Adrienne Rich's "Compulsory Heterosexuality and Lesbian Existence", originally published in 1980 and published in French in 1981, is without a doubt the most well-known illustration of this first current (Rich, 1981). For its part, the radical lesbian current in Quebec emphasised the political and ideological unity of the lesbian movement. Stein (1992) interprets the development of the separatist stream in the United States as a narrowing and hardening of the boundaries around the category 'lesbian' in order to establish common norms. According to Stein, who interprets the lesbian movement as an identity affirmation movement, these tensions were inevitable due to the enlargement of the lesbian category following its diversification given that the production of community spaces could not have been achieved without fixed norms and the sharing of a specific lifestyle.

14 Language barriers and a greater adherence to French materialist feminism meant that Quebec's feminist and lesbian movements were less impacted by many of the issues facing their American counterparts such as the debates surrounding "Sex Wars".

15 For example, Montreal's gay, lesbian and feminist bookstore, L'Androgyne, as well as Vancouver's Little Sister's bookstores, saw their orders seized or held back by Canadian Customs on more than one occasion.

16 Founded in 1993, Divers/Cité was Montreal's primary gay pride
    organisation until 2007 when Fierté Montréal took over organising the
    city's gay pride parade. The organisation was finally disbanded in 2015.
17 In French, the terms 'mixte' and 'non-mixte' refer to whether an event,
    space or organisation includes both men and women. They have
    been translated here as 'mixed' (in terms of gender) and 'non-mixed'
    (women-only).
18 Originally written in 2002, this text precedes major landmark decisions
    regarding same-sex partnerships. At the time, the state recognised
    common-law same-sex partners and, in 2002, Quebec's National
    Assembly adopted an act recognising civil unions for both same and
    opposite sex partnerships. It was not until 2005 that the Canadian
    Marriage Act was amended to make it legal for same-sex couples to
    marry throughout Canada.

ELEVEN | Navel gazing: of hating men, loving women and fighting back in our time

Nitya V, in conversation with Nadika Nadja and Poorva Rajaram

> Love of Woman for Woman should increase Terror. I see that
> so far it does not. All is not as it should be! (Dame Musset,
> "March", in Barnes, 1992)

You often hear it said that if you stare at something long enough, it disappears. The boundaries around it dissolve, its text becomes grainy, unfocused and meaningless, the hardness and present-ness of it vanishes and you are left with yourself, your altered vision, your uncertainty.

How do we then stare at something that is said to have already disappeared or be rapidly disappearing? How do we reconcile the state of outer disappearance with an inner presence that informs action, thought and understanding?

What this paper demands is nothing less than an encompassing of all the galaxies that comprise a life – desire and law, time and space, self and otherness, appearing and disappearing, person-hood and politics. When I began thinking about what I wanted to say here, several phrases came rushing at me: melancholia, loneliness, suicide, loss, the death of the lesbian, the feminist life, Westernness, lost histories, *savarna* feminism,[1] sexual poli-tics, standpoints ... This chapter has been an effort in thinking through what has until now been largely felt, intuited, sensed, acted on, avoided, missed. An attempt to do justice to the multiple ways of narrating history, the complexities of political subjectivity, and to lives that are being lived in the everyday. And to discuss a term which has no traction in 'my' context. 'Lesbian feminism' in India has not taken shape in ways that parallel trajectories in North American and Western European countries in the 1970s and 1980s, though there are people, processes, feelings, ways of being and historical moments that *could* populate this term in the Indian context.

How do the two words in this coinage relate to each other? Is it a grammatical relationship, with lesbian being the adjective to feminism as a noun? This would imply that 'lesbian' is what describes a certain standpoint within, or inflection of, feminism. Or is it feminism understood as the older woman lending knowledge and practice to the younger, rendering the younger *political*, drawing what exists as a sexual practice within the boundaries of justice and transformation? Or is lesbian feminism here, as elsewhere, connotative of a historical period when, as has been narrated by several women who belonged to the early days of LGBT activism in the Indian context, the women's movement was asked to acknowledge the presence and politics of the lesbian as a challenge to the "compulsory heterosexuality" (Rich, 1980) that the movement reproduced? 'Lesbian feminism' can be read as a state of being, a historical moment, an analytical locus, a political space, a moral centre or, as we will later see, an umbrella.

What does this term (in all its Englishness) mean to us today? While earlier the term 'lesbian' felt English, with all of what that implies, today it feels outdated, and I need to understand why that is. The question of what these terms (gay, lesbian, bisexual, transgender) did and are doing to our lives, what kind of congealing has taken place around them and how they affect our ability to understand our own experiences and those of others, continues to loom large over our heads. The historical moment in which the placard "Lesbian & Indian" was held up following the protests against Deepa Mehta's film *Fire* (1996); the "timely" shot of TV news blaring the headline "Supreme Court makes homosexuality a crime again" (Mahapatra, 2013);[2] the era in which the *hijra* chooses to rename herself a trans woman – all of these moves carry the burden of Englishness, as does the sex education we are attempting to provide young learners in our education spaces. The lines between existing categories (lesbian, gay, transgender, sexual/not sexual) are gaining a clarity that buries different histories and endangers our grasp of our own experiences and actions.

How then do 'we' occupy the term lesbian feminism, want to use it, want it to inform social and political domains of life? In the age of new categories such as gender fluidity, gender-queerness, gender non-conformism or trans feminism, does lesbian feminism carry any lingering promise, either as a way of reaching back to past lives or reaching forward to the yet unlived? To answer these questions, I had conversations with two women who are friends of mine: one who identifies as a lesbian woman and the other who identifies as an intersex lesbian trans woman.[3] The rationale of these conversations was to open up the idea and practice of lesbian feminism and what it means to those who have a "lesbian existence", to borrow the second term from Adrienne Rich (1980). It is no coincidence that both these women and myself all belong to a dominant caste, a fact I will address later in the essay. The conversations arrived at the term 'lesbian feminism' from different angles: as rooted in the psyche, as a political position we take in the world every day, as what has remained unnamed, as a term of self-identification, and as a personal-political history. Before offering what came out of these lovely and tentative conversations, I want to begin here with what I myself have been troubled by for these last few years as someone who identifies as both lesbian and feminist, but who has never really called herself a 'lesbian feminist' in academic, personal or political spaces.

- The death of the lesbian.[4] How do we reconcile the symbolic death of the lesbian with the real deaths of lesbians (the suicides that we have been hearing of for many years[5]) within the same analytical frame?[6] And does the lesbian only speak through death and erasure?

- The political lesbian. What does it mean to be lesbian *politically* and how does this affect our everyday experiences of love, loss, sociality, recognition? Is the political lesbian separable from the 'just' lesbian in our context?

- The place of lesbian feminism. Why haven't 'we' been able to build lesbian feminism into a sustained ground of critique? How have we moved from feminism to queer and trans feminism with no continuing articulation of a lesbian feminist politics, a separate space for a lesbian standpoint that does not collapse into the 'larger' and more international demands for LGBT rights?

- Lesbian vs trans. Why, in this day and age, is there a growing tension between those who see themselves as trans activists and those who see themselves as queer feminists (who had identified as lesbian in the past), i.e. between trans politics and feminist politics? Why and how does the emerging trans discourse claim affinity with Dalit movements in the face of the '*savarna* lesbian'?[7] If lesbian feminism had been able to build a movement across class and caste and language barriers, would the history of the LGBT movement have been different?

- The derivative discourse. Are all of the above questions heavily determined by radical lesbian feminist histories and terms that belong to North America of the 1970s? Do we need to return to ground zero for an understanding of what the history of the 'lesbian' has been in India, and of the relationship between this figure and feminism? This is not to repeat an old charge that both 'lesbian' and 'feminism' are 'Western'; it is rather to halt the assumption that we can discuss lesbian feminism easily in India, that there is such a thing as the disappearing lesbian here, that the claim to 'lesbian' experience has been similar here.[8] Perhaps we need to find "alternative frames of reference" (to use a phrase deployed by Tejaswini Niranjana (2006:13) in her comparative research on India and the Caribbean) to even begin this conversation about lesbian feminism in India. Are easily borrowed languages and terms making practices vanish as loci of critique?

All of these questions were carried into the two conversations that were held.[9] The choice of interlocutors was governed by the following factors: both are my friends, both identify as lesbian (whether or not they do so publicly and often), both identify as feminist, both are political actors in their own right, their histories of entry into being lesbian and feminist are different, and one of them being trans-identified while the other is not dismantles entirely the notion that lesbian feminism (whatever I will make that out to be) is wholly biologically determined.[10] In a way, writing this chapter has been an exercise in having these two women *speak to each other through me.* Looking back on the ways in which the conversations have been woven together, it was clear that while there is divergence in how both of them approach the question of lesbian life, feminism, language, belonging, death, identity, I chose to pull them together, to the extent that I felt I was almost forcing them to agree or feed each other's narratives. In retrospect, this was not a facetious attempt at bridging a perceived divide between trans woman and cis, trans lesbian and cis lesbian. For one, this pulling together would not have been possible if there had not already been some commonality of 'consciousness' (we will return to this term shortly). Second, viewing our articulations as tangentially crossing, glancing off or burrowing into ideas of feminism and lesbian life, and lying alongside one another occasionally, offered a richer way of presenting discussions that were already rich to begin with. There was no easy understanding of 'difference' possible here. I myself felt pulled into, and othered by, their narratives at various points, and our bodies, histories and current academic and personal trajectories all pushed the conversations in directions that did not allow for a vis-à-vis, an offence, a defence, all of which populate our social media universe to alarming degrees. While pulling their articulations together seemed at times 'convenient', it also seemed to be the only way of remaining true to this investigation into lesbian feminism.

As mentioned earlier, all three of us belong to a dominant caste. The fact that both my interlocutors and myself come from backgrounds of class and caste privilege did not involve a deliberate choice, but given both the social boundaries of my own circle of acquaintances and the corresponding history of lesbian activism being largely spearheaded by women from dominant caste and class backgrounds, it would be very difficult (though not impossible), even in research that seeks to be comprehensive (which this one does not) to find an equal number of working-class and Dalit women who are in the field of lesbian activism *as we know it*.[11] The difference between gay and lesbian activism and transgender and sex worker activism has always been marked by class and caste. Therefore, both interlocutors also address their own privilege and how it is related to their inhabitation of the term 'lesbian feminism'.

Habitation: the lesbian, the feminist and the lesbian feminist

Drink with me this bottle
And with the last drop we will go away
I want to see what your oblivion means,
Please don't cover my eyes with your hands
I'm not going to beg you tonight

("El Ultimo Trago" – Chavela Vargas[12])

Me: What does this term 'lesbian feminist' capture and not capture if you think of it from your own position?

P: It's feeling much more right now for me than earlier.

Me: Why is that?

P: In the Weinstein moment, the only people with umbrellas who are not getting the rain on them are lesbian feminists, theoretically speaking (laughs).

(Exchange with Poorva Rajaram, 2018)

We begin here with the question of how we inhabit the terms lesbian, feminist and lesbian feminist, to understand how real or not these terms are in our daily lives, when they are occupied, whether we cling to them, whether they are forced on us and whether they are superseded by each other.

It is inconceivable for me, given the ways in which I started loving women, to separate out the lesbian in me from the feminist, in fact to even try to analyse the bringing together of them. It is inconceivable because of the bodily, psychic, material, symbolic ways in which they curl around each other. In a 1980 interview with Karla Hammond, Audre Lorde said, "The true feminist deals out of a lesbian consciousness whether or not she ever sleeps with women" (Lorde and Hammond, *American Poetry Review*, 1980). Here lesbian *consciousness* becomes the mark of a true feminist and I am forced to ask: is the reverse also true? That the true lesbian deals out of a feminist consciousness? That feminist consciousness can become the measure of being truly lesbian?

Consciousness here is not identity, it is a knowledge at the edge of our minds, it is instinct and feeling, sight and gesture. Lesbian feminism has been this: consciousness more than articulation or declaration or identity. I admit here that it is this for me, maybe not for others who were part of the initial movement building around lesbian identity within the women's movement in India.

In the dialogue we had, Poorva Rajaram historicises this question and argues that it is perhaps easier for a younger generation of feminists to not conceive of these terms separately:

> In spite of where I am now and the fact that I'm part of women's groups now, I hadn't thickly spent time in the women's movement. I maybe read about it and was on an e-list but I didn't have that level of social interface and proximity as I do now, so I think when you don't have that it's easier to imagine those two words together in some abstraction, whereas actually being a more card-carrying member of the feminist movement will bring up this issue and I see it in the previous generation of lesbian feminists.

She concedes that they "needed those spaces where 'lesbian' could take precedence, and obviously I could deal with those women's movement spaces because my personal life had enough recognition of this form of life".

While acknowledging this tension between the two terms that an older generation of feminists experienced, she simultaneously marks out the Indian context as different from the West in that the telescoped nature of lesbian activism here also made/makes it impossible for these two terms to live fully independently of each other:

> I think what is clear in the Indian context, simply because we don't have that thick history, is that lesbian is feminist, whereas in the US there's been enough of a movement for one strand to move towards the 'mainstream', who say 'we are just like you, we live in picket fences', who may not even be birthed in feminist spaces. At least as far as I could tell ten years ago – maybe I was in spaces that had to umbilically detach themselves from feminism – but they were definitely feminist spaces, in fact precisely because of their arguments with feminism that showed how bound up with it they were. And I think that was an important moment for me, to meet those spaces, which

were disparate. I don't think that separation is as possible here as it is in the West, the lesbian feminist separation, our spaces are too narrow and too indebted to current feminist NGOs, current feminist civil society, current feminist vocabulary.

When asked how she related to the term lesbian feminist in her own life, whether she described herself this way, whether she deployed the term in political spaces or in writing, she drew a connection to the idea of political subjectivity and the ethical weight carried by those who use these terms in self-description:

I actually feel like I can only describe my relationship with this term as a lack, especially now when I am feeling and have been feeling for a few years – and there's no distinction between academic personal and to some extent what I will publicly self-identify – that separatist streak. That's how I would go back and read me and my friends, the relationship with identity and identification ... so much so that we didn't have to identify, and that it was fun to manipulate different contexts and it was also fun to imagine yourself as more than these identities but I'm actually thinking it came from fear, it came from a sense that the minute you commit yourself to this the rigour of a lived politics goes up.

Me: But in saying that you avoided self-identifying, you gave it a certain weight ...

P: Ya it's the thing I was, it's the purloined letter!

My other interlocutor, Nadika Nadja, approached the question of feminism through her recollection of how she came to terms with her gender identity as a woman.

I started using and started believing this idea of feminism much after I even began transitioning, it was there but it sort of became a bigger thing, started directing a lot of my later politics because it gave me a framework of understanding why my gender identity becomes a problem for people, be it my family or my boss and work colleagues or people on the street. And that critical look at the system of patriarchy and why there's a premium placed on womanhood and a lot of slack given to being a man but that same slack is not given to expressions of femininity in a certain way.

Feminism seemed to offer her a way of explaining how gender operated in the world and therefore the difficulties and confusion she was facing as an intersex lesbian trans woman. This confusion also came from desiring women, something that steps outside the conventional boundaries of the trans woman's narrative, which restricts itself to the story of the trans woman who loves men.

So initially when I started coming out or when I was going through this whole question of gender this was a question I was trying to fight – is my attraction to a woman determining my gender or not, and therefore am I not trans enough or not woman enough? If I'm not trans then what are the other things that are going on, but if I am trans then why am I doing this? I didn't find that many expressions of this doubt in a lot of Indian trans women that I have met. The question of attraction – is attraction gender and gender attraction, it comes from a very specifically trans perspective of 'I know and I am ok with whatever identity I have now, but am I being seen as that identity when I am seen as a lesbian and I have a girlfriend'?

This inner conflict between the body-gender you identify with and the gender you're attracted to (but which is also the sexual partner that your assigned gender would have been allowed) is revealing in that it throws up the question of how a lesbian identity emerges and the entry points we use to understand this figure. For Nadika, the lesbian relationship and lesbian self-hood offer a space in which she does not have to 'perform' her gender in prescribed ways (this taking us back to the idea of feminist consciousness):

Much less should I use the word oppressive – for me at least –
the lesbian framework for a relationship seems to be much
more accepting of who I am because if it were not then I would
probably have to pay a higher price in terms of presentability
and what kind of femininity I can occupy. That I do not need to
conform to a certain idea of femininity, either in a relationship or
not, I don't have to perform a certain kind of femininity in order to
be seen as woman. I can express that in different ways – a lot more
fluidity and a lot more ability to find that fluidity, it's not even that
I need to show that fluidity, that room for doing that is there.

Yet, Nadika describes herself more as a trans feminist than a lesbian
feminist (and clearly the term 'lesbian trans feminist' does not exist!).

'Lesbian feminist' is not particularly a term that I would use or talk
about for myself but the idea of sexuality and a sexual orientation
and a desire that is not influenced or not hetero-centred is
something that I'm trying to talk about a lot more. Especially the
assumption that trans women are automatically assumed to be
attracted to men which is a sort of position that I am trying to
[counter] which therefore means that a lesbian-centred feminism
is part of my thing but not something I'm actively using as a term.

She is able to speak/act as a lesbian to distance herself from the
heterosexuality that she sees as taken for granted even within
trans movements in the country, where an encouragement of her
gender transition simultaneously potentially fixes her within the
ambit of a heterosexual relationship.

For Poorva, identifying as lesbian has, as she put it, "been primary" to her feminist self.

It does influence, it is hard to be around women who identify
with men so much, it just is. In other words all these transactions
within the women's movement come from a position of strategy
because of that, because of a fear of being burnt, because of fear
that overinvestment will lead to some sort of psychic betrayal.

The lesbian selfhood of both women enables a distancing from both an automatic assignation of sexual partners or a forced participation in the heterosocial domain, and it offers them a standpoint from which to examine these phenomena and to inhabit feminism.

In recent years there has been an intensification of the polarisation between trans women and lesbian women in contexts like the US and the UK, a trend that has not left us untouched here in India. Feminists who are now referred to as TERFs (trans-exclusionary radical feminists) have been arguing for quite some time that trans women are born and have experienced 'male privilege' in this world and therefore cannot be granted the same place within feminism as 'real' women have.[13] In the Indian context, though, this opposition has not been transplanted in quite the same way because of the *hijra*[14] having existed as a certain kind of figure historically and socially, complicating any evolutionary narrative of sexual politics. But there has been (a) the lack of attention given to questions of *hijras*' and trans persons' gender identity rights, housing, employment, education, medical care and so on within the women's movement, and the consequent ghettoisation of trans issues within the LGBT organisations; and (b) within lesbian groups themselves, unease around the figure of the trans man or trans woman, *an unease strongly related to class and caste biases that are not visible on the surface.*

I feel the real danger here, in this moment, is a false opposition being set up between transgender and lesbian 'consciousness' (if not people or groups). And this false opposition might very well be informed by the history of this conflict in the West and the re-emergence of anti-trans lesbianism there today. One can understand the conditions that created this opposition in several ways: (a) that with the 'new' language of trans rights came something that no longer located itself within the 'LGBT' spectrum entirely or comfortably, as just another alphabet, with trans activists no longer willing to be represented by those they saw as *not of them*, seeking self-representation instead of being spoken for by gay and lesbian activists; (b) that the operation of class and caste difference is finally being *made apparent* within LGBT activism, and the consignment of working-class trans people to the roles of 'animator' or 'peer educator' within the NGO discourse (as different from gay and lesbian activists, who were/are directors, researchers, lawyers, programme supervisors, funder liaisons) is now being actively rejected; (c) that just as with lesbian and gay rights we inherited the assumptions created by a "discourse of globality" (Mani, 2008:42) – namely that 'gay' and 'lesbian' are coherent identities – with the language of trans rights another set of assumptions has come into play, with the trans–cis binary helping the above opposition take shape; (d) that the splitting of 'gender' from 'sexuality' (when they were united in Kate Millett's (1969) term "sexual politics") has led to our separating out trans/lesbian/feminist politics from each other as ways of describing the world.

Both of my interlocutors were asked if they would like to respond to the battles between trans activists and those who are seen as resurgent radical feminists in locations such as North America and the UK. Poorva spoke about how she had recently felt the need to return to 1970s lesbian feminist texts to deal with what is happening now; "I think we are at a moment of greater recognition that we need the pre-Butler era of feminism". When asked what has led to this recognition, she explained:

> We have lived through two decades of seminars all over the world on whether women can be the subject of feminist politics, which actually implicitly in that framework is a taunt and a push towards saying women are not the subject of feminist politics. Then, I'm sorry, who is? Fifty per cent of the world, give or take a few people in Haryana. So I think it's exhaustion with that moment, with that leading male question.

Her two statements might be referring to both the shift from a 'feminist' politics to a 'gender' politics, and the arrival of queer theory and the discourse of 'queerness' that has put into question the fact of women being at the centre of this politics.

> Just because we imagine drag would save us for three years in the early '90s doesn't mean that biology went anywhere and science and the pharma industry aren't actually controlling us, so I think there is more recognition of these things. This would be the American feminists, I don't think we have the same, but maybe to some extent also, like this fear of the medical ... I think that's why the trans question has been so good for feminism, hopefully, which is that implicit fear of medicine, pharma industries testing on Third World women ... Trans had the HIV question, right? We really have to change that relationship with science, we can't be anti-science, anti-science is like a leftover legacy of anti-Nehruvianism[15] and this moment calls for something else.

It is clear here that Poorva is not taking the position of a return to a biologically female lesbian body but is instead cautioning against the erasure of a *feminist* critique of economic and social conditions by the current discourse of identity.

When asked whether she thinks that queer theory as a field that emerged elsewhere erased the possibility of a lesbian feminist discourse emerging here in India in the period of the 1990s, she replied,

> I think it's faster here not because we never had a hold in the first place. If at the height of the possibility of the lesbian we were so few, then what would we be now that queer has taken over? I really think given my biography, given that I was a tomboy or called that, and basically looked like a boy, ten years later I might be calling myself queer or trans, I don't know. But then the interesting thing is that, and I also understand why we did it, identify politically [as lesbian] – this is keeping in mind that all said and done, whether it was historic misfiring at a kind

of humanist level where the concept of sexual orientation is
misfiring, we're[16] still more drawn to it than other things, and
specifically us, we're drawn to the lesbian one not the queer.
I think the better form of queer has been a backlash against this
idea, against the linearity of certain forms of sexual orientation,
but I think when one is faced with the choice of two we've picked
our path with all its troubles.

In an essay titled "Separating Lesbian Theory from Feminist
Theory", Cheshire Calhoun argues that

> separating sexuality politics from gender politics is exactly
> what must happen if there is to be a specifically *lesbian* feminist
> theory rather than simply feminist theory applied to lesbians
> ... A lesbian feminist theory would need, among other things,
> to focus on what is distinctive about the lesbian's relation to
> heterosexuality, to the category 'woman', and to other women.
> (Calhoun 1994:562)

What she means here is that lesbian experience cannot become
absorbed into existing descriptions of patriarchy and (heterosexual) feminism, and a lesbian feminist theory needs to
emerge in a way that is capable of separately addressing patriarchy and heterosexuality. Calhoun rejects the equation of
"lesbian escape from heterosexuality with women's escape
from male control" (1994:564). This is precisely the kind of
dangerous splitting off of gender from sexual practice, feminist
from lesbian, trans from lesbian, trans feminist from lesbian
feminist, that queer theory has enabled and that we need to
avoid deploying in this context. This is not to say that *difference* does not operate and has not operated, or that the ground
of feminism cannot be shaken. Perhaps Calhoun's attempt
here is to invest the term 'lesbian' with an ability to critique
that *parallels* 'feminist', to render it more than just a description of a sexual identity/'preference'. But any lesbian critique of

heterosexual relations is always already feminist in its premise, even if it departs from all existing feminist scholarship. The breaking apart of 'gender' and 'sexuality', as if they existed as separate domains of experience and action, is a historical mistake that needs to be corrected *after* acknowledging the several other mistakes we have made in the course of developing or borrowing languages to describe ourselves.

In speaking back to the new radical anti-trans position, Nadika arrives at this exact point, namely that lesbian theory is always already feminist:

> Your gender is not your genitals ... 'To be a true lesbian you
> need to have bled once a month' and all these things – it's
> very patriarchal, it's limiting experiences to bodies, which is
> what early, not even early, much later feminism is trying to
> break out of. At least in California and other places trans men
> are seen as women who've escaped patriarchy and have been
> successful in that (here also if you look at the trans men in our
> community). So, the thing is that then this person[17] is again
> reducing experiences to anatomy, which is, first, biologically
> false – biology does not have x or y, it's not neat boxes, it's a very
> messed up broken box with leaks everywhere. Second, that can't
> be a political stance, because it's politics of division and politics
> of hate which is again something that feminism questioned at
> various points, how can you then go back and claim that as
> feminism and as a feminist stance?

She picks on the exact idea that Calhoun has problems with, except through the example of the trans man, not the lesbian – that trans men are seen as having escaped patriarchy. This is true of the narratives of many trans men in India who were forcibly married off, even had children, before they literally 'escaped', ran away to shelters and places of refuge, leaving their families behind and later trying to re-establish relationships with their children.

When Nadika says experiences cannot be reduced to bodies, I read this not as meaning that experience is now detached from the body, but that the same feminist argument against biology determining a woman's experience of the world now can be rephrased to "biology does not determine being a woman". The facts of biology, although they are "leaky", still exist and need to be accounted for, and the trans and intersex person's experience of biology, the effect of medicines, the neglect faced within the health care system, the determination of sex, all still call for attention, as do sex selection, maternal mortality, forced hysterectomies, malnutrition and other issues. Nadika also acknowledges that in the context of India, where the battle against gender-biased sex selection is still raging and sex ratios are still skewed, making a demand such as "You should not record sex at birth" (as the intersex community elsewhere has done) is impossible, one can only say that if a child has intersex variations, the sex should not be recorded at birth and even this is difficult since both the means of identifying complex variations and the understanding that can make this happen do not exist in a large part of the country.

In light of these returns to what lesbian, trans, intersex, feminist truly mean – loci of critique, realms of experience, modes of interrogation – it becomes clear that we cannot dilute these terms or reduce them to just 'who we are', however much this assertion of a self is required. The work that these terms are doing, need to do, need to stop doing, could further do, takes us back to the question that this essay started out with – what is it that a term like 'lesbian feminism' gives us?

The question of the margin: identity and privilege

Poorva pushes the question from lesbian feminism onto the broader terrain of what identity politics is doing and has done, the effect of which is becoming recognisable in this moment in time.

> There is something wrong, something about certain forms of
> identity politics that have not lived up to their promise,
> so there is a critique, something in the air ... a critique of
> identity and how it is to be lived more generally, lesbian
> feminism in some ways is, I think, too narrow a discursive
> range here.

She says this while recognising that the figure of the lesbian, in our present time and in her academic and social circles, takes on a certain ethical and moral aura.

> It was a new moment for me also, watching people's reactions,
> I said, 'Oh, it connotes something to them' ... the
> incorruptibility of the lesbian, the integrity of lesbian, the
> basketball teams that stick with each other whatever it is,
> they have some of this imagination, in very leftover
> forms and in this moment it is attractive to them and my
> life is attractive to them, which is hard for me to say,
> but it is.

What she is referring to here as attractive is what she calls a certain "distance from normative political subjectivities", and it is this distance that she then focuses on to discuss what the problem with the idea of marginalised identities is. The recent history of social movements in India has seen them being pitted against each other and this is true of feminist and Dalit movements, LGBT and feminist movements, trans and feminist movements, sex worker and Dalit movements. While this complex history cannot be wished away, recognising that part of the problem lies in how we occupy the terrain of identity politics is a start in thinking through why these oppositions came to be. Poorva refers to the discussions that have been taking place around the sexual harassment list and #metoo in her women's hostel and gives us an instance of commonality that can offer an alternative way of framing the question of the margin.

We had this unfortunate history of some feminist groups taking completely different positions from Dalit feminists,[18] which has actually made that antagonistic. Even for me, personally going by just my hostel or whatever, it is more ripe for those kinds of political alliances, not just friendships – friendships may or may not have happened depending on the person – but forms of actual similar lived politics, that's why I'm happy all said and done that I engaged in this process,[19] of talking to different people at this moment, because it really felt like *who else doesn't feel at the heart of hetero academia?* [emphasis added] It is also the non-*savarna* woman, and there's something we have to say to each other, and it's very hard, you have to have that conversation around two things. One is a history of distrust, which is normal given that I am *savarna*, but the more complicated 2017 one is that you have to have that conversation around naïve social media ideas of alliances, you have to really bring words like 'in solidarity with' or 'retweeting' or whatever passes for solidarity in social media to a kind of lived terrain, so it is difficult, because that hangs in the air, it's not cut off from how young people are living.

In saying this she makes a shift *from an emphasis on an identity (lesbian or Dalit) as marginalised to seeing what stands outside of dominant caste heterosexuality, a lived terrain of politics*, implying that this terrain is where people who occupy these identities work, live, are kept out, are unable to belong, are ashamed or scared, are affected physically and mentally.

What has happened with the marginalised identities thing is that – it's not a politically correct thing to say but – it's a free for all, so how do we take this question … so of course in that sense we are people who believe in standpoint, standpoint not as something inherently authentic to someone but basically literally standpoint, what are you in the social structure, what is your relationship to these things, to turn that into something productive, to imagine something within the space of feminism, not just in the abstract, not just politically aligning … I guess it's the difference between saying I'm an 'X' and I'm an outsider.

This last statement refers to the fact that within this frame you are looking at the thing that is affecting you, the nexus of caste and heterosexuality and how it operates to position you in certain ways, not at yourself and what identity you belong to vis-à-vis someone else. At the same time Poorva does acknowledge that self-identification or social identification do not work the same way with everyone, that caste is thrust on you as an identification whereas the same does not happen when it comes to identifying as lesbian or gay, and that the two forms of identification are treated very differently in the world of academia in the Indian context.

While Poorva offers this shift from marginalised identity to speaking as outsider, Nadika offers the idea of crisis as the point at which languages of identification and self-description can change. When asked where she would begin to think through the morass of identity, she says, "Just talk of personal crises maybe, of experiential personal things, and see how many people it can find some kind of resonance in, I guess that's where to start from". I was intrigued by why she chose the crisis as the possible starting point of analysis. Crises have been seen as exceptional states, and 'crisis intervention' is a term that has become submerged in the NGO language of rescue and rehabilitation, so why would she return to it now? "Because questioning one's own anything does not happen without a jolt to the status quo, especially if you're in India and have some kind of privilege, either caste, class or gender privilege, these are not things you're going to ever question." It was staring hard at her own moments of crisis that allowed her to link the seemingly separate aspects of her life, her caste and her chosen gender.

> That is also one of the things I have questioned about myself, if I didn't have a Brahmin middle-class upbringing would I have come to terms with my gender much earlier? Because why did it take so long, was I afraid to lose that privilege, of being a Brahmin boy and a Brahmin man, especially in

Madras society? Or would it have been easier, would my
parents have been much more accepting and open were they
not themselves Brahmin?[20] Which is also one
point of understanding how you work with your
own privilege.

Her definition of crisis is "a jolt to a trajectory or narrative that
has been set for me by my birth and my privilege. Even if I had
been trans I would not have questioned or adopted a critical
understanding of gender but for other crises, even within the
trans movement, so I think that jolt is a personal crisis". Privilege
is then something that you 'work with', something that becomes
apparent in your analysis of personal crises, not a stable set of
characteristics that make you the same as some and different from
others. According to Nadika, it is through close reading of these
moments of crisis, of whether other people find resonance in
them, that we can begin again to describe the nature of our bodies, minds, practices, desire and so on, without getting trapped in
languages that impose coherent and fully delivered identities and
damage our ways of relating to the world.

Both women offer alternative frames through which to begin,
frames which might be partial, but they are consciously trying to
avoid the traps laid by the English-ness of identity politics. The
conversation with Nadika included a small discussion on what it
would mean if we abandoned English altogether in our descriptions. She tried to think of the word for 'lesbian' in Tamizh, and
realised that whatever words do exist are inventions necessi-
tated by the desire to disseminate the English terms that claim to
describe us. I pointed out that the term used in Kannada, 'samlaingikathe', is a translation of homosexuality and already carries the burden of that term. "Exactly, there's 'orinacherkai' [in
Tamizh], but like 'lesbian' expresses both attraction and gender
in that, that term doesn't exist in Tamil or Kannada. You have the
larger conceptual translation." ('Orinacherkai' roughly translates

as the bringing together of the same.) Here she refers to the fact that the term *orinacherkai* (like *samlaingikathe*) is a translation of the larger idea of homosexuality rather than a reference to specific identities (gay, lesbian, bisexual, etc.) If we were to extend this thought, we would go into an examination of how these terms came to us already shaped by modernity's idea of the self and of personhood,[21] and how we continue to carry this idea of what a person is.

Back to the future of lesbian feminism

After navigating the ways in which we are lesbian/feminist/ lesbian feminist, the inhabiting of terms and the possible ways of retooling identity politics, we return now to lesbian feminism, with two questions. Is lesbian feminism a useful term for our pres-ent moment and do we seek to bring it to social life in a way in which it has not lived so far? And, second, do we want the con-sciousness that lesbian feminism invokes to make itself felt more within current political scenarios in India? Nadika says that,

> I definitely want the concept if not the term to take shape. Terms I'm a little [apprehensive about] because what's happening is we're only starting now to talk about trans men and intersex people, so far trans means *aravani* means *hijra* / trans woman, but at the same time now groups are being pushed into a SOGIE [22] framework, again for funding reasons and other reasons. Politically I think SOGIE is a more intuitive thing to take up than LGBTQI, or even trans versus non trans/cis … Where even in India people have not taken up transgender that well, they're taking it up because it's an easy term to take up, but criticising that term and seeing how it's an umbrella term but how many ways it can apply, people are not using it. So at this point of time I don't know if a term taking root will cause more problems or not or what kind of issues it might [lead to] – will there be criticism of that? Which is the easiest criticism that this is Western, this is not culture, this is not India, this is not tradition.

What Nadika refers to here is the aforementioned shift in the last decade to self-identifying as 'transgender' and how this shift is taking place without questions being put to the self-description you choose. Many young *hijras* now call themselves trans women and while this can be explained through the idea that they think it is a term that offers more dignity and also sheds the connotations of the person being embedded in cultural ideas of auspiciousness, or in networks of begging and sex work, there is still the question of what else this shift means in the context of the international human rights discourse trying to establish a standard for trans rights, and funding being pumped into this area.[23]

While Nadika describes a world in which trans discourse is mushrooming and mutating in various ways, Poorva addresses the world in which the lesbian is said to be disappearing or dying, the cryogenetic state of it, so to speak. Though this idea exists largely in the West, many of 'us' (English-speaking, largely middle- and upper-middle-class lesbians who believe in a lesbian politics) who identify as such in India feel a lack,[24] a lack that makes a lesbian life seem unviable, unliveable, politically either irrelevant or too relevant. So much so that Poorva quips that, "Ten years. Lorde[25] would have turned twenty-five and lesbians would have died out".

For her, the death of the lesbian in the symbolic order is a moment at which we need to 'desacralise death', to use an analogy from the end-of-life-care discourse.

As people watching a death, what can we do? You have to think about death in new ways, that's how we inject life into lesbian feminism ... Process is as important as the actual content of politics, but I think there might be a value in modelling these forms of life however small, like these breakaway things, but I think they will only be seductive models if they speak to the times, with some amount of self-consciousness about all these other things[26] ... As people, how do we make sure it has an element of self-renewal built into it?

Nadika does not choose to speak in terms of death and erasure while Poorva does (and my own dogged pursuing of this question signals that it is a living concern in my own head and experience of the world). This difference could perhaps be explained by the ways in which each of us invests in the category of lesbian feminism and the demands we place before it: to alter personal life, public life and the nature of our relationships with the world. But each of us has moonlighted as lesbian feminist in our own separate ways, which has meant that a certain kind of consciousness *underlies* how we understand heterosexual relations, different forms of sexism, otherness and its deployment in personal and political domains, the value of relationships between women, marriage as an institution and how it affects women, what popular culture does with gender, the continued devaluing of femininity, the danger in revering legal change, the kinds of care that are needed to protect those living a precarious life, and so on.

How do you make an argument about something that is not apparent, has not been given the solidity or authority of history? How do you rescue something from being a lost cause when it has never been acknowledged as a cause? Turning to the idea of the lived terrain of politics and the analytical jolt that is a crisis in a person's life, writing this paper has felt like taking a series of missteps, with doubts plaguing the mind about whether we can use the same language that we are trapped in (like answers to *Jeopardy*[27] questions, namely "What is a lesbian. What is gender and sexuality politics. What is transgender identity") to move away from the corners into which we have painted ourselves. Yet, there has also been the sensation of arriving at calmer depths and moving past the choppiness of social media, the clamouring of 'international' LGBT language, and the nagging feeling of something being not quite right in the world.

What is clear is this – at this moment, after two decades of shifting identity politics and the encroachment of development and right-wing discourse, more than ever we need a return to the experiential narrative, the process, the crisis and the relation. It is here that lesbian feminism can exist.

Notes

1 The term '*savarna* feminism' has emerged in the last decade as a reference to feminist thought and action that has been led and given shape by feminists from dominant caste backgrounds. The term also implies that feminist history, ideological articulation and scholarly focus in this arena of *savarna* feminism have all been constituted by a wilful blindness to the ways in which the caste system operates alongside, and in, gender relations in the Indian society.

2 This is what news headlines read like after the 2013 judgment in which the Supreme Court refused to repeal Section 377 (the law that addresses "criminal intercourse against the order of nature"). On 6 September 2018, a five-judge bench of the Supreme Court read down Section 377, citing "transformative constitutionalism" as their basis.

3 The two conversations took place in January–February 2018.

4 Also the title of a *Huffington Post* article (Anderson, 2015). The article speaks of the shrinking of the lesbian life and community in the US. This whole anthology feels like a response to this notion of the death of the lesbian and, by extension, of lesbian feminism.

5 12 June 2018: Asha Thakor and Bhavna Thakor took their own lives by jumping into the Sabarmati river (Ahmedabad). September 2016: Roshini Tandel and Rujukta Gawand (Mumbai) tried to kill themselves when their parents separated them from each other. Roshini died as a result of this attempt. 16 November 2013: Radha (name changed in the media report) committed suicide because of being separated from her 'friend' Rani (name changed) in Madurai, Tamil Nadu. 24 January 2011: Bobby Saha and Puja Mondal commit suicide in Boral, West Bengal. 22 February 2011: Sucheta and Swapna Mondal consumed poison in Sonachura, Nandigram (West Bengal).

6 Melancholia is an affective state that is often associated with lesbianism. "Acute Melancholy is noticeable in those who have gone a long Way into this Matter." ("April" in Barnes, 1992).

7 Transgender communities have historically belonged to the working classes and Dalit or non-Brahmin castes.

8 The history of lesbianism is tied to the discourse of culture here. Women marrying women in temples, women being brought up as men, women who live as men, women who do not call themselves 'lesbian' in any known sense, relationships that are named and recognised in

languages other than English, attempts that have been made to recover the lesbian within history and mythology, the discourse of female friendship – while many of these might find resonance in Western histories, we cannot assume that India moves in a parallel line or that the 1970s radical feminist and lesbian frameworks of the US and Europe can be easily laid over the specificity of 'Third World-ness', caste, class, language.

9   Both were held in English and I transcribed them myself.

10 This was meant to address what one of the interlocutors called the symptom of the criticism that has been levelled at trans women by those who see themselves as 'real' women, i.e. TERFs (trans-exclusionary radical feminists) in the USA. For more see MacDonald (2017). Less vitriolic pieces lament the disappearance of the lesbian as if she were a mammoth or a condor.

11 Maya Sharma's *Loving Women: Being Lesbian in Underprivileged India* (2006), was the first and only book to examine what it means for women to love women in working-class and non-dominant-caste ways. The book includes narratives that question what I have framed as the problem of language in the Indian context.

12 Translated by Aldefina, 2014. http://lyricstranslate.com/en/el-%C3%BAltimo-trago-last-drop.html#ixzz59koQbAgc. Accessed 10 March 2018.

13 For a short explanation of this conflict, see Jones (2016). The conflict seems to have come to a head in the UK at the London Pride March on 7 July 2018, when a few cis-gender women started sloganeering against trans women during the march (Necati, 2018).

14 In India and regions like Bangladesh and Pakistan, *hijra* is the name given to, and adopted by, women who were born male and decided they wanted to live as women (now called trans women). *Hijras* are part of specific cultural formations, since they live as distinct communities and in separate spaces (i.e. *hamaams*, where they live together as one family with a guru or teacher, and her *chelas*, disciples). These and other community practices of the *hijra* are said to be around 4,000 years old. The *hamaam* system is changing now, with younger *hijras* choosing to stay independent of *hamaams* and refusing the cultural meanings that have been attached to the figure of the *hijra* in the past (that she is auspicious and therefore invited to weddings and births to give her blessings and accept money). Other terms like *thirunangai* are used by *hijras* to self-name, especially in south India.

15 Jawaharlal Nehru (1889–1964), the first Prime Minister of India, is remembered as a strong advocate of the Indian society developing what he called a "scientific temper". He believed that science alone was capable of solving the problems of poverty, illiteracy, the unequal distribution of resources, and superstition. Towards this end he funded, planned and inaugurated institutes of scientific research and

technology centres all over the country. Anti-Nehruvianism refers to the backlash of opinion against Nehru's approach to development, progress and scientific rationality.

16 Here she ropes me in as part of a 'we' that would rather call ourselves lesbian than queer, with all our misgivings and knowledge of where the term trips up. Why this is the case returns us to the heart of this paper and the question whether self-identification as a 'lesbian' feminist is something to hold on to in the proliferation of identities in the twenty-first century. 'Lesbian' here is not anti-trans, it seeks to be a reference to something else, a consciousness that combines loving women with the critique of patriarchy and its various operations.

17 The reference being made here is to the aforementioned Jocelyn MacDonald's (2017) article.

18 Here she refers to the debates on sex work and bar dancing, in which *savarna* and Dalit feminists took a range of positions, but two clear ones were the ones that saw sex work and bar dancing as livelihoods, in which women participated in carving out some degree of autonomy for themselves versus the one that saw these practices as part of caste-based exploitation of Dalit women, and as sexual slavery.

19 What she is referring to here is the discussions around the #metoo campaign and the list of sexual harassers in the Indian academia that was released on social media by Raya Sarkar, a feminist lawyer based in the US.

20 Patriarchy works in a certain way in a Brahmin house and the expectations of a 'first born' Brahmin son are greater.

21 Here I thank Nithin Manayath for the discussion on this term and for introducing me to an older term that seemed to have been used in the contexts of Calcutta and Bangladesh – '*samakami*' (based on '*kama*' as connoting love or erotics), and for his conjecture that this term did something quite different (the *hijra* was also seen as *samakami*) until it also became a translation of homosexuality (the *hijra* then being split off from this homosexual subject and rendered something else). For more on homosexuality and modernity, a return to Michel Foucault's (1978) *History of Sexuality* is always useful.

22 Sexual Orientation and Gender Identity – a phrase that first took shape in the Yogyakarta Principles (2007) and is now the basis on which the UN and other international bodies frame policy and address laws on human rights in relation to gender and sexual practices.

23 All of these questions should be and have been asked, even of the 'earlier' moment of 'sexual minority' rights, so it is not just trans communities who are asked here to scrutinise what they choose as a way of self-description.

24 For example, I am on the organising committee of the Bangalore Queer Film Festival and for two years in a row, in 2016 and 2017, the number of

lesbian films that came in as entries could be counted on the fingers of one hand. This year, in 2018, we saw a sudden surge in the number of films, a fact that we will be able to explain only in the next few years, when we are able to tell whether this was a trend or an exception.

25 Just to make it clear for those as clueless about pop culture as I am, this refers to the New Zealand-born singer Lorde (birth name Ella Marija Lani Yelich-O'Connor).

26 About language, privilege, caste, the history of distancing ourselves from other movements.

27 A 1960s American quiz show, where the question was in the form of an answer and the answer in the form of a question.

TWELVE | Reflections on historic lesbian feminisms in France

Natacha Chetcuti-Osorovitz

> Sex is a fundamental division that burdens all societies to an
> unrecognized degree. Our sociology, in this sense, is very
> inferior to what it could be. We should say to our students,
> especially to those who may one day do field observations, that
> we have only produced a sociology of men and not a sociology of
> women or of both sexes. (Marcel Mauss, 1969[1])

The 1970s and 1980s in France were marked by the refinement
of sociological theories through the development of different
approaches to the concept of 'sex' and its articulation in relation
to the system of sexuality. Divergent perspectives in the analysis
of the relationships between sex/gender/sexuality were developed both from within social movements and lesbian and feminist
theorising. These forms of analysis were concurrent with feminist
and lesbian movements and theories of the period, both in terms
of the collective and individual construction of bodies and the
social organisation of domestic and public space. The primary
objective of such research was to critique the 'naturalisation' of
feminine and masculine roles with a desire to disassociate sexuality from reproduction. Later authors (Hurtig, Kail and Rouch
[1991] 2002; Tahon, 2004; Sullerot, 2006) interrogated the use
of the notion of gender because it relegates sex to a fixed biological realm and reduces it to anatomy, and because gender had the
tendency to neutralise it by masking the relations of power that
govern relations between the sexes.

Work on categories of sex and sexuality, therefore, permitted the investigation into what seemed to reveal the 'natural' order. The use of the term gender and the various theorisations of sex permitted a focus on a whole system that included sex but was not directly determined by nor determining sexuality in its entirety. As Bazin, Mendès-Leite and Quiminal (2000:14) have argued:

> Sexuality appears, to use the expression coined by Mauss, as a total social phenomenon. It is in this sense that it is established as an actual anthropological object. This understanding creates very rich possibilities for revealing and analysing the social, symbolic and imaginary production of all society, not from a cultural perspective that positions it as an immobile whole, but more from the perspective of initiating an understanding of social transformations, tensions and disruptions: indeed, sexuality is always and everywhere understood as a central issue in the most diverse confrontations that operate at the micro and macro scales.

This chapter examines lesbian feminist critiques of this total social phenomenon from the radical and materialist perspectives that developed in France in the 1970s and 1980s. During this period, a variety of lesbian feminist critiques of the institution of heterosexuality permitted the exposure of its instability and illustrated how it might be modified both individually and collectively. Furthermore, the work of critiquing and producing lesbian feminist social theories fuelled a vibrant social movement in France for these two decades. Often described as essentialist and exclusionary, however, the disruptive potential of French lesbian feminist theories and activism is currently underappreciated. Thus, the goal of this chapter is to re-examine the contribution of these movements and the political theory that they generated in order to potentially contribute to contemporary gender and sexuality politics.

The radical lesbian perspective

Within feminist movements in France, radical lesbianism found expression in political lesbian groups formed during the 1970s in relation to the second-wave feminist movement.[2] By 1971, discussion groups on sexuality[3] had appeared such as Les polymorphes perverses or Les gouines rouges. In 1971, the FHAR (Front homosexuel d'action révolutionnaire) was also born out of an initiative of the lesbians within *Arcadie*.[4] Lesbians were participating in the FHAR because they could not find a place for themselves within the MLF (Mouvement de libération de femmes) due to a lack of consideration of the analysis of heterosexuality as social norm. But the publication of Issue 12 of *Tout!* (an extreme left publication where, for the first time, gays and lesbians were given a voice) gave a great deal of publicity to FHAR, and men and their concerns came to dominate the group, provoking the departure of most of the lesbians (Bonnet, 1998).

Lesbian groups such as Les gouines rouges and Front lesbien international simultaneously denounced the "heterosexism" of feminist movements and the misogyny of gay movements, as "the institutional and discursive practices that construct and maintain the hegemony of heterosexuality for the benefit of male domination" (Chetcuti, 2006:286). They were inspired by the 1974 compilation of Ti-Grace Atkinson's essays (written between 1967 and 1972) that were brought together under the title *Amazon Odyssey*, which analysed the institutionalisation of male/female relationships:[5] founded upon an arbitrary classification by sex, it depended on a social structure that impeded the advancement of women. Atkinson advanced the idea of a deinstitutionalised sexuality that would have no social function. Her framework distinguished lesbianism from feminism: "We call 'lesbianism' this voluntary and total engagement of a woman towards other members of her class. It is this absolute engagement, indifferent to all considerations of the individual order that confers political meaning to 'lesbianism'" (Atkinson, 1975:152).

From 1978,[6] political lesbian groups, who described themselves as "radicals" (Les Lesbiennes radicales in Belgium, Les lesbiennes de Jussieu (1979) in Paris, the Front des lesbiennes radicales in France), were inspired by materialist and Wittigian theory and articulated this commitment through political actions and theorising. Due to a lack of resources many texts were circulated in the form of photocopied collections, for example: *Les Lesbianaires* (review publication of the Centre for the Documentation and Research on Radical Lesbianism, 1980–1996); *Espace* (1982–1983); *Chroniques aiguës et graves* (Autumn 1982–January 1984); and the Franco-Quebecois *Amazones d'hier, lesbiennes d'aujourd'hui* (1979–2015).

From this political perspective, homosexuality was understood through social relations between the genders (versus the social relations between the sexes) and was thus inscribed in a strategy of resistance such as that expressed by same-sex couples who refuse to adopt a binary division of gender expression or adopt 'masculine' and 'feminine' roles. This is what Nicole-Claude Mathieu calls *the subversion of gender*.

> Homosexuality is no longer envisioned as an individual accident (Mode I), nor as something marginal that is as foundational for identity as the norm, and is hence to be reclaimed as the right to exist and the right to have a group culture (Mode II), but rather as a political position (conscious or unconscious) in the struggle against the heterosexual and heterosocial gender that underlies the definition of women and their oppression. (Mathieu, [1989] 1991:260)

The debates at the heart of these political movements regarding the status given to heterosexuality marked a decisive turn in the relationship between lesbianism and feminism.[7] Indeed, they made it possible to conceptualise what the activists practised and thought throughout the 1970s, but they also called into question feminist and sociological approaches to the analysis of the relationships between sex/gender and sexuality. "Thus, lesbianism, abandoned for strategic reasons in the 1970s, started to be thought of in political terms at the beginning of the 1980s" (Turcotte, 2003:36). Louise Turcotte highlights this point when she states that "all feminist struggles were established from the 'point of view of women'. Feminists had actually fought against the patriarchy as a system based on the domination of women by men, but they had never interrogated 'men' and 'women' as classes" (Turcotte, 1998:373). According to Monique Wittig's analysis, politicised lesbianism calls for "the universalizing of a minority point of view".

Heterosexual "biologism" and the place of lesbianism

In the 1970s, core critical texts on materialist feminist thought also addressed essentialist and cultural feminism. One of the principal references on the subject is a text first published in 1975 by Gayle Rubin, "The Traffic in Women: Notes on the 'Political Economy' of Sex". Situated within the critical Marxist tradition, Rubin proposed the idea of a sex/gender system providing an innovative analysis of the social organisation of biological sex and the social production of the feminine and masculine: "A 'system of sex/gender' is the set of dispositions by which society transforms biological sexuality into the products of human activity and in which these transformed sexual needs are satisfied" (Rubin, 1998a:8). She argues that the social organisation of sex depends on gender, compulsory heterosexuality and the constraints imposed on women's sexuality. "Gender is a socially imposed division of the sexes" (Rubin, 1998a:6). What she calls the *traffic in women* is the use of women as a means of exchange. Building on the above and what was implicitly the question in Claude Lévi-Strauss' analysis of the social organisation of sexuality, she shows that "compulsory heterosexuality" is defined as the systematic production of sexual need between the two sexes: heterosexuality.

> Lévi-Strauss comes dangerously close to saying that heterosexuality is an instituted process. If biological and hormonal imperatives were as overwhelming as popular mythologies would have them, it would hardly be necessary to insure heterosexual unions by means of economic interdependency. (Rubin, 1998a:33)
>
> [W]e can deduct from an analysis of the kinship theories of Lévi-Strauss some basic generalities regarding the organization of human sexuality. These include the incest taboo, compulsory heterosexuality and the asymmetrical division of the sexes. The asymmetry of gender – the difference between 'exchanger' and 'exchanged' – serve to constrain women's sexuality. (Rubin, 1998a:36–37)

Rubin then calls for a "political economy of sex". We must, she writes, "…study each society to determine the exact mechanisms by which particular conventions of sexuality are produced and maintained. The 'exchange of women' is an initial step toward building an arsenal of concepts with which sexual systems can be described" (Rubin, 1998a:29). According to her, we need to understand the existing links between imposed norms and intimate relations, kinship systems, matrimonial systems and "political and economic arrangements" within all societies because the different systems of sexuality cannot be considered in isolation. This approach permits an understanding of what determines the mechanisms of sexuality. Moreover, she concludes her article by stating: "But I must suggest, tentatively, a next step on the agenda: a Marxian analysis of sex/gender systems. Sex/gender systems are not ahistorical emanations of the human mind; they are products of historical human activity" (Rubin, 1998a:63).

Following Gayle Rubin, the radical feminist critique of heterosexuality, defined as a political regime, was developed through

Monique Wittig's writing. In 1976 she wrote "The Category of Sex"[8] (Wittig, 1982), an article translated and published in French in 2001 under the title "La catégorie de sexe" (Wittig, 2001). Here, she analysed the political dimension of heterosexuality and critiqued the assumed difference between the sexes that structures thinking on *difference* and gives *innate* and *a priori* status to heterosexuality. She showed that this sexual difference, stemming from the body, is nothing more than the justification of an ideology that informs an arbitrary system of classification structuring the unequal power relations between men and women. The consequence of naturalist thinking that considers the distinction between masculine and feminine to be logical and inevitable is to maintain the social imbalance in the distribution of power between men and women. Wittig argued that the distinction between homosexuality and heterosexuality depends upon the distinction constructed between man and woman and feminine/masculine, with that distinction being *the base of heterosexual society*.

> The category of sex is a political category that founds society as heterosexual. As such it does not concern being but relationships (for women and men are the result of relationships) ... The category of sex is the one that rules as 'natural' the relation that is the base of (heterosexual) and through which half of the population – women – are 'heterosexualised' ... and submitted to a heterosexual economy society. (Wittig, [1982] 2001:46)

For Monique Wittig, social change can only happen if we abolish the use of the category of sex as a tool for understanding the social. Moreover, the eradication of categories of sex would erase the binary of homosexuality/heterosexuality.[9] She concludes her article with these words:

> [T]he category of sex is a totalitarian one ... It shapes the mind as well as the body since it controls all mental production. It grips

our minds in such a way that we cannot think outside of it. This is why we must destroy it and start thinking beyond it if we want to start thinking at all, as we must destroy the sexes as a sociological reality if we want to start to exist. (Wittig, [1982] 2001:49)

As clearly stated by Claire Michard: "as Guillaumin has rightly noted ... Wittig did not, strictly speaking, produce a discourse critical of naturalist thought and its categories – 'sex', 'gender', 'woman', 'man', 'difference', 'heterosexuality' – but rather, a discourse of their destruction. A war was waged to liberate the discourse from these categories" (Michard, 2009).

"One is not born a woman"

For both Simone de Beauvoir and Monique Wittig, women's bodies are shaped through the intervention of the social. However, Wittig distinguished herself from the Beauvoirian statement "One is not born, but rather, becomes a woman" in an article written thirty years after the publication of the *Deuxième sexe*, where she used the following aphorism: "One is not born a woman".[10] By suppressing the "but rather becomes", she created an epistemological rupture. From a materialist perspective, she shows that a natural group of 'women' does not exist and thus questions 'the woman' which, according to her, was nothing but a myth. This is why she contested the way that certain feminist currents and lesbian feminists adopted the Beauvoirian approach by continuing to think that the basis of the oppression of women was as much biological as it was historical.

Some of them even claim to find their sources in Simone de Beauvoir. The belief in mother right and in a 'prehistory' when women created civilization (because of a biological predisposition) while the coarse and brutal men hunted (because of a biological predisposition) is symmetrical with the biologizing interpretation of history produced up to now by the class of men. It is still the same method of finding in women and men a biological explanation of their division, outside of other facts. For me this could never constitute a lesbian approach to women's oppression, since it assumes that the basis of society or the beginning of society lies in heterosexuality. Matriarchy is no less heterosexual than patriarchy: it is only the sex of the oppressor that changes. Furthermore, not only is this conception still imprisoned in the categories of sex (woman and man), but it holds onto the idea that the capacity to give birth (biology) is what defines a woman. (Wittig, [1980b] 2001:52–53)

Wittig distanced herself from essentialist and cultural feminist theories[11] by rejecting the term 'woman'. She showed the necessity of distinguishing between *women* fighting for women as a social class (and for the abolition of this class), and women fighting for 'the' woman as an essentialist concept – which was, from her point of view, an anti-feminist position because the notion of *woman* naturalises the subordination of *women*. She denounced the myth of 'the' woman and the use of 'her' by some groups of women or feminists who used the feminine point of view as a positive value that reinforced this myth. By nurturing a discourse of difference, the mythification of 'the' woman removes the political dimension contained in 'the women'. In this regard, Wittig wrote:

In 1949, Simone de Beauvoir destroyed the myth of the woman. For the last ten years, we have been fighting for a society without sexes.[12] Having stood up to fight for a sexless society, we now find ourselves entrapped in the familiar deadlock of 'woman is wonderful'. Simone de Beauvoir underlined particularly the false consciousness which consists of selecting among the features of the myth (that women are different from men) those which look good and using them as a definition for women. What the concept 'woman is wonderful' accomplishes is that it retains, for defining women, the best features which oppression has granted us, and it does not radically question the categories 'man' and 'woman', which are political categories (and not natural givens). (Wittig, [1980b] 2001:56–57)

In her article, "The Straight Mind", Wittig critiques the social science discourse, which she describes as apolitical and ahistorical, that does not question concepts such as 'man', 'woman', 'difference' and especially the concept of heterosexuality, which is always presented as inevitable and never critically examined:

> Yes, straight society is based on the necessity of the different/ other at every level. It cannot work economically, symbolically, linguistically, or politically without this concept. This necessity of the different/other is an ontological one for the whole conglomerate of sciences and disciplines that I call the straight mind. (Wittig, [1980a] 2001:72)

Wittig emphasises the 'violence' shaping the 'heterosexual discourse' for lesbians and homosexuals. The expression "the straight mind" was chosen as a reference to Lévi-Strauss' (1969) *The Savage Mind*. Within this framework, Wittig notes that the straight mind refuses to examine heterosexual relations or the obligatory relations between *the* man and *the* woman and thus will interpret history, language, culture and society in a totalising manner. General laws have therefore been established, that are applied to all time periods, all individuals, all societies: *the* exchange of women,[13] *the* sexual difference, *the* unconscious, *the* desire and *the* culture. To break with this philosophical and political dogma, Wittig concluded:

> [L]et us say that a new personal and subjective definition for all humankind can only be found beyond the categories of sex (woman and man, and that the advent of individual subjects demands first destroying the categories of sex, ending the use of them, and rejecting all sciences which still use these categories as their fundamentals (practically all social sciences)). (Wittig, [1980b] 2001:63)

Also, this required route "to becoming a woman" in the Beauvoirian sense was called into question by Wittig who proposed lesbianism in an alternative position. Refusing to become or to stay heterosexual is a mode of resistance to becoming a woman. She compares the lesbian escape from the heterosexual system to the African American slaves who escaped enslavement by crossing the Mississippi. She calls for the amplification of such forms of flight to destroy the property relations that are constitutive of the sexes:

> [O]ur survival demands that we contribute all our strength
> to the destruction of the class of women within which men
> appropriate women. This can be accomplished only by the
> destruction of heterosexuality as a social system which is based
> on the oppression of women by men and which produces
> the doctrine of the difference between the sexes to justify this
> oppression. (Wittig, [1980b] 2001:63-64)

This extract explains Wittig's now famous model "lesbians are not women": "'lesbian' is the only concept ... that is beyond categories of sex (woman and man), because the designated subject (lesbian) is *not*[14] a woman, either economically, or politically, or ideologically" (Wittig, [1980b] 2001:63). Indeed, although subjected to all the effects of the collective ownership of women – lower salaries, aggression, rape, etc. – lesbians escape being the private property of one man. If, for the author, lesbians are not women, it is precisely because they escape private ownership:

> For what makes a woman is a specific social relation to a man,
> a relation that we have previously called servitude, a relation
> which implies personal and physical obligation as well as
> economic obligation ('forced residence', domestic chores,
> conjugal duties, unlimited production of children, etc.), a
> relation which lesbians escape by refusing to become or to stay
> heterosexual. (Wittig, [1980b] 2001:63)

Wittig affirms that, to escape private ownership, it is not sufficient to position oneself as an 'individual': we must be "escapees from our class in the same way as the American runaway slaves were when escaping slavery" (Wittig, [1980b] 2001:63). But for Wittig, the connection between an awareness of sexual classes and actually obtaining the status of a 'subject' is not sufficient either: "Class consciousness is not enough. We must try to understand philosophically (politically) these concepts of 'subject' and 'class consciousness' and how they work in relation to our history" (Wittig, [1980b] 2001:61).

For Wittig, it is not a question of proposing a lesbian *society* – lesbianism is not an end in itself – but it is currently the only possible type of relationship[15] that permits the destruction of the heterosexual system.[16] Wittig positions lesbians within a set of resistances to diverse forms of oppression, within which she also positions relations of slavery, capitalism and the sexual exploitation. This position of individual and collective resistance would end in the eradication of these systems of power.

Following Colette Guillaumin and her analysis of the naturalisation of sex, Wittig argues that there are not two genders, because women are *the* sex: "the feminine carries the mark of gender and can never be beyond gender" (Wittig, 2001:131), in so far as the masculine gender "fundamentally signifies all of humanity" (Michard, 2009). Lesbianism is not perceived as a fixed category, but as a bearer of an emergent human who is neither gendered nor sexualised, someone who is not included in the reproductive heterosexual contract.

Wittig uses utopia as a heuristic tool that permits us to envision the social dynamic and its changes. By proposing a way of thinking beyond sex categories that make it impossible to conceive of women beyond said categories, she distances the present reality and thus evades thinking of it as natural, necessary or even inevitable. The social break imagined by the Wittigian proposal allows for a rethinking of the current order and renders an epistemological break possible. As Paul Ricœur writes, "the only way to exit the circle into which ideology pulls us is to adopt utopia, to declare it and judge ideology from this perspective" (Ricœur, [1986] 1997:231).

Heterosexuality, according to the perspective proposed by Rubin and Wittig, is no longer analysed as a simple sexual practice, but as "a social system, the cornerstone of the ownership of women from which lesbians partially escape" (Turcotte, 2003:38). For Wittig, giving lesbians an essentialist 'identity' is out of the question: lesbianism becomes a concept for the elaboration of a theory that permits an exit from "the *a priori* analogy between the (gender) feminine/sex/nature" (Wittig, [1982] 2001:112), rendering the genders obsolete and deleting them. Thus, it is in Wittig's proposed approach, that of bringing about the subject through a process of escaping the ownership of women as a class, that the lesbian becomes the inaugural figure of that disappearance, located somewhere beyond the category of sex. This would be, in Pascale Molinier's terms (2007), the initial crack in the masculinocentric system.

Starting in the 1980s, the premise of Wittig's proposal, that in a *lesbian society*, there would be no more sexual oppression, was contested by migrant lesbian movements. According to some of these detractors (for example, Moraga and Anzaldúa, 1981), the disappearance of sexual oppression does not imply the disappearance of oppression per se (i.e. relations of class, 'race', or even sexualities), nor, they noted, could there be a sexuality without power or beyond power. Thus, according to the philosopher Maria Lugones, "separatism, expressed by some feminists, idealizes feminine subjects, supposedly homogeneous and unified around only one identity, disregarding fragmented subjects, subjects inhabiting the border zones of plural identities, therefore the 'mestizo' is the paradigm" (cited by Dorlin, 2008:77–78).

"Compulsory heterosexuality" and the "lesbian continuum"

At the beginning of the 1980s, another current emerged, and it was distinct from materialist feminism and/or radical lesbianism. This position proposed that lesbian feminism should reject the political use of the categories heterosexuality and homosexuality because it considered them to be nothing more than practices that are inscribed in polarised power relations, historically detrimental to women, that can be diversely codified according to relations of sex, gender, class or 'race'. Thus, in response to Wittig's two articles ("One Is Not Born a Woman" and "The Straight Mind"), Adrienne Rich's article "Compulsory Heterosexuality and Lesbian Existence" (1981[17]) was published in *Nouvelles Questions féministes*[18] in March 1981. In this text, Rich talks about the "institution of heterosexuality", which depends on social conditioning and the system of belief generally circulated by the social sciences, but also through some feminist texts, that adopted the following premise: women are presupposed to have a heterosexual inclination, "a 'preference' or a 'choice' that draws women toward men" (Rich, 1981:20), which Rich describes as a mystical/biological discourse linked to the necessity to reproduce the species and to maternal desire. For Rich, "heterosexuality,[19] like motherhood, needs to be recognized and studied as a political institution – even, or especially, by those individuals who feel they are, in their personal experience, the precursors of a new social relation between the sexes" (Rich, 1981:20–21).

The bias of "compulsory heterosexuality" consolidates itself by erasing lesbianism in feminist research and in the social sciences in general. Rich shows that compulsory heterosexuality is also transmitted by what she calls heterosexual romance, the ideal form of love presented in literature, and particularly literature directed toward women, which presents love for men as simultaneously the prototype of duty and fulfilment, as the grand adventure of the feminine. To the elements involved in controlling the consciousness of women Rich adds the power of men to prohibit women from having any autonomous sexuality. The denigration of female pleasure is manifest by a series of oppressions that ensure women's dependence upon and identification with men. Among the series of actual sanctions, Rich refers to the practice of clitoridectomy, infibulation, the condemnation of female masturbation, the destruction of historical evidence of lesbianism, 'pseudo-lesbian' clichés in the media and in literature, etc. She insists that heterosexuality gains validity through violence against women, the control of their consciousness, the subjection of women to daily eroticisation and the censorship of lesbian existence. By denying the difficulties that can exist between men and women, 'the sexual revolution', with its model of a woman who is 'free and sexy', has as its corollary the internalisation of masculine values by women and is an impediment to their liberation, because this normative framework maintains their relationship with those who dominate them. These coercive measures, according to the author, do not permit the qualification of heterosexuality as a choice or a 'preference', because these terms obscure the social pressure that pushes women to be or become heterosexual.

Rich discusses what she calls "feminism's big question", which does not only address gender inequality or "the domination of culture by males", the silences and "the taboos against homosexuality", but should also question "the enforcement of heterosexuality for women as a means of assuring male right of physical, economic, and emotional access" (Rich, 1981:31). She proposes the concept of a "lesbian continuum" as a means of "survival relations". It is not only about practising exclusive and sexual lives between women, or conscious or unconscious desire of one woman for another, but all experiences of identifying with women (the capacity for personal autonomy and/or the sharing of practices, political solidarity) that she analyses as a means of resistance to masculine domination.

The notion of a "lesbian continuum" encompasses wider register ranging from the frigidity of women – considered by Rich as a form of resistance to "the imposition of male sexuality" – to puritanism, to comradery and friendship between women. However, Rich's article has been subject to critique by some branches of political lesbianism, notably regarding the notion of a *lesbian continuum*. The main critique is that this concept does not call into question the foundations of the heterosocial system: if "the existence of lesbians, in a political sense, must be defined as an identification-with-women in order to enter the continuum of resistance" that would permit heterosexuals to "contest heterosexual sexuality 'liberated and free' and lesbians to resist the patriarchy by always identifying with women" (Turcotte, 2003:39). In an article published in *Amazones d'hier, lesbiennes d'aujourd'hui* Danielle Chagnon adds that Rich's proposal denies "the strategic and subversive role of lesbiennes, because although widowhood, camaraderie, or frigidity are 'permitted' in a heterosexual system, lesbianism is not" (Chagnon, 1986:32).

Conclusion

These early lesbian feminist theories and their associated movements ultimately contributed to the denaturalisation and questioning of the biological determinism of categories of gender, sex and sexuality. They also permitted the questioning of the supposed neutrality of the sciences as a whole, the reproducers of androcentric thought, a doxa that had yet to be asked to provide evidence for its logic and prove its findings. They also consistently provided the theoretical and political foundations for diverse lesbian feminist, feminist and LGBT movements (the fight against violence towards women, abortion, contraception, professional equality, homosexual visibility, the decriminalisation of homosexuality).

In France, in particular, a combination of French and American lesbian feminist theories and an interchange between activists and theorists gave rise to a vibrant Francophone lesbian movement that began in the 1970s and flourished well into the 1990s.

But by the 1990s, Teresa de Lauretis (2007) would extend feminist post-structuralist theories and develop queer theory[20] by reinterpreting the relationships between sex, gender and sexuality as products of hegemonic forms of representation, providing new avenues for the critique of heteronormativity. The influence of Foucault (1984a; 1984b) and a new focus on the interplay between the subject and its subjugation via hegemonic representations of heterosexuality would mark a significant turn in sexuality politics and theory. However, the conceptual work begun by lesbian feminist activists and theorists in France in the 1970s would provide its foundation specifically because of its early attempts to denaturalise heterosexuality by exploring the role of gender and sex in producing heteronormativity.

Notes

1 Marcel Mauss' statement at a conference in 1931 at the Institut français de sociologie, published in "La cohésion sociale dans les sociétés polysegmentaires" and republished in *Œuvres III. Cohésion sociale et division de la sociologie* (Paris: Minuit, 1969), pp. 11–26.

2 At that time, one symbolic action made the broader public aware of the MLF: on 26 August 1970, a dozen activists attempted to lay a floral wreath in memory of the wife of the unknown soldier at the Arc de Triomphe in Paris. Many overlapping testimonials confirm that most of the activists at this 'birth' of the MLF's media presence were lesbians. This date was chosen in solidarity with the demonstration of American women who, on that day, celebrated the fiftieth anniversary of their right to vote.

3 In 1970, the essayist Kate Millett was one of the first to present an explicit critique of heterosexuality. Analysing the works of Henry Miller, Norman Mailer and Jean Genet, she demonstrated the links between masculine domination and heterosexuality and invented the concept of 'sexual politics'. She wrote that it is impossible to think of any transformation of the individual without "liberating humanity from the tyranny of socio-sexual categories and the obligation to conform

with sexual stereotypes (the couple, the family); this is as necessary as the abolition of the racial caste system and economic classes" (Millett, 1971:394).

4 The "homophile" movement surrounding the publication *Arcadie* (created in 1954) had almost no women "and, in terms of their politics, focused solely on the homosexual (male) question in terms of their practices of integration and their leveraging of political power … This is why *Arcadie*, despite itself and with the MLF as its midwife, could give birth to the movement for gay liberation" (Chauvin, 2005:111–113).

5 The institutionalisation of relations imposed on women as a function of their role in reproduction restrains their choices.

6 The same year, the first lesbian magazine, *Quand les femmes s'aiment*, appeared. It would be published until June 1980.

7 The decade of the 1980s and the years that followed were a time of cultural, political and theoretic effervescence for the lesbian movement in the Francophone world. This period was marked by the birth of a lesbian subculture that was organised and ritualised to permit collective lesbian identification which contrasted with the weak collective legitimacy shared by many lesbians who took part in the feminist movement in the 1970s (Lesselier, 1991:87–103). Many associations emerged in Paris including the Front des lesbiennes radicales (1981–1982), the MIEL (Mouvement d'information et d'expression des lesbiennes) (1981), the Archives lesbiennes (1984). In Toulouse, Bagdam Café (1988) was founded. Publications also appeared including *Les Lesbianaires* (Belgium) (1980–1996), *Lesbia Magazine* (January 1982) and *Vlasta* (Spring 1983). This movement continued until the end of the 1990s. As an extension of the MLF, it served as an alternative to feminist movements which were weakened by the changing economic, ideological, social and political context.

8 This text was, without a doubt, initially part of a presentation at Berkeley in 1976. Berkeley, 1976, is mentioned at the end of the article published in *Feminist Issues*.

9 However, for Monique Wittig, the idea of a society without sex categories, where everyone would have an undetermined sexuality, was also undesirable. Getting rid of the category 'woman' did not exclude the 'lesbian body'. See also Chetcuti and Amaral (2008) and Chetcuti (2009).

10 This article stemmed from the paper that Monique Wittig presented in 1978 at the conference of the Modern Language Association.

11 Monique Wittig and the 'radical' feminist current distinguished themselves from essentialist feminism through their critique of heterosexuality. For the essentialist current, the critique of heterosexuality required more than demonstrating that heterosexuality, in reality, contradicted the very essence of *hetero-sexuality*. "There is no question of Same and Other in heterosexuality, individually lived and

socially organized, but of the authoritarian lowering of the Other at the hands of the Same. If all sexuality is an experience of alterity, the actual heterosexuality is an unfortunate experience and is always akin to the negation of the feminine, as the figure of the Other" (Dorlin, 2008:64; see also Schor, 1993).

12　The author is referring to a Ti-Grace Atkinson text that was also translated into French: "Si le féminisme a une logique quelconque, il ne peut tendre que vers une société sans sexes" (Atkinson, [1974] 1975:6).

13　In the same period, an article was published in *Les cahiers du Grif* that explained what lesbians had brought to the feminist movement and non-mixity, permitting the creation of links beyond those undertaken with men. It also analysed homosociality in heterosexual society: "the power of the women's liberation movement was less its focus on fighting for female homosexuality than on demanding non-mixity ... A homosocial movement against heterosexual society, based on relations between men, in which the exchange of women created the link and furnished the matrix for all other transfers of goods" (Braidotti, Bonis and Ménès, 1985:51). That same year, an article by Eve Sedgwick was published which demonstrated how "flattering" attention given to women in romantic poetry is simultaneously a diversion and an elaboration of male homosexual desire (Sedgwick, 1985).

14　In italics and underlined in the text.

15　This suggests that, in the abstract, there could be other possible forms of relationships, but their terms are still unknown.

16　Heterosociality is understood here as a social and political order established against women, and whose operation makes heterosexuality, the total linking of the woman to the man understood in most societies as natural and unchanging, invisible.

17　Adrienne Rich's (1980) article "Compulsory Heterosexuality and Lesbian Existence" was published in an issue of *Signs: Journal of Women in Culture and Society* and then in French under the title "La contrainte à l'hétérosexualité et l'existence lesbiennes" in *Nouvelles Questions féministes* in 1981.

18　The beginning of the 1980s was marked by a very important shift in terms of the theory and politics informing the relationship between lesbianism and feminism. The two Wittig articles that formalised the analysis of heterosexuality as a political regime, "The Straight Mind" (February 1980) and "One Is Not Born a Woman" (May 1980) were the catalysts of an explosion of latent conflict, present since the beginning of the women's liberation movement, that rested on the political status of heterosexuality and its hegemony in the women's movement, and on the political alliance between lesbians and heterosexual women. See "Lettre au mouvement féministe", a text written by the radical lesbian feminists of the former collective *Questions féministes* in Paris in 1981 republished as "Politiques culturelles lesbiennes" in Natacha Chetcuti and Nelly Quemener (eds) (2015) *Miroir/Miroirs: Revue des corps contemporains*. It dealt with the rupture between the members of the *Questions féministes* editorial collective which dissolved on 24 October 1980 when the last issue was published. In 1981, Christine Delphy, Claude Hennequin and Emmanuèle de Lesseps decided to create another publication by adding the term *Nouvelles* to the former title *Questions féministes*.

19 A heterosexuality that is paired with the economic system and cultural propaganda (post-industrial economy of sex, pornographic clichés, the mythification of privacy, etc.).

20 Teresa de Lauretis, who coined the phrase "queer theory", organised the first Queer Theory conference in 1990 at the University of California at Santa Cruz, and later published one of the first articles on the topic in the journal *Differences* in 1991. At the same time, the emblematic group Queer Nation, which was organised to fight homophobic, lesbophobic, transphobic and racist and sexist violence, was formed in New York.

THIRTEEN | Looking for the lesbian: some notes for a lesbian feminist politics in the time of the girl child

Asha Achuthan

Introduction

This essay is located in the gap created by the difficulty of lesbian feminism as a critical lens, particularly with respect to engagements with the state.[1] I locate this difficulty vis-à-vis what I term the management of the gender question in the Indian nation-state. At the centre of this management, I suggest, is the 'girl child'.[2] I focus on this girl child as she has been historically produced at different moments in Indian nation-state contexts; as she appears in policy, as she is celebrated within and/or disappears from the natal family unit, as she performs in education, as she is marked for sexual protection, as she recovers space in the context of caregiving and as she – as a same-sex desiring young person – is rendered abject. I go on to mark a few aspects of women's and queer movements and women's studies as interlocutors of the state, where, in the focus on the adult agential heterosexual woman, and in the talk around the 'queer', the category of the girl child has received scant critical attention. My attempt is to mark this figure as normative, as the inaugural moment of the 'good woman' symbolic of the heteronormative family unit, and in many ways the success story of the 'Third World nation' status that India would no longer claim. Rather than the homonationalist impulse as laid out in Puar (2005; 2017), *this* figure is, I suggest, the peg on which the Indian nation-state today gains admittance to global responsibility and power, while managing criticism of its aggression, misogyny and homonegativity.[3] It follows that the lesbian woman stands erased in this management of the gender question. A keener attention is, I suggest, needed to unpack this category and make visible the young person as a not necessarily biologically or historically static being – a movement that is vital to any feminisms that might wish to mark entry under the sign of a lesbian politics in India today.

The woman of transnational politics, mainstream development and national state policy

As signatory, in 1992, to the UN Convention on the Rights of the Child, that came into effect in 1990, the Indian state has instituted various constitutional and legal measures that protect girl children from discrimination in India. These include the Prohibition of Child Marriage Act, 2006, the declaration of a National Girl Child Day (January 24), various schemes for empowerment of the girl child, the Juvenile Justice (Care and Protection of Children) Act, 2000, Protection of Children from Sexual Offences Act, 2012 and the National Policy for Children, 2013. Successive governments have reported in international forums on the legal machinery put in place to correct both the skewed Sex Ratio at Birth and the Child Sex Ratio. An example is the PCPNDT Act[4] of 1994, that has been much discussed in scholarly and popular literature (Menon, 1995; Rao, 2001; Luthra, 1999; Patel, 2007). The Beti Bachao Beti Padhao scheme,[5] a government flagship programme specifically aimed at the girl child, was instituted in January 2015 (Ministry of Women and Child Development, 2015).

Who is this girl child? What are the frameworks within which this category is understood? How does she fare as a citizen? One of the key claims of the Beti Bachao Beti Padhao scheme (hereafter BBBP), among other recent schemes, is that it takes the rights approach rather than the lifecycle approach; in other words, an approach to education as a fundamental right for the girl child, referring to Article 14 of the Indian Constitution that guarantees the right to equality, and to the right to life that is infringed in sex-selective abortion. To that end, it also offers goals other than marriage to the girl until age 18, and targets advocacy campaigns at parents, particularly fathers, in an attempt to suggest that marriage before 18 curbs opportunities and must therefore be delayed as a goal. The perceived benefits of educating the girl child include "elimination of child marriage, delay of pregnancy of young girls along with low maternal mortality rate, low infant mortality rates, balanced CSR, economic independence" (Ministry of Women and Child Development, 2015:15). The campaign material also suggests, almost as a matter of course, that the girl child who has completed secondary education will be a more equipped member of the family unit. The people responsible for this, of course, are primarily the natal family.

The BBBP scheme, although located in the Ministry of Women and Child Development, is to be supported also by the ministries of Health and Family Welfare, Human Resources, and Information and Broadcasting. Using a "multi-pronged approach to involve youth, adolescents, men, Panchayati Raj Institutions,[6] community leaders, judiciary and media for achieving behaviour change" (Ministry of Women and Child Development, 2015:16), the scheme proposes a three-tier training module involving master trainers from national to district officials from concerned departments, the lowest tier of which includes the ANM (auxiliary nurse midwife), ASHA (accredited social health activist) workers, AWW (*anganwadi* workers) – considered the "first line of contact for the community" (Ministry of Women and Child Development, 2015:17). The module for master trainers speaks of patriarchal mindsets that value sons over daughters as one of the primary causes of gender-based sex-selective abortion, and talks about the role of ANMs and ASHA workers in speaking to the community about the importance of girl child education, the status of girl children, the reasons for skewed sex ratios and the consequences of skewed sex ratios.

What are the parameters of success for such a scheme? How is responsibility allocated? What is the language within which it is framed? In guidelines for implementation, the suggested measures to enable girl child education and operationalise the scheme include having sufficient toilets for girls in schools, the efficient implementation of the midday meal scheme, the setting up of village-level *Gudda-guddi* display boards,[7] the issue of Pink cards for parents having (a maximum of two) girl children that can be used for ease of registration of births and marriages or driving licences. In other words, a mix of incentives and convergence with other pre-existing schemes. A quick survey of the present status of these other schemes produces ambiguous results. Drèze and Khera (2017), Drèze and Goyal (2003), Swaminathan et al. (2004), Khera (2002), Thorat and Lee (2005) speak of the positives as well as negatives of the midday meal scheme. Evidence for increased enrolment based on toilets being provided for is not forthcoming. As regards the *Gudda-guddi* boards or Pink cards, the question of pride in educating the girl child, the honour seemingly associated with better figures on child sex ratios, and the concomitant shame associated with the failure to do so, begs several questions. While patriarchy is named on paper as one of the primary causes of gender inequality, and son preference named somewhat weakly, the language of constitutional rights is never mobilised in the service of empowerment. Rather, family honour, a father's pride, a brother's efforts to convince the natal family to delay marriage for the young girl or the honour of the village are mobilised and acknowledged, alongside the very modern and market-generated stereotypes of 'pink'ness[8] to empower the girl child. Biology and gender hierarchies and binaries, as we see, are consolidated in and through this exercise, and this is where my questions on the consolidation of heteronormativity via this category begin. The girl child, in this formulation, is also the 'innocent', to be *re-valued* historically in order to qualify her for protection. This re-valuation is exhorted till the legal age of marriage; milestones do not change here, they are merely moved ahead by a bit. Indeed, the girl child here is the *beti*, the daughter, whether of the nation or the heteronormative family or the village, and it is in relation to these entities that her rights are defined. We might recall here some of the debates around women's or *zenana* education in the colonial period. Chakravarti traces the nationalist construction of 'woman', in the construction of a "national identity for women" (Chakravarti, 1989:52), in the early twentieth century. The woman can no longer, she suggests as she explores the literary output of the period, be the passive *sahadharmini*, the suitably educated companion for the nationalist man in a period of crisis; rather, she must take an active role, be the nationalist man's moral compass, and if necessary shed domesticity to be his public helpmate. It is in this control, this publicness as sublimation, that the woman is honoured; it is also in the service of this honour that her sexuality must be controlled. The pride that a father, a family, a village, a community is in today's nation exhorted to experience in allowing their daughter an education, written as it is in continuing reference to these tropes, may be read as continuing maps of control over her sexuality.

What are some of the other contexts within which this re-valuation becomes possible? The Prohibition of Child Marriage Act, 2006, marking eighteen years as the legitimate age of marriage for women, is one of the key gender commitments the Indian state makes to international bodies like the United Nations. This involves Child Marriage Prohibition Officers from the District Collector down to the ASHAs and AWWs, who must notify authorities and prevent the conduction of marriages of women below 18 years and men below 21. The rules mark 'early marriage' or 'child marriage' as a punishable offence, as also a reason for deprivation from education and other opportunities for the young girl, or a cause of ill-health owing to early pregnancy following marriage. Interestingly, it is *early* marriage that is the offence; questions of consent to marriage, or questions of choice, are not foregrounded here. Only one of the ways in which heterosexual marriage as a given for women is naturalised is evident in the ASHAs and AWWs being primary contact points for community under this Act. In this gendered allocation of labour alongside several other gender awareness-building responsibilities, these women become default nurturers for young girls. Not only is the woman-child hyphen a naturalised one here, any woman who shifts the goalpost of marriage ever so slightly, albeit at the behest of the state, particularly in underpaid and vulnerable work conditions that these workers find themselves in, puts herself at further than usual risk.[9]

The re-evaluation in policy runs alongside what Sangari (2015) calls re-traditionalisation – contemporary shifts in the heteronormative family, while retaining gender roles and relations, that reflects in a slew of newer developments and legislations. A key example is of commercial surrogacy,[10] which writes into the market women's reproductive labour in a renewed consolidation of the heteronormative, while seemingly offering ways out of biological motherhood. Another example that Sangari (2015) points to is the Maintenance and Welfare of Parents and Senior Citizens Act, 2007,[11] where, in a strange and surely unintended paean to gender equality, daughters are equally financial responsible for elderly relatives. When does the girl child get drafted into caregiving? When 'single', and therefore not seen as responsible in the heterosexual family unit, when abandoned after the birth of a daughter, when widowed or unmarried, she was anyway the ex-officio burden who must earn her keep in the natal household. In the typical middle-class upper-caste family, which seems to be the primary constituency that the Act refers to, as or before this girl child turns into an adult woman with the capacity to earn, considered to have access to equal status, she not only turns into the dependable decision-maker, but also retains the lot of the girl child who will never leave, who embodies filial loyalty, who can be held up against the son who is disloyal or who has left. A third example of the phenomenon of re-traditionalisation could be the Transgender Persons (Protection of Rights) Bill, 2016. There have been multiple iterations of this Bill from 2015, following the Supreme Court judgment of 2014 that had enjoined upon the government to deploy measures supporting gender self-identification and schemes for livelihood, as well as measures against discrimination. One of the clauses that have been actively critiqued in this Bill includes that of kidnapping – which marks biological family as the only site of nurturance for the young person, and which makes any removal from such family a criminal offence. Given the realities of many lives where children leave home to join *hijra*[12] families, driven either by overt familial violence, sexual or gendered (Panchal and Ajgaonkar, 2015) or a complete absence of gender non-conforming models of life and living in mainstream society (Shah et al., 2015), this clause is a telling reminder of the manner in which the heteronormative family model continues to be enforced.

I would now like to return, with these understandings, to the question of what the category of the girl child is, and what such a biologically, historically and nationally static category offers to the Indian nation-state. This category refers to the young person assigned gender female at birth who exists definitionally in relation to the family unit. The girl child is an occupant of the familial domestic domain, on whose continuing protection the honour of the family rests, who may be given educational opportunity such that her marriage may be *delayed*. The girl child deserves to be valued, and is also being *re-evaluated* as more economically useful in the contemporary family unit. This is clearly a heterosexual girl child, well within the gender binary, amenable to being *managed* within the boundaries of normative family. A Haryana study talks about families who marry off their daughters when they "start looking grown up (*thadi ho gayi*)" (Panchal and Ajgaonkar, 2015:xv), and who justify child marriage as a way of protecting young girls from sexual harassment. The study also finds that early marriages are sometimes forced on a young girl if she is brought back from an attempted elopement (Panchal and Ajgaonkar, 2015:xv) – what we might see as a source of coerced corrective endogamy. But as we look at the apprehensions around sexual autonomy here, we find that it is the cis-heterosexual young girl who is described as endangered, both by communities and by the state. It is this person who must be provided heterosexual anchor and protection through marriage, as messaging both to other men and to young women in general. As men, their families and communities are engaged with, therefore, 'early' or 'child' marriage is named as the problem; not the normalised sexual violence that forced marriages are, and apathetic redressal mechanisms (this does not appear once in all the training manuals), not natal families and intimate relations as a site of violence, not the link between familial and societal violence and its links to gendered violence, and certainly not the child's sexuality or gender identity that is being managed in a framework of "compulsory heterosexuality".[13] How, then, is the gender non-conforming child or the cis girl desiring another, being understood here? Are these children not at risk? Is the family a site of protection and nurturance or a site of violence? – of perhaps more terrifying kinds – for them too (Shah et al., 2015)? Is this a case of exclusion through invisibilisation, is it a case of being the 'miniscule' minority?[14] The minister-in-charge of the Ministry of Women and Child Development spoke in 2015 of the symbol of the Beti Bachao scheme, that it was 'simple'. A schematic drawing of a normatively feminine face, long hair in two ponytails, a centre parting of the hair,[15] neat and symmetrical, with a book in front of her.[16] Simple indeed; instantly recognisable, the innocent, classical and complete (read able-bodied) figure. Recognisable not on account of how most girl children in India may look, but on account of how we would like them to, as they *ought* to, this 'we' referring to socially dominant groups and normative positions. Recognisable in iteration, as "part of a regulatory practice that produces the bodies it governs ... whose regulatory force is made clear as a kind of productive power, the power to produce – demarcate, circulate, differentiate – the bodies it controls" (Butler, 1993:1). To put Butler to further use here, the productive constraints within which the girl child as subject-citizen is rendered intelligible, then, also are the conditions within which an excluded "domain of unthinkable, abject, unlivable bodies" is produced (Butler, 1993:ix). The young person who steps out of or is rendered single vis-à-vis the institution of marriage is more vulnerable than the young cis woman within marriage who is closer to the centre of Gayle Rubin's charmed circle (Rubin, 1984:109). However, the gender non-conforming child or the young cis girl experiencing same-sex desire cannot hope to find space or meaning anywhere in this discourse. The symbol that is the BBBP logo is indeed as simple as it is normative, and in the frame of biological developmentalism, the same-sex desiring person is leached out at the outset.

How then may we understand the idea of time and developmental milestones, or the claim to a lifecourse perspective in these documents? Earle and Letherby (2007:236, quoting Cohen, 1987:1) speak of the difference in approach between a lifecycle and lifecourse perspective: "the concept of a lifecycle 'implies fixed categories in the life of the individual and assumes a stable social system, whereas the [lifecourse] allows for more flexible biological patterns within a continually changing social system'". They go on to speak of how a lifecourse allows a non-linear approach to life events, as well as one that allows the analysis to interlink structure and agency. Of course, even in lifecourse approaches, 'expected' biomedical events like puberty, pregnancy, motherhood continue to be the markers with respect to which individuals locate their experiences, as the authors argue. Yet, treating time as a process experienced rather than as a commodity enjoined in expert language and controlled by experts like that of the medical practitioner, for instance, offers ways of unsettling even these expected events somewhat from their fixities. Halberstam's notion of queer time challenges these fixities more effectively (2005). Halberstam speaks of queer time and queer space, "as useful terms for academic and non-academic considerations of life, location and transformation" (Halberstam, 2005:4). 'Queer', in her understanding, constitutes "non-normative logics and organizations of community, sexual identity, embodiment, and activity in space and time" (Halberstam, 2005:6), and both time and space in her frame are about having different temporalities and milestones outside of puberty, pregnancy, motherhood, caregiving within family and inheritance, as also about place-making outside of the placeholders that, say, the category of 'girl child' creates. It is about seeking roots but also making home in non-places within natal/marital family spaces, or in collectives. The idea of forced marriage rather than early or child marriage, then, becomes a way of challenging a key placeholder[17] through this exercise.

The woman of dominant feminism

What have been dominant feminist[18] engagements with the category and state agendas on the girl child? How do we understand the ambivalent nature of this engagement in the context of the invisibilising of the same-sex desiring young person, and how does this connect with the invisibility of the lesbian adult woman in women's movements and feminisms? For one, feminists in India have been painfully aware of the natu-ralised mother-child connection and consolidation of biological motherhood-as-women's-identity in policy documents, with the accompanying protectionism and infantilisation that infringes any autonomy women might experience in their everyday lives. As such, the push for autonomy in decision-making has been part of the demand for full citizenship. The question I would pose here, however tentatively, is if the *adult woman* has been the primary subject of dominant feminisms. The campaigns against femicide – the patriarchal destruction of female foetuses (Menon, 2004:80), or against sexual violence are a case in point. Feminist movements have been ranged categorically against a state that, while appearing to court a pro-woman agenda in these contexts, was largely interested in the agendas of family planning, as the discourse around the MTP Act or amniocente-sis, suggests (Menon, 2005:73).[19] Was it the *woman* who must be allowed birth, who must be allowed *adulthood* and agency, who was our concern, then? As we dominant feminists agitated against the custodial rape of the 14-year-old Mathura and the impunity enjoyed by state-supported perpetrators of sexual violence, against the promiscuity stereotypically attached to the tribal woman or to the woman in a relationship outside of marriage,[20] we missed, perhaps, the question of the sexual autonomy of the young girl that was also being disallowed in the state narrative. It was the trope of innocence that we seemed to share with the patriarchal state in order to indicate the heinous-ness of sexual crimes against children. Even when speaking of sexual rights and autonomy in other campaigns, did we privilege the invisible qualifier – heterosexual autonomy?

What have our alternative, feminist queer, models of articulat-ing gendered childhoods been (Ranade, 2018)? A focus on the girl child as well as on early marriage does motivate some of the academic and activist feminist work *with/in* systems. The *Special*

Cells[21] set up in police stations across the country since 2007 recognise child marriage as a form of violence against women, even as they work with the legal age of marriage. This brings in the question of such marriages being non-consensual, and helps unsettle the idea of marriage as an inevitable milestone in women's lives. This also establishes the connect between forms of violence faced by young women and young girls, and the traditional erasure of their voices in families and communities, while retaining the specificity of each. It makes connections with the prospective risk of domestic violence, sexual abuse and reduced reproductive autonomy. In doing so, and in the manner of doing so, it also marks the young girl as active agent, holding structures and systems accountable for not enabling this agency. The state thus becomes the interlocutor in addition to the family. This is in sharp contrast to the cajoling language of the schemes intended to 'save' the girl child, addressed to the moral compass of heteropatriarchy rather than to the state as restorer of legal-constitutional rights. That said, the heterosexual placeholding does not become more than a compartmental recognition; as young women in same-sex relationships who are able to escape familial surveillance through *Special Cells* and related mechanisms and who access shelter homes for women attest. The extreme homonegativity of most of these shelters, whether state-run or otherwise, leaves these women mostly on their own – disowned by or escaped from family, sometimes pushed back into families with tacit support from law enforcement, or treated with extreme othering in the shelters if they choose to come out. In fact, part of the strategy employed by lesbian rights groups while accessing these shelters for women is the 'forced marriage' criterion *alone*, since any mention of non-heterosexual desire, evoking as it must the woman-outside-family, can challenge familiar, safe tropes. For those of us working *with/in* systems then, the knowledge that the network of referrals are incomplete and that safety is absent for some, that young persons in same-sex relationships are unintelligible in this network, and thereby socially abject too, is a political reality as well.

This brings me to the question of what such unintelligibility in framings of violence against women might mean for young persons. 'Expected biomedical events' like menarche, pregnancy and motherhood, experienced in dominant ways, continue to be the placeholders for investigating and intervening in the lives of women in families, communities, development agendas, biomedicine and public health, as well as dominant feminist discourse. This is accompanied by ghettoised talk around 'LGBTQ lives', as though these lives are entirely about sexual preference and its specific effects, and as though these persons do not experience menarche as trauma, or sexual violence, or gendered violence, or forced marriage. It is unsurprising, then, that we are unable to speak of young personhood as inclusive of these experiences, and that we continue to frame even our intersectional campaigns primarily around cis-heterosexual adult women's lives, so that gender non-conforming children become abnormal outliers, and same-sex desires become deviant. Ranade draws our attention to journeys of gender non-conforming and non-heterosexual young persons who, in the absence of alternative placeholders and milestones, occupy in-between spaces, both metaphorically and literally (2018:59–92), and forces us to look at what 'growing up' may therefore mean for these young persons in India.

A very brief exploration into the journeys and placeholders in women's studies, and their links to feminist and queer movements might be useful here, to explore other contexts of abjection.[22] Women's studies in India has moved from primarily an extradisciplinary mandate in Indian contexts, to a more institutionalised disciplinary presence today (John, 2009; Rege, 1997; Anandhi and Swaminathan, 2006). The *Towards Equality* report of 1974[23] had proposed new research on 'invisible' women in a bid to expand the category 'women'. With the entry of ideas of feminist standpoint via Sharmila Rege, John and others, as dominant feminism and its occupation of the women's studies spaces and agendas in the 1990s began to be called out, this agenda of expansion produced research by and on marginal and invisibilised women's lives, following their presence and voice in movements, curricula and pedagogy – albeit an uneven and fraught set of histories. In addition to invisibilisation and marginality, some research also dismantled the dualism of good woman / bad woman; discussions of sex work as labour, as also questions of pleasure and desire, found place, however contested, in women's studies curricula and movement spaces (Shah, 2014). Another form this question took is of gender never being an isolated experience, and multi-perspectival, interdisciplinary approaches therefore being a need.

The question that I am not sure was asked, however, was of the *ontological heterogeneity*[24] *of what and who we were calling women.* While questions about the fractured nature of subject categories[25] were well received from Western feminist contexts into dominant feminism in India, and some of us were instrumental in practising this understanding in our research agendas in the late 1990s–early 2000s, whispers of what possibilities of gender location and bodies this category 'woman' also definitionally excluded – those outside the gender binary, for instance – had barely reached the urban metropolitan university.

Did the lesbian figure find entry into women's studies curricula, despite the availability of research on violence faced by lesbian women, or narratives of lesbian invisibility generated since the 1990s (Fernandez and Gomathy, 2003; Shah et al., 2015), under the term "unproper sexuality" Butler names it (in Meijer and Prins, 1998:284)?[26] Experientially we knew that critiques of marriage in feminist academia had not necessarily extended to critiques of heterosexism and lesbian invisibility. The embodied heterosexism and ways of life in largely cis-women-occupied women's studies spaces enabled perhaps the habit of, and desire for, the heterosexual subject position; in the event, the entry of the stereotyped 'bad woman' into dominant feminism too was a heterosexual entry (as the discussions on women in sex work show).

Alongside this embodied heterosexism, however, the marked-as-queer practitioner-teacher-student is more intelligible-legible-visible in the urban metropolitan university today than even a few years ago, and a combination of interested rumour and embodied 'difference' may combine to mask prejudice towards this figure. Meanwhile, in the unguarded practice of classroom conversation, following Spivak (1988),[27] 'opposites attract' continues to function as the norm, and the word 'queer' is less minced in its articulation or delivery, is in fact preferred over the word 'lesbian' in these classrooms. In a very short time, in the urban metropolitan university space, the 'queer' word has become the catch-all and placeholder for both non-heterosexual and non-conforming gender identities as a new object of study, as exciting theoretical frameworks, as a way to 'talk about 377' without talking about other laws that impact lesbian lives. The distance from identities in this context – its vagueness rather, at a time when identity politics is witnessing a resurgence – is confusing at best. 'Queer talk', then, is as much a part of women's studies as other disciplinary spaces, and this might be another manner of the management of gender in institutionalised feminist work. I would like to leave this as a question.

Looking for lesbian feminism in *this* time of the nation

I have been speaking of the intersections of state and feminist discourse in multiple locations on gender and sexuality, and the manner in which the trope of the cis-heterosexual younger person is constructed through iteration and a constitutive outside. With the historically static trope of the girl child as the meter of national time, we have, it would seem, a 'reproductive being-in-waiting' brought into being, protected and nurtured, and assuming centrality, while presented as a being-for-itself. This figure consolidates, in miniature, what the 'woman' is of and for the state, and for community and family too. Through this consolidation, committed to in international documents, the state's commitment to gender too gets read. And through this commitment, the binary, heterosexual model gets reiterated as the normative. Jasbir Puar, in her articulation of homonationalism, asks how we may "conceptualise queer sexualities in Afghanistan, Iraq, and other parts of the 'Middle East' … without reproducing neocolonialist assumptions that collude with U.S. missionary and savior discourses" (Puar, 2007:xiii), and goes on to say that "[r]ather than emphasizing the resistant or the oppositional, [she would] exhume the convivial relations between queernesses and militarism … surveillance technologies … nationalism, globalization, fundamentalism, secularism … and neoliberalism" (Puar, 2007:xiv), as she names the "contemporary war machines" (Puar, 2007:xiv). If we were, following her impulse somewhat, to examine the frameworks of nationalism and globalisation that are the confusing face of development in India today, and re-examine fundamentalism, in Indian contexts, in a 'peacetime' that is not really peace, it might strike us that a conviviality or collusion, in other words, the deal that might have been struck, is not so much with queerness, although that word now populates our horizons. Rather, it is on the consensus around what the 'woman' is. To that end, while queerness may hover on our horizons, and while gay or trans lives might be grudgingly acknowledged, the *woman* is cis, heterosexual, *reproductive, familial*. As long as that is clear, and as long as that is read as the primary agenda of gender in India today, the masculine privileges of the state are both intact and hailed. This might be useful for us to think about, as we, in queer feminist spaces, examine our political and disciplinary languages, their zones of uninhabitability, and how those constitute, through exclusion and abjection, the subjects of these spaces (Butler, 1993:3). In other words, it may help us understand the contexts within which a critical lens like lesbian feminism is to be considered. We may need to recognise that there is, in the negotiation between the state and the social, this consensus around 'woman'.

What else does this trope do for the nation-state as such? Menon notes in 2009, following Balibar (2009), that various kinds of mobilisation of the nation-state, "that have historically been associated with emancipatory projects" (Menon, 2009b:77), have now become the very conditions of their refusal. In offering the idea of the post-national as counter-hegemonic, Menon then asks if these counter-hegemonic impulses might be traced 'over' – that is across – the nation (all boundaries) as well as 'under' – resisting "inclusion into the 'larger' national identity" (Menon, 2009b:77). Mary E. John has suggested that one way to think about the post-national is to recognise that there are multiple and divergent narratives, including feminist, than the straight line from the nation-to-globalisation that is generally spoken of in the critical literature (John, 2009:46–49). Spivak has spoken, earlier, with reference to Dopdi, the tribal woman protagonist of Mahasweta Devi's short story of the same name, of those experiences and identities that resist such inclusion, that fall outside "empire-nation exchanges" (Spivak, 1990: 90), and thus could be read as both socially and constitutively abject. Does a recovered narrative of young lesbians or same-sex desiring persons, then, depending on the languages and categories under consideration here, offer scope to articulate a counter-hegemonic stance 'under' or 'over' the nation? What are the spaces from which such a counter-hegemonic stance may be made possible? As far as the 'over' is concerned, the furore over the UN Special Rapporteur's report on violence against women in India comes to mind, where caste, same-sex relationships, disability, all figured as unfavourable contexts for women in India (Manjoo, 2014). Queer feminist activists in India and elsewhere have been articulating the 'feminist queer' position as a necessary opposition to some more convivialities – to use Puar's term again. Corporatised gay politics, misogyny and entrenched and essentialist religious-cultural positions that model a 'good queer' are some of these convivialities, most publicly visible in the pride marches in some urban metros. In the framework of such convivialities, an event like the vandalism of theatres at the time of the showing of the film *Fire* in 1997[28] does not require a calling out of Hindu fundamentalist politics alongside a calling out of homo-negativity, and is the ground for the continued refusal by cor-poratised gay politics to engage or ally with other movements against discrimination or oppression. In the present moment, where the idea of the nation is symbolically, literally, visibly, legitimately tied to the notion of the dominant and upper-caste Hindu majority as never before, even these 'feminist queer' counter-hegemonic articulations look uncertain. In such a sce-nario, the girl child is indeed the nation's honour rather than state responsibility, and references to patriarchy, as a passing nod to feminist language, can be made without commitment to structural change. As to whether the bleak picture afforded by this analysis can change, is possibly up to our feminist queer politics, and the languages within gender studies, to attempt.

Notes

1 I invoke here this difficulty, not to refuse acknowledgement of or delegitimise the work of lesbian collectives in the country; the difficulty I pose is of lesbian feminism as a frame of reference for political work.

2 I use the term 'girl child' as a state category throughout the chapter; this category emerged since the 1990s in development and policy worldwide, and gained increasing visibility since the 'International Day of the Girl Child' celebrated by the United Nations in 2012. The Beijing Platform was "the first UN World Conference on Women document to specifically mention 'the girl child' as a separate category" (Hendricks and Bachan, 2015:895).

3 At the time of writing, we have received a favourable judgement on Section 377 of the Indian Penal Code, which faced its latest challenge through a new group of petitions submitted in the Supreme Court this year, by feminist queer activists and mental health professionals, among others. A legacy of colonial law, Section 377 has had a complicated history, having been used literally and as a threat against queer-identified people on the grounds of acts that are considered "against the order of nature". In a far-reaching judgment on 6 September 2018, the Supreme Court read down Section 377 as unconstitutional.

4 The Preconception and Prenatal Diagnostics Techniques (Prohibition of Sex Determination) Act, 2003.

5 The slogan translates roughly as "Save the girl child, educate the girl child". It is not clear if it means – "save her by educating her", or "save her, and educate her".

6 Institutions of local self-government formalised in the 1990s in India.

7 One of the incentives suggested at the village level – boards that would indicate the numbers of girl and boy children born, as a way of reflecting on protection for girl children.

8 Maglaty (2011) offers a fascinating account of the emergence of gender-specific and binary clothing trends in the United States in the 1940s, curiously linked to the emergence of the child as consumer and prenatal testing as a means of 'knowing' and therefore shopping for the baby to come. As we are well aware, this knowledge has had different effects in Indian contexts.

9 Bhanwari Devi's experience in a situation such as this is seared into the memory of the women's movement; but what she was being punished for, in the familiar script of sexual punishment for flouting the norms of heteropatriarchy, is what I am concerned with here. Bhanwari Devi was a village-level worker or *Saathin* (roughly translating as woman friend) in the women's development programme of the government of Rajasthan, and a Kumhar (Dalit). This also gives a sense of where women who are village-level workers stand in caste and gender hierarchies in any community, while being considered first point of contact. See Kumar (1997), Sen (2014), and Jaising (2014), for detailed discussions of this history.

10 Commercial surrogacy is now illegal with the Surrogacy Bill of 2016 by the Indian state; however, with a continuing consolidation of kinship and biological ties, and the rendering illegal of same-sex parenthood through surrogacy.

11 The Act stipulates that parents or elderly relatives who are unable to provide for themselves, can apply to be taken care of by their children or younger relatives, failing which the younger relatives may face imprisonment. The Act prompted several commentaries, including a survey by HelpAge India, an NGO, that claimed that the main abusers of the elderly in homes were daughters-in-law, followed by sons and daughters (HelpAge India, 2015:135).

12 A term indicating a cultural, social and professional identity for a particular group of transfeminine persons in India, who have historically had family structures outside of the traditional heteronormative ones. They have been written about in multiple scholarship, in orientalist (Nanda, 1999) and more enabling ways (Revathi, 2010).

13 A phrase introduced by Adrienne Rich (1980).

14 The Supreme Court in 2013 argued this in response to the plea against the reading down of Section 377 by the Delhi High Court; it said that "a miniscule fraction of the country's population constitute lesbians, gays, bisexuals or transgenders" and therefore could not be grounds for declaring the section invalid (Joseph, 2013).

15 That centre parting has, in normative Hindu marriages, a special significance, as the site of the *sindoor*, the symbol of marriage linked in myth as the mark of ownership of her body.

16 Images: Ministry of Women and Child Development, Government of India. Available at http://www.wcd.nic.in/ (Accessed 12 August 2018).

17 Both placeholder and place-making are Halberstam's terms. The idea of the placeholder would seem to refer to the normative category, while place-making might indicate, extending Halberstam, alternative ways of claiming space within heteropatriarchal households. See Ranade (2018) for an evocative discussion of some of these aspects of growing up for lesbian and gay children.

18 I use the term 'dominant feminism' to indicate, within the heterogeneous and uneven character of feminisms, the presence of a particular strand that is inhabited by socially dominant perspectives – cis-heterosexual women, upper-caste, able-bodied, to name a few. I suggest that, in addition to these perspectives being primarily held up by people occupying these locations, they have also been normatively accommodated, and therefore made the standard.

19 She refers to The Forum Against Sex Determination and Sex Pre-selection, a coalition and campaign started in 1984, to make this point.

20 The Mathura rape case, as it is commonly referred to, is of a young tribal woman who was sexually assaulted within a police station in a small town in Maharashtra, India, in 1979. There were large-scale protests in the women's movement and amongst feminist academics against the Supreme Court judgment that pronounced that she had consented, since she was found to be 'habituated' to intercourse. For a detailed discussion, see Gothoskar et al. (1982) and Baxi (2000).

21 The *Special Cell for Women and Children* is an initiative of the social work discipline of a university in Mumbai, India, which, through "strategic collaboration with the Police Department, aims at integrating social services with the police system to provide a co-ordinated, coherent and in-depth response to the issue of violence against women" (Panchal and Ajgaonkar, 2015:11). While the expected coherence with an inherently patriarchal police system can at best be pragmatic, and while

social services are not geared to overturning the system, the programme has been able to introduce the language of rights for women, multiple kinds of negotiated solutions in individual women's lives, and in shared language with feminist movements, acknowledge the heteronormative structure of families and systems.

22 I have attempted a more extended discussion on these connections, with other disciplines as well, elsewhere (Achuthan, 2017), and will only be flagging them here.

23 This report, considered a watershed document in India's feminist history, was prepared by a Committee on the Status of Women and submitted to the Ministry of Education and Social Welfare in December 1974, in the run up to the International Women's Year, as a commentary on the failed promise of constitutional equality.

24 Longino's term, used to urge an attentiveness to "individual difference among the individuals and samples that constitute the objects of study" (Longino, 1992:337).

25 Butler speaks of "[t]he production of the unsymbolizable, the unspeakable, the illegible [as] ... a strategy of social abjection" (Butler, 1993:190).

26 "If lesbianism were to be understood as one among many forms of impropriety, then the relationship between sexuality and gender remains intact in the sense that we don't get to ask under what conditions lesbianism actually unsettles the notion of gender. Not simply the question of what is a proper woman or an improper woman, but what is not thinkable as a woman at all!" (Butler in Meijer and Prins, 1998:283–284).

27 Spivak speaks of the "unguarded practice of conversation" in another context of representation (1988).

28 A film made by Canadian Indian filmmaker Deepa Mehta, that was released in 1997, that spoke of an intimate relationship between sisters-in-law. Screenings in Delhi and Bombay were vandalised and shut down by Hindu right-wing activists on the grounds of dishonour and misrepresentation of Hindu culture. Protests and massive mobilising against this vandalism is marked as India's lesbian moment in many histories (Dave, 2012).

FOURTEEN | Activist past, theoretical future

Valérie Simon

As registration for the series on lesbian theory and activism opened, what I was asked most often were variations of one question: how many people are in the collective? What was most surprising about this question was not only how often it came, but people's reaction when I would tell them that this lecture series on lesbian theory and activism was a solo project: shock and confusion. On the one hand, this is understandable. Many of Montreal's activist projects are the work of affinity groups. Even if the project starts as a solo endeavour there is more often than not potential for the project to become a group thing. On the other hand, however, this question was mystifying to me because the main reason why I was organising the series was to try something different in my efforts to build community around this shared interest in lesbian theory and activism. So, I wondered: who and where are all these people with whom I could have built a collective to organise this series? And if they do exist in great numbers: will they come to the series? Will they see themselves in it?

The series took place over the course of twelve weeks in Montreal, from January to April 2016 at Concordia University's Simone de Beauvoir Institute, which houses the Women's Studies department. Throughout it, as I document the series' existence with this essay, these questions remained open and mostly unanswered. They are, however, central to the project of which the lecture series was only one manifestation: LEARNING HOW

TO SCREAM (LHTS), an activist, zine[1] and archival project that focuses on the relationships between sexuality, theory, activism and life. Whereas the zine project is a critical engagement with lesbian activism, the aim of the lecture series titled "LEARNING HOW TO SCREAM: A Lecture Series on Lesbian Lives, Theory and Activism" was to explore the possibility of doing lesbian studies in an academic context and testing out in practice what this would look like. As such, the series had two parts. The first part focused on key themes in lesbian studies such as lesbian bar culture and compulsory heterosexuality. The second part focused on specific lesbian practices such as lesbian cultural productions, lesbian narratives and testimony practices, and lesbian archiving.

This essay aims to archive, not by way of simply giving an account of what was, what is and what could have been, but by way of nuanced reflections from an activist and academic perspective. I will first describe the series of choices that shaped the structural elements of the series, i.e. its description and its syllabus and the main issue they engage with: the question of the (lesbian) past. This discussion will be followed by a synthetisation of an approach to lesbian studies, i.e. lesbian theory and lesbian activism, that I will refer to as a logic of engagement. Such a logic aims to open up lines of thought concerning the relationship between gender, sexuality, lesbophobia and a critique of heterosexuality through an engagement with, rather than a revaluation of, lesbian theory and activism.

"LEARNING HOW TO SCREAM: A Lecture Series on Lesbian Lives, Theory and Activism" was not the first effort to think through the possibility of lesbian studies at Concordia University's Simone de Beauvoir Institute. Indeed, founded in 1987 by Carolyn Gammon (1993) and active until 1993, the Lesbian Studies Coalition of Concordia (LSCC) aimed to create lesbian studies classes at Concordia University and Lesbian

Studies programmes in Canada. Their motto was: "Lesbian Studies, PhD, year 2000!" Theoretically influenced by Adrienne Rich (Lesbian Studies Coalition of Concordia, 1988), the LSCC understood lesbian feminism in terms of women identification and resisted perspectives that would interpret being a lesbian as the "female version" of "male homosexuality" (Lesbian Studies Coalition of Concordia, 1988).

In conjunction with this history of the LSCC and its activism, the series had two structural elements: a description and a syllabus. Both elements aimed to address a question that confronts lesbian feminist[2] activism and theory in our contemporary moment, i.e. what to do with a problematic past? The specific lesbian feminist tradition that I'm concerned with is the radical lesbian materialist position that can be identified with Monique Wittig (1992) as well as with a specific strand of lesbian feminist activism and movement in Montreal. As such, this radical lesbian materialist position is, as I have come to understand it, on the one hand, suspicious of feminism and its use of lesbian labour while throwing lesbians and their issues under the bus, and, on the other hand, constituted by a deep commitment to the fight against the heteropatriarchy and the violence women face every day. In its classical deployment, radical lesbian materialism uses non-mixity, i.e. lesbian-only spaces and not simply women-only spaces as a way to organise around issues concerning lesbians and women. This is the only kind of lesbian feminism (understood as an umbrella term) to which the questions of the lecture series were addressed and that I understand as lying at the centre of the question posed by this anthology: should it, i.e. radical lesbian materialism, be engaged with and if so, at what cost?

Within the series' structural elements, this question of what to do with a problematic lesbian past was framed as the series' starting point through a question and a definition. Indeed, the series' description opened with the following question: *in face of the transmisogynistic, whitewashed, biphobic and classist official history of lesbian theory and activism, what does it mean that it is the very people excluded from that history who are digging up that history, engaging with it and critiquing it?* This question was immediately followed by an inclusive definition of who 'lesbian' refers to:

> lesbian refers to any person who identifies as such, meaning cis, trans, or intersex women who identify as lesbian, dyke, bisexual, pansexual, lesboromantic, and/or queer as well as any non-binary identified people who are queer, genderqueer, intersex or two-spirited and who identify as lesbian, dyke, bisexual, pansexual, lesboromantic and/or queer. (LEARNING HOW TO SCREAM: A Lecture Series on Lesbian Lives, Theory and Activism, 2016)

What emerged in discussions with participants from this question and this definition as a starting point for the series was a first characterisation of what I will refer to, for the remainder of this essay, as the 'Other' of lesbian feminisms. Indeed, the bold and unambiguous challenge to transmisogynistic and biphobic logics and the inclusive definition of lesbian were both revered and reviled by participants. Had the definition and question not been stated in those terms, people would not have come to the series. At the same time, however, those terms were not seen as enough to fully address those problematic elements and their current manifestations in lesbian communities.[3] Thus, the 'Other' of lesbian feminisms refers to those for whom denunciation of transmisogynistic and biphobic logics and an inclusive definition of 'lesbian' (as a sexual orientation) are necessary starting points for exploring ways to engage with a problematic past. Furthermore, for those 'Other' of lesbian feminisms, lesbian communities are understood as sexual communities made of people who identify in different ways (in terms of sexual orientation and gender identity) and who have a relationship (good, bad, broken or severed forever) with the word lesbian and the communities that organise themselves around the word either because it speaks to part of their identity and/or the people in that community are part of their dating/kinship pool.

Building off this question and this definition, the second structural element of the series, its syllabus, was shaped by the assumption that work on lesbian sexuality and communities never stopped, but rather took different forms, was less centralised and was expanding other narratives. It is for this reason then, that following the discussion of classical texts such as *The Straight Mind* by Monique Wittig (1992), "Compulsory Heterosexuality and Lesbian Existence" by Adrienne Rich (1980), "The 'Empire' Strikes Back: A Posttranssexual Manifesto" by Sandy Stone (1987/2014), and "Poetry Is Not a Luxury" and "The Transformation of Silence into Language in Action" by Audre Lorde (1984/2007), contemporary authors (both academic and non-academic) such as Julia Serano (2013), Sara Ahmed (2006b; 2017), Yasmin Nair (n.d.), Erin J. Rand (2014) and Viviane Namaste (2015), whose work engages with lesbian theory and activism or specific practices such as cultural productions, narratives, testimony and archiving were examined.

What the structural elements of the series highlighted was that this past that the 'Other' of lesbian feminisms tries to wrestle with is both activist (e.g. the LSCC) and theoretical (e.g. the works of Rich and Wittig). Moreover, because of the ways in which lesbian theory and activism open lines of thought and the imagination, this grappling with a lesbian past is paired with an uneasiness with such an engagement. A tension then emerges between a problematic past and engagement with this past. Indeed, I come from a generation of people, post-1980s and post-1990s, for whom, as Teresa de Lauretis (2007) puts it in an essay she wrote to mourn Wittig's passing, "today's lesbians are many things and only rarely women" (de Lauretis, 2007:73). From this standpoint, Wittig's "lesbians are not women" (Wittig, 1992:32) not only opens up ways to understand gender in nonessentialist terms, but also ways to understand one's gender identity as *not* woman. This latter interpretation is not so much about theoretical accuracy as it is about how the text opens a door that cannot be closed and shapes one's understanding and reading of radical lesbian materialism. After spending time identifying with a queer movement in our local cities and working on queer festivals, zines, shows, we found ourselves at a standstill; somehow neither queer nor lesbian, in the classical sense, was enough to capture what it is that we are, what it is that we want, what it is that we need. So, we got to work and read some more, talked to different people, worked on different projects, went back to the lesbian, the queer and the trans archive to find answers. However, the uneasiness brought by diving into work not made for us persisted.

The challenge then, is not just to point to this uneasiness, but to further characterise this tension between lesbian feminisms' problematic history and a rigorous engagement with that history and its texts, meaning with lesbian theory. But what constitutes specifically lesbian theory? For Cheshire Calhoun, in her 1994 article "Separating Lesbian Theory from Feminist Theory", there is a lot at stake in asking this question because if lesbian feminism is the use of feminist tools to analyse lesbianism then there is no specifically lesbian theory as lesbian theory is *really* feminist theory (Calhoun, 1994:559). Indeed, a feminist theory that neither understands "heterosexuality as a political structure separable from patriarchy" (Calhoun, 1994:559) nor differentiates between heterosexual and nonheterosexual women and their different relationship to heterosexuality can't do otherwise but theorise "lesbian oppression as a special case of patriarchal oppression" (Calhoun, 1994:559). For Calhoun then, there are barriers to the creation of specifically lesbian theory, i.e. "to [the treating of] sexual orientation on a par with gender, race, and economic class – that is, as a distinct and irreducible dimension of one's political identity" (Calhoun, 1994:562). What this discussion of Calhoun's concern with specifically lesbian theory points to is first, that how we conceptualise the relationship between gender, sexuality, lesbophobia and a critique of heterosexuality as well as the (lesbian) past matters to the kind of theory we can and do produce. Second, that from different understandings of the (lesbian) past and of gender, sexuality, lesbophobia and heterosexuality emerge different specifically lesbian theories and forms of activism.

The question is then, what is the relationship between this tension resulting from lesbian feminisms' problematic past and a rigorous engagement with that past and the different ways lesbian theory understands the relationship between gender, sexuality, lesbophobia and heterosexuality? How can this tension and these relationships be further characterised? Initially, they can be characterised through critical questions asked both to oneself as one engages with that work and to this problematic (lesbian) past. These questions, which map onto the themes of the past and the relationship between gender, sexuality, lesbophobia and a critique of heterosexuality, are:

- Regarding the past: Are transmisogyny and biphobia an unfortunate trope or an integral part of lesbian feminisms' history?
- Regarding the relationship between gender and sexuality: Is lesbian about women identification or about desire and sexuality with its own codes and history?
- Regarding the relationship between lesbophobia and heterosexuality: Are lesbians aiming to be visible within the feminist movement or within the LGBTQ+ movement?

These critical questions are neither exhaustive nor yes or no. However, their either/or form echoes the uneasiness that results from the tension between a problematic (lesbian) past and an engagement with lesbian theory. As such, to better understand this tension as well as to open up ways to do lesbian theory, what is needed is an examination of those binaries when the question of specifically lesbian theory and activism is posed.

In "Homo Sum", Wittig aims to interrogate dialectics from a "lesbian political philosophical point of view" (Wittig, 1992:49) and therefore examines Aristotle's table of opposites and singles out those she sees as terms of evaluation (right/left, male/female, light/dark, good/bad). At work for her with those categories of opposition (or difference) is that for thinkers of our modern age (philosophers, linguists, psychoanalysts, anthropologists), "one cannot reason or think or, even better, that outside of them meaning cannot shape itself" (Wittig, 1992:52). By listing what I see as a non-exhaustive list of categories of opposites that make up a table of lesbian feminist opposites and function as a more succinct version of the critical questions asked above, I aim to articulate the ways in which current discussions and conceptualisations of lesbian feminisms stay trapped in those categories. This is so because each side of the binary forms a set of organising categories around which thinking, theorising but also discussions regarding lesbian feminisms are structured. This, in turn, limits how we can engage with lesbian feminisms and evaluate their theoretical legacy and contemporary developments. Each pair listed below relates (in order) to the past, the relationship between gender and sexuality, and the relationship between lesbophobia and heterosexuality:

Monique Wittig	Patrick Califia
Adrienne Rich	Joan Nestle
Feminist activism	LGBTQ+ activism

This table functions differently from the Aristotelian table of opposites that Wittig is interrogating. Indeed, the usual interpretation of such binaries and their categories (right/left, male/female, light/dark, good/bad) is to understand one side (the left side of the dichotomy) as socially, politically and materially valued and superior while the other side (the right side of the dichotomy) is devalued and inferior. The particularity of this table of lesbian feminisms' opposites is that each half of the binary is both valued and devalued. There is no consistency, i.e. both the left side and the right side are valued/devalued in no particular pattern by a variety of groups and/or individuals coming from different perspectives. What then, is lesbian theory to do with this double devaluation in its work of interrogating the binaries that characterise the tension between a problematic (lesbian) past and an engagement with that past?

To illustrate what this double devaluation can look like, I briefly return to Calhoun's discussion of specifically lesbian theory. Indeed, as discussed above, for her, it is important that gender politics be separated from sexuality politics for specifically lesbian theory to emerge. However, the consequence of such a separation, for Calhoun, is that sometimes they are in disagreement with one another, i.e. what is valued/devalued in each perspective regarding the past, and the relationship between gender, sexuality, lesbophobia and heterosexuality differs. In her discussion of debates surrounding butch and femme relationships and their roots in 1950s working-class bars, Calhoun simultaneously devalues and values such relationships. Indeed, she devalues such relationships as she adheres to a certain feminist critique (Calhoun, 1994:570) for whom even if butch and femme relationships challenge heterosexuality, they do not challenge patriarchy (Calhoun, 1994:572). At the same time, however, she disagrees with the characterisation, by certain lesbian feminist theories that she associates with Adrienne Rich that "butches and femmes, lesbian sex radicals who promote pornography and s/m, lesbian mothers and married lesbians fail to measure up" politically and are either politically uninteresting or assimilationists (Calhoun, 1994:577). Rather, they correspond, in my reading of Calhoun, to further specificy to whom the 'Other' of lesbian feminisms refers.

These 'Others' of lesbian feminisms did not remain silent as they faced the violent ostracisation by lesbian feminisms of their lives, theories and activism. Indeed, drawing a poignant picture of this exclusion in his 1994 introduction to *Public Sex: The Culture of Radical Sex*, Patrick Califia describes the work of and the exclusion of these 'Others' of lesbian feminisms in the following way:

> Most of them had never had to come out because people had started telling them they were queers when they were just little kids. They could not and would not hide their identities. They were committed to living in the company of and for the good of other women. They had kept a lesbian community alive through very hard times. They defended the bars where women's studies majors who despised them went cruising. Their physical and emotional scars from those battles frightened middle-class white girls who formed their lesbian identities over books by Ti-Grace Atkinson, Kate Millet, and Shulamith Firestone. But Amazons always have scars. It drove me crazy that these women, who were my ancestors and heroes, were being written off and ignored. *Not only did they get beaten up, ridiculed, and pathologized by straight society, but their own intelligentsia, wanted to deny them a place in our history. This was just plain wrong.* (Califia, 2000:xvii, emphasis added)[4]

In articulating this relationship between lesbians who were part of 1950s lesbian communities, lesbian feminist theory, and a lesbian feminist critique that devalued those communities and their history, Califia highlights a reversal at work with the ways in which lesbian feminisms has found footing in academia and outside of it. Indeed, at the time of writing Califia's 1994 introduction, those most visible lesbian members were in fact silenced by being rendered irrelevant to the lesbian feminist project, while, at the same time, they were being repackaged through sociological studies that made it possible for the very few lesbian scholars that are still at work today to establish themselves and a kind of lesbian scholarship which, in turn, became a mandatory starting point for anyone who came after them who would like to also do lesbian scholarship. As such, the most visible members of the lesbian community, those rendered superfluous to the lesbian feminist project, were repackaged and their lives and activism was put to work to make space for lesbian theory in academia and now, those people who can trace their lesbian lineage back so to speak to those who were rendered superfluous are now wrestling with what to do with a lesbian past that was never for or about them in the first place as this past has established itself as the main (or only) starting point to think through lesbian feminisms and its possibilities. It is here then, that the uneasiness that is the result of the tension between a problematic lesbian past and an engagement with that past emerges.

Following this illustration of the double devaluation that characterises the tension between a problematic lesbian past, an engagement with that past and the uneasiness that results from such engagement for the 'Others' of lesbian feminism, the question remains: how can the work of interrogating the binaries of the table of lesbian feminist opposites that are doubly devalued take place? This work will be made possible by a change of relationship to valuation, i.e. a move from a logic of reclaiming to a logic of engagement. Indeed, I use these terms to identify what constitutes, in my view, two attitudes one can take (both personally and in one's work) while interrogating the binaries that make up the table of lesbian feminist opposites. A reclaiming logic aims to show that both sides of the table of opposites should not be either valued or not valued, and as such aims to bring nuance to the examination and potential contribution of each category. In contrast, a logic of engagement uses the double devaluation of each part of the table as a starting point for thinking about lesbian feminisms as well as a descriptor of the current political, social and theoretical landscape where each half of these respective dichotomies is valued or devalued but never in a consistent way. In so doing, a failed revaluation is not an obstacle to a renewed lesbian feminist project, but rather a further descriptor of the current state and context for contemporary sexuality politics. This interrogation of binaries through a logic of engagement, is not, however, a queering of those binaries and of lesbian feminisms: it does not involve a reflexive critique of the norms that structure lesbian feminisms, an attention to the inconsistencies and queer moments within lesbian feminisms, or an intertwining of queer theory with lesbian feminist theory. This is so because queer theory and queer movements have their own others: lesbians and bisexual people.[5] Therefore, an engagement with lesbian feminisms requires a decentralising of queer as the main or only way to engage with, theorise and critique contemporary sexuality politics to make space for not only the 'Other' of lesbian feminisms but also the 'Other' of queer theory.

At the start of the chapter, I noted that its task is two-folded. On the one hand, it offers a characterisation of the tension that results from a problematic lesbian past and an engagement with that past through a table of lesbian feminist opposites made up of a list of non-exhaustive binaries that shape meaning and thinking around issues of lesbian feminisms. As each half of the binary is not valued/devalued in any consistent way, I proposed a logic of engagement to open ways to continue the work of interrogating such binaries and to describe the landscape of contemporary sexual politics. On the other hand, this essay is an archive: it documents a lecture series on lesbian lives, theory and activism that took place in 2016. This need to archive an event that took place so recently is also an element that makes up contemporary sexuality politics. Indeed, a logic of engagement not only aims to describe this contemporary terrain, but also asks, through this description: what is the effect of this engagement with lesbian feminisms?[6] Even though this question is left unanswered, one thing is clear: the success of this engagement cannot simply be measured by how ubiquitous the ideas put forth and the projects that shape such an engagement become. It is fine if no one, in Montreal, does a lecture series on lesbian theory and activism for another twenty or more years. New standards need to be imagined. But in the meantime, a logic of engagement and its success can be measured by the strength of the commitment to the 'Others' of lesbian feminisms and queer theory, to ending biphobia and transmisogyny in lesbian communities, and to a theorising of the landscape of contemporary sexuality politics that goes beyond the building of a more exhaustive table of lesbian feminisms opposites. This means asking: what would our thinking, our theorising and our lives look like if, through our engagement with lesbian feminisms, we committed ourselves to ourselves?[7]

Notes

1 The zine currently has two issues. The first issue (completed in December 2015) documents and reflects on the history of dyke marches in Montreal from 2012 to the present. The second issue (completed in August 2018) is a series of reflections on loss and activism.

2 In this essay, when I refer to lesbian feminisms, I use it as an umbrella term, following the definition given by Browne, Olasik and Podmore (2016) in the article 'Reclaiming Lesbian Feminisms: Beginning Discussions on Communities, Geographies and Politics', which is itself based on JoAnne Myers' (2003) account in *Historical Dictionary of the Lesbian Liberation Movement: Still the Rage*: "lesbian feminism includes a wide array of practices ranging from lesbian feminism (claiming a lesbian position within feminism), radical lesbianism (claiming a separate and autonomous movement for lesbians) and cultural feminisms (the creation of women-only spaces for the production of a women-centred culture)" (Browne, Olasik and Podmore, 2016:113).

3 Julia Serano speaks to the workings of monosexists and transmisogynistic logics in lesbian communities in *Excluded: Making Feminism and Queer Movements More Inclusive* (2013). Specifically, she discusses what she refers to as FAAB (Female-Assigned-At-Birth)-mentality which she defines as lesbian/queer desire in terms of not dating or being sexual with cis men. According to this logic, one is not queer if one engages in relationships with cis men. Thus, FAAB-mentality justifies simultaneously the marginalisation of bisexual people who do date cis men and the disavowal of trans women as potential romantic and/or sexual partners.

4 Joan Nestle also speaks to this issue when she writes, in the introduction to *Persistence: All Ways Butch and Femme*, that one of her goals in editing, in 1992, *Persistent Desire: A Femme-Butch Reader* was to "reconstitute lives fragmented by the small-minded, by those trapped by gender or class conventions, by those so taken with prevailing ideologies of liberation that they repeated new mantras of dismissal" (Nestle, 2011:17).

5 Regarding lesbians, Erin Rand (2014) makes the case for lesbians as the 'Other' of queer theory in her book *Reclaiming Queer: Activist and Academic Rhetorics of Resistance* where she discusses the absence of the Lesbian Avengers as a "proper" queer direct-action group in academic queer theory. Viviane Namaste (2015) discusses the othering of bisexual identities in her book *Oversight: Critical Reflections on Feminist Research and Politics*.

6 Here, I am more specifically referring to this question as it was asked in the article "Reclaiming Lesbian Feminisms: Beginning Discussions on Communities, Geographies and Politics", where the authors concluded: "beyond recovering lost lesbian feminist histories and practices, the extent to which lesbian feminist political ideas are being embraced and reconsidered remains unclear" (Browne, Olasik and Podmore, 2016:121).

7 I further flesh out the question of commitment to lesbian theory and activism in the first issue of the LEARNING HOW TO SCREAM zine titled *LEARNING HOW TO SCREAM*, Issue #1: *It Breaks My Heart, But It Had To Be Said* (Simon, 2015).

FIFTEEN | From separation to dialogue/ dangerous love

Mamatha Karollil

While writing this paper, I had an argument with a friend over what she felt was my political obligation in going to a meeting of queer academics and activists. While I was only too eager to avoid the gay male domination[1] that I anticipated therein, she thought this engagement crucial for troubling dominant androcentric frameworks of knowledge and politics. I remarked with irony that I was acting against the key ethical tenets that I was attempting to develop in this paper – of staying in relation, in *dangerous* relation with the other against whom one is cast in a hierarchical relationship and whose power derives from this difference (man and woman in this instance). Feeling grateful for queer women's[2] and women's collectives, we however had a moment of pause when we thought of how our *dalit-bahujan* sisters may be similarly suspicious and avoidant of our company (we are both *savarna*).[3]

My primary objective in this paper is to reconsider the basis of collective organising in various kinds of identity politics in the face of an intersectional troubling/enriching of it. Before I do that, in the interest of minimising epistemic violence, I'd like to locate myself intellectually/ideologically and also relatedly, briefly describe the material political context of the world and work I am attempting to theorise. I'm an academic with a higher degree in psychology, but I also consider myself an activist in the queer-feminist critical theory and pedagogy that I pursue in the classroom and in my participation in a few queer, LBT, feminist and anti-fascist collectives in the city of Delhi, in the faculty union and in the primarily student-filled, informal queer collective that some of us faculty and students set up in the university five years ago. These groups, although being city-based and composed largely of English-speaking middle-class Indians, also see a diversity of political consciousness in terms of class, caste and region, and many of us are therefore placed in multiple activist groups working on a range of issues.[4]

It also becomes important to contextualise these efforts against the big other of the progressive academic-activist circles in the country's urban centres – the revival of the Hindu right-wing in electoral politics in India. This is to say that as activists and academics of various ideological frameworks, as feminists, Marxists, queer activists and anti-caste activists, in this climate of almost constant war and fire-fighting against injustice on various fronts, we often find ourselves working side by side – petitioning, holding strikes, waving banners – as we walk arm in arm on the streets, sometimes for democratic and civil liberties such as the right to criticise the government, or to eat food of one's choice, or to marry who one chooses; at other times, against de-regularisation and privatisation that displaces and dispossesses already precarious lives, defending the autonomy of art, cultural and educational institutions, or protesting state violence against its citizens in insurgent states such as Kashmir and Chattisgarh.

If my solidarity is with a diverse political agenda, my primary and most organic political perspective on the world is of feminism, and lesbian feminism[5] in particular has been of enormous personal influence. However, solidarity, as we know, is not a matter of a liberal inclusion of perspectives or an easy lending of voice to a range of left-liberal or progressive issues. An intersectional interrogation of theoretical positions and politics necessarily threatens collectivisation – difference promises to overwhelm the commonality to our experiences along any stable axis of identity, such experience being the starting point of many forms of collective organising and resistance. I use the words "necessarily" and "promises", because, while intersectionality has the potential to threaten concerted organised action, I wish to foreground its necessity at the same time.

In LGBTQ (...)[6] political organising, the turn to non-identitarian *queer politics*, paralleling and/or informed by poststructuralist critique, with its unstable fragmented subject-in-process, was imagined to be inaugurating such a logic of intersectional political organising:

> If identities were no longer fixed as the premises of a political syllogism, and politics no longer understood as a set of practices derived from the alleged interests that belong to a set of ready-made subjects, a new configuration of politics would surely emerge from the ruins of the old. (Butler, 1990: 149)

Yet, the promise hides a danger: once we accept the poststructuralist critique of essentialism, we open up a veritable avalanche of identity perspectives. From *savarna* woman to queer *savarna* woman, to cis queer *savarna* woman and onwards, in a more and more particularising and differentiating manner. Carried to its logical end, queer theory and intersectional politics can, in practice and in its categorical differences, devolve to a consideration of the life and context of a unitary being in all its irreducible unique difference – in the suspicious manner of the humanist project, where human beings are seen as possessing a unique potential that he/she/they have a right to and an obligation to fill. As academics and activists,[7] we often see how this plays out practically in the everyday living of this intersectional ideal. In our striving (not nearly enough) to be threatened by our non-privileged others or in our engagements with those we see as positioned higher than us in the hierarchy, in the harsh interrogation of erasures, prejudices, violence, we often find that difference threatens to eclipse commonality, that it threatens to atomise and isolate us.

The dilemmas that mark these new forms of identity politics are old ones – how does one stand witness to experience, yet resist the narcissistic, individualising pull of such an examination of experience and move beyond, to the hidden collective structures through and against which these are articulated? How does one resist the lure of being mired in experience and move towards political action for a re-articulation of these structures (e.g. see hooks, 1997). The questions are also new ones. In seeing the limits of these imaginations and these actions, drawn as they are from our limited discursive fields, often against a singular dominant other (race/caste/class/ability/religion), in recognition of the production of the subject by "hybrid transformations generated by the horizontal coexistence of a number of symbolic systems" (Canclini, 1992), what will be the new foundations for collective action towards social justice? In this new postmodern world, where power is *also* nonsovereign, where it is locatable not only outside of us, and where therefore separation is not viable as a political strategy, how does one survive within relations of power, either as the oppressor or the oppressed? Locating ourselves in the pyramid of power, as we turn our gaze upwards and downwards, the questions keep changing. On the one hand, how do we allow ourselves to be threatened by beings whose lives and wor(l)ds are illegible or unknown to us, whose realities are as yet eclipsed by our re-articulations of our world/s? On the other hand, how do we risk engaging with those served by hegemonic meaning systems that erase or overwhelm us, that threaten to annihilate us, that deny us our claim to the symbolic and material world?

Here I attempt to articulate an everyday ethic of staying in relation that has as its foundation a movement from 'woman-identification' to 'other-identification' or a constant striving for identification with those situated in marginalised locations in relation to us. Where assertion of certain epistemic frameworks over others is a way in which dominant groups gain and maintain power, the attempt here will be to first reassert the site of the personal as the site of the political (for race, caste, ability, gender and sexuality) as well as to briefly examine a feminist psychoanalytic analysis of the feminine mode of being and relating,[8] with all its dangers and potentials, as a resource for 'being with' those differently placed on the power hierarchy in relation to us as people of all genders, as black or white or brown, as *dalit-bahujan* or *savarna*. I enter this problematic through an examination of the debates that accompanied the #metoo campaign in Indian academic and activist circles; a debate that, as I will show, lesbian feminism in its critique of heterosexuality is uniquely placed to inform.

On the sites, objects, methods and *limits* of politics/knowledge

The world-wide reverberations of the #metoo campaign, though perhaps largely restricted to those on the World Wide Web and those working in modern organisational/institutional contexts, is a testament to the endurance of patriarchy – the rule of one class of people (men) over another (women). It is a testament to the endurance of the category 'woman', the common everyday sexual violence through which the woman and womanly bodies are shaped and controlled in everyday sites. In real and virtual spaces in activist-academic India, in this period and continuously so, there seemed to occur a foregrounding of gender politics and a backgrounding of other axes of politics – women across caste, region, religion and sexuality, seemed to briefly accommodate their *difference* in a manner that allowed them to be alive to the *commonality* of their experiences as women, calling truth to power. One way in which the university I work at responded was via a consolidation of the identity 'woman academic' in the sharing of experiences and stories of academic journeys among women faculty,[9] the felt need to have woman-only spaces and a renewed sensitivity to how subtle and non-subtle gendered violence constructs academic spaces.

Yet, this moment was not without its exclusion, the forgetting of this commonality. For example, a bid in a newly formed women's collective in the university to include a caste audit alongside a gender audit was met with doubt. In another instance, an online debate saw a well-meaning gay man desist from sharing his experiences of sexual violence, ceding space to women who as per him the #metoo moment served. However, gender non-conforming people (non-binary/trans) as a group threaten and therefore face as much or more sexual violence from hegemonic masculinity as cis women. Here the failure was in not moving beyond the experiences of some kinds of women (*savarna* women and cis women in the above instances) to intersections of structures that produce sexual violence. In either case, one can speculate how much richer an analysis of, and resistance to, the operation of hetero-brahminical-patriarchy would have been possible had such an exclusion been avoided. Such an excision of certain kinds of experiences as being of a different order of power and oppression fails to see, for instance, how hegemonic masculinity relies on a violent othering and exclusion of not just women but a range of femininities – including transfemininities, also seen as 'incomplete masculinities' in order to secure its own symbolic and relatedly material power (e.g. Kimmel's (1997) analysis of masculinity as homophobia under capitalism). It fails to see how the domination of *savarna* men at the higher rungs of an organisation and Dalit women (and men) at the lower rungs demonstrates that in the sexualised corporate-like university in modernity, the labouring body of the woman is subject to the intersecting influence of men's sexual control alongside that of capital's economic control (e.g. MacKinnon, 1979). It could see, following other feminist analyses, how such a control of female sexuality or sexual control of females is a means whereby women are barred from the public sphere, relegating her to the devalued private sphere, which she enters disenfranchised, her devalued labour contributing surreptitiously to surplus value, her body policed and trafficked in aid of consolidating wealth along protected lines of caste (patri)lineage (Rubin, 1975; Franco, Macwan and Ramanathan, 2007) .

The consolidation of the woman-academic identity in academic circles during the #metoo movement accompanied and was, in part, a response to the reactions of male academics of a Marxist socialist leaning (and some well-known gay men were not exempt from this), who somewhat blind to the sex/gender system and its interrelations with flow of capital, often showed a defensive dismay, anger and distancing from the #metoo campaign as a "trend", as "fascist identity politics",[10] as divisive and oppositional, as a bourgeois distraction that needs to be waited out, before the *real* work of politics began. A parallel to such an erasure of modes of everyday feminist resistance and politics is the erasure of certain kinds of feminist scholarship, seen as staying too close to the experiential and the micro-political, as that which neither reaches theoretical sophistication nor political efficacy. Thus, a comment by a young male student (it may well have been from a 'male-identified' female student as well) in a class reading a complex reflexive piece by a post-colonial feminist on the polysemic rhetoric of the veil in Iran, is revealing: "But where is the theory, professor? This reads like an op-ed piece".

Classical radical feminist and lesbian feminist analysis such as was emergent in North America and Western Europe (e.g. Firestone, 1970; Greer, 1970; Rich, 1980; Lorde, 1984) would see these as the many routes through which dominant societal values that define what is legitimate scholarship and what is legitimate political action are identified with male values, serving to consolidate power to serve male needs – the revolutionary has clear and concrete targets in the public sphere, he moves with an unflinching rational force towards goals with real and material consequences. Countering this, lesbian feminism presents the feminist revolutionary as the everyday militant, keenly attuned to the flow of micropower in everyday sites – the street, the factory, the field, the board room and the bedroom, on social media, in who populates and/or dominates these spaces, in whose voice is heard and whose gaze sought. The political aim is to question and rearticulate the criteria by which higher and lower forms of knowledge, labour and art are legitimated, in whose image 'success'/'the good life' is drawn and whose route to this is therefore always already eased (and whose violently prohibited). Turning from a male-identification at these sites and in these technologies of power, such a feminist re-channels her energies and efforts into *woman-identification*. Recognising the production of female subjects in subjugated relation to male subjects (especially through pervasive heterosexuality – in forced intimacies such as 'consensual marriage/relationship' or sexualisation at the work place and in the street), and the impossibility of resisting the pressures of such production in relation, she pursues separation (temporary or long-term, limited or absolute) from men, forging sisterhoods both personal and professional, espousing and living communitarian values and an ethics of care, interdependence and the sharing of psychic and material resources.

Such a language and method of politics, as we know, serves well the aims and concerns of many marginalised and disenfranchised communities. As an upper-caste feminist academic, my keenest entry into caste politics has been through a conscious attempt to recognise these technologies of power through which I am made a subject, limited as these efforts can be (for I can be ignorant, this ignorance fortified by resistance to knowledge that casts me as oppressor, this time in ways that are advantageous to myself). As we start to break apart in recognition of the non-commonality of our experiences as women, can we again start coming together in recognition of the common modus operandi of power relations that produce us in various relations as man and woman, as *savarna* and Dalit, as Hindu and Muslim, as white and brown, as straight and queer? How would a commitment to interrogation of power and social justice in our everyday and long-term relationships and investments translate to the sharing of power and resources at the various material sites of these investments?

From such a perspective, the purported epistemic incommensurability and imagined methodical incompatibilities between various political ideologies do not seem to be unbridgeable. It accommodates on the one hand forms of politicking typically associated with resistance to *sovereign power*: taking to the streets protesting the increasing withdrawal of state funds for higher education, re-ordering institutional/organisation policies in ways that redistribute power and resources, organising to protect welfare measures of the state. There is little cognitive dissonance between these and our individual negotiation of normalising *disciplinary power* in our everyday life: patronising the local vendor rather than the chain store, remunerating 'low skill' labour we access above the market rate for these, broadening notions of what counts for knowledge when evaluating in the classroom, consciously investing in friendships and love relationships across social divisions, sharing and parting with material and cultural resources accrued from our social positions, embodying resistance through 'queering' attire and demeanour.[11] These efforts may thus slide between those seeking 'redistribution' and those seeking 'recognition'; they are sometimes overtly political-economical, at other times seeming 'merely cultural'.[12]

The point to note is that this form of a political awakening involves not just a rising awareness of the structural bases of our own subjugation as women in relation to men but also being alive to the particularity of this subjugation as *savarna* or able-bodied women and, relatedly, gaining knowledge of our participation in other intersecting structures of oppression, even as the oppressor. In other words, where woman-identification is the cultivated mode of political consciousness that some strands of lesbian feminism strive for, here the ethical imperative is towards the conceptually and experientially difficult broad-based notion of (marginalised) *other-identification*. Such a mode of queer resistance to normalisation across a broad swathe of social registers that our multiply-messaged subjecthood traverses invokes what Chela Sandoval (2000) has called *differential consciousness* in her book, *Methodology of the Oppressed*.[13] Derived from locations of multiple oppression such as is the standpoint of feminists of colour in the US, by those who occupy in-between spaces of social categories (not the 'woman' in white feminism, nor the 'black' in masculine anti-race movements), this involves a kinetic and self-conscious mobility across and between different political ideologies and programmes for action, foregrounding and backgrounding of identities, a mode of "guerrilla warfare" as Cherrie Moraga (1981, cited in Sandoval, 2000) puts it:

> Our strategy is how we cope ... how we measure and weigh what is to be said and when, what is to be done and how, and to whom ... daily deciding/risking who it is we can call an ally, call a friend (whatever that person's skin, sex, or sexuality).

Where differential consciousness has been articulated from the perspective of those located at the far peripheries or margins of power, for those closer to the centres of power the ethical imperative in differential consciousness as a method would be to push ourselves to be acquainted with histories of domination and violence and our unknowing and continuing complicity in those, something that many members of the urban-based political collectives that I participate in often attempt to do and many others fail to do equally often.

The ways of failing are many. Sometimes it is about an epistemic arrogance, the lack of an epistemic humility or a poor admission to the limits of our knowledge and the everyday violence it wreaks. In 'progressive' circles, there is sometimes indignation and defensiveness when these limits are observed: "but I consider myself a feminist/anti-caste!" "Admit to your ignorance, manifest your openness to learning, nobody will file a complaint of discrimination against you", I tell a colleague. At other times, epistemic humility mis-translates to a withdrawal from true engagement with the other, where there is an addition of standpoints but no real mutual listening and inter-subjective change. For instance, holding an "I'll cover my *savarna* corner that I know best, you cover yours" orientation in a queer collective, by mapping politics too closely onto sub-divisions in identities/experiences. Often, however, failure is inevitable. Where power flows in the everyday and marks *all* aspects of being and relating, of labour and production in *all* realms of love, work and play, the ethical responsibility towards redistribution of power can become a tremendous burden, the work never-ending.

Failure is inevitable, for there are limits to liberal, rational and conscious efforts towards negotiating relations of power. Failure to bear this intersectional burden then translates to anger and lashing out – in the classroom, meeting room and the bedroom, in the organised political groupings, between friends and family members. Histories of pain translated to anger can catalyse and energise many forms of political action against the origins of that pain, the structures of oppression. Yet, in the context of a heightened and painful awareness of the mediation of our lives through multiple and intersecting relations of power, anger has the potential to become a tool less for forging solidarities and communities than for breaking them.

Failure is also inevitable – and this is not recognised enough – simply because people are differently placed in terms of power and privilege in bearing this burden, something that is often forgotten in the radical race in the political circles I am familiar with. One example of this is the misplaced and what I see as uncharitable criticism of *hijra* women, among the most disenfranchised category of queers in India, for reproducing "regressive (upper) caste Hindu" markers of femininity in their dance performance in the university recently (Chettri, dance performance, 2018). Another is the virulent social media take-down of a feature on lesbians living together in butch–femme roles and speaking of marriage in a mainstream magazine some years ago (Sen, 2013). This is the same feature a close lesbian friend left discreetly around her home for her very traditional middle-class parents to find and thus realise that queers are not only promiscuous seekers of fleeting sexual pleasure, they also pursue (heterosexual) marriage-like stable domesticity. As Shah, Raj and Nevatia (2012) note, for many queer women in precarious social and economic circumstances, attaining a sophisticated intersectional political consciousness and vocabulary is secondary to matters of everyday survival and negotiation. Indeed, it is poor intersectional sensitivity that results in a failure to see the enormous revolutionary effort that *hijra* women and cis queer women who choose to embrace their queer selves demonstrate even in acts of everyday survival, in the absence of networks of class and caste privilege available to those higher up in the class and caste hierarchy.

In the ideological policing that we subject each other to, can this seeing of the entirety of our beings, our beginnings and our social locations be understood as a form of love? Can we extend this compassion in the face of failure and imperfection to all beings, including those we see as more powerful than us? Would this humanising of the oppressor rob us of the radical edge to our questioning structures of oppression? Is love then a political anathema?

Focus on love as a method of politics/knowledge

At a recent talk by Gayatri Spivak in Delhi (Spivak, 2018), in response to a question about the relevance of love in political organising, she said that for her as a feminist love is only a four-letter word. If recognition of the oppressive function of marriage and family in the exploitation of women's labour or in the recruitment of women into the hetero-patriarchal (Hindu) nationalist project are the re-articulations offered by many traditions of feminist analysis, the counter-intuitive and radical insight a lesbian standpoint feminism offers is that of the hidden politics of love and desire.

In this relational view of gender, men and women are produced in a relation of power with each other that is called heterosexuality (sex between gendered opposites, rather than race or class opposites); gender in other words is the eroticisation of domination and submission. Patriarchy constructs female pleasure and desire in a manner that serves itself; women are thus seduced into their own oppression. Moreover, sexual domination through which people with vaginas are made women occurs as a pervasive feature of women's lives, and is a means to control them, even in contexts where her identity as woman is irrelevant, such as the work place. Heterosexual love thus is not only compulsory, it is also dangerous, it confounds oppression with love.

Separation is a logical response to the recognition of the unavoidably power-inflexed/violent nature of the relationships between men and women, and the compulsory heterosexuality that meets the woman in the private and public spheres (Rich, 1980). Turning from man and thereby heterosexuality, however, can she really imagine herself as having escaped relations of domination and subjugation? On the contrary, she is already imbricated in relations of power with her sisters along other axes such as race and class. Perhaps we can begin to see that what lesbian feminism offers to politics is not to reveal the sado-masochistic nature of heterosexuality and separation as a political response and solution to this insight, but the essentially power-ridden nature of *all* relationships. Indeed, desire or the process of formation of the subject stipulates loss and exclusion (one cannot be both boy and girl, old and young, hetero and homo, Dalit and *savarna*) as the very basis of its operation. Moreover, if a relationship/identification of any kind is necessarily threatening of our selves – this self-transformation being the very *sine qua non* of a relationship – social power defines this in a way that casts self and other in an always already binary symbolic hierarchy, the hierarchy that the work of progressive politics attempts to trouble. This work then becomes interrupted in separation. In other words, the unavoidably violent nature of all relationships in this analysis posits not just the unviability of separation as a political strategy, but also posits staying in relation as a political obligation.

If social relations are dangerous, since they cannot escape the function of power, how do we stay in relation in a way that if it does not excise power, then manages it in a way that democratises relations, in a way that doesn't finish us off? Some psychoanalytic feminists (e.g. Chodorow, 1978; Benjamin, 1988; Dimen, 2013) may suggest a way in which to reconsider the strategy of staying in relation; the key argument here posits a relational, intersubjective mode of the self as an ideal that transcends the logic of domination and submission marking social relations.

Gayle Rubin (1975) observes how the division of labour by sex upholds the taboo against the sameness of men and women, a method through which gender is produced. Psychoanalytic feminism suggests that the psychic pathway to masculinity and femininity constructs the former to be more threatened by the collapse of this difference than the latter, an observation borne out by several researches.[14] This is because such accounts posit, in a context where the mothering function is borne by the woman in the early years of life when gender identity develops, boys achieve autonomous selfhood in a context of separation and difference from the mother, whereas girls achieve the same in a context of relationship and similarity. For masculine psyches therefore, emotional attunement to another (a feminine function and the basis of relationality) is threatening to their sense of masculinity and indeed, their very sense of self – this is especially so in a culture that is sexist and devalues the qualities associated with femininity.

Thus, the valuing and cultivation of separation and independence in certain kinds of people (those with penises) contributes to a fragile self that is threatened by intimacy in relationship, the radical difference of the other, for this involves a self-threatening attunement and identification with the other. On the other hand, a feminine mode of being weathers better the assault of difference, for such an individual has been socialised to retain their sense of self even while being attuned to others, being in dialogue with others; this is especially so in a culture that will value the qualities associated with femininity, where desire is not phallic independence but feminine interdependence.

I end this paper by sharing here a post on social media where a feminist is speaking of her developing relationship in dialogue with her mother, someone whose values may be read as male-identified in the lesbian feminist framework.[15] I share this, leaving aside for now the question of whether family relationships are to be distinguished in some essential manner from other forms of relationships.

Observe here the seeing of the other in their entirety, their origins. Observe, also, the epistemic humility, the openness to the risk of transformation in oneself that both parties show and a respect for the limits of that, all of which I'd like to call love:

> I am the youngest one among three daughters & I think my mom loves me the most. Not that she doesn't love the other two, but I think love has to be cultivated. I see that she and I invested in each

other way too much. After quitting her job when I was 13 and my eldest sister was 25 then, my sister started distancing herself for obvious reasons of privacy and other issues. I am now 27 and during my 19–22 yrs of age I noticed how I am distancing myself from her for the very same reasons. And then I started sharing my world out to her. Not that I share all my private stuff with her but I shared everything about my world. Not that she liked everything that I said or did but yeah, it kept us both connected, near even when we were in different states and in all of these I can sense the presence of love.

Initially things went wrong with me as well as I expected her to understand everything I say, and understand it the way I want her to understand. But soon I realised that I should just leave her and give her time to generate her own opinions on what I say. I also started sharing reading that she can connect to, mostly translated ones or read out some good articles for her. I also constantly kept her involved in meeting my world whether she liked it or not. Slowly slowly she got adapted, in later phase she also changed her stands (when she, on her own understood things) and then in the present time, even if she disagrees with what I say at least we hold mutual respect for each other's view. What's important while you share your world is that you don't pull her down, or disagree so strongly that no space of interaction is left. Sometimes it's good to leave a person with a idea, not try to convince them at that particular point but continue the conversation over a longer duration. Like, it took me a continuous conversation for almost two years to make her understand how it is okay for someone to be an unwed mother (the conversation was sometimes in bits and pieces, sometimes the conversation would last just for 10 minutes and sometimes for couple of hours). I don't know if she can actually accept this if her daughter decides to be an unwed mother but I have seen her overcoming her anxiety, fears and judgements.

Notes

1 Or alternatively, the domination of people identified gender male at birth, including those who identify as trans and non-binary genders.
2 Or groups of people identified gender female at birth, including those who identify as trans and non-binary genders. In Indian urban political organising, there is a tendency (barring some exceptions) for allegiances and collectives to form along these lines – thus, trans men

form collectives with cis women who love women more than they do with gay men.

3   In the Hindu caste system, brahminism is a system of power relations, an ideology, that casts *savarna* people in a hierarchical relationship of domination over *dalit-bahujan* people.

4   Though the mapping of the political-economical-historical forces that produced such a forging of solidarities is beyond the scope of this paper, it is important to note the contributions of affirmative action towards diversity and equal opportunity in higher education in India towards the same. The political consciousness that arises in such academic spaces also has a productive if not always easy connection with activist and non-governmental organisations outside academia that are working on a range of issues.

5   Anzaldúa (1987), Lorde (1984), Rich (1980).

6   The ellipses in brackets in LGBTQ (...) stand for the potential and existing multiplicity of identities around which political organising occurs in a particular cultural context.

7   This paper primarily addresses fellow academics and activists, and the pronouns 'we', 'our' and 'us' will henceforth address this collective; the striving is for engagement with each other in academic activist circles but also with those outside, such as friends, family, neighbours and the online community via social media.

8   The feminine here is to be understood not as a static, universal, timeless essence associated with certain kinds of bodies but as produced in relation to its many others – the masculine, the classed and raced others.

9   This proliferation of sharing of experiences of sexual harassment and gendered violence and exclusion at places of work and study followed the publication of LoSHA (List of Sexual Harassers in Academia), a listing of male academics in universities in India and abroad on social media by Raya Sarkar, a US based student of Indian origin. For weeks and months following this, all informal conversations – in office cubicles, in corridors, while commuting back home, over dinner, over phone and email centred with much emotion (pain, rage, fear) on this issue and related experiences of sexism in many dimensions of academic life.

10 In electoral politics, this can be noted in commentaries that bemoan the appeasement of the Dalits and the Muslims by the left/left-of-centre forces, thereby, it is claimed, losing the masses to the right.

11 Where "queer" denotes anti-heteronormativity defined against local contexts, where reproductive heteronormativity becomes the conduit for maintenance of hegemonic understandings of the nation, culture and tradition, queer bodies not only suggest deviant sexuality, but may also 'fuck' / 'play' with caste markers, with religious markers, with ideal femininity. Some embodiments provoke violence and censure, and under a conservative, extreme right-wing tyranny as India is currently

writhing under, these include the trans -masculine or -feminine body, the 'slutty' body, the burqa-clad body.

12 See Butler (1997) for a rebuttal of the characterisation of LGBTQ (...) politics as "merely cultural" identity politics as against those that attempt to reconfigure political-economical material worlds.

13 It needs to be noted that Butler's queer call for a new mode of post-identity politics as quoted from her 1990 work, *Gender Trouble*, was preceded by modes and methods developed by feminists of colour in the US on which Sandoval bases her work *Methodology of the Oppressed*. Differential consciousness recalls the "new mestiza" (Anzaldúa, 1987), "the outsider within" (Hill-Collins, 1986) and "strategic essentialism" (Spivak, 1996 [1985]).

14 A social analysis may observe how the powerful in any society are keen to maintain the difference – symbolic and material – that confers on them their superiority, while the disenfranchised aspire toward acquiring these and minimising difference, or more radically, to resignify difference.

15 This social media post was published by R. Singh on 15 December 2017. The original is no longer available. Reprinted with permission from the author.

SIXTEEN | Lesbian feminism

Sara Ahmed

I speak today from a conviction: in order to survive what we come up against, in order to build worlds from the shattered pieces, we need a revival of lesbian feminism. This lecture is an explanation of my conviction.

Right now might seem an odd time to ask for such a revival. It might seem we are offered more by the happiness of the queer umbrella. I think the erasure of lesbians as well as lesbian feminism (often via the assumption that lesbian feminism is a naïve form of 'identity politics') would deprive us of some of the resources we need because of what is not over, what is not behind us. In some recent queer writing, lesbian feminism appears as a miserable scene that we had to get through, or pass through, before we could embrace the happier possibility of becoming queer. For instance, Paul Preciado (2012) in a lecture on queer bulldogs refers to lesbians as ugly with specific reference to styles, fashions and haircuts. The lesbian appears here as elsewhere as an abject figure we were all surely glad to have left behind. I suspect this referencing to the ugliness of lesbians is intended as ironic, even playful. But of course, much contemporary sexism and homophobia is ironic and playful. I don't find it particularly amusing.

We need to refuse this passing by holding onto the figure of the lesbian feminist as a source of political potential. Lesbian feminism can bring feminism *back to life*. Many of the critiques of lesbian feminism, often as a form of 'cultural feminism', were precisely because of how lesbian feminists posed feminism as a life question, as a question of how to live. Alice Echols in her book *Daring to be Bad*, which gives a history of radical feminism in the United States, describes: "With the rise of lesbian-feminism, the conflation of the personal with the political, long in the making was complete and unassailable. More than ever, how one lived one's life, not commitment to political struggle, became the salient factor" (1989: 240). *Note this not*: the question of how we live our lives is separated from a commitment to political struggle; more than that, it is implied that focusing on living our lives would be a withdrawal of energy from political struggle. We can hear a similar implication in Juliet Mitchell and Rosalind Delmar's argument: "the effects of liberation do not become the manifestations of liberation by changing values or for the matter by changing oneself, but only by challenging the social structure that gives rise to the values in the first place" (cited in Echols 1989:244). The suggestion is not only that life change is not structural change but that focusing on how one lives one's life might be how structures are *not* transformed.

I want to offer an alternative argument. When a life is what we have to struggle for, we struggle against structures. It is not necessarily the case that these struggles always lead to transformation. But to struggle against something is to chip away at something. Many of these structures are not visible unless you come up against them and this makes doing the work of chipping away, I call this work 'diversity work', a particular kind of work (Ahmed, 2014a). The energy required to keep going when you keep coming up against these structures is how we build things, sometimes, often, from the shattered pieces.

Walls

I am currently writing a book, *Living a Feminist Life*, which concludes with a chapter on lesbian feminism. One of the aims of the book is to bring feminist theory 'home' by generating feminist theory out of ordinary experiences of being a feminist. The book could have been called "everyday feminism". Feminist theory is or can be what we might call following Marilyn Frye "lived theory", an approach that "does not separate politics from living" (1991:13). Living a lesbian life is data collection; we collect information about the institutions that govern the reproduction of life: it is almost too much data; we don't have time to interpret all the material we collect. If living a lesbian life generates data, then lesbian feminism provides the tools to help us interpret that data.

And by data I am referring to walls. I first began thinking about walls when completing a research project on racism and diversity within institutions. Diversity practitioners would talk of how the very institutions that appointed them would block their efforts. Diversity work was described by one practitioner as "a banging your head against a brick wall job". A job description becomes a wall description. And what I learnt from doing this research was that unless you came up against the walls, they did not appear: the university would seem as happy as its mission statement, as willing as its equality statement.

In one interview I conducted quite late in the research process, a practitioner described one of her experiences of a brick wall. It was a click moment: you know that kind of moment, when something is revealed to you that you realise retrospectively you had been trying to work out or to work through. She described to me what happened within her university when they tried to change a policy around appointment procedures: she had got the change agreed at the diversity committee, but the agreement went missing from the minutes; when the minutes were sent to council someone noticed because she had chaired the diversity committee; the minutes were rewritten and resubmitted and the policy was approved by council; but then people within the institution acted as if the change had not been agreed. The diversity officer said that when she pointed out there has been a change of policy "they looked at me as if was saying something really stupid". I learnt so much from her account: I learnt how the mechanisms for blocking structural transformation are *mobile*; things can be stationary because what stops things from moving moves. I learnt how an effective way of stopping something from happening is by agreeing to something. A "yes" can be said when or even because there is not enough behind that "yes" to bring something about.

It is the process of trying to transform a situation that allows this wall to become apparent. And I realised that this was the difficulty I had been trying to describe throughout my work: how you come up against things that are not revealed to others. Indeed, what is hardest for some (I mean literally, ouch) does not even exist for others. I now use diversity work to refer not only to the work that aims to transform institutions, but the work we do when we do not quite inhabit the norms of an institution. When we fail to inhabit a norm (when we are questioned or question ourselves whether we are 'it', or pass as or into 'it') then it becomes more apparent, rather like that brick wall: what does not allow you to pass through. A life description can be a wall description.

Things are fluid if you are going the way things are flowing. Think of a crowd: if you are going the right way, you are being propelled forward; a momentum means you need to make less effort to keep going. If you are not going that way, a flow is something solid, a wall; an obstruction. Lesbians know a lot about obstruction. And it might seem now for lesbians that we are going with the flow. Hey, we can go; hey, we can get married. And if you talked about what you come up against now, those around you may blink with disbelief: hey what's up, stop complaining dear, smile. I am not willing to smile on command. I am willing to go on a smile embargo, if I can recall Shulamith Firestone's "dream action" for the women's movement (1970:90).

Talking about walls matters all the more when the mechanisms by which we are blocked are less visible.

The everyday is our data.

A lesbian experience: you are seated with your girlfriend, two women at a table; waiting. A straight couple walks into the room and is attended to right away. This might also be a female experience: without a man present at the table, you do not appear. I have experienced my female solidarity around these sorts of experiences: say, you are pressed up against a busy bar; two women who do not know each other, and over and over again, the men are served first. You look at each other both with frustration but sometimes affection, as you recognise that each other recognises that situation, as one in which we are perpetually thrown: she too, me too, "we" from this too. For some, you have to become insistent to be the recipient of a social action, you might have to announce your presence, wave your arm, saying: "Here I am!" For others, it is enough just to turn up because you have already been given a place at the table before you take up that place.

Of course, more than gender is at stake in the distribution of attention. But gender is at stake in the distribution of attention. Every now and then you encounter something that reveals that distribution: that allows the feminist groan of recognition. One time I was at the London feminist film festival. They were showing *A Question of Silence*. It is a table scene, of course: there is one woman seated at a table of men; she is the secretary. And she makes a suggestion. No one hears her: the question of silence is in this moment not a question of not speaking but of not being heard. A man then makes the exact same suggestion she has already made: and the other men turn to him, congratulating him for being constructive. She says nothing. It is at that moment she sits there in silence, a silence which is filled or saturated with memories of being silenced: her memories, ours, having to overlook how you are looked over. Sexism: a worn thread of connection. And yes: there was a collective groan.

Feminist philosophers has taught us for over a century how men becomes universal; women particular. Or perhaps we might say women become relatives, female relatives, existing by existing in relation to men. To become woman is to become relative. Women encounter the universal as a wall when we refuse to become relative. Note how we come to know these distinctions (such as universal and relative) not as abstractions, but in everyday social life, which is to say, in being in a world with others.

I want to add here that the requirement to become a female relative is not simply about the privileging of heterosexuality. Working in the academy I have noticed this expectation that to progress you must progress through male networks: you have to declare your love for one dead white male philosopher or another (if not Derrida, then Lacan, if not Lacan, then Deleuze, if not Deleuze, then, who Sara, who are you following?). You have to cite men and give more time and attention to their work; you have to have references by men in order to validate your own work. Of course, we do not "have to do" what we "have to do". But if it is easier to refuse that requirement from a position of relative security then we learn how that requirement is enforced through insecurity, the sense that, to reach somewhere, you have to go in this direction, or you might not get anywhere at all.

For her to appear, she might have to fight. If this is true for women, it is even truer for lesbians. Women with women at a table are hard to see (and by table here I am referring to the mechanisms of social gathering, a table is what we are assembled around). For a gathering to be complete a man is the head. A table of women: a body without a head. Male privilege is not simply about being seen but being *seen to*, having your needs attended to. This is why I describe privilege as an energy-saving device: less effort is required when a world has been assembled to meet your needs. You don't need to raise your arm to have a standing. I will return to wilful lesbian arms in my conclusion.

Data as wall.

You turn up at a hotel with your girlfriend and you say you have booked a room. A hesitation can speak volumes. This reservation says your booking is for a double bed, is that right madam? Eyebrows are raised; a glance slides over the two of you, catching enough detail. Are you, sure madam? Yes that's right; a double bed. You have to say it, again; you have to say it, again, firmly. Some have to insist on what is given to others. In previous work (Ahmed, 2014b) I have offered a formula:

Rolling eyes = feminist pedagogy

When you are known as a feminist, you do not even have to say anything before eyes roll. You can hear them sigh "oh here she goes". I now have another formula.

Raised eyebrows = lesbian feminist pedagogy

The raising of eyebrows: lodged as a question: Really, are you sure? This happens again and again; you almost come to expect it, the necessity of being firm just to receive what you have requested. One time after a querying, are you sure madam, are you sure, madam, you enter the room; twin beds. Do you go down; do you try again? It can be trying. Sometimes it is too much, and you pull your two little beds together; you find other ways of huddling.

Questions follow you, wherever you go. For some to be is to be in question (Ahmed, 2014c). Is that your sister or your husband? Are you sisters? What are you? Who are you? As a brown woman I am used to be asking "where are you from?" as a way of being told I am not from here. There are many ways of being made into strangers, bodies out of place. "Are you a boy or a girl?" they ask her, this time, a question that drips with mockery and hostility. Some of these questions dislodge you from a body that you yourself feel you reside in. Once you have been asked these questions, you might wait for them. Waiting to be dislodged *changes your relation to the lodge*.

It can be exhausting this constant demand to explain yourself. A desire for a more normal life does not necessarily mean identification with norms but can be simply this: a desire to escape the exhaustion of having to insist just to exist. A history can become concrete through the repetition of such encounters, encounters that require you to put the whole of your body, as well as your arms, behind an action. Maybe these actions seem small. Maybe they are small. But they accumulate over time. They feel like a hammering, a chip, chip, chip, against your being, so that eventually you begin to feel smaller, hammering as hammered down. Actions that seem small can also become wall.

An ordinary battle

An ordinary is what we might be missing when we feel that chip, chip. An ordinary can be what we need to survive that chip, chip. Susan Griffin remembers a scene for us, a scene that has yet to happen:

> I remember a scene … This from a film I want to see. It is a film made by a woman about two women who live together. This is a scene from their daily lives. It is a film about the small daily transformations which women experience, allow, tend to, and which have been invisible in this male culture. In this film, two women touch. In all ways possible they show knowledge of. What they have lived through and what they will yet do, and *one sees in their movements how they have survived*. I am certain that one day this film will exist. (cited by Becker et al., 1981)

Lesbian feminism: to remember a scene that has yet to happen, a scene of the ordinary; of the movements, little movements, which tell the story of our survival. It is a touching scene. Sometimes you have to battle for an ordinary. When you have to battle for an ordinary, when battling becomes ordinary, the ordinary can be what you lose.

But you have a glimpse of it even when you lose it.

Think of this: how for many women, life has been understood as a sphere of *immanence*, as *dwelling in* not rising above; she is there, there she is; not transcending things by creating things. A masculinist model of creativity is premised on withdrawal. She is there, there she is: engaged in the endless repetitive cycle of housework. We can follow Adrienne Rich who makes this starting point into an instruction: "begin with the material", she says, with "matter, mma, madre, mutter, moeder, modder" (1986:213). Lesbian feminism is materialist right from the beginning. If women are expected to be here, in matter, in materiality, in work, at work, this is where lesbian feminism begins. We begin in the lodge *where* we are lodged. We begin with the lodge *when* we are dislodged.

A poignant lesbian scene of ordinary life is provided by the first of the three films that make up, *If These Walls Could Talk 2* (2000). We begin with that ordinary: we begin with its warmth. Edith and Abby: they have been together a long time. The quietness of intimacy: of going to see a film together, of coming home together. Yes, maybe there are comments made by some kids on the street, but they are used to it: they have each other, a place to return to; home as shelter, a place to withdraw to. If the walls could talk, they would tell their story, photographs cover the walls, photographs not only of each other, of their friends, but of lesbian and gay marches, demonstrations. A wall can be how we display a lesbian feminist history.

Everything shatters, when Abby slips and falls.

Everything shatters. A life can shatter.

We are in the hospital waiting room. Edith is waiting to hear how Abby is. Another woman arrives. She says: "they just took my husband in, he had a heart attack". When this woman asks about Edith's husband, Edith replies, "I never had a husband". And the woman says, "That's lucky, because you won't have the heart break of losing one". The history of heterosexuality becomes a history of broken hearts, or even just the history of hearts. To be recognised as having a heart is to be recognised as the one who is broken. With such recognition, comes care, comfort, support. Without recognition, even one's grief cannot be supported or held by the kindness of another.

We know this history; it is a history of what we know.

And so, Edith waits. When she asks the hospital staff to see Abby they say, "only family are allowed". The recognition of family ties, as the only ties that are binding, means Abby dies alone; it means Edith waits all night, alone. When lesbian grief is not recognised, because lesbian relationships are not recognised, you become "non-relatives". You become unrelated, you become not. You are left alone in your grief.

Heterosexuality could be described as an elaborate support system. Support is how much you have to fall back on when you fall. To leave heterosexuality can be to leave those institutional forms of protecting, cherishing, holding. You have less to fall back on when you fall. When things break a whole life can unravel.

When family is not there to prop you up, when you disappear from family life, you have to find other ways of being supported. When you disappear from family life: does this happen to you? You go home, you go back home and it feels like you are watching yourself disappear: watching your own life unravel, thread by thread. No one has willed or intended your disappearance. Just slowly, just slowly, as talk of family, of heterosexuality as the future, of lives that you do not live, just slowly, just slowly, you disappear.

They welcome you, they are kind, you are the lesbian aunties from London, say, but it is harder and harder to breathe. And then when you leave you might go and find a lesbian bar or queer space; it can be such a relief. You feel like a toe, liberated from a cramped shoe (Ahmed, 2014d). And we need to think about that: how the restriction of life when heterosexuality remains a presumption can be countered by creating spaces that are *looser, freer* not only because you are not surrounded by what you are not but because you are reminded there are so many ways to be.

So much invention comes from the necessity of creating our own support systems. Note here the significance of fragility to this history: how we too can be shattered, how we need each other to put our lives back together again. And: if we are recognised as fragile, breakable, broken, we are often assumed to have caused our own damage. We after all have willingly left the apparently safer paths, the more brightly lit paths of heterosexuality. What did you expect, dear: what did you expect? Feminists are often assumed to cause their own damage, as if she, rather like a broken pot, flies out of hand. When we say she "flies out of hand" we usually means she speaks out of anger, caught up by a destructive impulse, and that in breaking ties, she breaks herself.

Shattering; it is shattering; she is shattered.

There are many ways of telling the story of the struggle for recognition because there are many stories to tell. The struggle for recognition can be about having access to a good life. It can be about wanting inclusion in the structures that have been oppressive, wanting inclusion in the very structures that remain predicated on this dispossession of others. But that's not the only story. The struggle for recognition can also come from the experience of what is unbearable, what cannot be endured, when you lose your bearings, becoming unhoused. The struggle for recognition can be a struggle for an ordinary life, an ordinary that is far more precious than property; indeed, an ordinary as what is negated when things become property, when things become alienable things. We learn this from *If These Walls Could Talk 2*: when Abby's family ask what things are hers so her things can become theirs, Abby's things, her loved worn things, her memories, can become family possessions. A family possession is a dispossession. Perhaps a lesbian feminist struggle for recognition comes out of rage against the injustice of how some dwell by the dispossession of others. We want the walls to come down. Or, if they stay up, we want the walls to talk, to tell this story. A story too can shatter: a tiny thousand little pieces, strewn, all over the place.

Lesbian feminism: in making an ordinary from the shattered pieces of a dwelling we dwell. We dwell, we tell. How telling.

A wilfulness archive

In this first part of this lecture I noted how actions that are small can also become wall. Lesbian feminism might also involve small actions. Maybe the chip, chip, chip of hammering can be transformed into a hammer: if he is a chip off the old block, we chip, chip, chip away at that block. Chip, chip, chip, who knows, eventually it might come right off. To persist in chipping at the blocks of heteropatriarchy, we have to become wilful. I want to think of lesbian feminism as a wilfulness archive, a living and a lively archive made up and made out our own experiences of struggling against what we come up against.

Why wilfulness? Let me share with you a typical definition of wilfulness: "asserting or disposed to assert one's own will against persuasion, instruction, or command; governed by will without regard to reason; determined to take one's own way; obstinately self-willed or perverse" (OED). To be called obstinate or perverse because you are not persuaded by the reasoning of others? Is this familiar to you? Have you heard this before?

Lesbian, feminist and anti-racist histories can be thought of as histories of those who are willing to be wilful, who are willing to turn a diagnosis into an act of self-description. Let's go back: let's listen to what and to who is behind us. Julia Penelope describes lesbianism as wilfulness: "The lesbian stands against the world created by the male imagination. What *wilfulness* we posses when we claim our lives!" (1992:42, emphasis in original). Marilyn Frye's radical feminism uses the adjective wilful: "The willful creation of new meaning, new loci of meaning, and new ways of being, together, in the world, seems to me in these mortally dangerous times the best hope we have" (Penelope, 1992:9). Alice Walker describes a "womanist" in the following way: "A black feminist or feminist of color ... Usually referring to outrageous, audacious, courageous or *willful* behavior. Wanting to know more and in greater depth than is considered 'good' for one ... Responsible. In charge. *Serious*" (2005:xi, emphases in original). Together these statements can be heard as claims to wilfulness: wilfulness as audacity; wilfulness as standing against; wilfulness as creativity.

Wilfulness is usually a charge made by someone against someone. Wilfulness becomes a charge in Alice Walker's sense, to be "in charge". If we are charged with wilfulness, we can accept and mobilise this charge. To accept a charge is not simply to agree with it. Acceptance can mean being *willing to receive*. A charge can also be thought of as electricity. *The language can be our lead*: wilfulness can be an electric current, passing through each of us, switching us on. Wilfulness can be a spark. We can be lit up by it. It is an electric thought.

We can distinguish here between wilfulness assumed as behind an action, and wilfulness required to complete an action. Sometimes to stand up you have to stand firm. Sometimes to hold on you must become stubborn. Remember my example of going the wrong way in the crowd? For some bodies mere persistence, "to continue steadfastly", requires great effort, an effort that might appear to others as stubbornness or obstinacy, as an insistence on going against the flow. You have to become insistent to go against the flow and you are judged to be going against the flow because you are insistent. I think of this as a life paradox: *you have to become what you are judged as being. You might have to become what you are judged as being to survive what you are judged as being.*

We are often judged as wilful when we are not willing; not willing to go with the flow, not willing to go. To become lesbian might require not being *willing women*; lesbians as wilful women. Monique Wittig's (1992) audacious statement "lesbians are not women" could thus be read through the lens of wilfulness. She argues that lesbians are not women because to be "women" is to be – is being – in relation to men: "women" for Wittig is heterosexual term or a heterosexual injunction. Remember woman becomes from the conjunction of *wif* and man: wif as wife, as female servant. To be a woman with a woman or a woman with women (we do not need to assume a couple form) is to become what she, Wittig, calls an "escapee" or a stray. To be a lesbian is to stray away from the path you are supposed to follow if you are to reach the right destination. To stray is to deviate from the path of happiness. So if lesbians are women, if we wrestle woman away from this history of women as being for men, we are wilful women.

Wilful women: how striking. Wilfulness as a style of politics might involve not only being willing not to go with the flow but being willing to cause its obstruction. Political histories of striking are indeed histories of those willing to put their bodies in the way, to turn their bodies into blockage points that stop the flow of human traffic, as well as the wider flow of an economy.

Wilfulness might seem here to be about an individual, the one who has to become wilful just to keep going, although we see how a strike only works when it becomes collective, when others too are lit up by that spark. We might think of characters like Molly Bolt from *Rubyfruit Jungle* (Brown, 1973) as part of our wilfulness archive: girls who want girls are often those girls whose wills are deemed wanting. As a lesbian feminist reader, it was characters like Molly Bolt with a spring in their step that picked me up; feisty characters whose vitality is not at the expense of their lesbian desire, but is how their desire roams across the pages.

If we think of lesbian feminism as a wilfulness archive we are not simply directing our attention to characters such as Molly Bolt, however appealing. A wilfulness archive would derive as much from our struggle to write ourselves into existence, as from who appears in what we write. This intimacy of audacity, standing against and creativity can take the form of a book.

A wilful girl in a book
A wilful girl as a book
I am rather taken by you

Gloria Anzaldúa describes her book *Borderlands* as follows: "The whole thing has had a mind of its own, escaping me and insisting on putting together the pieces of its own puzzle with minimal direction from my will. It is a rebellious, willful entity, a precocious girl-child forced to grow up too quickly" ([1987] 1999:88). A book, a survival strategy, comes alive, acquires a life of its own, a will of its own, a wilful will; history by the bone, own but not alone. Words are sent out: wilful words; they pile up, they make something. Words can pulse with life; words as flesh, leaking; words as heart, beating.

Lesbian feminism of colour: the struggle to put ourselves back together because within lesbian shelters too our being was not always accommodated. Where does she take me? Not white, lesbian out of not; here she comes. I think of a brown history, a mixed-history as a lesbian history, another way in which we can tell a history of women being in relation to women. I think of my own history, as a mixed lesbian, with so many sides, all over the place. I think of all that lesbian potential, as coming from somewhere. Brownness has a lesbian history; because there are brown lesbians in history, whether or not you could see us, whether or not you knew where to find us. As Camel Gupta (2014) has noted, it is sometimes assumed as brown queers and trans folk that we are rescued from our unhappy brown families by happy white queer communities; but not, what if not, what if not; what if brownness is what rescues us from the white line, the line takes us in a direction that asks us to give up part of ourselves?

> I will not give you up
> A wilful will; not willing as willing not

Lesbian feminism of colour is a lifeline made up out of wilful books that insist on their own creation. Books themselves are material, paper, pen, ink, blood, the sweat of the labour to bring something into existence. Words come out of us.

> A poem weeps

Audre Lorde spoke of herself as a writer when she was dying. For Lorde, writing and speaking and living as a Black lesbian (Lorde never refused the demands of this "as", nor assumed it can abbreviate an experience), survival is militancy; words are her weapons. She says: "I am going to write fire until it comes out of my ears, my eyes, my nose holes – everywhere. Until it's every breath I breathe. I'm going to go out like a fucking meteor!" (1988: 76–77).

> And so she did
> And so she did

She goes out, she makes something. She calls this capacity to make things through heat "the erotic". Lorde notes: "There is a difference between painting a black fence and writing a poem, but only one of quantity. And there is, for me, no difference between writing a good poem and moving into sunlight against the body of a woman I love" (1984:8).

A love poem
A lover as poem

I am warmed by the thought. I am warmed by Cherrie Moraga's poem, "The Welder". Moraga speaks of heating being used to shape new elements, to create new shapes, "the intimacy of steel melting, the fire that makes sculpture of your lives, builds buildings" (1981:219).

We build our own buildings when the world does not accommodate our desires. When you are blocked, when your very existence is prohibited or viewed with general suspicion or even just raised eyebrows (yes, they are pedagogy), you have to come up with your own systems for getting things through. You might even have to come up with your own system for getting yourself through.

How inventive
Quite something
Not from nothing
Something from something
A kitchen table becomes a publishing house.

To stand against what is we have to make room for what is not. Lesbian feminist world-making is nothing extraordinary; it is quite ordinary. We might think of the work of making room as wiggling, a corporeal wilfulness. Remember that toe, liberated from its cramped shoe. She does not toe the line. Lesbians (as lesbians well know) have quite a wiggle; you have to wiggle to make room in a cramped space. We can be warmed by the work required to be together even if sometimes we wish it was less work. To recall the vitality of lesbian feminism as a resource of the present is to remember that effort required for our shelters to be built. When we have to shelter from the harshness of a world we build a shelter.

I think of lesbian feminism as *wilful carpentry*: she builds with her own hands; she is handy. What we build to survive what we come against, the very materials, are how values materialise or are given expression. How easily though without foundations, without a stable ground, the walls can come down. We keep them up by keeping up with each other. A fragile shelter, a looser shelter: walls made from lighter materials, blowing haphazardly in the wind. It is a movement. We might recognise this fragility not so much as what we might lose, or will lose, *but as a quality of what we have*: values that do not derive or depend on making things safer, more secure or more permanent. There are other ways to survive. Lesbian feminism is another way to survive.

Conclusion: a lesbian feminist army

I want to share a "lesbian lives" story with you. I gave my very first lecture from my research project on will and wilfulness in Dublin at the 17th Lesbian Lives conference in 2010. I shared a story I found because I was on a trail, I was following wilful girls, going wherever they went. Yes I did end up all over the place. Because I was on this trail, I found this story: a Grimm story, about a wilful child. This is not a lesbian story. But perhaps there is a lesbian in this story. Let me share it again.

Once upon a time there was a child who was wilful, and would not do as her mother wished. For this reason, God had no pleasure in her, and let her become ill, and no doctor could do her any good, and in a short time she lay on her death-bed. When she had been lowered into her grave, and the earth was spread over her, all at once her arm came out again, and stretched upwards, and when they had put it in and spread fresh earth over it, it was all to no purpose, for the arm always came out again. Then the mother herself was obliged to go to the grave, and strike the arm with a rod, and when she had done that, it was drawn in, and then at last the child had rest beneath the ground.

What a story. It is quite a story. My book (Ahmed, 2014e) opens with this story, with this figure of the wilful child, the one who disobeys; as the one who is punished, who is beaten into the ground. It is the story of a child but also of an arm: the child's wilfulness is inherited by an arm, an arm that keeps coming up, until it too is beaten down. Is the wilful child a lesbian feminist? Or is the wayward arm a lesbian feminist?

We could tell a few lesbian stories about arms. One story: a butch lesbian enters the female toilets. The attendant become flustered and says "you are not supposed to be here". The butch lesbian is used to this: how many of her stories are toilet stories; to pass as male becomes a question mark of your right to pass into female space. "I am a woman", she says. We might have to assign ourselves with gender if we trouble the existing assignments. With a re-assignment, she can go to the toilet. When she comes out, the attendant is embarrassed; the attendant points to her arm, saying "so strong". The butch lesbian allows the moment to pass by joking, giving the attendant a "show of her arms".

With arms we come out; with arm we come in. These moments do not always pass so easily. Many of these histories of passing or of not passing are traumatic. Arms can be beaten; they can be straightened. Jack Halberstam in *Female Masculinity* notes with some surprise how Havelock Ellis uses the arm as a gender test in the case of Miss M:

Miss M. he thinks, tries to cover over her masculinity but gives herself away to Ellis when he uses a rather idiosyncratic test of gender identification: 'with arms, palmed up, extended in front of her with inner sides touching, she cannot bring the inner sides of the forearms together as nearly every woman can, showing that the feminine angle of the arm is lost'. (1998:80)

If the muscular female arm is measured by a straightening rod, the arm is not straightened. An arm becomes a wayward gift.

So maybe I am thinking too of your arms, your strong butch arms and what they can do, who they can hold. I think of being held by your arms. Yes, I do.

Judith Butler includes the arm in a list of limbs that can symbolise the phallus. Although I always have had sympathy for Judith Butler's "The Lesbian Phallus" (1993:88), and by this I mean her argument, I wonder if we make arms into phallic symbols, that we might miss lesbian arms in all their fleshy potential.

Let me share another "lesbian lives" story. When I gave that first paper on wilfulness at Lesbian Lives in 2010, Kath Browne said to me afterwards, I am not sure if she remembers this, that my lecture concluded with a real "call to arms". I think you were referring to my call for us to be wilful, to be killjoys, to be willing to cause the unhappiness we are assumed to cause. It took me a long time before I heard the arms in that expression "call to arms", even though I had already been struck by the wayward arm from the Grimm story. Once I heard the arms, the call sounded differently: the call *to* arms as the call *of* arms. A call can mean a lament, an accusation; a naming, as well as a visitation (in the sense of a calling upon). Can we put the "arms" back into the "miserable army" of the inverted described in Radcliffe Hall's (1982) *The Well of Loneliness*? Can we hear in the sorrow of their lament a call?

A wayward arm is a call of arms. A call of arms can be a recall. Just recall Sojourner Truth speaking to the suffragettes, having to insist on being a woman activist as a Black woman and former slave, having to insist that abolitionism and suffrage can and should be spoken by the same tongue: "Ain't I a woman", she says. "Look at me", she says, "look at my arm". And in brackets, in the brackets of history, it is said that Sojourner Truth at this moment: "bared her right arm to the shoulder, showing her tremendous muscular power" (cited in Zackodnik 2011:99).[1] The muscularity of her arm is an inheritance of history; the history of slavery shown in the strength of the arm, the arm required to plough, to sow the field. The arms of the slave belonged to the master, as did the slave, as the ones who were not supposed to have a will of their own. No wonder we must *look to the arm*, if we are to understand the history of those who rise up against oppression.

Those who have to insist on being women are wilful women, and the arm becomes your resource, something that can lend its hand in a battle to be. Trans women are wilful women; women who have to insist on being women, who have to keep insisting, again and again, often in the face of violent and repeated acts of misgendering. Any feminists who do not stand up, who do not wave their arms to protest against this misgendering, have become straightening rods. When I ask for a revival of the militancy of the figure of the lesbian feminist I am imagining lesbian feminism as in a fundamental and necessary alliance with transfeminism. Transfeminism has also brought feminism back to life. And can I add here that an anti-trans stance is an anti-feminist stance; it is against the feminist project of creating worlds to support those for whom gender fatalism (boys *will be* boys, girls *will be* girls) is fatal; a sentencing to death. We have to hear that fatalism as punishment and instruction: it is the story of the rod, of how those who have wayward wills or who will waywardly (boys who *will not* be boys, girls who *will not* be girls) are beaten. We will not be beaten. We need to drown these anti-trans voices out by raising the sound of our own. Our voices need to become our arms; rise up; rise up.

There are many arms, they keep coming up, arms that are muscular, strong, labouring arms, arms that refuse to be employed, striking arms, arms that break, Gloria Anzaldúa said once, "I'm a broken arm" (1983:204); arms that are lost in service to the industrial machine. Wilful arms not only have a history; they are shaped by history. Arms are history made flesh. Arms that exceed an idea of the arm (an idea, say, of how a woman's arm should appear) have something to say to us. It is the arms that can help us make the connection between histories that otherwise do not seem to meet. *Intersectionality is army.* If histories meet in arms, then histories meet in the very limbs of our rebellion. The arms that build the master's residence are the arms that will bring the walls down. Audre Lorde entitled an essay with a proclamation: "the master's tools will never dismantle the master's house" (1984:110–113). In that unflinching "will never" is a call to arms, do not become the master's tool!

Chip, chip, chip, when our arms become tools, we hammer away at the house of his being. We make our own houses, lighter, looser; see how the walls move; it is a movement. Chip, chip, chip, a lesbian feminist army is being assembled.

Here we are; here we come; here we arm.

Thank you.

Note

1 Zackodnik is citing here from Frances Dana Gage's *Reminiscences* in which Gage, a leading feminist, reformer and abolitionist, gives us this account of Truth's speech as well as "bodily testimony" that has been crucial to how it has been remembered. It is important to note the status of this description as citation: our access to Sojourner Truth's address is through the testimony of others, in particular, the testimony of white women. Maria Zackodnik notes that other accounts of this event did not include references to Truth baring her arm (2011:99). We learn from this to be cautious about our capacity to bear witness to arms in history: we might only be able to read (of) arms through the mediation of other limbs.

SEVENTEEN | An exploration of counter-hegemonic discourses in an expanding queer archive

Nadine Lake

Corrective rapes and the homophobic everyday

'Corrective rape', a phrase that describes the rape of lesbian women by heterosexual men, emerged with the first reports of violence against lesbians in South African print media in 2003. Gender-based violence in South Africa has received enormous scholarly attention since the country's adoption of a democratic constitution in 1996, where the high incidence of rape and sexual violence constitutes what Pumla Dineo Gqola has coined a "rape culture" (Gqola, 2015). According to the South African Police Services, 39,828 cases of rape were recorded for the period 2016–2017,[1] which is an alarming figure given the fact that many rapes are left unreported because of police insensitivity and the low number of prosecutions for perpetrators of the crime.

South Africa has been defined as unique in relation to the rest of the African continent because of its democratic constitution which proscribes discrimination against sexual minorities. The violence and abuses associated with the country's racist history have compelled a distinct intolerance to the slightest possibility that these injustices may be repeated, with Helen Moffett asserting in 2006 that "[t]he recent history of legislated inequality was so abhorrent that rights were endorsed and guaranteed across the spectrum of race, gender, class, ethnicity, religion, language, level of ability, sexual orientation or preference" (Moffett, 2006:141). However, while South Africa's constitution – as is common for constitutions which are aspirational declarations rather than reflect actuality – appears impeccable on paper, it has become clear that there is a significant disconnection between the proposed rights and reality.

This disconnection between lived experiences and reality has become increasingly apparent in the proliferation of reports and scholarly research on the phenomenon of corrective rapes (Gunkel, 2010; Brown, 2012; Swarr, 2012; Morrissey, 2013). Scholar and activist Graeme Reid comments on this, arguing that "gay and lesbian equality has come to occupy a paradoxical place" (Reid, 2010:38); this paradox featuring prominently in the South African press. Reid explores the issue further, writing that, "[o]n the one hand, it [gay and lesbian equality] is a litmus test for the success of constitutional democracy – emblematic of a human rights-based social order. On the other hand, homosexuality is cast as untraditional, as unAfrican and as unChristian – a dangerous threat to the social fabric" (2010:38). This stance occupies a large part of the debate on sexual minorities with the result that violence against lesbian women is eclipsed by the country's polarised socio-political perspectives, leaving little room to challenge the racist and sexist status quo.

In 2003, South African journalists Yolanda Mufweba and Xolile Bhengu reported on a staggering number of lesbians coming forward with accounts of rape, assault and homophobia-driven attacks. Their news article (Mufweba and Bhengu, 2003) comments on the fact that Black lesbians feel unsafe in Johannesburg townships and that they do not report the crimes for fear of revictimisation. Black lesbians are identified as the primary targets of corrective rape and like other news reports of this period (Mufweba, 2003; Dugmore, 2004), the article highlights that deviating from a presumed African standard of heterofemininity is often met with contempt and punishment. The press piece provides a very necessary context for understanding how violence against lesbians has been represented in the media. Black lesbians often emerge as voiceless victims while the perpetrators, Black men, are reported as being remorseless and acting with impunity.

Furthermore, the term 'corrective rape' remains unproblematised and is understood by the media as a legitimate form of punishment perpetrated against lesbians in the African context. In the insightful article titled "Crimes and Corrections: Bride Burners, Corrective Rapists, and Other Black Misogynists", Madhumita Lahiri (2011) problematises the language used to define violence against lesbians, arguing,

> [t]he "corrective" portion of "corrective rape" refers to the alleged motivations of the perpetrator, and this desire for correction is usually glossed as being a belief that the exposure to heterosexual intercourse, even under conditions of coercion, would "correct" the deviant sexual orientation of a woman presumed to be lesbian. To some extent, this terminology is only as problematic as its purported explanation. It would be quite reasonable, for example, to affirm that these sorts of attacks are correctional in that they punish those who challenge dominant ideas of gender and sexuality. (Lahiri, 2011:122)

The emphasis on the phenomenon of 'corrective rapes' and the spectacular representations of violence against lesbians in the media has resulted in a specific form of 'othering', which is revealing of prevailing racist and sexist political ideologies. Instead of interrogating the violence perpetrated against lesbian women, newspapers contribute to stereotypes about African bodies and sexualities in the name of upholding a heterosexual norm. A discursive analysis of corrective rape from a postcolonial and feminist perspective illustrates that the common message conveyed is that women's bodies are not their own and that African men are homophobic rapists. The failure to interrogate hegemonic discourses of power thus results in the (re-)emergence of racialised and sexualised master narratives that had been present during the apartheid years.[2]

In her critical engagement with the representation of African sexualities, Desiree Lewis (2011) argues that Black men and women have been defined in relation to sexual excess and that gender constitutes an additional form of othering (Lewis, 2011:205). For Lewis, "to explore African sexualities carefully means first exploring how they have been thought about; it requires what Kwame Appiah (1992:240) describes as a 'discursive space-clearing', a way of both acknowledging and analysing how others have historically been imagined" (Lewis, 2011:200). Stereotypes about African female and lesbian sexualities have come strongly to the fore in the South African print media. In a short YouTube video clip titled "South African Women Fall Victim to 'Corrective Rape'", a young man interviewed about the phenomenon is revealed to share the sentiments of men perpetrating corrective rape crimes in his confident statement that, "my idea is to say let's turn their minds to be normal because right now they're being inhuman".[3] This comment reveals much about the discursive construction of corrective rape and the specific frames within which the matter is reported. In other words, this discursive example reinforces the notion that Black lesbian women's minds and bodies are represented as being open to attack, and heterosexuality is used to co-construct the definition of what it means to be human. Discourses that prescribe heterosexuality for women are ubiquitous in South African print media and strengthen the assumption that lesbian sexuality is unAfrican. In this chapter I argue that lesbian feminism with an emphasis on "non-heterosexual, woman-connected existence" (Rich, 1980:635) and positive representations of Black lesbian women in the South African public sphere constitute a powerful counter-narrative.

Reframing lesbian life

In an attempt to better understand the frames within which corrective rape and Black lesbians are reported on, it may be more productive to focus on "compulsory heterosexuality" (Rich, 1980:632) for women than to foreground homophobia in the African context. Corrective rape has been depicted as something perpetuated specifically against lesbian *women*, making it clear that there is a patriarchal logic embedded in this punitive act. Lewis takes this argument further, reminding us that "discourses of national belonging have been anchored in familial scripts and the invention of nations as biological families" (Lewis, 2008:107). In a post-apartheid context where discipline and punishment remain part of the social fabric and where the heterosexual norm is perceived to maintain social order (Moffett, 2006), those who deviate from this norm and assume a sense of autonomy are by implication defined as *un*African, unnatural and vulnerable to rape (Lewis, 2008). Therefore, a prescriptive heterosexual norm contributes to the definition of Black lesbians as unintelligible victims of violence.

A lesbian feminist approach enables us to reimagine this one-dimensional representation of lesbian life. To speak from a subject position is central to reconceptualising lesbian liveability and I argue along with Teresa de Lauretis that "in the very act of assuming and speaking from the position of subject, a woman could [and can] concurrently recognize women as subjects *and* objects of female desire" (1988:155). Lesbian feminism is therefore important for regarding women loving other women as an entity that stands apart from heteropatriarchal assumptions and definitions of lesbians' lives.

Furthermore, Judith Butler provides a productive argument around frames and representation in her book titled *Frames of War* (2009). Here she illustrates how frames have been used to legitimise war and violence against certain bodies. For Butler, a differential allocation of precarity to certain lives plays an influential role in framing some people as less valuable than others. While Butler's argument focuses on war, I argue that it is equally relevant to a reading of rape and LGBTQ lives in South Africa. An examination of news reporting on corrective rape shows that Black lesbians and their lives are framed in ways that detract from their liveability and intelligibility. Butler's definition of intelligibility as "the historical schema or schemas that establish domains of the knowable" is particularly relevant for investigating how Black lesbians have become framed as the most vulnerable victims of homophobic violence. In her theorisation of frames Butler considers it important not to simply create space to add more people into existing norms, but that we problematise the differential allocation of precarity to certain bodies within existing norms (Butler, 2009:6). This differential allocation of precarity is prominent in the representation of Black lesbians where their race, gender, class, social location and sexuality combine to frame them as essentialised victims of violence. Socio-political power dynamics is central to the frames by which we recognise certain lives and bodies and in the present analysis it becomes clear that Black lesbians fall outside of normative frames of recognition, thus acquiring an unintelligible status.

For Butler, the frame itself signifies something existing outside of the frame. She writes that "to call the frame into question is to show that the frame never quite contained the scene that it was meant to limn" (2009:9). In other words, calling the frame into question forms part of calling the power dynamics into question and illustrates that there is potential to reimagine the 'framed' scene or subject. The framing of Black lesbians as 'special' victims (Matebeni, 2013) of corrective rape has contributed to their representation as vulnerable and precarious victims. Black lesbians' vulnerability is therefore directly tied to their representation in relation to a heteronormative and misogynistic frame. Lesbian feminism which foregrounds women's sexuality as independent of men has the potential to challenge these dominant frames and orders (Matebeni, 2013:343–344). In the section that follows

I focus on Zanele Muholi's portraits and how they provide an alternative discourse on lesbian sexuality.

Zanele Muholi's *Faces and Phases* 2006–14

A prominent example of queer activism that transcends hetero-normative modes of recognition constitutes the work of acclaimed South African artist and photographer, Zanele Muholi. In 2014, Muholi published 258 portrait photographs of Black lesbians and transgender men in a collection titled *Faces and Phases 2006–14*. Muholi's work has been heralded as a queer archive and occupies a central role in challenging normative modes of recognition, and the unintelligible status ascribed to Black lesbian and transgender life.

Faces and Phases is a celebration of queer visibility where black and white portraits of Black lesbians and transgender men are accompanied by short stories, narratives and poems authored by the project's participants. In Muholi's words, *"Faces and Phases* is both highly personal and deeply political to me: an act of searching, resisting, transgressing the boundaries of oppressive racial, sexual, class and gender power structures" (Muholi in *Faces and Phases*, 2014:6). Muholi is sensitive to the homophobic gaze confronting Black lesbian lives and refuses to reinforce the emerging status of victimhood that is at play when these women are represented by others. Muholi clearly articulates this when she writes, "each time we are represented by outsiders, we are merely seen as victims of rape and homophobia" (Muholi, 2013:169). Muholi's queer archive is a project of unprecedented prominence that speaks to a long history of marginalisation and violence perpetrated against Black queer lives.

Faces and Phases constitutes what Ann Cvetkovich refers to as "an unusual archive" (2003:7). In *An Archive of Feelings* (2003), Cvetkovich makes a compelling case for redefining our understanding of the archive and what belongs there. For Cvetkovich, trauma is a productive category for analysing and documenting queer lives and she attaches significant value to feelings which she considers integral to creating and recognising new lesbian cultures (Cvetkovich, 2003:7). Cvetkovich's argument about the psychic, unspeakable and lose-able nature of trauma resonates with the difficulties of documenting lesbian lives in Muholi's work. The unspeakable and invisible status of Black lesbians in South Africa prior to 1994[4] underlines, all the more, the importance of documenting Black lesbian life in contemporary times.

The queer archive problematises the dominant homophobic frames that define Black lesbian life. Gabeba Baderoon observes that "the visionary spaces in Muholi's 'intimate archive' of Black lesbians redefine[s] belonging and normalcy in South Africa and beyond" (Baderoon in *Faces and Phases*, 2014:327). This reconceptualisation of belonging thus queers heteronormative standards embedded in nationalist familial scripts. Muholi's visual activism counters dominant modes of knowledge; the dedication of her book to all mothers of LGBTI children furthermore challenges prescriptive forms of family in the post-apartheid context:

> To my late mother, Bester Muholi, and to all mothers who gave birth to LGBTI children in Africa and beyond. And to those mothers who lost their children to hate-crime-related violence, we continue to mourn with you – you are not alone. (Muholi in *Faces and Phases*, 2014)

This dedication interrupts the patriarchal logic that continues to reinforce a heterosexual norm and reclaims the significance of mothers who bear, love and mourn LGBTI children who become the victims of homophobia-driven attacks in South Africa, and in the rest of the world. Furthermore, the existence of LGBTI people within and beyond South Africa's borders represented in Muholi's work makes an important statement about the global impact of homophobia; something that is not unique to Africa. *Faces and Phases* includes portraits of Black lesbians and transgender men from Mafikeng, Durban, Gaborone, Johannesburg, Toronto, Harare, Paarl, London and Cape Town (Baderoon in *Faces and Phases*, 2014:333). The transnational focus in this archive directs one's attention to the forgotten narratives of the global Black LGBTI community. The transnational inclusion of LGBTI narratives from places such as London and Toronto problematises the representation of Western democracies as always liberal, democratic and gay-friendly; a homonationalist move that detracts from Western conservatism by critiquing homophobia in the rest of the world, especially in Africa. Transnational LGBTI inclusion in Muholi's collection furthermore draws our attention to the superficiality of the borders between LGBTI communities and alerts us to how these imagined borders can work to erode transnational LGBTI solidarity and queer activism.

This unprecedented collection of portrait photographs and accompanying narratives provides insight into the multiplicity of stories and identities of Black lesbians and transgender men. Baderoon provides an eloquent definition of the archive in commenting that, "[t]hese are not mechanically produced portraits, but a choreography of presence" (Baderoon in *Faces and Phases*, 2014:335). Both the bodily presence in terms of faces staring back as well as the narratives, poems and short stories of Black lesbians and transgender men comprise an archive that resists the homophobic frames and murderous scripts prevalent in the media. A well-known lesbian activist that is featured in *Faces and Phases*, Funeka Soldaat, describes the importance of lesbian women speaking for themselves and for the LGBTI community in starting to write their own chapter in history.

Lesbians and transgender men who form part of this archive are aware of the potential of their portraits and narratives to challenge one-dimensional representations of their lives. The archive documents desire, struggle, hope, disappointment, love and rage. Muholi insists that "photographic images produced within her community constitute a powerful political and epistemological act against the erasures of the dominant national culture" (Baderoon in *Faces and Phases*, 2014:329). As part of this political and episte-mological act I wish to identify three themes in Muholi's collection that contest hegemonic modes of representation: survivability, mourning and belonging. In the section that follows I discuss counter-narratives documented in *Faces and Phases*. These sto-ries form part of a queer archive that challenges normative modes of recognition and intelligibility for the LGBTI community.

Survivability, mourning and belonging

A prominent theme in the narratives documented in *Faces and Phases* is the ever-present spectre of fear. Some of this includes the fear of corrective rape and homophobia as well as the fear of merely surviving as a Black lesbian or transgender man in a homophobic or transphobic community. Muholi expresses some of these fears in the introduction to her collection when she states:

> As black lesbian women and gay men today we are resisting homophobia, queerphobia and transphobia simply by living our lives. We put ourselves at risk in the townships by coming out and being seen, but we refuse to comply and to deny our own existence. (Muholi in *Faces and Phases*, 2014:7)

The stories, narratives and poems in Muholi's collection all confirm that although Black lesbian women and transgender men are victi-mised because of their sexuality they continue to "live their lives", referencing a strong sense of survivability. Narratives of survival include both physical and psychic traumas such as rape, contract-ing HIV, losing partners and experiencing rejection from family members. However, these are narratives of survival, not defeat. For example, one of the participants in the collection, Nonhlanhla Sigasa, writes, "I have two birthdays: I was born on 10 October and

I was diagnosed HIV positive in February, so each and every 15 February my HIV status turns a year older and I get to live another year" (Sigasa in *Faces and Phases*, 2014:63). In contrast to representations of violated and abused bodies in the print media, Sigasa's narrative is a positive one and foregrounds lesbian survivability. While a large number of narratives reference a painful past, they simultaneously speak of liveability and hopeful futures. For instance, Funeka Soldaat, LGBT activist and founder of the South African organisation Free Gender, hopes for a future where there will not be any need for gay and lesbian organisations in Khayelitsha, Cape Town; a sentiment that resonates with Muholi's aspiration to find "a history in which she can claim part and which would also allow her to envisage a future" (Baderoon in *Faces and Phases*, 2014:334). Survivability thus constitutes a significant counter-narrative in that it speaks back to frames that detract from the liveability and intelligibility of Black lesbian and transgender life.

The second theme in *Faces and Phases* is that of mourning. The act of mourning and remembering the lives of Black lesbian women and transgender men who are represented as ungrievable in the public sphere plays an important affective role in restoring the intelligibility of queer life. The archive includes portraits, poems and narratives of lesbians who were murdered for their sexuality. The first photograph taken for the *Faces and Phases* project is that of Busi Sigasa, a lesbian who contracted HIV from rape and died a year after her photograph was taken at the age of 25. In her moving poem, Sigasa articulates a central feature of the archive when she writes "Remember me when I'm gone" (Sigasa in *Faces and Phases*, 2014:315). Mourning those who have already passed thus challenges the erasure of memory. Memory furthermore acts as a method of living on beyond the boundaries of the body. The first poem included in *Faces and Phases*, by Sindiwe Magona, is titled "Please, Take Photographs!" and underscores the urgency of documenting queer lives. The young age at which Black lesbian women and transgender men are raped and murdered for their sexuality is remembered in Magona's poem and the mourning of lives terminated prematurely emerges as an important affective theme.

Finally, I identify the theme of belonging in Muholi's collection. It can be argued that all elements of the archive combine to form a new type of belonging that resists heteronormative and national scripts of conformity and belonging. Belonging is scripted into *Faces and Phases* where participants define their place in families. Amogelang Senokwane writes about her coming-out process, asserting that most of her family members accepted her sexuality. Senokwane's story problematises the stereotype that homosexuality is unAfrican and in describing the benefits of forming part of a collective project she comments,

> *Faces and Phases* has helped me a lot, because when my family saw the book and saw me and other lesbians there, it made them more proud of me and made them understand that there are lesbians out there and we are here to stay. (Senokwane in *Faces and Phases*, 2014:22)

Furthermore, Black lesbian women and transgender men make it clear that they see themselves as playing an active role in the production of Muholi's queer archive, all asserting a strong sense of belonging to the expanding narrative. An important contribution in this regard is written by Pamella Dlungwana,

> I wanted to insert myself into an archive that was still learning its ABCs. There are all kinds of African queers out there: dominatrixes and leather boys and tranny lesbian MTFs – the vocab and the archive are growing, and I'm glad that Zanele Muholi is standing in front and centre with a Canon gawd-knows-what in her hand ready to help with the script. (Dlungwana in *Faces and Phases*, 2014:148)

Portraits, poems, narratives and biographies in this collection constitute a central part of the expanding chapters authored by the LGBTI community challenging lesbian erasure and loss. These chapters celebrate Black lesbian and transgender existence and survival, and through practices of mourning and queer affiliations a new LGBTI script and a positive frame and future is starting to emerge in Africa and beyond. Muholi's photography and visual activism forms part of a growing body of literature that contests the single narrative often ascribed to African lesbian sexualities.[5]

Conclusion

In this chapter I explored ways in which common understandings of corrective rape and Black lesbian sexuality are being challenged. The dominant narrative that has attached itself to lesbian sexuality in the South African public sphere is that Black lesbians are particularly vulnerable to homophobic violence and rape, and that 'corrective rape' is a legitimate form of punishment reserved for these women. This one-dimensional frame applied to Black lesbians in South Africa has contributed to their status as unintelligible figures. In challenging negative representations of Black lesbian life I suggest that Butler's theorisation around frames, Cvetkovich's contribution to queer publics and finally the act of reclaiming lesbian feminisms constitute productive elements for reimagining Black lesbian life in post-apartheid South Africa. Such a reconceptualising becomes possible through a queer archive and, as demonstrated in Zanele Muholi's work, the deconstruction of superficial boundaries between LGBTI communities and an unusual archive of feelings offer an opportunity to strengthen lesbian and queer, transnational solidarity.

Notes

1   The rape statistics for the 2016–2017 period are available online at www. saps.gov.za/services/crimestats.php.

2 Apartheid was a political system of racial segregation and discrimination against all non-whites. It was established in 1948 and abolished in 1994 when South Africa became a democratic country.

3 The YouTube video "South African Women Fall Victim to 'Corrective Rape'" is available online at www.youtube.com/watch? v=wefnH1SGDLM&t=213s.

4 The overwhelming focus on race relations during apartheid resulted in the silencing and marginalisation of Black lesbian identities. Black lesbians have become more visible since the advent of democracy in 1994.

5 This growing body of literature on the Black lesbian community in South Africa also includes: *Only Half the Picture* (2006) by Zanele Muholi, *The Writing Circle* (2007) by Rozena Maart and *Black Bull, Ancestors and Me: My Life as a Lesbian Sangoma* (2008) by Zandile Nkunzi Nkabinde.

About the editors and contributors

ASHA ACHUTHAN presently teaches at the Advanced Centre for
Women's Studies, School of Development Studies, Tata Institute
of Social Sciences, Mumbai, India. Her research areas include
feminist science and technology studies, feminist queer politics
and women-centred childbirth practices and their positioning
vis-à-vis modern medicine. Some of her recent writing includes
the editing of a special issue on gender and science in *Economic
and Political Weekly* in 2017, a book chapter on integration and
interdisciplinarity in *Integrated Science Education* from Orient
Blackswan in 2017, and on feminist standpoint epistemology in a
volume on feminists and science in India from Sage in 2017. She
is presently concluding a research study on discrimination based
on gender and sexuality in healthcare with particular focus on the
institution and the expert model.

SARA AHMED is an independent feminist scholar and writer. Her
work is concerned with how power is experienced and challenged
in everyday life and institutional cultures. She has recently completed the book *What's the Use? On the Uses of Use*, which is forthcoming with Duke University Press and is currently working on a
project on complaint. Her previous publications include *Living a
Feminist Life* (2017), *Willful Subjects* (2014), *On Being Included:
Racism and Diversity in Institutional Life* (2012), *The Promise of
Happiness* (2010), *Queer Phenomenology: Objects, Orientations,*

Others (2006), *The Cultural Politics of Emotion* (2014, 2004), *Strange Encounters: Embodied Others in Post-Coloniality* (2000) and *Differences That Matter: Feminist Theory and Postmodernism* (1998). She blogs at www.feministkilljoys.com.

NIHARIKA BANERJEA teaches at the School of Liberal Studies, Ambedkar University, Delhi. Working across and drawing from sociology, social anthropology and geographies of sexualities, Niharika writes about gendered institutions, queer feminist collective imaginaries, notions of community and queer politics in the context of contemporary India. She identifies as an academic-activist, as a way to critically address familiar binaries between academia and activism – in classrooms, in activist spaces and in writing practices. Across all these sites, along with her co-thinkers, co-writers and co-workers, Niharika tries to make 'theory' relevant to the interrogation of everyday hegemonic relations, as well as self-referential understandings of 'lived experiences'. At the same time, she invests in bringing the complexity of lived experiences to question familiar theoretical endeavours. Niharika also identifies as queer, and this identification includes an assemblage of socio-political histories of varied journeys, rather than as an already arrived at moment.

PARAMITA BANERJEE opted out of academics nearly three decades ago to work with young people from marginalised communities – to push boundaries together with them for a world where Every Young Voice Counts. She is the Co-founder and Chief Functionary of DIKSHA, which grew out of an experiment Paramita had started in three red-light areas of Kolkata, India, in 1999 with a MacArthur Fellowship for Leadership Development. Her ability to be 'the mid-wife who facilitates the birth of new leaders' resulted in her being elected an Ashoka Fellow in 2016. Paramita is recognised as a gender-sexuality expert for adolescents, skilled in research, training and evaluation. Writing and translation are

Paramita's passions. She has translated and published a collection of short stories for children by the Magsaysay Award-winning writer Mahasweta Devi titled *Our Non-veg Cow and Other Stories* (Seagull Books, 1998) and translated into English and published many poems by women poets from Bengal. Some of her translations appear in Elizabeth Bumiller's *May You Be the Mother of a Thousand Sons* (Random House, 1990). She has written columns and articles for noted online and printed journals, including an article in *Friendship as Social Justice Activism: Critical Solidarities in a Global Perspective* (University of Chicago Press, 2018; Indian edition by Seagull Books, 2018). One of her articles is forthcoming in the two-volume *The Idea of the University: Histories and Contexts* (Routledge), scheduled for publication later this year.

SUMITA BEETHI is a queer feminist activist, traveller, writer, member of Sappho for Equality.

RANJITA BISWAS is a queer feminist academic-activist. She also practices psychiatry. She is a member of Sappho for Equality.

KATH BROWNE is a professor of Geographies of Sexualities and Genders at Maynooth University Ireland. Her work explores lesbian, gay, bisexual and trans liveabilities, and with Niharika Banerjea and others she works on the project "Making Lives Liveable: Rethinking Social Exclusion". She has written on lesbian geographies (including the book *Lesbian Geographies* co-edited with Eduarda Ferreira), gender transgressions and women's spaces, including Michigan Womyn's Music Festival. She also works with Catherine Nash and Andrew Gorman Murray on understanding transnational resistances to LGBT equalities.

LINE CHAMBERLAND, a sociologist, is a professor in the Sexology Department and the Director of the Research Chair on Homophobia at the Université du Québec à Montréal. Her earliest work examined Montreal's lesbian histories, including her oral history project, *Mémoires lesbiennes*. Broadly speaking, her research projects have focused on various forms of social exclusion affecting sexual minorities in particular institutional contexts ranging from education, the workplace, health care and social services. Her most recent research projects include "SAVIE-LGBTQ: Understanding Inclusion and Exclusion of LGBTQ People", as well as a collaborative research project with l'Astérisk, a safe space for queer youth (14–25 years old).

KARUNA CHANDRASHEKAR is a psychodynamic psychotherapist. She is currently a doctoral candidate in the Department of Social and Political Thought at York University, Toronto. Her research work is on psychoanalysis and mourning.

SHRADDHA CHATTERJEE is currently a doctoral candidate in Gender, Feminist and Women's Studies at York University, Toronto. Her/Their research focuses on the resignifications of contemporary discourses of sexuality in relation to globalisation and neoliberalism in India. Shraddha has previously been trained in psychology, cultural studies and gender studies. She/They are the author of *Queer Politics in India: Towards Sexual Subaltern Subjects* (2018).

NATACHA CHETCUTI-OSOROVITZ is a sociologist who works as a senior lecturer at Centrale Supélec, and as a research associate at Laboratoire IDHES (Institutions et Dynamiques Historiques de l'Economie et de la Société – UMR 8533) at Université Paris-Saclay in France. Her current research focuses on the relationship between gender and violence. Her most recent publications include: "New Forms of Antisemitism, the Law, and the Politics of Gender and Sexuality in Contemporary France" (with Fabrice Teicher; 2018) in *Analysis of Current Trends in Antisemitism*; "Subvertir les scénarios hétéronormés de la sexualité: pratiques et savoirs lesbiens", in Delphine Gardey and Marilène Vuille (eds) *Les Sciences du désir: La sexualité féminine, de la psychanalyse aux neurosciences*; and "La notion de personne sexuée dans l'œuvre de Nicole-Claude Mathieu" (with Martine Gestin; 2017), in Dominique Bourque and Johanne Coulomb (eds) *Penser "l'arraisonnement des femmes": vivre en résistance, Nicole-Claude Mathieu (1937–2014).*

JULES FALQUET is an associate professor at Paris Diderot University and member of the CEDREF (Centre for Teaching, Documentation and Research in Feminist Studies) – LCSP (Research Group on Social and Political Change). Her research has been published in a number of feminist and gender studies, Latin American studies and political science journals including *Nouvelles Questions féministes, Cahiers du genre, Cahiers du CEDREF, Travail, Genre et société, Clio, Cahiers d'Amérique latine, Futur antérieur, Contretemps, Mouvements, Lutas sociais, Universitas Humanísticas* and *Descentradas*. She has published two books in both French and Spanish: *Pax neoliberalia* (2016) and *De gré ou de force: Les femmes dans la mondialisation* (2008). She is currently pursuing research on gender and globalisation, the continuum of violence and the interweaving of sex, race and class relations – both from an epistemological perspective and by observing labour-market transformations.

EDUARDA FERREIRA is a researcher at the research group "Gender and Sexuality" of CICS.NOVA – Interdisciplinary Centre of Social Sciences, at FCSH/NOVA, Portugal, with an active involvement in LGBTI rights movements. With a background in Educational Psychology and a PhD in Social and Cultural Geography, she has published and presented on gender, sexualities, lesbian studies and equality policies, and participated in diverse conference organising committees, such as: "European Geographies of Sexualities Conference" and "Geographies of Inclusion: Challenges and

Opportunities". She is a founding member of "REGGSILA – Iberian and Latin American Network of Geography, Gender and Sexuality", and an editorial member of the section LES Online of the *Latin American Journal of Geography and Gender* (RLAGG).

SUBHAGATA GHOSH is a queer feminist activist by passion and a scientific worker by profession. She is a co-founder of Sappho and Sappho for Equality.

MAMATHA KAROLLIL has a PhD in Social Sciences (Psychology and Sociology) from TISS, and teaches at the School of Human Studies at the Ambedkar University Delhi. Her interests and commitments include feminism, psychoanalysis, queer politics, pedagogy, stories (as methodology and outside academy, sustenance), sex and sexuality, intimacies and community.

NADINE LAKE is the director of the Gender Studies Programme at the University of the Free State, South Africa. She was awarded a twenty-two-month Erasmus Mundus scholarship to complete her PhD at the Centre for Gender Research (CfGR) at Uppsala University, Sweden. Nadine's doctoral dissertation, titled *Corrective Rape and Black Lesbian Sexualities in Contemporary South African Cultural Texts*, troubles the precarious status ascribed to black lesbian life as well as identifying counter-narratives that form part of a queer cultural archive in Africa. Her research is invested in debunking the myth that homosexuality is unAfrican. Nadine is currently involved in a Swedish International Development Agency (SIDA) research project titled "Gender Mainstreaming: Developing Competencies in Higher Education for Gender Equality, Peace-Building and Gender-Sensitive Research Coordinators". Her participation in this project includes presenting gender-based violence workshops, developing gender studies curricula and supervising postgraduate students at the University of Eduardo Mondlane, Mozambique.

SHALS MAHAJAN is a writer, layabout, part feline, somewhat hooman, queer feminist fellow who lives in Bombay, but mainly lives in their head. They have been part of LABIA – Queer Feminist LBT Collective – for the past two decades. Shals is genderqueer and has worked on issues of gender, sexuality, caste and communalism as trainer, teacher and activist. They have also published several children's books, including *Timmi in Tangles* and *Timmi and Rizu* (Duckbill, 2013, 2017), and *A Big Day for the Little Wheels* (Pratham, 2017). They also co-authored *No Outlaws in the Gender Galaxy* (Zubaan, 2015).

NADIKA NADJA is a writer and researcher with interests in cities, history and archaeology, gender and the internet. She is currently a news editor for a web-based magazine.

KATHERINE O'DONNELL is Associate Professor, History of Ideas, UCD School of Philosophy and one of the five members of the group Justice for Magdalenes Research (JFMR jfmresearch.com). For ten years she was the Director of UCD Women's Studies Centre and she has published widely on the History of Ideas in Eighteenth Century Ireland, on the history of sexuality and on Irish literature. She has won a number of awards for her teaching which include the UCD President's Gold Medal for Excellence in Teaching and with TrueTube the British Universities Learning on Screen Award for Teaching materials relating to Ireland's Magdalene Laundries; with JFMR she has won a number of activist awards including the Irish Labour Party's Thirst for Justice Award; she has held a number of research grants from the Irish Research Council as well as a number of grants from the EU. She has been a lesbian activist since the late 1980s and has been a prime organiser of the Lesbian Lives Conference which was first held in UCD in 1995.

MARTA OLASIK received a PhD in Social Sciences (Sociology) from the University of Warsaw. Her area of expertise is lesbian studies, which primarily involves reflecting on the subject from the perspectives of the sociology of knowledge and geographies of sexualities. Her dissertation is a pioneering interdisciplinary work on lesbian subjectivities and citizenships that aims to establish a distinct lesbian-studies discourse in Poland. The next step for her will be to conduct a proper and first-ever empirical research into the question of lesbian subjectivities and citizenships in Poland. Marta's general objective is to promote an intertextual attitude, where lesbianity (sic!) is an open field of possibilities for emotional and sexual self-creation.

JULIE PODMORE is a professor at John Abbott College in Montreal. She is also an affiliate assistant professor at Concordia University and a research associate of the Research Chair on Homophobia at the Université du Québec à Montréal. Her research has been published in a number of urban studies, geography and sexuality studies journals and as chapters in collections such as *The Routledge Research Companion to Geographies of Sex and Sexuality*, *The Ashgate Research Companion to Gay and Lesbian Activism* and *Queer Mobilizations: Social Movement Activism and Canadian Public Policy*. Her current research projects include "Queering Mile End: Sexuality, Generation and Neighbourhood Change in Montreal" and "Queering Canadian Suburbs: LGBTQ2S Place-making Outside of Central Cities" with Alison Bain and Brian Ray.

POORVA RAJARAM is a freelance journalist and an organising member of the Bangalore Queer Film Festival. She is currently finishing her PhD in History at Jawaharlal Nehru University (New Delhi).

SOPHIE ROBINSON teaches women's and gender studies and history at the University of New South Wales (Sydney, Australia). In 2018, she submitted her PhD thesis titled *The Lesbian Presence in Australian Feminist, Gay and Queer Social Movements,*

1970s–1990s. Sophie has published on Australian lesbian history, feminist history and masculinity politics. She is also the secretary of Sydney's Pride History Group, which records and preserves the oral histories of Sydney's LGBTIQ+ communities.

RUKMINI SEN is an associate professor in the School of Liberal Studies at Ambedkar University, Delhi. She teaches and writes at the intersections of sociology, law, movements and narratives. Her most recent publications include: "Interrogating (Non) Consent in Sexual Intimacies and Infringements: Mapping the Socio-legal Landscape in India", in Gita Chadha and Joseph MT (eds) *Re-Imagining Sociology in India: Feminist Perspectives* (Routledge, 2018); "Re-imaging Kinship in Disability Specific Domesticity: Legal Understanding of Care and Companionship", in Anita Ghai (ed.) *Disability in South Asia: Knowledge and Experience* (Sage, 2018); (a co-editor) *Indian Feminisms, Law Reform and the Law Commission of India: Special Issue in Honour of Lotika Sarkar, Journal of Indian Law and Society*, vol. 6 (Monsoon, 2018). She has been involved with women's movements in Kolkata and New Delhi. She is in a heterosexual companionship and takes care of neighbourhood dogs.

VALÉRIE SIMON is a queer and lesbian activist from Montreal currently working on a PhD in Philosophy at the University of Oregon. Her academic interests situate themselves at the intersection of phenomenology, sexuality studies and the philosophy of technology, and her activism focuses on issues of safe(r) space, sexuality, sexual health and activist history.

ROSIE SWAYNE is a British theatre composer, sound designer, songwriter and performer whose professional life is currently divided between the theatre/arts scene in Helsinki and the UK grassroots/folk festival circuit. Her ongoing projects include "Adventures in White Privilege", a collaborative writing/theatre/

film project involving members of the Romanian Roma community that seeks to shed a light on what 'travelling' in the EU means for different ethnic groups. She is also currently touring songs from her evolving musical show *FOSSILHEADS: The Future Is Petrifying* – a comical, political commentary on the relationship between climate change and global capitalism, with some lesbian angst. There always needs to be some lesbian angst.

NITYA V is currently working as faculty member at the Centre for Wellness and Justice, Baduku Community College (Samvada, Bangalore). She is also on the organising committee of the Bangalore Queer Film Festival along with a bunch of others who all do it out of a mad love for good cinema.

Bibliography

Aarmo M. (1999) How homosexuality became "un-African": the case of Zimbabwe. In: Wieringa S and Blackwood E (eds) *Same Sex Relations and Female Desires: Transgender Practices across Cultures*. New York: Columbia University Press, 255–280.

Achuthan A. (2017) "Queer talk" in Indian academia: some notes on the politics of naming. *National Queer Conference, Sappho for Equality, 2017*. Kolkata.

Achuthan A, Biswas R and Dhar A. (2007) *Lesbian Standpoint*. Calcutta: Sanhati.

Ahmed, S. (2006a) Orientations: towards a queer phenomenology'. *GLQ: A Journal of Lesbian and Gay Studies* 12: 543–574.

Ahmed S. (2006b) *Queer Phenomenology: Orientations, Objects, Others*. Durham, NC: Duke University Press.

Ahmed S. (2014a) Practical phenomenology. https://feministkilljoys. com/2014/06/04/practical-phenomenology/. Accessed 2/11/2018.

Ahmed S. (2014b) Feminist complaint. Available at: https://feministkilljoys. com/2014/12/05/complaint/. Accessed 2/11/2018.

Ahmed S. (2014c) Being in question. Available at: https://feministkilljoys. com/2014/04/01/being-in-question/. Accessed 2/11/2018.

Ahmed S. (2014d) Wiggle room. Available at: https://feministkilljoys. com/2014/09/28/wiggle-room/. Accessed 2/11/2018.

Ahmed S. (2014e) *Willful Subjects*. Durham, NC: Duke University Press.

Ahmed S. (2017) *Living a Feminist Life*. Durham, NC: Duke University Press.

Akanksha and Malobika (2007) Sappho: a journey through fire. In: Bose B and Bhattacharyya S (eds) *The Phobic and the Erotic: The Politics of Sexualities in India*. London: Seagull Books, 363–368.

Amadiume I. (1987) *Male Daughters, Female Husbands: Gender and Sex in an African Society*. London: Zed Books.

Anandhi S and Swaminathan P. (2006) Making it relevant: mapping the meaning of women's studies in Tamil Nadu. *Economic and Political Weekly* 41: 4444–4454.

Anderson A. (2015) The death of the lesbian. *HuffPost*. www.huffingtonpost. com/aimee-anderson/the-death-of-the-lesbian_b_7699284.html. Accessed 8/8/2018.

Anderson J. (2018) 300 women "quit" the Labour Party because self-identifying trans women are being included. *Pink News*, 2 May. www. pinknews.co.uk/2018/05/02/300-women-quit-the-labour-party-because-self-identifying-trans-women-are-being-included/. Accessed 2/11/2018.

Anonymous Collective. (1981) La contrainte à l'hétérosexualité. *Nouvelles Questions féministes* 1: Editorial.

Anzaldúa G. (1983) La Prieta. In: Morago C and Anzaldúa G (eds) *This Bridge Called My Back: Writings by Radical Women of Color*. Watertown, MA: Persephone Press, 198–209.

Anzaldúa G. ([1987] 1999) *Borderlands/La Frontera: The New Mestiza*. San Francisco, CA: Aunt Lute.

Appiah K. (1992) *In My Father's House: Africa in the Philosophy of Culture*. New York: Oxford University Press.

Aquinas T. (1947) *Summa Theologica*. New York: Benzinger Brothers Inc.

Arcos GLV. (2016) Subjetividad y experiencia: el caso de una lesbiana feminista. *LES Online* 8: 2–12.

Ardill S and Neumark N. (1982) Putting sex back into lesbianism. *Gay Information* 11: 4–11.

Ardill S and O'Sullivan S. (1986) Upsetting an applecart: difference, desire and lesbian sadomasochism. *Feminist Review* 23: 31–57.

Atkinson TG. (1975 [1974]) *Odyssée d'une amazon*. Paris: Des femmes.

Banerjea N. (2011) Reflections on "being queer" in India. Available at: http://humanitiesunderground.org/reflections-on-being-queer-in-kolkata. Accessed 2/11/2018.

Barnes D. (1992 [1928]) *Ladies Almanack*. New York: New York University Press.

Barthes R. (1978) *A Lover's Discourse: Fragments*. New York: Hill and Wang.

Bashford K, et al. (1993) *Kink*. Strawberry Hills, NSW: Wicked Women Publications.

Baxi P. (2000) Rape, retribution, state: on whose bodies? *Economic and Political Weekly* 35: 1196–1200.

Bazin L, Mendès-Leite R and Quiminal C. (2000) Déclinaisons anthropologiques des sexualités. *Journal des anthropologues* 82–83: 9–24.

BBC. (2018) Trans inmate jailed for Wakefield prison sex offences. *BBC News*, 11 October. www.bbc.com/news/uk-england-leeds-45825838. Accessed 13/10/2018.

Becker E, Citron M, Lesage J, et al. (1981) Lesbians and film. *Jumpcut* 24–25: 17–21.

Bélanger D. (2000) *Les droits clandestins: les enjeux de l'intégration des lesbiennes dans les organismes communautaires intervenant auprès des femmes*. Montreal: Réseau des lesbiennes du Québec/Quebec Lesbian Network.

Bell D and Valentine G. (1995) *Mapping Desire: Geographies of Sexualities.* London and New York: Routledge.

Bell L. (1987) *Good Girls, Bad Girls: Sex Trade Workers and Feminists Face to Face.* Toronto: The Women's Press.

Benjamin J. (1988) *The Bonds of Love: Psychoanalysis, Feminism, and the Problem of Domination.* New York: Pantheon Books.

Berlant L and Edelman L. (2014) *Sex, or the Unbearable.* Durham, NC: Duke University Press.

Biswas R. (2007) The lesbian standpoint. In: Bose B and Bhattacharya S (eds) *The Phobic and the Erotic: The Politics of Sexualities in Contemporary India.* London, New York and Calcutta: Seagull Books, 263–290.

Biswas R. (2011) Of love, marriage and kinship: queering the family. In: Sen S, Biswas R and Dhawan N (eds) *Intimate Others: Marriage and Sexualities in India.* Kolkata: Stree, 414–435.

Blackman I and Perry K. (1990) Skirting the issue: lesbian fashion for the 1990s. *Feminist Review* 34: 67–78.

Blackwood E. (1999) Tombois in West Sumatra: constructing masculinity and erotic desire. In: Wieringa S and Blackwood E (eds) *Same Sex Relations and Female Desires: Transgender Practices across Cultures.* New York: Columbia University Press, 181–205.

Blanchard R. (1989) The concept of autogynephilia and the typology of male gender dysphoria. *The Journal of Nervous and Mental Disease* 177: 616–623.

Boehringer S. (2014) Female homoeroticism. In: Hubbard TK (ed) *A Companion to Greek and Roman Sexualities.* Chichester: Wiley Blackwell, 150–163.

Bonneau M and Demczuk I. (1998) *Des droits à reconnaître: les lesbiennes face à la discrimination.* Montréal: Éditions du remue-ménage.

Bonnet M-J. (1998) De l'émancipation amoureuse des femmes dans la cité: lesbiennes et féministes au XXe siècle. *Les temps modernes* 598: 85–112.

Bose B. (2006) Introduction. In: Bose B (ed) *Gender and Censorship.* New Delhi: Women Unlimited, xiii–xlvi.

Bose B and Bhattacharya S. (2007) *The Phobic and the Erotic: The Politics of Sexualities in Contemporary India.* London, New York and Kolkata: Seagull Books.

Boucheron B. (2007) Introduction à une histoire du mouvement lesbien en France. *Visibilité/invisibilité des lesbiennes,* Coordination lesbienne en France. Hôtel de Ville de Paris.

Boulila SG. (2015) What makes a lesbian salsa space comfortable? Reconceptualising safety and homophobia. In: Browne K and Ferreira E (eds) *Lesbian Geographies: Gender, Place and Power.* Farnham: Ashgate, 149–168.

Bourassa H. (1925) *Femmes-hommes ou hommes et femmes? Études à bâtons rompus sur le féminisme.* Montreal: Imprimerie du Devoir.

Braidotti R, Bonis O and Ménès M. (1985) Des reconversions libidinales: femmes en fin de droits. *Les Cahiers du GRIF* 32: 36–56.

Brown R. (2012) Corrective rape in South Africa: a continuing plight despite an international human rights response. *Annual Survey of International and Comparative Law* 18: 45–66.

Brown RM. (1973) *Rubyfruit Jungle*. New York: Bantam Books.

Brown-Saracino J and Ghaziani A. (2009) The constraints of culture: evidence from the Chicago Dyke March. *Cultural Sociology* 3: 51–75.

Browne K. (2011) Beyond rural idylls: imperfect lesbian utopias at Michigan Womyn's music festival. *Journal of Rural Studies* 27: 13–23.

Browne K and Ferreira E. (2015a) *Introduction to Lesbian Geographies*. Farnham: Ashgate.

Browne K and Ferreira E. (2015b) *Lesbian Geographies: Gender, Place and Power*. Farnham: Ashgate.

Browne K and Olasik M. (2016) Feminism, lesbian. *The Wiley Blackwell Encyclopedia of Gender and Sexuality Studies*. Hoboken, NJ: John Wiley & Sons, 1–3.

Browne K, Olasik M and Podmore J. (2016) Reclaiming lesbian feminisms: beginning discussions on communities, geographies and politics. *Women's Studies International Forum* 56: 113–123.

Bunch C. ([1976] 1987) Learning from lesbian separatism. In: Bunch C (ed) *Passionate Politics: Feminist Theory in Action, Essays, 1968–1986*. New York: St. Martin's Press, 182–191.

Butler J. (1990) *Gender Trouble: Feminism and the Subversion of Identity*. New York: Routledge.

Butler J. (1993) *Bodies That Matter: On the Discursive Limits of "Sex"*. London: Routledge.

Butler J. (1997) Merely cultural. *Social Text* 15: 265–277.

Butler J. (1999) *Gender Trouble: Feminism and the Subversion of Identity*, 2nd ed. New York and London: Routledge.

Butler, J. (2002). Is kinship always already heterosexual? *differences: A Journal of Feminist Cultural Studies* 13: 14–44.

Butler J. (2004) *Undoing Gender*. London: Routledge.

Butler J. (2009) *Frames of War*. London: Verso.

CALERI. ([1999] 2011) *Lesbian Emergence: Khamosh! Emergency Jari Hai! A Citizens' Report*. New Delhi: CALERI.

Calhoun C. (1994) Separating lesbian theory from feminist theory. *Ethics* 104: 558–581.

Calhoun C. (1996) The gender closet: lesbian disappearance under the sign "women". In: Vicinus M (ed) *Lesbian Subjects: A Feminist Studies Reader*. Bloomington, IN: Indiana University Press, 209–232.

Califia-Rice P. (1980) *Sapphistry: The Book of Lesbian Sexuality*. Tallahassee, FL: Naiad Press.

Califia-Rice P. (2000) *Public Sex: The Culture of Radical Sex*. San Francisco, CA: Cleis Press.

Cameron D. (2016) What makes a word a slur? https://debuk.wordpress. com/2016/2011/2006/what-makes-a-word-a-slur/. Accessed 2/11/2018.

Canclini NG. (1992) Cultural reconversion. In: Yúdice G, Flores J and Franco J (eds) *On Edge: The Crisis of Contemporary Latin American Culture*. Minneapolis, MN: University of Minnesota Press, 29–43.

Caprio F. (1954) *Female Homosexuality*. New York: Citadel Press.

Carby H. (1996) White woman listen! Black feminism and the boundaries of sisterhood. In: Baker HA Jr, Diawara M and Lindeborg RH (eds) *Black British Cultural Studies: A Reader*. Chicago, IL: University of Chicago Press, 61–86.

Centre Lyonnais d'études féministes. (1989) *Chronique d'une passion: le mouvement de libération des femmes à Lyon*. Paris: L'Harmattan.

Chagnon D. (1986) Lesbianisme et féminisme. *Amazones d'hier, lesbiennes d'aujourd'hui* 4.

Chakravarti U. (1989) Whatever happened to the Vedic Dasi? Orientalism, nationalism and a script for the past. In: Sangari K and Vaid S (eds) *Recasting Women: Essays in Colonial History*. New Brunswick, NJ: Rutgers University Press, 27–87.

Chamberland L. (1989) Le lesbianisme: continuum féminin ou marronnage? Réflexions féministes pour une théorisation de l'expérience lesbienne. *Recherches féministes* 2: 135–146.

Chamberland L. (1997) Du fléau social au fait social: l'étude des homosexualités. *Sociologie et sociétés* 19: 5–20.

Chamberland L. (2000) Québec. In: Zimmerman B (ed) *Lesbian Histories and Cultures*. New York: Garland Publishing, 627–629.

Chatterjee S. (2018) *Queer Politics in India: Towards Sexual Subaltern Subjects*. London: Routledge.

Chauvin S. (2005) Les aventures d'une "alliance objective": quelques moments de la relation entre mouvements homosexuels et mouvements féministes au XXe siècle. *L'Homme & la société* 4: 111–130.

Chetcuti N. (2006) Lesbianisme. In: Andrieu B (ed) *Dictionnaire du corps en sciences humaines et sociales*. Paris: CNRS Éditions, 286–287.

Chetcuti N. (2008) *Normes socio-sexuelles et lesbianisme: définition de soi, catégories de sexe/genre et script sexuel*. Paris: École des hautes études en sciences sociales.

Chetcuti N. (2009) De "on ne naît pas femme" ... à "on n'est pas femme": de Simone de Beauvoir à Monique Wittig. *Sexualité, Genre et Société* 1.

Chetcuti N. (2010) *Se dire lesbienne: vie de couple, sexualité, représentation de soi*. Paris: Payot.

Chetcuti N and Amaral MT. (2008) Monique Wittig, la tragédie et l'amour. *Corps: revue interdisciplinaire* 4: 93–98.

Chetcuti N and Michard C. (2003) *Lesbianisme et féminisme: histoires politiques*. Paris: L'Harmattan.

Chetcuti N and Quemener N. (2015) Politiques culturelles lesbiennes In: Chetcuti N and Quemener N (eds) *Miroir/Miroirs. Revue des corps contemporains* 4.

Chiesa L. (2007) *Subjectivity and Otherness: A Philosophical Reading of Lacan.* Cambridge, MA: The MIT Press.

Chodorow N. (1978) *The Reproduction of Mothering.* Berkeley and Los Angeles, CA: University of California Press.

Chow R. (2001) Gender and representation. In: Bronfen E and Kavka M (eds) *Feminist Consequences: Theory for the New Century.* New York: Columbia University Press, 38–57.

Clarke J. (1975) Life as a lesbian. In: Mercer J (ed) *The Other Half: Women in Australian Society.* Ringwood, Vic: Penguin, 333–346.

Cohen CJ. (1997) Punks, bulldaggers and welfare queens: the radical potential of queer politics? *GLQ: Gay and Lesbian Quarterly* 3: 437–465.

Collins P. (1986) Learning from the outsider within: the sociological significance of Black feminist thought. *Social Problems* 33: 14–32.

Combahee River Collective. ([1977] 1997) A Black feminist statement. In: Nicholson L (ed) *The Second Wave: A Reader in Feminist Theory.* New York: Routledge, 63–70.

Combahee River Collective. (1979) A Black feminist statement. In: Eisenstein Z (ed) *Capitalist Patriarchy and the Case for Socialist Feminism.* New York: Monthly Review Press, 362–372.

Committee on the Status of Women in India (1974) *Towards Equality: Report of the Committee on the Status of Women in India.* Ministry of Education & Social Welfare, Department of Social Welfare.

Connell R. (2012) Transsexual women and feminist thought: toward new understanding and new politics. *Signs* 37: 857–881.

Conrad K. (2001) Queer treasons: homosexuality and Irish national identity. *Cultural Studies* 15: 124–137.

Cooper SE and Trebra CJ. (2006) Teaching transgender in women's studies: snarls and strategies. *Journal of Lesbian Studies* 10: 151–180.

Covina G and Galana L. (1975) *The Lesbian Reader: An Amazon Quarterly Anthology.* Oakland, CA: Amazon Press.

Crone J. (1995) Lesbians: the Lavender Women of Ireland. In: O'Carroll, Í and Collins E (eds) *Lesbian and Gay Visions of Ireland: Towards the Twenty-First Century.* London and New York: Cassell, 60–70.

Currans E. (2012) Claiming deviance and honoring community: creating resistant spaces in US dyke marches. *Feminist Formations* 24: 73–101.

Cvetkovich A. (2003) *An Archive of Feelings: Trauma, Sexuality, and Lesbian Public Cultures.* Durham, NC: Duke University Press.

Daly M. (1968) *The Church and the Second Sex.* New York: Harper and Row.

Daly M. (1973) *Beyond God the Father: Toward a Philosophy of Women's Liberation.* Boston, MA: Beacon Press.

Daly M. (1978) *Gyn/ecology: The Metaphysics of Radical Feminism.* Boston, MA: Beacon Press.

Daly M. (1984) *Pure Lust: Elemental Feminist Philosophy.* Boston, MA: Beacon Press.

Daly M. (1987) *Websters' First New Intergalactic Wickedary of the English Language, Conjured in Cahoots with Jane Caputi (with Jane Caputi and Sudie Rakusin).* Boston, MA: Beacon Press.

Daly M. (1992) *Outercourse: The Bedazzling Voyage, Containing Recollections from My Logbook of a Radical Feminist Philosopher.* San Francisco, CA: Harper.

Daly M. (1998) *Quintessence ... Realizing the Archaic Future: A Radical Elemental Feminist Manifesto.* Boston, MA: Beacon Press.

Daly M. (2006) *Amazon Grace: Re-Calling the Courage to Sin Big.* New York: Palgrave Macmillan.

Dansereau M. (1957) À propos du Deuxième sexe de Simone de Beauvoir. *Cité libre* 17: 57.

Dave N. (2011) Indian and lesbian and what came next: affect, commensuration, and queer emergences. *American Ethnologist* 38: 650–665.

Dave NN. (2012) *Queer Activism in India: A Story in the Anthropology of Ethics.* Durham, NC: Duke University Press.

Davis M and Kennedy E. (1989) History and the study of sexuality in the lesbian community: Buffalo, New York, 1940–1960. In: Duberman MB, Vicinus M and Chauncey G (eds) *Hidden from History: Reclaiming the Gay and Lesbian Past.* New York: Penguin Books, 426–440.

De Gallier T. (2018) Brian Paddick is right: Karen White is not an excuse to label transgender people sex offenders. *TalkRADIO.* https://talkradio. co.uk/opinion/opinion-brian-paddick-right-karen-white-not-excuse-label-transgender-people-sex-offenders#EHJTyrH3ceRYOotz.99. Accessed 13/10/2018.

De Lauretis T. (1988) Sexual indifference and lesbian representation. *Theatre Journal* 40: 155–177.

De Lauretis T. (2007) *Théorie queer et cultures populaires: de Foucault à Cronenberg.* Paris: La Dispute.

De Lauretis T and White P. (2007) *Figures of Resistance: Essays in Feminist Theory.* Urbana, IL: University of Illinois Press.

De Veaux A. (2004) *Warrior Poet: A Biography of Audre Lorde.* New York: W.W. Norton.

Delphy C. (1996) L'invention du "French feminism": une démarche essentielle. *Nouvelles Questions féministes* 17: 15–58.

Demczuk I. (2000) Marcher pour le droit des lesbiennes à l'égalité. *Recherches féministes* 13: 131–144.

Demczuk I and Remiggi FW. (1998) *Sortir de l'ombre: histoires des communautés lesbienne et gai de Montréal.* Montreal: VLB éditeur.

Derrida J. (2005) *The Politics of Friendship.* London: Verso.

Deshpande A. (2015) "Queer Azadi March" protests against forced reconversions. *The Hindu*, 1 February.

Dhejne C, Lichtenstein P, Boman M, Johansson ALV, Långström N and Landén M. (2011) Long-term follow-up of transsexual persons undergoing sex reassignment surgery: cohort study in Sweden. *PLoS One*, 22 February. https://doi.org/10.1371/journal.pone.0016885.

Dimen M. (2013) *Sexuality, Intimacy, Power*. Hillsdale, NJ: The Analytic Press.

Doan L. (1994) *The Lesbian Postmodern*. New York: Columbia University Press.

Dodds L. (2016) Britain needs to stop freaking out about transgender kids. *The Telegraph*, 13 May.

Donoghue E. (1995) Noises from woodsheds: tales of Irish lesbians, 1886–1989. In: O'Carroll Í and Collins E (eds) *Lesbian and Gay Visions of Ireland*. London: Cassell, 158–170.

Donohoe K. (2018) Ireland says no to TERFs. *GCN*, 24 January. https://gcn.ie/ireland-says-no-to-terfs/.

Dorlin E. (2008) *Sexe, genre et sexualités: introduction à la théorie féministe*. Paris: Presses Universitaires de France.

Drèze J and Goyal A. (2003) Future of mid-day meals. *Economic and Political Weekly* 38: 4673–4683.

Drèze J and Khera R. (2017) Recent social security initiatives in India. *World Development* 98: 555–572.

Drydakis N. (2017) How transitioning leads to better mental health – and job satisfaction. *The Conversation*, 27 September. http://theconversation.com/how-transitioning-leads-to-better-mental-health-and-job-satisfaction-84617. Accessed 15/3/2018.

Duffy N. (2017) Radical feminists team up with right-wing evangelicals to oppose trans rights protections. *Pink News*, 8 February. www.pinknews.co.uk/2017/2002/2008/radical-feminists-team-up-with-right-wing-evangelicals-to-oppose-trans-rights-protections/. Accessed 2/11/2018.

Duggan L and Hunter ND. (2006) *Sex Wars: Sexual Dissent and Political Culture*. New York: Routledge.

Duggan M. (2016) *Queering Conflict: Examining Lesbian and Gay Experiences of Homophobia in Northern Ireland*. London: Routledge.

Dugmore H. (2004) We're not comfortable. *Sunday Tribune*, 8 August.

Dunne P and Hewitt T. (2018) Gender recognition, self-determination and segregated space. *Oxford Human Rights Hub*, 16 January. http://ohrh.law.ox.ac.uk/gender-recognition-self-determination-and-segregated-space. Accessed 2/11/2018.

Dworkin A. (1974) *Woman Hating*. New York: EP Dutton.

Dykes on Bikes. (2018) *Welcome!* www.dykesonbikes.org/. Accessed 2/11/2018.

Dykes on Bikes. (n.d.) *Our History*. www.dykesonbikes.org/history. Accessed 2/11/2018.

Earle S and Letherby G. (2007) Conceiving time? Women who do or do not conceive. *Sociology of Health and Illness* 29: 233–250.

Echols A. (1984) The taming of the id: feminist sexual politics, 1968–1983. In: Vance C (ed) *Pleasure and Danger: Exploring Female Sexuality*. Boston, MA: Routledge and Kegan Paul, 50–72.

Echols A. (1989) *Daring to Be Bad: Radical Feminism in America, 1967–1975*. Minneapolis, MN: University of Minnesota Press.

Edelman L. (2004) *No Future: Queer Theory and the Death Drive*. Durham, NC: Duke University Press.

Ellis SJ and Peel E. (2011) Lesbian feminisms: historical and present possibilities. *Feminism and Psychology* 21: 198–204.

Engels F. (1972) *The Origin of the Family, Private Property and the State*. New York: Pathfinder Press.

Enke A. (2007) *Finding the Movement: Sexuality, Contested Space, and Feminist Activism*. Durham, NC and London: Duke University Press.

Enszer JR. (2016) How to stop choking to death: rethinking lesbianism as a vibrant political theory and feminist practice. *Journal of Lesbian Studies* 20: 180–196.

Faderman L. (1981) *Surpassing the Love of Men: Romantic Friendship and Love between Women from the Renaissance to the Present*. New York: William Morrow and Company.

Faderman L. (1991) *Odd Girls and Twilight Lovers: A History of Lesbian Life in Twentieth-Century America*. New York: Penguin.

Faderman L. (1992) The return of butch and femme: a phenomenon in lesbian sexuality of the 1980s and 1990s. *Journal of the History of Sexuality* 24: 578–596.

Faderman L. (1993) *Scotch Verdict*. New York: Columbia University Press.

Faderman L and Eriksson B. (1980) *Lesbian-feminism in Turn-of-the-Century Germany*. Weatherby Lake, MO: Naiad Press.

Falquet J. (2004) Lesbianisme. In: Hirata H, Laborie F, Le Doaré H, et al. (eds) *Dictionnaire critique du féminisme*. Paris: Presse Universitaires de France, 102–108.

Falquet J. (2008) *De gré ou de force: les femmes dans la mondialisation*. Paris: La Dispute.

Faye S. (2017) If you really want women to be safe in prisons, it's not transgender prisoners you need to be wary of. *The Independent*, 11 September. www.independent.co.uk/voices/transgender-prisons-jessica-winfield-gender-recognition-act-a7940561.html. Accessed 2/11/2018.

Ferguson A. (1984) Sex war: the debate between radical and libertarian feminists. *Signs: Journal of Women in Culture and Society* 10: 106–112.

Fernandez B and Gomathy NB. (2003) *The Nature of Violence Faced by Lesbian Women in India*. Mumbai: Research centre on violence against women, Tata Institute of Social Sciences.

Ferreira E. (2014) Lesbian activism in Portugal: facts, experiences, and critical reflections. *Lambda Nordica* 2: 53–82.

Ferreira E and Salvador R. (2015) Lesbian collaborative web mapping: disrupting heteronormativity in Portugal. *Gender, Place and Culture* 22: 954–970.

Ferreira E and Silva MJ. (2011) Equality policy in Portugal: the case of sexual orientation. In: Motmans J, Cuypers D, Meier P, et al. (eds) *Equal Is Not Enough: Challenging Differences and Inequalities in Contemporary Societies*. Antwerp: Policy Research Centre on Equal Opportunities: University of Antwerp – Hasselt University, 142–155.

Firestone S. (1970) *The Dialectic of Sex: The Case for Feminist Revolution.* New York: Bantam Books.

Fisher O. (2017) A recent study claimed that 41 percent of transgender prisoners are sex offenders – this is why it's false. *The Independent*, 23 November.

Ford R, Jones R, Isaac L and History Inverted Collective. (1996) *Forbidden Love – Bold Passion: Lesbian Stories 1900s–1990s*. North Fitzroy, Vic: History Inverted Collective.

Foucault M. (1978) *The History of Sexuality*. New York: Pantheon Books.

Foucault M. (1984a) *Histoire de la sexualité II: l'usage des plaisirs*. Paris: Gallimard.

Foucault M. (1984b) *Histoire de la sexualité III: le souci de soi*. Paris: Gallimard.

Foucault M. (1997) Friendship as a way of life. In: Rabinow P (ed) *Ethics: Subjectivity and Truth*. New York: The New Press.

Franco F, Macwan J and Ramanathan S. (2007) Marriage, sexuality and motherhood. In: Menon N (ed) *Sexualities*. New Delhi: Women Unlimited, 141–174.

Frye M. (1983) *The Politics of Reality: Essays in Feminist Theory*. Trumansburg, NY: The Crossing Press.

Frye M. (1991) Introduction. In: Murphy M. *Are You Girls Travelling Alone?* Los Angeles, CA: Clothes Spin Fever Press, 11–16.

Fuszara M. (2006) *Kobiety w polityce*. Warsaw: Wydawnictwo Trio.

Gammon C. (1993) Lesbian studies emerging in Canada. *Journal of Homosexuality* 24: 137–160.

Ghai A. (2002) Disabled women: an excluded agenda of Indian feminism. *Hypatia* 17: 49–66.

Ghai, A. (2005) Inclusive education: a myth or reality? In: Kumar R, Sethi A and Sikka S (eds) *School, Society, Nation: Popular Essays in Education*. New Delhi: Orient Longman, 244–262.

Ghosh S. (2011) *Fire*. Delhi: Orient Publishing.

Gilchrist C. (2015) Forty years of the Elsie Refuge for Women and Children. *Dictionary of Sydney*. https://dictionaryofsydney.org/entry/forty_years_of_the_elsie_refuge_for_women_and_children. Accessed 2/11/2018.

Gilligan A. (2017) Up to half of trans inmates may be sex offenders. *The Times*, 19 November. www.thetimes.co.uk/article/up-to-half-of-trans-inmates-may-be-sex-offenders-26rz2crhs. Accessed 27/1/2019.

Girls Own. (1984) Introducing S.O.W. *Girls Own*.

GLEN and NEXUS. (1995) *Poverty: Lesbians and Gay Men, the Social and Economic Effects of Discrimination*. Dublin: Combat Poverty Agency.

Gothoskar S, Patel V, Patel V, et al. (1982) Documents from the Indian Women's Movement. *Feminist Review* 12: 92–103.

Government of India, Ministry of Statistics and Programme Implementation. (2018) http://mospi.nic.in/sites/default/files/reports_and_publication/statistical_publication/social_statistics/Chapter_1.pdf. Accessed 13/7/2018.

Gqola PD. (2015) *Rape: A South African Nightmare*. Johannesburg: Jacana Media.

Graff A. (2001) *Świat bez kobiet. Płeć w polskim życiu publicznym*. Warsaw: Wydawnictwo W.A.B.

Greer G. (1970) *The Female Eunuch*. London: MacGibbon & Kee.

Guillaumin C. (1978) Pratique du pouvoir et idée de Nature. *Questions féministes* 2: 5–30 and 3: 5–28.

Gunkel H. (2010) *The Cultural Politics of Female Sexuality in South Africa*. New York: Routledge.

Gupta C. (2014) Presentation in Black British Feminism panel. Centre for Feminist Research, Goldsmiths.

Guru G. (1995) Dalit women talk differently. *Economic and Political Weekly* 30: 2548–2550.

Halberstam J. (1998) *Female Masculinity*. Durham, NC: Duke University Press.

Halberstam J. (2005) *In a Queer Time and Place: Transgender Bodies, Subcultural Lives*. New York: New York University Press.

Halberstam J. (2011) *The Queer Art of Failure*. London: Duke University Press.

Hall R. (1982 [1928]) *The Well of Loneliness*. London: Virago Press.

Harris G. and Witte J. (2018) A winter's tale. In: Marsden M. (ed.) *Mardi Gras 40th Anniversary Magazine*. Sydney: ABC Magazines, 11.

Harris G, Witte J and Davis K. (2008) *New Day Dawning: The Early Years of Sydney's Gay and Lesbian Mardi Gras*. Sydney: Pride History Group.

Harrison K. (2017) Email communication with Sophie Robinson, 11 April.

Hartmann HI (1979) The unhappy marriage of Marxism and feminism: towards a more progressive union. *Capital & Class* 3: 1–33.

Healey E. (1996) *Lesbian Sex Wars*. London: Virago.

HelpAge India. (2015) *State of Elderly in India, 2014*. New Delhi: HelpAge India.

Henderson L. (1993) Lesbian pornography: cultural transgression and sexual demystification. *Women and Language* 14: 3–12.

Henderson M. (2013) Pornography in the service of lesbians: the case of Wicked Women and Slit magazines. *Australasian Journal of Popular Culture* 2: 159–182.

Hendriks SE and Bachan K. (2015) Because I am a girl: the emergence of girls in development. In: Baksh R and Harcourt W (eds) *The Oxford Handbook of Transnational Feminist Movements*. Oxford: Oxford University Press, 895–918.

Higgins R. (1998) De la libération gaie à la théorie queer. In: Lamoureux D (ed) *Les limites de l'identité sexuelle*. Montreal: Remue-ménage, 109–133.

Higgs K. (2017) Email communication with Sophie Robinson, 11 April.

Hildebran A. (1998) Genèse d'une communauté lesbienne: un récit des années 1970. In: Demczuk I and Remiggi FW (eds) *Sortir de l'ombre: histoires des communautés lesbienne et gaie de Montréal*. Montreal: VLB Éditeur, 207–233.

Hill-Collins P. (1986) Learning from the outsider within: the sociological significance of Black feminist thought. *Social Problems* 33: 14–32.

Hinsliff G. (2018) The Gender Recognition Act is controversial: can a path to common ground be found? *The Guardian*, 10 May.

Hite S. (1987) *The Hite Report: Women and Love, a Cultural Revolution in Progress*. New York: Knopf.

Hoagland SL. (1988) *Lesbian Ethics: Towards a New Value*. Palo Alto, CA: Institute for Lesbian Studies.

Hoagland SL and Penelope J. (1988) *For Lesbians Only: A Separatist Anthology*. London: Onlywomen Press.

hooks b. (1997) Feminist politicization: a comment. In: Gergen M and Davis S (eds) *Towards a New Psychology of Gender*. New York: Routledge, 533–539.

Huggins J. (1987) Black women and women's liberation. *Hecate* 13: 77.

Hurteau P. (1991) *Homosexualité, religion et droit au Québec: une approche historique*. Department of Religion, Concordia University.

Hurtig MC, Kail M and Rouch H. (2002) *Sexe et genre: de la hiérarchie entre les sexes*. Paris: CNRS Éditions.

HWAG – Hobart Women's Action Group. (1973) Sexism and the Women's Liberation Movement, or, why do straight sisters sometimes cry when they are called lesbians? *Camp Ink* 3: 8–12.

In Her Voice. (2014) Interview with Malobika by Sayan Bhattacharya. http://kindlemag.in/voice. Accessed 2/11/2018.

Jaising I. (2014) Eliminating sexual harassment at the workplace: broadening the discourse on gender equality. *Commonwealth Law Bulletin* 40: 375–397.

Jay K. ([1999] 2013) *Tales of the Lavender Menace: A Memoir of Liberation*. New York and Plymouth: Basic Books.

Jeffreys S. (2003) *Unpacking Queer Politics: A Lesbian Feminist Perspective*. Cambridge: Polity.

Jeffreys S. (2006) Address to Andrea Dworkin Commemorative Conference, Oxford University's Centre for the Study of Justice. www.clarechambers.com/andrea-dworkin-commemorative-conference/. Accessed 2/11/2018.

Jeffreys S. (2018) *The Lesbian Revolution: Lesbian Feminism in the UK, 1970–1990*. London: Routledge.

Jennings R. (2008) "The most uninhibited party they'd ever been to": the postwar encounter between psychiatry and the British lesbian, 1945–1971. *Journal of British Studies* 47: 883–904.

Jennings R. (2009) Lesbians in Sydney. *Sydney Journal* 2: 29–38.

Jennings R. (2013) Womin loving womin: lesbian feminist theories of intimacy. In: Willett G and Smaal Y (eds) *Intimacy, Violence and Activism: Gay and Lesbian Perspectives on Australasian History and Society*. Clayton, Vic: Monash University Publishing, 133–146.

Jennings R. (2015) *Unnamed Desires: A Sydney Lesbian History*. Melbourne, Vic: Monash University.

John ME. (2009) Refraining globalisation: perspectives from the women's movement. *Economic and Political Weekly* 44: 46–49.

Johnston J. (1973) *Lesbian Nation: The Feminist Solution*. New York: Simon and Schuster.

Jones KB. (2014) Trans-exclusionary radical feminism: what exactly is it, and why does it hurt? *HuffPost*, 2 August. www.huffingtonpost.com/kelsie-brynn-jones/transexclusionary-radical-terf_b_5632332.html. Accessed 1/8/2018.

Jones Z. (2018) "Rapid onset gender dysphoria": what a hoax diagnosis looks like. *Gender Analysis*, 1 February. https://genderanalysis.net/2018/02/rapid-onset-gender-dysphoria-what-a-hoax-diagnosis-looks-like/. Accessed 2/11/2018.

Joseph S. (2013) Imperial morality of the Apex Court over shines the Constitutional wisdom. *LiveLaw*, 12 December. www.livelaw.in/imperial-morality-of-the-apex-court-over-shines-the-constitutional-wisdom/. Accessed 23/05/2018.

Kamikaze I. (1995) I used to be an activist, but I'm alright now. In: O'Carroll Í and Collins E (eds) *Lesbian and Gay Visions of Ireland*. London: Cassell, 117–137.

Kannabiran K and Kannabiran V. (2002) Looking at ourselves: Stree Shakti Sanghatana. In: Kannabiran K and Kannabiran V (eds) *De-Eroticizing Assault: Essays on Modesty, Honour and Power*. India: Stree, 25–54.

Kapur R. (2000) Too hot to handle: the cultural politics of *Fire*. *Feminist Review* 64: 53–64.

Karen. (1973) Radicalesbian weekend at Sorrento. *Vashti's Voice*: 12.

Khera R. (2002) Mid-day meals in Rajasthan. *The Hindu*, 13 November.

Kimmel MS. (1997) Masculinity as homophobia: fear, shame and silence in the construction of gender identity. In: Gergen M and Davis S (eds) *Toward a New Psychology of Gender*. New York: Routledge, 223–242.

Kingston B. (1974) Lesbianism and feminist theory. *Refractory Girl* 5: 3–5.

Kitchin R and Lysaght K. (2003) Heterosexism and the geographies of everyday life in Belfast Northern Ireland. *Environment and Planning A* 35: 489–510.

Koedt A. ([1968] 2000) The myth of the vaginal orgasm. In: Coulter GB and Crow B (eds) *Radical Feminism: A Documentary Reader*. New York: New York University Press, 371–377.

Kossowska M and Van Hiel A. (2003) The relationship between need for closure and conservative beliefs in Western and Eastern Europe. *Political Psychology* 24: 501–518.

Kotha A. (2010) *Our Words*. www.sapphokolkata.in/wp-content/uploads/bsk-pdf-manager/SWAKANTHEY-JAN-2010. Accessed 2/11/2018.

Krishna P. (2010) Sexuality, queerness and internet technologies in Indian context. *The Centre for Internet and Society*, 13 September. https://cis-india.org/raw/histories-of-the-internet/blogs/queer-histories-of-the-internet/sexuality-queerness-and-internet-technologies-in-indian-context. Accessed 2/11/2018.

Ksieniewicz M. (2004) Specyfika polskiego feminizmu. *Kultura i historia* 4.

Kulpa R and Mizielińska J. (2011) *De-centring Western Sexualities: Central and Eastern European Perspectives*. London: Ashgate.

Kumar R. (1997) *The History of Doing: An Illustrated Account of Movements for Women's Rights and Feminism in India 1800–1990*. New Delhi: Zubaan.

LABIA: A Queer Feminist LBT Collective (2010) *About LABIA*. https://sites.google.com/site/labiacollective/home. Accessed 2/11/2018.

Lahiri M. (2011) Crimes and corrections: bride burners, corrective rapists, and other black misogynists. *Feminist Africa* 15: 121–134.

Lake M. (1999) *Getting Equal: The History of Australian Feminism*. St. Leonards, NSW: Allen & Unwin.

Lamare N. (1965) *Problèmes sexuels de la femme*. Paris: Buchet-Chastel.

Lamoureux D. (1990) Les services féministes: de l'autonomie à l'extension de l'État. *Nouvelles pratiques sociales* 3: 33–43.

Lamoureux D. (1998a) La question lesbienne dans le féminisme montréalais: un chassé-croisé. In: Demczuk I and Remiggi FW (eds) *Sortir de l'ombre: histoires des communautés lesbienne et gai de Montréal*. Montreal: VLB Éditeur, 167–185.

Lamoureux D. (1998b) Agir sans "nous". In: Lamoureux D (ed) *Les limites de l'identité sexuelle*. Montreal: Remue-ménage, 87–108.

Lane N. (2015) All the lesbians are White, all the villages are gay, but some of us are brave: intersectionality, belonging, and Black queer women's scene space in Washington DC. In: Browne K and Ferreira E (eds) *Lesbian Geographies: Gender, Place and Power*. Farnham: Ashgate, 235–258.

Lang S. (1999) Lesbians, men-women and two-spirits: homosexuality and gender in Native American cultures. In: Wieringa S and Blackwood E (eds) *Same Sex Relations and Female Desires: Transgender Practices across Cultures*. New York: Columbia University Press, 91–118.

Laurie AJ. (2001) *Lesbian Studies in Aotearoa/New Zealand*. Binghampton, NY: Harrington Park Press.

Leeds Revolutionary Feminist Group. (1981) *Love Your Enemy? The Debate between Heterosexual Feminism and Political Lesbianism*. London: Onlywomen Press.

Lees P. (2017) Trans people already face a hostile world: now the media is making it worse. *The Guardian*, 12 November. www.theguardian.com/global/commentisfree/2017/nov/17/trans-people-children-suicide-bullying-rightwing-media. Accessed 2/11/2018.

Leidinger C. (2004) "Anna Rüling": a problematic foremother of lesbian herstory. *Journal of the History of Sexuality* 13: 477–499.

Lemoine C and Renard I. (2001) *Attirances: lesbiennes fems, lesbiennes butchs*. Paris: Éditions Gaies et Lesbiennes.

Lesbian Studies Coalition of Concordia. (1988) Lesbian Studies Documentation.

Lesselier C. (1991) Les regroupements de lesbiennes dans le mouvement féministe parisien: positions et problèmes, 1970–1982. In: Groupe d'Études Féministes de l'Université Paris VII (ed.) *Crises de la société, féminisme et changement*. Paris: Éditions Tierce, 87–103.

Lévi-Strauss C. (1949) *Les structures élémentaires de la parenté*. Paris: CNRS Éditions.

Lévi-Strauss C. (1969) *The Savage Mind*. Chicago, IL: University of Chicago Press.

Lewis D. (2008) Rethinking nationalism in relation to Foucault's *History of Sexuality* and Adrienne Rich's "Compulsory Heterosexuality and Lesbian Existence". *Sexualities* 11: 104–109.

Lewis D. (2011) Representing African sexualities. In: Tamale S (ed) *African Sexualities: A Reader*. Cape Town: Pambazuka Press, 199–216.

Lewis H. (2016) *The Politics of Everybody: Feminism, Queer Theory and Marxism at the Intersection*. London: Zed Books.

Longino HE. (1992) Taking gender seriously in philosophy of science. *Proceedings of the Biennial Meeting of the Philosophy of Science Association*. Chicago, IL: University of Chicago Press, 333–340.

Longino HE. (1995) Gender, politics, and the theoretical virtues. *Synthese* 104: 383–397.

Lorde A. (1981) *Uses of the Erotic: The Erotic as Power*. Tucson, AZ: Kore Press.

Lorde A. (1982) *Zami, a New Spelling of My Name: A Biomythography*. Trumansburg, NY: The Crossing Press.

Lorde A. (1983) An open letter to Mary Daly. In: Moraga C and Anzaldúa G (eds) *This Bridge Called My Back: Writings by Radical Women of Color*. New York: Kitchen Table/Women of Color Press, 94–98.

Lorde A. (1984) *Sister Outsider: Essays and Speeches*. Trumansburg, NY: Crossing Press.

Lorde A. (1988) *A Burst of Light: Essays*. Ithaca, NY: Firebrand Books.

Lorde A. and Hammond K. (1980) An interview with Audre Lorde. *American Poetry Review* 9: 18–21.

Loulan J. (1987) *Lesbian Passion: Loving Ourselves and Each Other*. San Francisco, CA: Spinsters Ink.

Love H. (2007) *Feeling Backwards: Loss and the Politics of Queer History*. Cambridge, MA: Harvard University Press.

Luthra R. (1999) The women's movement and the press in India: the construction of female foeticide as a social issue. *Women's Studies in Communication* 22: 1–24.

Maart R. (2007) *The Writing Circle*. Toronto: TSAR Publications.

MacDonald J. (2017) Today's shameless lesbians won't be queered. *Feminist Current*, 13 January. www.feministcurrent.com/2017/01/13/todays-shameless-lesbians-wont-queered/. Accessed 18/3/2018).

Macken D. (1988) Behind Cath Philips. *Sydney Morning Herald* 245.

MacKinnon CA. (1979) *Sexual Harassment of Working Women: A Case of Sex Discrimination*. New Haven, CT: Yale University Press.

Madsen C. (2000) The thin thread of conversation: an interview with Mary Daly. *Cross Currents* 50.

Magarey S. (2013) Sisterhood and women's liberation in Australia. *Outskirts* 28.

Magarey S. (2014) *Dangerous Ideas: Women's Liberation – Women's Studies – around the World*. Adelaide, SA: The University of Adelaide Press.

Maglaty J. (2011) When did girls start wearing pink? *Smithsonian.com*, 7 April. www.smithsonianmag.com/arts-culture/when-did-girls-start-wearing-pink-1370097/. Accessed 10/5/2018.

Mahapatra D. (2013) Supreme Court makes homosexuality a crime again. *Times of India*, 12 December.

Majewska E. (2017) *Tramwaj zwany uznaniem. Feminizm i solidarność po neoliberalizmie*. Warsaw: Instytut Wydawniczy Książka i Prasa.

Malinowitz J. (1996) Lesbian studies and postmodern queer theory. In: Zimmerman B and McNaron TA (eds) *The New Lesbian Studies: Into the Twenty-First Century*. New York: Feminist Press, 262–268.

Manayath N. (2013) Why marriage equality may not be that equal. *Tehelka*, 3 May. http://old.tehelka.com/why-marriage-equality-may-not-be-that-equal/. Accessed 8/8/2018.

Mani L. (2008) The phantom of globality and the delirium of excess. *Economic and Political Weekly* 43: 41–47.

Manjoo R. (2014) Report of the Special Rapporteur on violence against women, its causes and consequences, Twenty-sixth session, Agenda item 3. Human Rights Council.

Martin B. (1994) Sexualities without genders and other queer utopias. *Diacritics: Special Issue on Critical Crossings* 24: 104–121.

Matebeni Z. (2013) Deconstructing violence towards black lesbians in South Africa. In: Ekine S and Abbas H (eds) *Queer African Reader*. Dakar: Pambazuka Press, 343–353.

Mathew S. (2017) Understanding trans and queer issues in movements: an interview with Chayanika Shah. www.theypfoundation.org/news-2/2017/3/31/interviewing-chayanika-shah. Accessed 2/11/2018.

Mathieu N-C. (1991) *L'Anatomie politique: catégorisations et idéologies du sexe*. Paris: Côté-femmes.

Mathieu N-C. (1996 [1989]) Sexual, sexed and sex-class identities: three ways of conceptualising the relationship between sex and gender. In: Leonard D and Adkins L (eds) *Sex in Question: French Materialist Feminism*. London: Taylor & Francis, 42–71.

Mathieu N-C. (1999) Bourdieu ou le pouvoir auto-hypnotique de la domination masculine. *Les temps modernes* 604: 286–324.

Mathieu N-C. (2007) *Une maison sans fille est une maison morte: la personne et le genre en sociétés matrilinéaires et/ou uxorilocales*. Paris: Maison des Sciences de l'Homme.

Mathur S. (2010) Maya backtracks on dalit cooks for midday meals. *The Times of India*, 26 July. https://timesofindia.indiatimes.com/india/Maya-backtracks-on-dalit-cooks-for-midday-meals/articleshow/6216902.cms. Accessed 23/5/2018.

Matthews JJ. (2017) Good and mad women redux. *History Australia* 14: 461–471.

Mauss M. (1969) La cohésion sociale dans les sociétés polysegmentaires. *Œuvres III: Cohésion sociale et division de la sociologie*. Paris: Les Éditions de Minuit, 11–26.

McAuliffe M and Kennedy S. (2017) Defending Catholic Ireland. In: Kuhar R and Patternote D (eds) *Anti-Gender Campaigns in Europe: Mobilizing against Equality*. Lanham, MD: Rowman & Littlefield, 133–150.

Mehta D. (1996) *Fire*. India: Kaledescope Entertainment.

Meijer IC and Prins B. (1998) How bodies come to matter: an interview with Judith Butler. *Signs: Journal of Women in Culture and Society* 23: 275–286.

Melbourne Gay Women's Group. (1975) The Melbourne Gay Women's Group. In: Mercer J (ed) *The Other Half: Women in Australian Society*. Ringwood, Vic: Penguin Books, 441–446.

Mendelsohn D. (2015) Girl, interrupted: who was Sappho? *The New Yorker*, 16 March. http://docplayer.net/78440260-March-16-2015-issue-girl-interrupted-who-was-sappho-by-daniel-mendelsohn.html. Accessed 2/11/2018.

Menon N. (1995) The impossibility of justice: female foeticide and feminist discourse on abortion. *Contributions to Indian Sociology* 29: 369–392.

Menon N. (2004) *Recovering Subversion: Feminist Politics beyond the Law*. Urbana and Chicago, IL: University of Illinois Press.

Menon N. (2005) How natural is normal? Feminism and compulsory heterosexuality. In: Narrain A and Bhan G (eds) *Because I Have a Voice: Queer Politics in India*. New Delhi: Yoda Press, 33–39.

Menon N. (2007) Outing heteronormativity: nation, citizen, feminist disruptions. In: Menon N (ed) *Sexualities*. London: Zed Books, 3–51.

Menon N. (2009a) Sexuality, caste, governmentality: contests over "gender" in India. *Feminist Review* 91: 94–112.

Menon N. (2009b) Thinking through the postnation. *Economic and Political Weekly* 44: 70–77.

Michard C. (2009) Assaut du discours straight et universalisation du point de vue minoritaire dans les essais de Monique Wittig. *Genre, sexualité & société* 1.

Millett K. (1969; 1970) *Sexual Politics*. Urbana and Chicago, IL: University of Illinois Press; New York: Doubleday.

Millett K. (1971) *Le Politique du mâle*. Paris: Stock.

Millward L. (2015) *Making a Scene: Lesbians and Community across Canada, 1964–84*. Vancouver: UBC Press.

Ministry of Women and Child Development. (2015) Beti Bachao Beti Padhao Scheme: Module for Master Trainers. A module for survival, education and empowerment of the girl child. Government of India.

Minnis D. (2017) Interview with Sophie Robinson, Glebe, 30 July.

Moane G. (1995) Living visions. In: O'Carroll Í and Collins E (eds) *Lesbian and Gay Visions of Ireland*. London: Cassell, 86–98.

Moffett H. (2006) "These women, they force us to rape them": rape as a narrative of social control in post-apartheid South Africa. *Journal of Southern African Studies* 31: 129–144.

Mogrovejo N. (2000) *Un amor que se atrevió a decir su nombre: la lucha de las lesbianas y su relación con los movimientos homosexual y feminista en América Latina*. México City: Plaza y Valdés, CDAHL.

Molinier P. (2007) Préface. In: De Lauretis T. *Théorie queer et cultures populaires: de Foucault à Cronenberg*. Paris: La Dispute.

Montgomery LM. ([1908] 1976) *Anne of Green Gables*. New York: Bantam Books.

Moore DL. (2013) Structurelessness, structure, and queer movements. *Women's Studies Quarterly* 41: 257–260.

Moraga C. (1981) The welder. In: Moraga C and Anzaldúa G (eds) *The Bridge Called My Back: Writings by Radical Women of Colour*. Watertown, MA: Persephone Press, 219.

Moraga C. (2000) *Loving in the War Years: Lo que nunca pasó por sus labios*. Cambridge, MA: South End Press.

Moraga C and Anzaldúa G. (1981 / 1983) *This Bridge Called My Back: Writings by Radical Women of Color*. Watertown, MA: Persephone Press / New York: Kitchen Table/Women of Color Press.

Morgan R. (1970) *Sisterhood Is Powerful: An Anthology of Writings from the Women's Liberation Movement*. New York: Vintage Books.

Morgan R. (1972) *Monster: Poems*. Melbourne, Vic: Melbourne Radical Feminists.

Morgan, R. (2014) *Monster: Poems*. Newburyport, MA: Open Road Media.

Morris BJ. (1999) *Eden Built by Eves: The Culture of Women's Music Festivals*. Los Angeles, CA: Alyson.

Morrissey ME. (2013) Rape as a weapon of hate: discursive constructions and material consequences of black lesbianism in South Africa. *Women's Studies in Communication* 36: 72–91.

Moses C. (1996) La construction du "French Feminism" dans le discours universitaire américain. *Nouvelles Questions féministes* 17: 3–14.

Mufweba Y. (2003) Lesbians targets of rape war. *Saturday Star*, 8 November.

Mufweba Y and Bhengu X. (2003) Gay women hate crimes. *Independent on Saturday*, 8 November.

Muholi Z. (2014) *Zanele Muholi: Faces and Phases 2006–14.* Göttingen: Steidl.

Muholi Z and Perryer S. (2006) *Zanele Muholi: Only Half the Picture.* Cape Town: Michael Stevenson.

Mulcahy C. (2013) *An Examination of Irish Feminist Opinion on the Inclusion of Transsexual Women in Feminism.* Unpublished MA thesis in Women's Studies, National University of Ireland, Cork.

Mulhall A. (2015) The republic of love. *Bully Bloggers*, 20 June.

Mulholland M. (1995) Ghetto-blasting. In: O'Carroll, Í and Collins E (eds) *Lesbian and Gay Visions of Ireland: Towards the Twenty-First Century.* London and New York: Cassell, 131–137.

Mulligan M. (2018) Fight and flight: "butch flight", trans men, and the elusive question of authenticity. *Nursing Clio*, 11 January. https://nursingclio.org/2018/01/11/butch-flight-trans-men-and-the-elusive-question-of-authenticity. Accessed 2/11/2018.

Mumford A. (2018) Frequently asked questions: women's equality and the Gender Recognition Act. *Engender*, 29 January. www.engender.org.uk/news/blog/frequently-asked-questions-womens-equality-and-the-gender-recognition-act/. Accessed 2/11/2018.

Murray J. (2017) Be trans, be proud, but don't call yourself a real woman. *The Sunday Times*, 5 March. www.thetimes.co.uk/article/be-trans-be-proud-but-dont-call-yourself-a-real-woman-frtld7q5c. Accessed 2/11/2018.

Murray S. (2002) *More than Refuge: Changing Responses to Domestic Violence.* Crawley, WA: University of Western Australia Press.

Myers J. (2003) *Historical Dictionary of the Lesbian Liberation Movement: Still the Rage.* Lanham, MD: Scarecrow Books.

Nadeau C. (1997) Sexualité et espace public: visibilité lesbienne dans le cinéma récent. *Sociologie et sociétés* 19: 113–128.

Nair Y. (n.d.) Yasmin Nair: writer, academic, activist, commentator. www.yasminnair.net/.

Namaste V. (2015) *Oversight: Critical Reflections on Feminist Research and Politics.* Toronto: Women's Press.

Nanda S. (1999) *The Hijras of India: Neither Man nor Woman.* Belmont, CA: Wadsworth.

Narrain A and Bhan G. (2005) *Because I have a Voice: Queer Politics in India.* Delhi: Yoda Press.

National Crime Records Bureau. (2016) *Crime in India*. New Delhi: National Crime Records Bureau, Table 3A.5, p. 148.

Necati Y. (2018) The anti-trans protests at Pride were the latest in a long history of transphobia in the LGBTQ+ community. *Independent*, 15 July. www.independent.co.uk/voices/anti-trans-protests-london-pride-transgender-transphobia-terf-lgbt-feminist-a8448521.html. Accessed 1/8/2018.

Nestle J. (1981) Butch-fem relationships: sexual courage in the 1950s. *Heresies* 12: 21–24.

Nestle J. (1992) *The Persistent Desire: A Femme-Butch Reader*. Boston, MA: Alyson Publications.

Nestle J. (2011) Forward! In: Coyote IE and Sharman Z (eds) *Persistence: All Ways Butch and Femme*. Vancouver: Arsenal Pulp Press.

Nigianne C and Storr M. (2009) *Delueze and Queer Theory*. Edinburgh: Edinburgh University Press.

Niranjana T. (2006) *Mobilizing India*. Durham, NC: Duke University Press.

Nkabinde NZ. (2008) *Black Bull, Ancestors and Me: My Life as a Lesbian Sangoma*. Auckland Park, South Africa: Fanele.

Ntim Z. (2018) Mumsnet brings in tougher forum rules after transgender row. *The Guardian*, 13 June. www.theguardian.com/media/mumsnet.

O'Carroll Í and Collins E. (1995) *Lesbian and Gay Visions of Ireland*. London: Cassell.

O'Donnell K. (2003) Irish lesbian history. In: Lalor B (ed) *The Encyclopaedia of Ireland*. London: Yale University Press.

O'Donnell K and Giffney N. (2007) *Twenty-First Century Lesbian Studies*. London: Routledge.

O'Dwyer C and Schwartz K. (2010) Minority rights after EU enlargement: a comparison of antigay politics in Poland and Latvia. *Comparative European Politics* 8: 220–243.

O'Sullivan K. (1991) Sexually outrageous women. *Wicked Women* 2: 22.

O'Sullivan K. (1997) Dangerous desire: lesbianism as sex or politics. In: Matthews JJ (ed) *Sex in Public: Australian Sexual Cultures*. St. Leonards, NSW: Allen and Unwin, 114–126.

O'Sullivan K. (2015) Interview with Sophie Robinson, Newcastle, 3 October.

O'Toole T. (2013) Cé leis tú? Queering Irish migrant literature. *Irish University Review* 43: 131–145.

Olasik M. (2015a) Becoming a lesbian citizen: a path of reflection. *LES Online* 7: 28–36.

Olasik M. (2015b) Location, location: lesbian performativities that matter, or not. In: Browne K and Ferreira E (eds) *Lesbian Geographies: Gender, Place and Power*. Aldershot: Ashgate, 201–217.

Olasik M. (2017) Towards lesbian studies in Poland. In: Ostalska K (ed) *Women's Space and Men's Space*. Łódź: Wydawnictwo Uniwersytetu Łódzkiego, 55–71.

Olasik M. (2018) *Lesbian Studies at the Intersection of Sociology and Cultural Geography*. Doctoral dissertation submitted and defended in the Institute of Applied Social Sciences, University of Warsaw.

Panchal TJ and Ajgaonkar V. (2015) *Let Them Fly: A Multi-Agency Response to Child Marriages in Haryana*. Resource Centre for Interventions on Violence Against Women, Tata Institute Of Social Sciences, Supported by Government of Haryana.

Parke C. (2016) The Christian Right's love affair with anti-trans feminists. *Political Research Associates*, 11 August. www.politicalresearch. org/2016/2008/2011/the-christian-rights-love-affair-with-anti-trans-feminists/. Accessed 2/11/2018.

Patel T. (2007) Informal social networks, sonography and female foeticide in India. *Sociological Bulletin* 56: 243–262.

Penelope J. (1992) *Call Me Lesbian: Lesbian Lives, Lesbian Theory*. New York: Crossing Press.

Penney J. (2014) *After Queer Theory: The Limits of Sexual Politics*. London: Pluto Press.

Perreau B. (2016) *Queer Theory: The French Response*. Stanford, CA: Stanford University Press.

Phelan S. (1989) *Identity Politics: Lesbian Feminism and the Limits of Community*. Philadelphia, PA: Temple University Press.

Plaskow J. (2012) Lessons from Mary Daly. *Journal of Feminist Studies in Religion* 28: 100–104.

Podmore J. (2015) Contested dyke rights to the city: Montréal's 2012 Dyke Marches in time and space. In: Browne K and Ferreira E (eds) *Lesbian Geographies: Gender, Place and Power*. Aldershot: Ashgate, 87–106.

Podmore J and Tremblay M. (2015) Lesbians, second-wave feminism and gay liberation. In: Paternotte D and Tremblay M (eds) *The Ashgate Companion to Lesbian and Gay Activism*. Aldershot: Ashgate, 121–134.

Preciado P. (2012) Queer bulldogs. *Documenta (13)*.

Puar JK. (2005) Queer times, queer assemblages. *Social Text* 23: 121–139.

Puar JK. (2007) *Terrorist Assemblages: Homonationalism in Queer Times*. Durham, NC: Duke University Press.

Puar JK. (2017) Homonationalism as assemblage: viral travels, affective sexualities. In: Sircar O and Jain D (eds) *New Intimacies, Old Desires: Law, Culture and Queer Politics in Neoliberal Times*. New Delhi: Zubaan.

Radicalesbians. (1970) The woman-identified woman. In: Koedt A, Levine E and Rapone A (eds) *Radical Feminism*. New York: Quadrangle, 240–245.

Ranade K. (2018) Living life as a queer person: role of queer community/s in consolidation of identity. *Growing Up Gay in Urban India*. Singapore: Springer, 141–160.

Rand EJ. (2014) *Reclaiming Queer: Activist and Academic Rhetorics of Resistance*. Tuscaloosa, AL: The University of Alabama Press.

Rao M. (2001) Female foeticide: where do we go? *Issues in Medical Ethics* 9: 123–124.

Ray R. (1999) *Fields of Protest: Women's Movements in India*. Minneapolis, MN: University of Minnesota Press.

Raymond J. (1979) *The Transsexual Empire: The Making of the She-Male*. Boston, MA: Beacon Press.

Raymond J. (1986) *A Passion for Friends: A Philosophy of Female Friendship*. Boston, MA: Beacon Press.

Raymond J. (1994) *The Transsexual Empire: The Making of the She-Male*. New York: Teachers College Press.

Redmond S. (2018) An open letter to the organisers of the "We Need to Talk Tour" from a Group of Feminists in Ireland. *Feminist Ire*, 22 January, https://feministire.com/2018/2001/2022/an-open-letter-to-the-organisers-of-the-we-need-to-talk-tour-from-a-group-of-feminists-in-ireland/. Accessed 2/11/2018.

Rege S. (1997) Institutional alliance between sociology and gender studies: story of the crocodile and monkey. *Economic and Political Weekly* 32: 2023–2027.

Rege S. (1998) Dalit women talk differently: a critique of "difference" and towards a Dalit feminist standpoint position. *Economic and Political Weekly* 33: WS39–WS46.

Rege S. (2006) *Writing Caste Writing Gender*. New Delhi: Zubaan.

Reid G. (2010) The canary of the constitution: same-sex equality in the public sphere. *Social Dynamics* 36: 38–51.

Revathi A. (2010) *The Truth about Me: A Hijra Life Story*. India: Penguin Books.

Rich A. (1979) *On Lies, Secrets and Silence*. New York: Norton.

Rich A. (1980) Compulsory heterosexuality and lesbian existence. *Signs: Journal of Women in Culture and Society* 5: 630–660.

Rich A. (1981) La contrainte à l'hétérosexualité et l'existence lesbienne. *Nouvelles Questions féministes* 1: 15–43.

Rich A. (1986) Notes toward a politics of location. *Blood, Bread, and Poetry: Selected Prose 1979–1985*. New York: W.W. Norton & Company.

Richardson N. (2016) *Transgressive Bodies: Representations in Film and Popular Culture*. London: Routledge.

Ricœur P. ([1986] 1997) *L'idéologie et l'utopie*. Paris: Seuil.

Riley E. (1975) *All That False Instruction*. Sydney: Angus and Robertson.

Roden D. (2014) *Posthuman Life: Philosophy at the Edge of the Human*. London and New York: Routledge.

Roe J. (1971) Lesbians are women. *MeJane*: 4–5.

Ross BL. (1995) *The House That Jill Built: A Lesbian Nation in Formation*. Toronto: University of Toronto Press.

Ross BL. (2009) We were catalysts for change. *Journal of Lesbian Studies* 13: 442–460.

Rowe K. (1991) Sexually outrageous women. *Wicked Women* 24.

Rowe K. (2016) Interview with Sophie Robinson, Balmain, 5 July.

Roy C. (1985) *Les lesbiennes et le féminisme*. Montreal: Albert Saint-Martin.

Rubin G. (1975) The traffic in women: notes on the "political economy" of sex. In: Reiter R (ed) *Toward an Anthropology of Women*. New York: Monthly Review Press, 157–210.

Rubin G. ([1975] 1998a) L'économie politique du sexe: transactions sur les femmes et systèmes de sexe/genre. *Les Cahiers du CEDREF* 7: 3–81.

Rubin G. ([1984] 1998b) Thinking sex: notes for a radical theory of the politics of sexuality. In: Nardi PM and Schneider BE (eds) *Social Perspectives in Lesbian and Gay Studies: A Reader*. London: Routledge, 100–133.

Rueling (Rüling) A. ([1904] 1980) What interest does the women's movement have in the homosexual question? In: Faderman L and Eriksson B (eds) *Lesbian-Feminism in Turn-of-the-Century Germany*. Weatherby Lake, MO: Naiad Press, 81–91.

S K. (2016) Why lesbians tend to earn more than heterosexual women. *The Economist* (The Economist Explains), 15 February.

Saheli Women's Resource Centre. (2000) Conferences of women's movements: history and perspectives. Newsletter January 2000. https://sites.google.com/site/saheliorgsite/women-s-conferences/national-conferences-of-women-s-movements/conferences-of-womens-movements-history-and-perspectives. Accessed 2/11/2018.

Saheli Women's Resource Centre. (2003) Threatened existence: the international initiative for justice in Gujarat. Newsletter January–April 2004. https://sites.google.com/site/saheliorgsite/communalism/violence/threatened-existence-the-international-initiative-for-justice-in-gujarat. Accessed 2/11/2018.

Saladin d'Anglure B. (1985) Du projet "PAR.AD.I" au sexe des anges: notes et débats autour d'un "troisième sexe". *Anthropologie et sociétés* 9: 139–176.

San Francisco Dykes on Bikes. (2016) Our history. www.dykesonbikes.org/. Accessed 15/10/2018.

Sandoval C. (2000) *Methodology of the Oppressed*. Minneapolis, MN: University of Minnesota Press.

Sangari K. (2015) *Solid:Liquid: A (Trans)National Reproductive Formation*. New Delhi: Tulika Books.

Santos AC. (2012) *Social Movements and Sexual Citizenship in Southern Europe*. Basingstoke: Palgrave Macmillan.

Sappho (2010) Editorial (translated). *Swakanthey*, 7th Year, 1st Issue, Book Fair: 1.

Schor N. (1993) Cet essentialisme qui n'(en) est pas un: Irigary à bras les corps. *Futur Antérieur*: 1–20.

Scott J. (1992) Experience. In: Butler J and Scott J (eds) *Feminists Theorize the Political*. London: Routledge.

Sedgwick EK. (1985) *Between Men: English Literature and Male Homosocial Desire*. New York: Columbia University Press.

Sedgwick EK. (1990) *The Epistemology of the Closet*. Berkeley, CA: University of California Press.

Sen P. (2013) Waxing sapphic gently. *Outlook*, 15 April. www.outlookindia.com/magazine/story/waxing-sapphic-gently/284806. Accessed 2/11/2018.

Sen R. (2014) Resistances, reforms and (re)-creation. In: Fernandes L (ed) *Routledge Handbook of Gender in South Asia*. London: Routledge, 333–346.

Sen S. (2000) *Towards a Feminist Politics? The Indian Women's Movement in Historical Perspective*. Policy Research Report on Gender and Development.

Serano J. (2007) *Whipping Girl: A Transsexual Woman on Sexism and the Scapegoating of Femininity*. Berkeley, CA: Seal Press.

Serano J. (2013) *Excluded: Making Feminist and Queer Movements More Inclusive*. Berkeley, CA: Seal Press.

Serano J. (2015) The real "autogynephilia deniers". *juliaserano.blogspot.com*, 13 July.

Serano J. (2016) Detransition, desistance, and disinformation: a guide for understanding transgender children debates. https://medium.com/@juliaserano/detransition-desistance-and-disinformation-a-guide-for-understanding-transgender-children-993b7342946e. Accessed 2/11/2018.

Shah C. (2005) The roads that e/merged: feminist activism and queer understanding. In: Narrain A and Bhan G (eds) *Because I Have a Voice: Queer Politics in India*. Delhi: Yoda Press, 143–154.

Shah C, Merchant R, Mahajan S, et al. (2015) *No Outlaws in the Gender Galaxy*. New Delhi: Zubaan.

Shah C, Raj SM and Nevatia S. (2012) Breaking the binary: understanding concerns and realities of female assigned/born persons across a spectrum of lived gender identities. In: Wieringa SE (ed) *Women-Loving-Women in Africa and Asia*. Amsterdam: Rick Stienstra Fonds, 182–240.

Shah SP. (2014) *Street Corner Secrets: Sex, Work, and Migration in the City of Mumbai*. Durham, NC: Duke University Press.

Sharma M. (2006) *Loving Women: Being Lesbian in Underprivileged India*. New Delhi: Yoda Press.

Shumsky E. (2009) The Radicalesbian story: An evolution of consciousness. In: Mecca TA (ed) *Smash the Church, Smash the State: The Early Years of Gay Liberation*. San Francisco, CA: City Lights Books, 190–196.

Silva JS, Ornat MJ and Junior ABC. (2017) *Diálogos ibero-latino-americanos sobre geografias feministas e das sexualidades*. Ponta Grossa: Todapalavra Editora.

Simon V. (2015) *LEARNING HOW TO SCREAM*, Issue #1: *It Breaks My Heart, But It Had to Be Said*.

Simon V. (2016) *LEARNING HOW TO SCREAM: A Lecture Series on Lesbian Lives, Theory and Activism*. Eugene, OR: University of Oregon.

Singal J. (2016) What's missing from the conversation about transgender kids. *The Cut*, 25 July. www.thecut.com/2016/07/whats-missing-from-the-conversation-about-transgender-kids.html. Accessed 15/3/2018.

Singal J. (2018) Everyone, myself included, has been misreading the single biggest study on childhood gender dysphoria desistance and persistence. *Medium*, 28 March. https://medium.com/@jesse.singal/ everyone-myself-included-has-been-misreading-the-single-biggest-study-on-childhood-gender-8b6b3d82dcf3. Accessed 2/11/2018.

Sitka C. (1989) *A Radicalesbian Herstory*. http://users.spin.net.au/~deniset/ alesfem/s1sitka.pdf. Accessed 2/11/2018.

Sitka C. (2011) A herstory of the Radicalesbians. In: Willett G, Murdoch W and Marshall D (eds) *Secret Histories of Queer Melbourne*. Parkville, Vic: Australian Lesbian and Gay Archives, 122–125.

Smith B. (1983) *Home Girls: A Black Feminist Anthology*. New York: Kitchen Table/Women of Color Press.

Smith R. (2007) Interview with John Witte. *Sydney: Early Mardi Gras Interview Collection*. Sydney: Sydney's Pride History Group.

Smith Oboler R. (1980) Is the female husband a man? Woman/woman marriage among the Nandi of Kenya. *Ethnology* 19: 69–88.

Snitow A, Stansell C and Thompson S. (1983) *Powers of Desire: The Politics of Sexuality*. New York: Monthly Review Press.

Spivak GC. (1988) Can the subaltern speak? In: Morris RE (ed) *Can the Subaltern Speak? Reflections on the History of an Idea*. New York: Columbia University Press, 21–78.

Spivak GC. (1990) Theory in the margin: Coetzee's foe reading Defoe's "Crusoe/Roxana". *English in Africa* 17: 1–23.

Spivak GC. (1996 [1985]) Subaltern studies: deconstructing historiography. In: Landry D and MacLean G (eds) *The Spivak Reader*. London: Routledge, 203–236.

Spivak GC. (2018) Necessary and impossible? Culture as translation. Lecture posted on YouTube. www.youtube.com/watch?v=da9Zniv2T7I. Accessed 22/2/2018.

Środa M. (2009) *Kobiety i władza*. Warsaw: Wydawnictwo W.A.B.

Steensma TD, Biemond R, de Boer F, et al. (2011) Desisting and persisting gender dysphoria after childhood: a qualitative follow-up study. *Clinical Child Psychology and Psychiatry* 16: 499–516. www.ncbi.nlm.nih.gov/ pubmed/21216800. Accessed 2/11/2018.

Stein A. (1992) Sisters and queers: the decentering of lesbian feminism. *Socialist Review* 22: 33–55.

Stein A. (1993) *Sisters, Sexperts and Queers: Beyond the Lesbian Nation*. New York: Plume.

Stein A. (1997) *Sex and Sensibility: Stories of a Lesbian Generation*. Berkeley and Los Angeles, CA: University of California Press.

Stewart H. (2017) Women bearing 86% of austerity burden, Commons figures reveal. *The Guardian*, 9 March.

Stock K. (2017–2018) Arguing about feminism and transgenderism: an opinionated guide for the perplexed. https://medium.com/@ kathleenstock. Accessed 2/11/2018.

Stone S. (2014) The "empire" strikes back: a posttranssexual manifesto. *Camera Obscura* 10: 150–176.

Stonewall. (2017) Conversion therapy. www.stonewall.org.uk/campaign-groups/conversion-therapy. Accessed 2/11/2018.

Stonewall. (2018) LGBT in the UK: trans report. www.stonewall.org.uk/sites/default/files/lgbt-in-britain-trans.pdf. Accessed 26/1/2019.

Stryker S. (2008) Transgender history, homonormativity, and disciplinarity. *Radical History Review* 2008: 145–157.

Sukthankar A. (2004) The slow shifting of a collective identity. *Swakanthey: In Her Own Voice*. Kolkata: Sappho for Equality.

Sullerot E. (2006) *Pilule, sexe, ADN: trois révolutions qui ont bouleversé la famille*. Paris: Fayard.

Suresh Kumar Koushal & Anr vs Naz Foundation & Ors. Singhvi, G., Supreme Court (2013).

Swaminathan P, Jeyaranjan J, Sreenivasan R, et al. (2004) Tamil Nadu's midday meal scheme: where assumed benefits score over hard data. *Economic and Political Weekly* 39: 4811–4821.

Swarr AL. (2012) Paradoxes of butchness: lesbian masculinities and sexual violence in contemporary South Africa. *Signs* 37: 961–964.

Tabet P. (2004) *La grande arnaque: sexualité des femmes et échange économico-sexuel*. Paris: L'Harmattan.

Tahon MB. (2004) *Vers l'indifférence des sexes? Union civile et filiation au Québec*. Montréal: Éditions Boréal.

Tannehill B. (2014) Myths about transition regrets. *HuffPost*, 18 November. www.huffingtonpost.com/brynn-tannehill/myths-about-transition-regrets_b_6160626.html. Accessed 5/2/2018.

Tannehill B. (2016) The End of the Desistance Myth. *HuffPost*, 1 January. www.huffingtonpost.com/brynn-tannehill/the-end-of-the-desistance_b_8903690.html. Accessed 15/2/2018.

Tannehill B. (2018) "Rapid onset gender dysphoria" is biased junk science. *Advocate*, 20 February. www.advocate.com/commentary/2018/2/20/rapid-onset-gender-dysphoria-biased-junk-science. Accessed 2/11/2018.

Taylor J. (2008) The queerest of the queer: sexuality, politics and music on the Brisbane scene. *Continuum* 22: 651–665.

Taylor K-Y. (2017) *How We Get Free: Black Feminism and the Combahee River Collective*. San Francisco, CA: Haymarket Books.

Taylor V and Rupp LJ. (1993) Women's culture and lesbian feminist activism: a reconsideration of cultural feminism. *Signs: A Journal of Women in Culture and Society* 19: 32–61.

Taylor V and Whittier NE. (1992) Collective identity and social movement communities: lesbian feminist mobilization. In: Morris AD and Mueller CM (eds) *Frontiers in Social Movement Theory*. New Haven, CT: Yale University Press, 104–129.

Temple Newhook J, Pyne J, Winters K, et al. (2018) A critical commentary on follow-up studies and "desistance" theories about transgender and gender-nonconforming children. *International Journal of Transgenderism* 19: 212–224.

Thadani G. (1996) *Sakhiyani: Lesbian Desire in Ancient and Modern India*. London: Cassell.

The Maintenance and Welfare of Parents and Senior Citizens Act (2007). Government of India.

The Prohibition of Child Marriage Act (2006). Government of India.

Thompson M. (1991) *Leatherfolk: Radical Sex, People, Politics, and Practice*. Boston, MA: Alyson Publications.

Thorat S and Lee J. (2005) Caste discrimination and food security programmes. *Economic and Political Weekly* 40: 4198–4201.

Transgender Trend. (2018) Suicide facts and myths. www.transgendertrend. com/the-suicide-myth/. Accessed 26/1/2019.

Tremblay M and Podmore J. (2015) Depuis toujours intersectionnels: relecture des mouvements lesbiens à Montréal, de 1970 aux années 2000. *Recherches féministes* 28: 101–120.

Trigilio J. (2016) Complicated and messy politics of inclusion: Michfest and the Boston Dyke March. *Journal of Lesbian Studies* 20: 234–250.

Trujillo C. (1991) *Chicana Lesbians: The Girls Our Mothers Warned Us About*. Berkeley, CA: Third Woman Press.

Trujillo C. (1997) Chicana lesbians: fear and loathing in the Chicano community. In: García AM (ed) *Chicana Feminist Thought: Basic Historical Writings*. New York: Routledge, 281–287.

Trujillo G. (2008) *Deseo y resistencia. Treinta años de movilización lesbiana en el Estado español (1977–2007)*. Madrid: Egales.

Turcotte L. (1998) Itinéraire d'un courant politique: le lesbianisme radical au Québec. In: Demczuk I and Remiggi FW (eds) *Sortir de l'ombre: histoires des communautés lesbienne et gai de Montréal*. Montreal: VLB Éditeur, 363–398.

Turcotte L. (2003) Féminisme/lesbianisme: la nécessité d'une pensée radicale. In: Chetcuti N and Michard C (eds) *Lesbianisme et féminisme: histoires politiques*. Paris: L'Harmattan, 33–48.

Turn off the Red Light Campaign (TORL). (2018). www.turnofftheredlight. ie/. Accessed: 2/11/2018.

UN Women. (n.d.) *Why Is Climate Change a Gender Issue?* www.uncclearn. org/sites/default/files/inventory/unwomen704.pdf. Accessed 2/11/2018.

United Nations. (2014) Concluding Observations for India's Third and Fourth Periodic Reports. UN Convention on the Rights of the Child, 66th session.

Valentine G. (1997) Making space: separatism and difference. In: Jones JP, Nast HJ and Roberts SM (eds) *Thresholds in Feminist Geography: Difference, Methodology, Representation*. Oxford: Rowman and Littlefield, 65–75.

Valk AM. (2002) Living a feminist lifestyle: the intersection of theory and action in a lesbian feminist collective. *Feminist Studies* 28: 303–332.

Valk AM. (2008) *Radical Sisters: Second-Wave Feminism and Black Liberation in Washington*. Urbana, IL: University of Illinois Press.

Vance C. (1984a) *Pleasure and Danger: Exploring Female Sexuality*. Boston, MA: Routledge and Kegan Paul.

Vance C. (1984b) Pleasure and danger: toward a politics of sexuality. In: Vance C (ed) *Pleasure and Danger: Exploring Female Sexuality*. Boston, MA: Routledge & Kegan Paul, 9–27.

Vargas C. (2014) *"El último trago"*, translated by Aldefina. http://lyricstranslate.com/en/el-%C3%BAltimo-trago-last-drop.html#ixzz 59koQbA9c. Accessed 2/11/2018.

Walker A. (2005) *In Search of Our Mothers' Gardens*. Phoenix, AZ: New Edition.

Walters SD. (1996) From here to queer: radical feminism, postmodernism, and the lesbian menace (or, why can't a woman be more like a fag?). *Signs: Journal of Women in Culture and Society* 21: 830–869.

Ward E. (1984) *Father–Daughter Rape*. London: Women's Press.

Watson P. (1997) Civil society and the politics of difference in Eastern Europe. In: Scott JW, Kaplan C and Keates D (eds) *Transitions, Environments, Translations: Feminisms in International Politics*. New York: Routledge, 21–29.

Weinberg, J. et al. (August 27, 2018 at 9:48 am) Derogatory language in philosophy journal risks increased hostility and diminished discussion (guest post) (Update: Response from Editors). *Daily Nous: News for and about the Philosophy Profession*. http://dailynous.com/2018/08/27/derogatory-language-philosophy-journal-hostility-discussion/.

Wieringa S and Blackwood E. (1999) *Same Sex Relations and Female Desires: Transgender Practices across Cultures*. New York: Columbia University Press.

Willett G. (2000) *Living Out Loud: A History of Gay and Lesbian Activism in Australia*. St. Leonards, NSW: Allen and Unwin.

Willett G, Murdoch W and Marshall D. (2011) *Secret Histories of Queer Melbourne*. Parkville, Vic: Australian Lesbian and Gay Archives.

Willett G and Smaal Y (2013) *Intimacy, Violence and Activism: Gay and Lesbian Perspectives on Australasian History and Society*. Clayton, Vic: Monash University Publishing

Williams C. (2013) Cotton ceiling: uncovering the trans conspiracy to rape lesbians. *The Transadvocate*, 27 September. http://transadvocate.com/cotton-ceiling-uncovering-the-trans-conspiracy-to-rape-lesbians_n_10251.htm. Accessed 2/11/2018.

Williams C. (2015) Fact check: study shows transition makes trans people suicidal. *The Transadvocate*, 2 November. http://transadvocate.com/fact-check-study-shows-transition-makes-trans-people-suicidal_n_15483.htm. Accessed 2/11/2018.

Wills, S. (1990) I'm going down the road … some recollections of what it was like then. In: Lavender, *What Is Lesbian Discrimination: Proceedings of an October 1987 Forum Held by the Anti-Discrimination Board*. Sydney: Anti-Discrimination Board.

Wills S. (1994) Inside the CWA: the other one. *Journal of Australian Lesbian Feminist Studies* 4: 6–22.

Winters K. (2016) Media misinformation about trans youth: the persistent 80% desistance myth. GID Reform Weblog, 26 July. https://gidreform. wordpress.com/2016/07/26/media-misinformation-about-trans-youth-the-persistent-80-desistance-myth/. Accessed 2/11/2018.

Winterson J. (1992) *Written on the Body*. New York: Vintage.

Wittig M. (1980a) La pensée straight. *Questions féministes* 7: 45–54.

Wittig M. (1980b) On ne naît pas femme. *Questions féministes* 8: 75–84.

Wittig M. (1982) The category of sex. *Feminist Issues* 2: 63–68.

Wittig M. (1992) *The Straight Mind and Other Essays*. Boston, MA: Beacon Press.

Wittig M. (2001) *La pensée straight*. Paris: Balland.

Women's Refugee Commission. (2018) Facts & figures. www.womensre fugeecommission.org/empower/resources/practitioners-forum/facts-and-figures. Accessed 2/11/2018.

Woo E. (2004) David Reimer, 38: after botched surgery, he was raised as a girl in gender experiment. *Los Angeles Times*, 13 May.

Wright J. (1990) Cath Phillips: profile. *ALR*. February. http://ro.uow.edu. au/cgi/viewcontent.cgi?article=2785&context=alr. Accessed 15/6/2018.

Yasmin N. (n.d.) Yasmin Nair: writer, academic, activist, commentator. www.yasminnair.net/. Accessed 2/11/2018.

Yeung P. (2018) Loss of senior managers led to UK's prison crisis. *The Guardian*, 25 August. www.theguardian.com/society/2018/aug/25/staff-cuts-prison-leadership-crisis. Accessed 26/1/2019.

Zackodnik T. (2011) *Press, Platform, Pulpit: Black Feminist Publics in the Era of Reform*. Knoxville, TN: University of Tennessee Press.

Ziering A and Dick K. (2002) *Derrida*. USA: Zeitgeist Films.

Zimmerman B. (1996) Placing lesbians. In: Zimmerman B and McNaron TA (eds) *The New Lesbian Studies: Into the Twenty-First Century*. New York: Feminist Press, 269–275.

Index

ZED

Zed is a platform for marginalised voices across the globe.

It is the world's largest publishing collective and a world leading example of alternative, non-hierarchical business practice.

It has no CEO, no MD and no bosses and is owned and managed by its workers who are all on equal pay.

It makes its content available in as many languages as possible.

It publishes content critical of oppressive power structures and regimes.

It publishes content that changes its readers' thinking.

It publishes content that other publishers won't and that the establishment finds threatening.

It has been subject to repeated acts of censorship by states and corporations.

It fights all forms of censorship.

It is financially and ideologically independent of any party, corporation, state or individual.

Its books are shared all over the world.

www.zedbooks.net
@ZedBooks